LSAT
Law School Admission Test

A Wiley Self-Teaching Guide

LSAT
Law School Admission Test

A Wiley Self-Teaching Guide

RANDOLPH Z. VOLKELL, J.D.

with

DAVID M. WERTHEIMER, L.L.B. and L.L.M.

John Wiley & Sons, Inc.

New York · Santa Barbara · London · Sydney · Toronto

Produced by Ken Burke & Associates

Copyeditor: Gail Larrick
Artist: Douglas Luna
Compositor: Meredythe

Library of Congress Cataloging in Publication Data

Volkell, Randolph Z., 1950–
LSAT, law school admission test.

(Wiley self-teaching guides)
1. Law schools–United States–Entrance examinations.
I. Wertheimer, David M., joint author. II. Title.
KF285.Z9V64 340′.07′1173 77-9956
ISBN 0-471-02138-5

Printed in the United States of America

77 78 10 9 8 7 6 5 4 3 2 1

Credits

Pages	*Source*
69–70, 84–85 (passage 1) 87–88 (passage 3)	Passages from *River Through Time: The Course of Western Civilization,* by C. Warren Hollister, John F. H. New, James D. Hardy, Jr., and Roger L. Williams. Copyright © 1975, by John Wiley & Sons, Inc. Reprinted by permission of John Wiley & Sons, Inc.
72–73, 85–87 (passage 2)	Passages from *Ecology: Selected Concepts,* by David B. Sutton and N. Paul Harmon. Copyright © 1973, by John Wiley & Sons, Inc. Reprinted by permission of John Wiley & Sons, Inc.
75–76	Passage from "Islamic Religious Tradition," by Charles J. Adams, which appears in *The Study of the Middle East,* edited by Leonard Binder. Copyright © 1976, by John Wiley & Sons, Inc. Reprinted by permission of John Wiley & Sons, Inc.
76–77	Passage from *Life Science in The Twentieth Century,* by Garland E. Allen. Copyright © 1975, by John Wiley & Sons, Inc. Reprinted by permission of John Wiley & Sons, Inc.
78–79	Passage from *Paths to the Present: Thoughts on the Contemporary Relevance of America's Past,* by Thomas J. Osborne and Fred R. Mabbutt. Copyright © 1974, by John Wiley & Sons, Inc. Reprinted by permission of John Wiley & Sons, Inc.

Pages	*Source*
80–81	Passage from *Taira: An Okinawan Village,* by Thomas Maretzki and Hatsumi Maretzki, which is Volume VII in the *Six Cultures: Studies of Child Rearing* series edited by Beatrice B. Whiting. Copyright © 1966, by John Wiley & Sons, Inc. Reprinted by permission of John Wiley & Sons, Inc.
164–165	Passage from "Chapbook Influence on Irish Mummers' Plays," by Alan Gailey, which appears in *Folklore,* Vol. 85, 1974. Reprinted by permission of *Folklore.*
166–167	Passage from "The Nature of Comets," by Fred L. Whipple. Copyright © 1974, by Scientific American, Inc. All rights reserved. Reprinted by permission.
168–169	Passage from *Introduction to Psychology, 4th edition,* by Ernest R. Hilgard and Richard C. Atkinson. Copyright © 1953, 1957, 1962, 1967, by Harcourt Brace Jovanovich, Inc., and reprinted with their permission.
170–171	Passage from *The American Tradition in Literature, Volume 1,* edited by Sculley Bradley, Richmond Croom Beatty, E. Hudson Long, and George Perkins. Copyright © 1956, 1957, 1962, 1967, 1974, by Grosset & Dunlap, Inc. Used by permission of Grosset & Dunlap, Inc.
176	Graph "U. S. Energy Flow – 1980" from the pamphlet UCRL 51487, "U. S. Energy Flow Charts for 1950, 1960, 1970, 1980, 1985, and 1990," by A. L. Austin and S. D. Winter, dated November 16, 1973. Prepared for U. S. Atomic Energy Commission under contract No. W-7405-Eng-48. Designated TID-4500, UC-13, Nonnuclear Energy Sources and Energy Conversion Devices, Lawrence Livermore Laboratory. Reprinted by permission of the National Technical Information Service.
180–181 (passage 1)	Passage reprinted with permission from *Science News,* the weekly news magazine of science and the applications of science. Copyright © 1974, by Science Service, Inc.
181–182 (passage 2)	Passage from *The Family Herds,* by P. H. Gulliver, published by Routledge & Kegan Paul, Ltd., London, 1955, second impression, 1966. Reprinted by permission of Routledge & Kegan Paul, Ltd.
285–316	Foreword and Table from the booklet "Law Schools and Bar Admission Requirements: A Review of Legal Education in the United States – Fall 1977." Copyright © 1977, by the American Bar Association, Reproduced by permission of the American Bar Association, 1977.

Acknowledgments

Very special thanks to my parents.

For their contributions, thanks to Paul K. Stanton and Stuart Miller.

Thanks also to Elizabeth Boehm, Irene Brownstone, Joyce Campbell, Ellen Cooperman, Mark Kalman, Steve Madsen, Kurt Paul, Robert Raciti, Merton Reichler, Michael Ricky, Robert Shannon, Richard Spector, Sari Walker, Joshua Wallace, and Judy Wilson.

Special acknowledgment to Burt Neuborne for acknowledging me in his own book and for being my inspiration for a career in the Law.

Randolph Z. Volkell

Dedication

To the memory of Irene and Joseph Tax

INTRODUCTION

What You Need to Know

The grade you get on the Law School Admission Test (LSAT) may not have very much to do with how good a lawyer you will be, or even how good a law student you will be. However, it can have a great deal to do with how good a law school you can attend. The purpose of this book is to help you do as well as possible on the LSAT.

The LSAT is not an achievement test, a test of how much you know. On the contrary—you are cautioned *not* to rely on your outside knowledge in answering the questions. Nor is it really an aptitude test. In fact, the most important contributor toward your score will probably be your mental attitude when you take the test. Once you have finished working through all the materials in this book, you should feel comfortable with the types of questions you will see on the LSAT. You should be able to finish the book in a couple of weeks at an easy pace, or in a few days of intensive study. This Self-Teaching Guide is entirely self-contained—you need no other aids or courses to prepare you for the LSAT. It is streamlined to cover only what you *need* to know and is designed to be readable rather than highly technical. If you work the exercises and sample test sections carefully, you should have the confidence you need to do well on the test.

The LSAT questions themselves are usually not too hard—the real problem you will face is timing. Each section is designed so that an average student has about a 50% chance of finishing all of the questions. Each section is timed separately—if you finish early on one you cannot use the time to work on another. As you go through the practice materials in the book, you will learn how to pace yourself and to work at your optimum speed. Any time you are unable to finish a section or answer a particular question, be sure to fill in a guess—there is no penalty for wrong answers, and guessing can only help you.

The LSAT itself is about three and a half or four hours long and usually consists of seven sections. You will receive two separate scores—a three-digit LSAT score (ranging from 200–800) and a two-digit writing ability score (ranging from 20–80). The first four sections generally determine the LSAT score and the fifth and sixth, the writing ability. The last section is usually experimental, which means that it does not count in your score. You *must,* however, take every section seriously. Do your best on every question, even if you are sure it is experimental—it just might count.

Tests given on a different date, or even on the same date, can include a different selection of sections. As we go to press, the four sections that count toward your three-digit LSAT score are being drawn from the following list: Reading Comprehension, Reading Recall, Data Interpretation, Principles and Cases, Logical Reasoning, Practical Judgment, and Quantitative Comparison. The Principles and Cases section has always appeared, generally as the fourth section. The first and third sections usually test reading and reasoning skills. Typically, you will have Reading Comprehension and Reading Recall or Logical Reasoning and Practical Judgment. The second section usually tests mathematical skills—either Data Interpretation or Quantitative Comparison. The writing ability part consists of two sections—Error Recognition and Sentence Correction. The experimental section might be one of the sections we have already mentioned, a variation on a standard section, or a new type of section.

Of course, the test is always subject to change, but past experience indicates that you might expect the following:

Section I Reading Comprehension or Logical Reasoning

In Reading Comprehension, you will be given four passages to read, with 25 questions to answer. Questions are given after each passage, and you can refer back to the passages while answering the questions.

In Logical Reasoning, you will also have 25 questions, but the passages will be much shorter, with only one or two questions on each, and they will cover a variety of styles and question types.

Section II Data Interpretation or Quantitative Comparison

In Data Interpretation, you will be given a set of graphs with about six or seven questions about each one. To answer them, you will have to read the graph and do some calculation. The emphasis will be on estimation and quick thinking, not calculations.

In Quantitative Comparison, you are asked to compare two quantities and indicate if they are equal or unequal (and which is larger) or if there is no way to tell.

Section III Reading Recall or Practical Judgment

In the Reading Recall Section, you are given three passages to read in 15 minutes. You are then given 30 questions to answer in 15 minutes, *without looking back at the passages.*

In Practical Judgment, you are given two long passages with 25 questions on each one. The first 19 questions are called Data Evaluation, in which you are asked to categorize a list of items from the passage. The last six, the Data Application questions, ask you to interpret and calculate based on the passage.

Section IV Principles and Cases

There are several types of Principles and Cases sections, but the basic idea in most is to apply an imaginary principle to an imaginary case and determine what the result should be.

Section V Error Recognition

In this section, you are given 35 sentences and asked to indicate whether each contains a diction error, verbosity error, grammar error, or no error at all.

Section VI Sentence Correction

This section contains 25 sentences, each of which contains an underlined part. You are asked to select the *best* replacement for the underlined part, or to leave the sentence alone if it is better without any change.

Section VII This is generally the experimental section.

We must emphasize again that the Educational Testing Service (ETS) is under no obligation to follow this order—it is only a prediction based on past performance.

In this book, we will spend time on each of the standard section types. We begin with a background chapter to help prepare you for the mathematical sections, followed by chapters on those sections. The text chapters deal with the sections that test reading and reasoning skills (the Reading, Logical Reasoning, and Practical Judgment sections). These are followed by a chapter on Principles and Cases, and one chapter on Writing Ability (the Error Recognition and Sentence Correction sections). Appendix A contains samples of question types that have appeared experimentally on recent tests. Each chapter ends with one or more self-tests, complete with answers and explanations. Answer sheets are provided in the back of the book for all of the tests, if you want to practice under actual conditions.

The second part of the book contains two full-scale self-tests with answers and explanations. To make best use of these tests, you should go through all of the chapters and chapter self-tests first, to become thoroughly familiar with the question types. Then, when you are ready to try the full-scale test, try to simulate actual test conditions. Block off a period of about 4 hours in an undisturbed place and time yourself carefully for each section. That experience will let you learn how to pace yourself. Use the answer sheets at the back of the book. Then, as soon as possible while the questions are fresh in your mind, carefully go over the answers and explanations given in the book. If possible, then wait a day or so before you take the second sample test.

Use all of the material in this book to help you prepare, but do not try to predict your LSAT score based on how you do on these tests. You will find out soon enough, and you can accomplish nothing useful by trying to predict your score in advance. Just take each test as a learning experience, and when it is time for the actual LSAT you will know that you have prepared as well as you can.

In addition to this book, you should read the Law School Admission Bulletin, published by the Educational Testing Service (ETS) and available from them or any College Placement Office, and the description of the LSAT, which the ETS will mail to you free of charge as soon as you apply for the test. It contains a sample LSAT with answers, as well as a description of the various sections. Fur further information about the LSAT, write to:

Law School Admission Services
Box 944
Princeton, New Jersey 08540

In general, remember that time is of the essence. With this Self-Teaching Guide, you will learn to underline and highlight on the verbal sections and to estimate and use short cuts on the mathematical sections. Whenever a question looks as if it will take too much time, skip it and come back to it at the end if time allows. Each question has exactly the same value. If you guess, try first to eliminate any answers you can be sure are wrong. Every ten questions or so, check to make sure you are answering the correct question number.

Special Feature To make applying to law school easier for you, we have provided in the back of this book a table of law schools on the approved list of the American Bar Association, 1976. This table includes the address, enrollment and type of program, type and number of degrees awarded, costs, time and credits required, composition of teaching faculty, and total volumes in the library. This table is part of a booklet called "Law Schools and Bar Admission Requirements: A Review of Legal Education in the United States–Fall 1977" published by the American Bar Association, Section of Legal Education and Admissions to the Bar. Single copies of this booklet are available without charge upon request from the American Bar Association, 1155 East Sixtieth Street, Chicago, Illinois 60637.

Before you take the actual LSAT, review the page called Tips for Taking the LSAT for some last-minute reminders. Now turn to page 1 and start your preparation for the LSAT. Good luck!

Tips for Taking the LSAT

1. Be sure to bring your admission ticket with you.
2. Bring at least two soft lead pencils or a mechanical pencil with refills. Also, bring a pencil eraser so that you can change an answer you think is incorrect.
3. Bring a watch that keeps correct time and check it when you start so that you can pace yourself.
4. Read the instructions and each question very, very carefully—don't start until you're sure you understand what you are expected to do. Some questions will call for you to select one, or a combination of correct or incorrect alternatives. Be careful with all questions, but especially those which read "All of the following are correct *except—*."
5. As you go through the test, stop at every tenth question and make sure that you are entering the answer to that question in the right place on the answer sheet. That is, when you answer question 10, make sure you're putting the answer in the tenth answer place, and so on for the twentieth, thirtieth, etc. Otherwise it is too easy to slip by just one number and then to go on through the rest of the section, answering each question correctly, but in the wrong place.
6. In each section, start with the first question and continue right through to the end, answering those you're sure of, but skipping those you're not sure of the first time. Mark in the question booklet each one you skip. When you've finished the entire section, go back to those you skipped. This time you'll find you can answer many of them. You'll be less nervous and more confident. Watch your time carefully, to make sure you have enough time to go back to those you haven't answered. If you still don't know the answers, eliminate any choices you are sure are wrong, and guess. There's no penalty for wrong answers, so be sure to answer every question.
7. If you still have time, you might want to recheck your answers. But be very careful, and don't change an answer unless you're absolutely sure you were wrong the first time. Usually, your first impression is better than a later one.
8. You might wish to bring some hard candy to the test with you.
9. Do not panic.
10. Good luck!

Contents

CHAPTER ONE

Preliminary Math Review

To solve the mathematical problems in the Law School Admission Test (LSAT), you need know nothing more advanced than junior high school math. Some questions require only that you read a graph; others ask you to do some calculation. As a general rule where graphs are concerned, the more complex the visual display, the simpler will be the questions that follow it. The actual calculation will usually not be the most difficult task required by the question. This chapter presents background material to give you the foundation you need to solve math questions of the LSAT type to be given in the chapters which follow.

For example, try this simple problem:

> When a certain number is multiplied by 3, the result is 32 more than the number itself. What is the number?

The first and most important step in solving such a problem is to translate the words into mathematical symbols. Let's call the number n. Then,

$$3n = n + 32$$

Now that we have "set up" the problem, its solution is easy:

$$2n = 32$$
$$n = 16$$

Our "certain number" (n) was 16.

On the LSAT, you won't see any questions like the one we just answered. The data interpretation section will consist of four or five graphs, tables, or charts. Each graph will be followed by approximately seven questions referring to it. The quantitative comparison section will contain short-answer questions of a wholly different nature, as we shall see. All questions will be multiple choice.

Probably the most important factor in the test will be time. You don't have to finish every question, but the more you answer, the higher your score will be. (No penalty is given for guessing.) If you come to a question that looks as if it will take a disproportionate amount of time, go on to the next one, leaving the more time-consuming question for the end. The value of each question is the same, so your time is better spent in answering several easy questions than in answering one hard one.

ESTIMATION VERSUS CALCULATION

You should learn when to estimate and when to calculate. If you calculate every number, you will not finish the test section. On the other hand, if you always estimate, many of your answers will be wrong.

For example, if you knew that the answer was $\frac{243}{387}$ and your choices were 0.35, 0.40, 0.60, and 0.80, you could safely estimate the answer to be closest to 0.60. (The fraction appears to be about $\frac{2}{3}$—actually, a little bit less.) But if the choices were 0.60, 0.61, 0.63, 0.65, and 0.67, you would need to divide the fraction out to be sure that 0.63 is the best answer.

Often the same problem may be solved in an easy way and a hard way. The more shortcuts you know, the faster you will be able to work. For example, suppose you bowl 168 and 204 in the first two games of a three-game series. What score must you bowl in the third game to have a 200 average for the series?

Let's solve it the hard way:

$$\frac{204 + 168 + x}{3} = 200$$

$$\frac{372 + x}{3} = 200$$

$$372 + x = 600$$

$$x = 228$$

That method takes time, but you can obtain the same result without ever lifting a pencil.

In order to average 200, you could bowl three games of 200 each. If you bowl less in one game, you must make up the difference in another. The 168 game is 32 short of 200. The 204 game makes up 4 points. Thus you are still 28 points short going into the third game, so you need to bowl a 228 game.

$$\begin{aligned} &\text{Game 1:}\ 168 - 200 = -32 \\ &\text{Game 2:}\ 204 - 200 = \underline{\ \ +4} \\ &\qquad\qquad\qquad\qquad\ \ -28 \\ &\text{Game 3:}\ 228 - 200 = \underline{+28} \\ &\qquad\qquad\qquad\qquad\qquad 0 \end{aligned}$$

We will be discussing these problem-solving techniques, and many others, more fully. You may not want to use all of them, but some of them will undoubtedly be helpful. As you work through this book, you will have a chance to try them all and decide which ones you would like to adopt.

Those of you who are skilled mathematicians may now wish to move ahead to page 4. If you have been out of touch with the numerical world lately, or want to be sure of your methods, or want to try them just for fun, we present a few exercises to jog your mathematical memories.

Try these problems, timing yourself for 5 minutes. (Answers are given below the line of dashes.)

1. Bobby, Richie, and Mike each start with 50 marbles. If at the end of their game Richie has 67 marbles and Mike has 74, how many marbles has Bobby lost? ______

2. Wanda the Witch makes 600 predictions for 1984. If 120 of them come true, what percentage of the time is Wanda right? ______

3. Which number is the smallest: $\frac{284}{673}$, $\frac{1}{2}$, 0.6, 1, or $\frac{301}{652}$? ______

4. If a golfer plays rounds of 68, 70, and 67, what score does he need in the fourth round to bring his average down to 67? ______

5. In Ms. Wilson's kindergarten class, the tallest student is 5'2" tall; the shortest is 3'11" tall. How much shorter is the shortest student than the tallest student? ______

6. Which of the following numbers is not equal to all of the others: $\frac{16}{64}$, 0.25, 25%, $\frac{1}{4}$, $\frac{250}{10{,}000}$, or 7:28? ______

7. When 16 is added to a certain number, and the sum is divided by the original number, the result is 9. What was the original number? ______

8. If Superman can fly 15,000 miles per hour, how long does it take him to make a round trip to a city 3,000 miles away? ______

Let's look at the answers.

1. Richie gained 17 marbles and Mike gained 24. They won 41 marbles between them, so Bobby lost 41 of his marbles.

2. Of Wanda's predictions, $\frac{120}{600}$ are true. You might have recognized that this fraction is equal to $\frac{1}{5}$, or 20%. Otherwise, you could divide it out, in which case you would still get 0.20, or 20%. We'll talk more about percents later.

3. This problem can be done without computation. Since $\frac{284}{673}$ is obviously less than half, $\frac{1}{2}$, 0.6, and 1 are all out of the picture, and since $\frac{284}{673}$ has a smaller numerator and a larger denominator than $\frac{301}{652}$, it must be the smallest of the five numbers.

4. The golfer took one extra stroke in his first round (68) and three extra strokes in his second round (70), for a total of four strokes higher than if he had averaged 67. Therefore, in his fourth round, he must golf four strokes under 67, or a 63.

5. **To find the difference in height, we must subtract 3'11" from 5'2". To do this, we may conveniently think of 5'2" as 4'14". (That process is called borrowing—remember?)**

4'14"
- 3'11"
1' 3", or 15"

6. **All are equal to each other except $\frac{250}{10,000}$, which is 0.025, or $\frac{1}{10}$ as much as each of the other numbers.**

7. **Again, the trick is in the translation. Let's call the number *n* again. Then 16 plus *n*, all divided by *n*, equals 9.**

$$\frac{16 + n}{n} = 9$$

Now we can solve:

$$16 + n = 9n$$
$$16 = 8n$$
$$2 = n$$

So our original number was 2.

8. **The round trip is 6,000 miles long, so it takes Superman $\frac{6,000}{15,000}$, or $\frac{2}{5}$ of an hour, or 24 minutes.**

After this simple review, we are ready to talk a little about the LSAT. Two concepts—ratio and percentage—appear in many LSAT questions.

RATIOS

Once you understand what a ratio is, you should never again have trouble interpreting one. Basically, a ratio is just the answer to a simple division problem. It is, then, simply a number—the ratio of 3 to 5 (written 3:5) is just $\frac{3}{5}$, or 0.6. The ratio of 8 to 4 (8:4) is 2. To compare two or more ratios exactly, simply divide them out. The larger answer is the larger ratio, and the smaller answer is the smaller ratio.

Which of the following represents the smallest ratio? the largest?

8:4
1:1
623:717
19:38
2:7

You will begin by dividing them out, right? *Wrong.* Remember, we need not know exactly what each of these numbers is, only which ratio is the largest and which is the smallest. The first ratio is easy to determine—the ratio of 8:4 is 2. The second is 1. The third ratio, however, is not so easy to find without computation. But we can see that it is a bit less than 1. If it turns out that this ratio may be the smallest, we may have to be more accurate than that, but for now, why bother? The fourth is exactly the same as 1:2, or $\frac{1}{2}$. Since $\frac{1}{2}$ is clearly smaller than 623:717, we are saved from computing the complex division. Finally, the last is 2:7—less than $\frac{1}{2}$. This ratio is the smallest. (It is actually 0.286.) The largest was the first (8:4). Please note that the size of the numbers involved makes no difference—623:717 was not the largest ratio, and 1:1 was not the smallest.

Now, try these problems:

City A has a population of 50 and a Gross Annual Income (GAI) of $5,000. City B has a population of 6,000 and a GAI of $3,000,000. City C, with a population of 1,000, has a GAI of $1,000,000; City D has a population of 1 and a GAI of $3,000.

1. **Which city has the largest ratio of GAI to population? ______ the smallest? ______**

2. **Which city has the largest per capita annual income? ______ the smallest? ______**

3. **Which city has the largest ratio of population to GAI? ______ the smallest? ______**

4. **Which city has a per capita income exactly half that of another city? ______**

- -

The answers to those four questions are:

1. **The best way to start is to calculate the four ratios; you can do this in your head if you are careful with the zeroes.**

   City A: 5,000:50 = 100
   City B: 3,000,000:6,000 = 500
   City C: 1,000,000:1,000 = 1,000
   City D: 3,000:1 = 3,000

   City D has the largest ratio, and City A has the smallest.

2. **This question asks for exactly the same information as the first one. *Per capita* means per person; you should remember this term. The income per person is equal to the total income divided by the number of people (or, the average income). We have calculated exactly this in the first question, and both answers are the same.**

3. **This question is basically the same as the first two, but the answer is reversed. City A has the largest ratio and City D has the smallest. If you calculated, the ratios are:**

   City A: 0.01 (50:5,000)
   City B: 0.002 (6,000:3,000,000)
   City C: 0.001 (1,000:1,000,000)
   City D: 0.0033 (1:3,000)

4. **By inspecting our original four ratios, we see that City B's per capita income ($500) is exactly half of City C's ($1,000).**

PERCENTAGES

Ordinary percentage problems are very simple. They come in only three types. For example, you could be asked:

1. **What percentage is 9 of 10? (What percentage of 10 is 9?)**

2. **What is 90% of 10?**

3. **Nine is 90% of what number?**

Once you learn to recognize the three problem types, you should have no difficulty solving them.

1. **What percentage is 9 of 10?**

This type of question is the easiest to answer. You need only divide the number associated with the word "is" by the number associated with the word "of": $\frac{9}{10} = 0.90$. To convert a decimal into percentage, multiply by 100 ($0.90 \cdot 100\% = 90\%$). Thus, 9 is 90% of 10.

2. **What is 90% of 10?**

Translate the question into an equation, substituting x for "what." You then have:

$$x = 90\% \text{ of } 10$$

or

$$x = \left(\frac{90}{100}\right)(10)$$

$$x = \frac{900}{100} = 9$$

So 9 is 90% of 10.

3. **Nine is 90% of what number?**

Again, make an equation:

$$9 = 90\% \text{ of } x$$

$$9 = \left(\frac{90}{100}\right) x$$

$$900 = 90x$$

$$\frac{900}{90} = x$$

$$10 = x$$

So 9 is 90% of 10.

Try these problems:

1. **What percentage of 8 is 3? ________**

2. **Forty-eight is 75% of what number? ________**

3. **What number is 60% of 80? ________**

4. **Bobby starts the day with 25 marbles.**

   a. **If he loses six to Duggan, what percent of his original marbles does he have left? ________**

   b. **If he loses eight more to Doug, what percentage of Bobby's marbles do Doug and Duggan have between them? ________**

   c. **If he loses 11 more to Connie, what percentage of his marbles has Bobby lost altogether? ________**

5. **If Sergeant Friday invites 19 police officers to his house, and 90% of the force is not invited, how many people are on the force? ________**

6. **The Batmobile has a fuel gauge which registers, in percent, how full the fuel tank is. If Robin takes the car out on Saturday night with a full tank (40 gallons) and comes back Sunday morning with the needle on 4%, how many gallons did he use?________**

- - - - - - - - - - - - - - - - - - - -

1. **Three is 37.5% of 8.**

$$\frac{3}{8} = 0.375$$

2. **When you can reduce easily, you should do so. You will find, then, that 48 is 75% of 64.**

$$48 = \left(\frac{75}{100}\right)x$$

$$48 = \left(\frac{3}{4}\right)x$$

$$\left(\frac{4}{3}\right)48 = x$$

$$(4)16 = x$$

$$64 = x$$

3. **Forty-eight is 60% of 80.**

$$x = \frac{60}{100}(80)$$

$$x = \frac{4{,}800}{100} = 48$$

4. a. **If he loses 6, he has 19, or 76%, left.**

$$\frac{19}{25} = 0.76$$

b. **Doug and Duggan between them have 14 of the 25 marbles, so they have 56% of Bobby's marbles.**

$$\frac{14}{25} = 0.56$$

c. **Altogether, Bobby has now lost 25 marbles. Poor Bobby has lost all of his marbles.**

$$\frac{25}{25} = 1, \text{ or } 100\%$$

5. **Nineteen police officers are equal to 10% of the force, so the entire force has 190 members.**

$$19 = 10\% \text{ of } x$$

$$19 = \left(\frac{1}{10}\right) x$$

$$190 = x$$

6. **Robin used 96% of the 40 gallons, so he used 38.4 gallons.**

$$x = \left(\frac{96}{100}\right)(40) = \frac{(96)(4)}{10} = \frac{384}{10} = 38.4$$

Percent change. As you consider percentages, be aware of the notion of percent increase and percent decrease, or, more generally, percent change. Clearly, before we can talk about the percent change, some sort of change must be suggested. If nothing changes, then the change is zero, and the percent change is zero.

Suppose Mike starts out with 10 marbles and ends up with 15. By what percent has he increased his collection?

He started with 10 and showed an increase of 5. In other words, he finished with half again as many marbles as he had when he started. This change is a 50% increase.

The formula is very simple:

$$\text{percent change} = \frac{\text{actual change}}{\text{original}} \text{ or } \frac{\text{difference}}{\text{original}}$$

Note that we did not ask "what percent of Mike's starting total was his final total?" The answer then would have been 150% $\left(\frac{15}{10} = 1.5\right)$.

Try these sample problems:

Seth, Gary, and Bimbo each start with a stake of $10 and play pinochle. At the end of the game, the money is distributed this way:

Bimbo	$28
Gary	$ 2
Seth	$ 0

1. **What was Bimbo's percent gain? ________**

2. **What percentage of Bimbo's stake was his final total? ________**

3. **What was Gary's percent loss? ________**

4. **What percentage of Gary's stake was his final total? ________**

5. **What was Seth's percent loss? ________**

6. **What percentage of Seth's stake was his final total? ________**

– – – – – – – – – – – – – – – – – – – –

1. **Bimbo started with $10 and ended with $28—an increase of $18, which is 180% of $10.**

2. **Since $\frac{\$28}{\$10}$ equals 2.8, then $28 is 280% of $10.**

3. **Gary had an $8 loss. This $8 is 80% of his original $10.**

4. **Since $\frac{\$2}{\$10}$ equals 0.2, then $2 is 20% of $10.**

5. **Seth lost all of his $10: $\frac{\$10}{\$10} = 1$. He lost 100% of his money.**

6. **Since Seth had no dollars left, he retained 0% of his original stake $\left(\frac{0}{\$10} = 0\right)$.**

Averages. Let's take a look at one more useful trick. If you study it for a few minutes and then practice it, you should be able to calculate averages with great speed, ease, and accuracy. The idea is basically the same one we used on page 2.

Suppose Lizzy bowls games of 172, 167, 147, and 210. The first step in figuring out her average is to take a guess. Whether the guess is correct doesn't matter; any guess will serve as a starting point. But in practice, the better the guess, the easier the arithmetic. Let's guess 170. In the first game, then, Lizzy came out 2 ahead of our guess. In the second game she was 3 behind, in the third 23 behind, and in the fourth 40 ahead. By adding, we find she was ahead 42 and behind 26; altogether, she was 16 ahead.

172	**170**	+2
167	**170**	−3
147	**170**	−23
210	**170**	+40
		+16

Those 16 points, though, were accumulated over a period of four games, which means that she beat our guess by 4 points per game. Her average was 174.

Once you get used to it, this technique is much easier than the conventional method which yields the same result but involves somewhat lengthy and error-prone arithmetic:

$$\frac{172 + 167 + 147 + 210}{4} = \frac{696}{4} = 174$$

Suppose we had guessed 180 instead of 170; would the technique still work? Let's see:

172	**180**	−8
167	**180**	−13
147	**180**	−33
210	**180**	+30
		−24

Since $\frac{-24}{4}$ equals −6, the average for four games is 180 minus 6, or 174.

Now determine the average of these numbers:

140 121 131 116

If we guessed the average to be 130, we could make the following mental calculations:

140	**130**	+10
121	**130**	−9 (altogether +1)
131	**130**	+1 (altogether +2)
116	**130**	−14 (altogether −12)

Since $\frac{-12}{4}$ equals −3, the average is 130 minus 3, or 127.

Average the following sets of numbers, without writing, if possible.

1. **136 113 111** ______

2. **91 57 70 68 69** ______

3. **1 24 18 21** ______

The answers are:

1. **120**

2. **71**

3. **16**

Preliminary Math Review Self-Test

Directions: These problems will help you review what we have discussed in this chapter. Circle the best answer to each problem. (Don't worry about timing in this review. As noted earlier, the problems in this chapter review basic skills that you will use in various parts of the LSAT. For the moment, just concentrate on the problem-solving techniques.) Answers follow the test.

1. If $\frac{x}{250}$ equals 2.4%, then x equals:

   (A) 0.6 (B) 6 (C) 60 (D) 104.2 (E) 144

2. If halvah that usually sells for $1.20 a pound is on sale for $.90 a pound, what is the percent reduction?

   (A) 25% (B) 30% (C) $33\frac{1}{3}\%$ (D) $66\frac{2}{3}\%$ (E) 75%

3. What part of a yard is one half of a foot?

   (A) $\frac{1}{12}$ (B) $\frac{1}{4}$ (C) $\frac{1}{6}$ (D) $\frac{1}{3}$ (E) $\frac{1}{2}$

4. Which of these fractions has the largest value?

   (A) $\frac{2}{5}$ (B) $\frac{21}{32}$ (C) $\frac{11}{16}$ (D) $\frac{55}{64}$ (E) $\frac{7}{8}$

5. During his first 6 weeks as an attorney, Perry earned $45 per week; during the next 4 weeks, he earned $52 per week. What was his average weekly earning for the entire period?

   (A) $47.80 (B) $48.50 (C) $48.70 (D) $50.30 (E) $52.00

6. When a dealer sells a hat for $22, he makes a $33\frac{1}{3}\%$ profit over cost. The hat is now on sale, and the dealer is making only a 20% profit. The current price is:

   (A) $13.20 (B) $16.50 (C) $19.80 (D) $20.00 (E) $21.00

7. Nine out of 10 members of the graduating class at the local high school are going to college. Of these, $\frac{3}{5}$ are going to Kings College. What part of the class is going to other colleges?

   (A) $\frac{3}{10}$ (B) $\frac{9}{25}$ (C) $\frac{2}{5}$ (D) $\frac{4}{9}$ (E) $\frac{1}{2}$

8. What percent of $\frac{1}{4}$ is $\frac{1}{3}$?

   (A) $\frac{3}{4}\%$ (B) $1\frac{1}{3}\%$ (C) $8\frac{1}{3}\%$ (D) 75% (E) 133%

9. What is 0.5% of 2,800?

(A) 0.14 (B) 1.4 (C) 14 (D) 140 (E) 1,400

10. What percent of 4 is x?

(A) $\frac{x}{4}\%$ (B) $\frac{4}{x}\%$ (C) $\frac{400}{x}\%$ (D) $\frac{x}{400}\%$ (E) $25x\%$

11. Eighteen is 9% of:

(A) 1.62 (B) 20 (C) 162 (D) 180 (E) 200

12. If 6.25% of the people in a city are silly, and 2,000 people are silly, how many people are in the city?

(A) 3,200 (B) 17,000 (C) 32,000 (D) 34,000 (E) 320,000

13. Captain Mike bowled an average of 150 points per game for 12 games. If he bowls 6 more games, how high an average must he maintain in these games to raise his average for the 18 games to 160?

(A) 170 (B) 180 (C) 190 (D) 210 (E) 225

14. Thirty-two is $\frac{2}{7}$ of what number?

(A) $9\frac{1}{7}$ (B) 14 (C) 64 (D) 112 (E) 224

15. A chocolate bar costs $4.40 including the 10% candy tax. How much does it cost without tax?

(A) $3.60 (B) $3.96 (C) $4.00 (D) $4.04 (E) $4.20

16. Bill gets $1.10 per hour for work in the candy store, and a 20% bonus after 6:00 p.m. How much does he earn between 4:00 p.m. and 8:20 p.m.?

(A) $2.71 (B) $4.76 (C) $5.28 (D) $5.71 (E) $7.50

17. During the holiday season, Mr. Miggle increases his staff by 20%. If 150 people are employed during the holidays, how many are employed at other times?

(A) 100 (B) 120 (C) 125 (D) 130 (E) 180

18. Milenko takes a French test every week. In the fifth week, his average drops from 72% to 70%. His grade on the fifth test was:

(A) 59 (B) 60 (C) 61 (D) 62 (E) 63

19. At St. Kenneth Hospital, an average of one baby is born every 5 hours. Approximately how many are born in a year?

(A) 250 (B) 1,600 (C) 1,750 (D) 2,000 (E) 2,500

20. Mr. Loman, a salesman, is paid $50 per month plus 4% of all his sales. If he earns $200 in July, what are his total sales that month?

(A) $375 (B) $600 (C) $800 (D) $3,750 (E) $5,000

21. If the population of Sleepy Hollow increases from 3,000 to 12,000, what is the percent increase?

(A) 25% (B) 75% (C) $133\frac{1}{3}$% (D) 300% (E) 400%

22. A man paid $44.10 for a fake beard, after receiving successive discounts of 10% and 2% from list price. What was the list price?

(A) $49.39 (B) $49.48 (C) $49.96 (D) $50.00 (E) $50.11

23. Acme Furniture offers a chair for $63 cash, or $5 down and $6.50 a month for 10 months. The installment price is greater than the cash price by:

(A) 1% (B) 7% (C) 9% (D) 10% (E) 11%

24. In a three-candidate race, one candidate gets $\frac{3}{5}$ of the votes, and another gets $\frac{3}{4}$ of the remainder. What portion of the total vote does the third candidate get?

(A) $\frac{1}{10}$ (B) $\frac{1}{5}$ (C) $\frac{3}{10}$ (D) $\frac{1}{4}$ (E) $\frac{9}{20}$

25. On a $9,840 bill, what is the difference between a discount of 30% and successive discounts of 20% and 10%?

(A) No difference (B) $195.20 (C) $196.80 (D) $787.20
(E) $2,755.20

Answers to Preliminary Math Review Self-Test

Our solutions are given below. You may have solved a problem in a different way. You should use whatever shortcuts you know, in addition to those we've covered.

1. (B) **You can easily do this problem without calculating. The fraction $\frac{2.5}{250}$ would be 1%, so $\frac{5}{250}$ would be 2%. What we need, then, is a number a little bigger than 5; only 6 appears in the answers. If you wanted to calculate this solution, you would have to multiply each side of the equation by 250 to get *x*.**

   $$x = (250)(2.4\%) = 6$$

2. (A) **The *original* price is $1.20. The *new* price is $.90. The *actual change,* then, is $.30.**

   $1.20 → $.30 → $.90

   The percent change is the actual change, or difference, divided by the original.

   $$\frac{\text{difference}}{\text{original}} = \frac{0.30}{1.20} = \frac{1}{4} = 25\%$$

3. (C) $$\frac{\frac{1}{2}\text{ foot}}{1\text{ yard}} = \frac{\frac{1}{2}\text{ foot}}{3\text{ feet}} = \frac{1}{6}$$

4. (E) **You could convert all of these fractions to decimals, but to do so would take much more time than it is worth. The fraction $\frac{2}{5}$ is less than $\frac{1}{2}$; all the rest are more than $\frac{1}{2}$. The fraction $\frac{11}{16}$ is $\frac{22}{32}$, so it is larger than $\frac{21}{32}$. On the other hand, it is only $\frac{44}{64}$, so it is much smaller than $\frac{55}{64}$. Since $\frac{7}{8}$ is the same as $\frac{56}{64}$, it is the largest.**

5. (A) **Since he has worked 10 weeks altogether, it is probably easiest just to work out the answer by the traditional method—in your head, if possible.**

   $$(6)(\$45.00) = \$270.00$$
   $$(4)(\$52.00) = \underline{\$208.00}$$
   $$\$478.00 \div 10 = \$47.80$$

6. (C) **First, we must determine the cost. We know that cost plus $33\frac{1}{3}\%$ (or $1\frac{1}{3}$ cost) is $22. Let cost equal *c*. Then $\frac{4}{3}c$ equals $22.00, and *c* equals $16.50. The**

current price is 20% more than cost, or $\frac{6}{5}$ ($16.50). The current price is $19.80 (alternatively, 20% of $16.50 = $3.10; $16.50 + $3.10 = $19.80).

7. (B) Two-fifths of the college-bound graduates are going to colleges other than Kings, so $\frac{2}{5}$ of $\frac{9}{10}$ of all the students in the class interest us.

$$\left(\frac{2}{5}\right)\left(\frac{9}{10}\right) = \frac{18}{50} = \frac{9}{25}$$

8. (E) The fraction $\frac{1}{3}$ is larger than $\frac{1}{4}$. Therefore, it must be more than 100% of $\frac{1}{4}$, and only 133% fits that description. To compute it, remember the rule of thumb: *is* over *of*.

$$\frac{1}{3} \div \frac{1}{4}$$

Invert and multiply:

$$\frac{1}{3} \cdot \frac{4}{1} = \frac{4}{3} = 133\frac{1}{3}\%$$

On the LSAT, once you know an answer is correct, you should mark it and go on to the next question, without working it out the rest of the way.

9. (C) One percent of 2,800 would be $\frac{2{,}800}{100}$, or 28. The decimal fraction 0.5% (or $\frac{1}{2}$%) is exactly half as much, or 14. Or, you can say $\frac{0.5 \cdot 2{,}800}{100} = 14$. Just as you multiply by 100 to convert numbers to percents, you divide by 100 to convert percents to numbers.

10. (E) Remember, *is* over *of!*

$$\frac{x}{4} \cdot 100\% = 25x\%$$

11. (E) Make an equation:

$$18 = \frac{9x}{100}$$

$$1{,}800 = 9x$$

$$200 = x$$

12. (C) Again, make an equation:

$$2{,}000 = 6.25\% \text{ of } x$$

$$2{,}000 = \frac{6.25}{100}x$$

$$200{,}000 = 6.25x$$

$$32{,}000 = x$$

13. (B) If he is to finish with an average of 160, the good captain has bowled 10 points per game (or a total of 120 points) too little in the first 12 games. He must make them up in the last six games. To do so, he must average 20 points a game more than 160, or 180. You can also do this the hard way, but we do not recommend that method.

14. (D)

$$32 = \frac{2}{7}x$$

$$\left(\frac{7}{2}\right)32 = x$$

$$112 = x$$

15. (C) Let's call the cost c.

$$c + 10\%c = \$4.40$$

$$110\%c = \$4.40$$

$$1.1c = \$4.40$$

$$c = \$4.00$$

(You should not write out all of these steps. If you are really catching on to our estimating techniques, you probably shouldn't have to lift your pencil to do a problem like this one.)

16. (C) From 4:00 to 6:00, Bill earns \$2.20. From 6:00 to 8:20—that is, for $2\frac{1}{3}$ hours—he makes \$1.32 per hour.

$$\left(\frac{7}{3}\right)(\$1.32) = \$3.08$$

All told, Bill earns \$2.20 plus \$3.08, or \$5.28.

17. (C) A staff of 150 people is more than the regular staff (S) by 20%, or $\frac{1}{5}$.

$$\left(\frac{6}{5}\right)S = 150$$

$$S = \frac{5}{6}(150) = 125$$

18. (D) For 4 weeks, Milenko averaged 72 points per week—a total of 288 points. After 5 weeks, he averaged 70 points per week, for a total of 350 points. The difference—62 points—is what he scored the fifth week.

19. (C) A day has 24 hours, and a year has 365 days. A year, then, has 24 times 365, or 8,760, hours. Since one baby is born every 5 hours, divide by 5 to find the number of babies born in a year—1,752.

It is sometimes helpful to work out a problem like this using the units:

$$\frac{24 \text{ hours}}{\text{day}} \cdot \frac{365 \text{ days}}{\text{year}} \cdot \frac{1 \text{ baby}}{5 \text{ hours}}$$

Cancelling $\frac{\text{days}}{\text{days}}$ and $\frac{\text{hours}}{\text{hours}}$, we are left with:

$\frac{24{,}365 \text{ babies}}{5 \text{ years}}$, or 1,752 babies per year

20. (D) If Mr. Loman earns \$200 in all, \$150 must come from commissions. In other words, \$150 represents 4% of Mr. Loman's sales for the month of July.

$$\$150 = 4\% \text{ of } x$$

$$\$150 = \frac{4}{100}x = \frac{1}{25}x$$

$$x = \$3{,}750$$

21. (D) Remember the rule: *difference* divided by *original.*

3,000 → 12,000 (difference 9,000)

Since $\frac{9{,}000}{3{,}000} = 3$, we have a 300% increase in production.

22. (D) This problem is tedious; you must do two successive calculations:

$$\$44.10 = 98\% \text{ of } x$$
$$x = 90\% \text{ of } y$$

Then y is the original price. But the hit-and-miss method is probably better. Start with \$49.96, or \$50.00, and see if your answer is too big, too small, or just right. You probably won't be asked to do anything quite like this on the LSAT and, if you are, you might wisely decide to skip the question until you are sure you have had time to finish all of the others. If you got the answer, you have an excellent understanding of percentages.

23. (E) The installment price comes to a total of \$70 (\$5 down + \$6.50 · 10). The "*difference* over *original*" rule is in order.

63 → 70 (difference 7)

$$\frac{7}{63} = \frac{1}{9} = 11\%$$

24. (A) After the first candidate's votes, only $\frac{2}{5}$ remain. The loser gets $\frac{1}{4}$ of these.

$$\left(\frac{1}{4}\right)\left(\frac{2}{5}\right) = \frac{2}{20} = \frac{1}{10}$$

25. (C)

$$30\% \text{ of } \$9{,}840 = \frac{3}{10} \cdot 9{,}840 = \$2{,}952.00$$

$$20\% \text{ of } \$9{,}840 = \frac{1}{5} \cdot 9{,}840 = \quad \$1{,}968.00$$

$$9{,}840 - 1{,}968 = 7{,}872$$

$$10\% \text{ of } 7{,}872 = (787.20) \qquad \underline{787.20}$$

for a total of $2,755.20

The difference is $2,952 – $2,755.20, or $196.80.

CHAPTER TWO
Data Interpretation

The data interpretation section is standard on the LSAT. All data interpretation problems involve some sort of visual display—a graph, chart, or table (we will often use the term *graph* to include the other two). Four or five graphs will be presented with about seven questions relating to each one. Usually, the more difficult the graph, the easier the question; surprisingly, the simpler graphs have more difficult questions.

The instructions you should follow for the data interpretation section are shown below:

Directions: **This section consists of various displays of data. Each display is followed by questions based on its content. After studying the display, select the best answer to each question on the basis of the information presented or implied in the display.**

If you come to a question that looks as if it will take you an inordinate amount of time to solve, skip it and go on to the next one; all are equal in value. To spend a long time on one question does not pay when you can do several others in the same amount of time. If you finish early, you can always go back and do the ones you skipped. If you don't finish, then you were certainly better off not spending all your time in one place.

Let's take a look at a few simple graphs of various types.

THE BAR GRAPH

GROSS ANNUAL INCOME OF MONEY CORP., 1984–1990

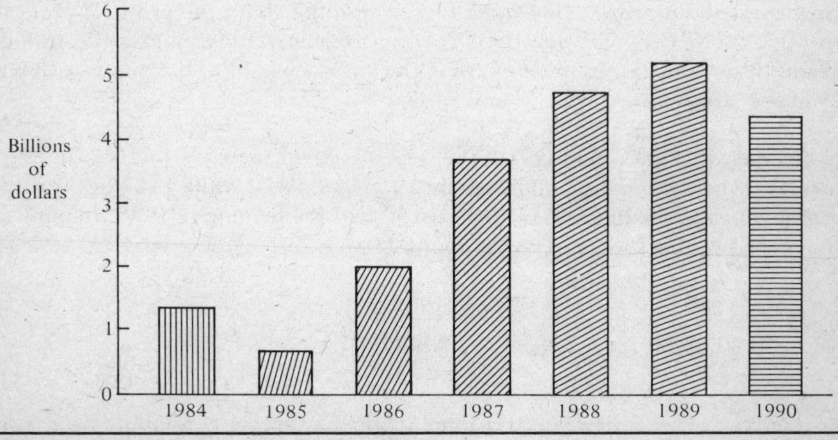

See how many of these questions you can answer with the information given by the graph. (On the LSAT, you will be given multiple-choice questions. The questions in this chapter aim to give you practice in drawing correct information from graphs.) Answers are given below the line of dashes.

1. **In which year did Money Corp. have the largest gross income? ________**

2. **In which year did Money Corp. have the smallest gross income? ________**

3. **In how many years did Money Corp. show a decrease in profit from the previous year? ________**

4. **In which year did Money Corp. show the largest percent increase in gross income compared to the previous year? ________**

5. **If expenses were one billion dollars per year, in how many years did Money Corp. show a loss? ________**

– –

Whenever you face a series of questions about a graph, the best way to begin is to look at the graph itself. Read the title and any explanatary notes (this graph had none).What does the graph represent? In this case, the *horizontal axis* represents time; each year has its own bar. The *vertical axis* represents the gross annual income of Money Corp., in billions of dollars (as the *scale* at the left tells us). The taller the bar, the larger the gross income for the year the bar represents.

Once you have made these observations, you may safely go on to the questions, but the half-minute or so that they take is usually time well spent.

1. **The question is easy. We have only to look for the tallest bar, which happens to be 1989, when the gross income of Money Corp. was about $5.3 billion.**

2. **This question asks for similar information, except that we must look for the smallest bar–1985, when Money Corp. grossed only $0.8 billion. (That's $800 million, by the way.)**

3. **Did you say "2 years"? Let's hope not. Gross income decreased twice, but the question asked about *profit.* This graph tells us nothing about the profit of Money Corp., so we cannot answer the question. You must read carefully on every section of the exam. In some instances on the LSAT, the answer will be: "It cannot be determined from the information given."**

4. **Notice that this question asks for the largest *percent* increase, not the largest increase. The only two possibilities are 1986 and 1987; while 1987 has the largest actual increase, the increase in 1986 is 150% of the income in 1985. In contrast, the increase from 1986 to 1987 is about 75%.**

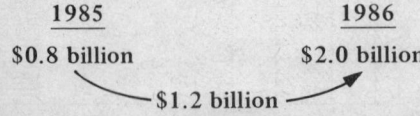

1985		1986
$0.8 billion		$2.0 billion
	→ $1.2 billion →	

$$\% \text{ increase} = \frac{1.2}{0.8} = 150\%$$

1986 — **$2.0 billion** → **$1.5 billion** → **1987** — **$3.5 billion**

$$\% \text{ increase} = \frac{1.5}{2.0} = 75\%$$

5. **The only year in which Money Corp. had a gross income of less than one billion dollars was 1985. Therefore, 1985, the year in which expenses exceeded gross income, was the only year in which Money Corp. showed a loss.**

THE LINE GRAPH

PRICE IN KWACHAS OF A POUND OF ICE CUBES, JANUARY, 1991–FEBRUARY, 1992

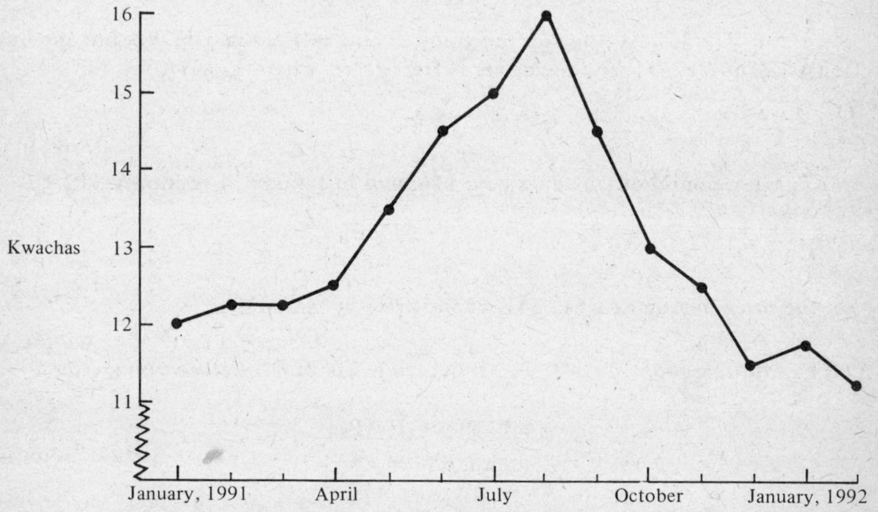

Try these questions using the above graph:

1. **How much did a pound of ice cubes cost in May, 1991?** ______________

2. **Why do ice cubes cost more during the summer months?** ______________

3. **In what month does the weather begin to get hot?** ______________

4. **In which month in 1991 did a pound of ice cubes cost the least?** ______________

5. **The price of a pound of ice cubes in August, 1991, was what percent of the price of a pound of ice cubes in January, 1991?** ______________

This graph tells us the price (in Kwachas) of a pound of ice cubes during the 14-month period from January, 1991, to February, 1992. A line graph is generally the most effective way to show variation. Notice that the vertical scale begins at 11; the fact that there are numbers below 11 is indicated by the zig-zag lines at the bottom of the vertical scale. Each division on the horizontal axis represents one month, even though only every third month is labeled.

1. **This question is easy. All you have to do is read the graph. In May, 1991, a pound of ice cubes cost $13\frac{1}{2}$ Kwachas.**

2. **This question is tricky, but the graph does not give us this information. You should make no assumptions when you get a question like this. Again the best answer will be "It cannot be determined from the information given."**

3. **This question is tricky, but you still can't answer it. What is meant by "hot"? Is heat the only factor that causes a change in the price of ice cubes? The graph does not tell us.**

4. **Be careful. The lowest price on the graph occurs in February, 1992, but the question asks about 1991, so the answer is December, when the price fell to $11\frac{1}{2}$ Kwachas.**

5. **In August, a pound of ice cubes cost \$16, and in January it cost only \$12.**

$$\frac{16}{12} = 1.33$$

So, the price in August was 133% of the price in January.

If you had trouble with the last question, review Chapter 1 before you go on.

THE PIE GRAPH

PUDGIE'S BUDGET
(Week of March 6, 1949)

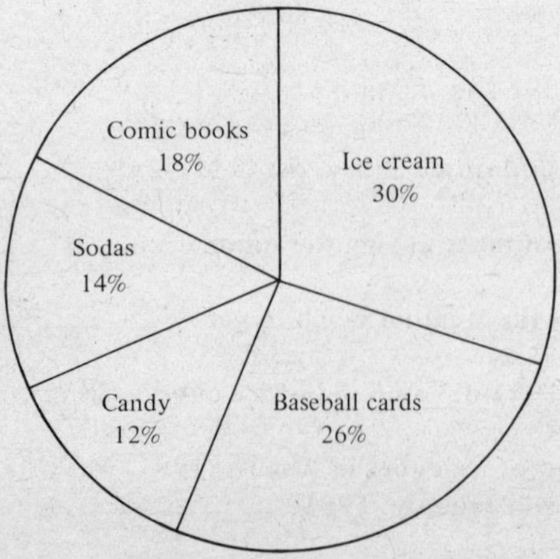

Note: Total amount included in budget = 50¢.

As always, before going on to answer the questions, read the graph and any notes. Be careful. Some of these questions are a bit more difficult.

1. **How much did Pudgie budget for comic books during the week of March 6, 1949? ________**

2. **What is the most that Pudgie spends on any one item in an average week? ________**

3. **Assuming that Pudgie's ice cream expenses remain constant, by what percent would he have to increase his candy expenses in order to make them equal to his ice cream expenses? ________**

4. **If comic books cost 3¢ each, how many can Pudgie buy if he has to use 5¢ of his comic book money to meet an emergency expense? ________**

5. **If Pudgie budgets 20% for each of the five items in his budget next week, which item would undergo the largest percent change? ________**

\- -

In this case, the graph is very simple, almost self-explanatory. The entire "pie" represents Pudgie's budget for the week, and each "piece of pie" represents a portion of Pudgie's budget. Remember, the whole pie always equals 100% of whatever it represents. The note below the graph tells us that the whole pie is 50¢. In other words, Pudgie's budget for sodas for the week is 14% of 50¢, or 7¢.

1. **This answer is a snap—18% of 50¢, or 9¢.**

2. **Though this question may look almost the same, don't be fooled. The graph tells us nothing about an average week; it is valid only for the week of March 6, 1949, which, for all we know, may be a very unusual week.**

3. **Pudgie's ice cream expenses are 30% of the budget. At the moment, his candy expenses are only 12%. Bringing them up to the level of his ice cream expenses would involve an increase of 150%.**

   12% → Difference = 18 → 30%

   $$\frac{\text{difference}}{\text{original}} = \frac{18}{12} = 1.5$$

   So a 150% increase is needed. Note that we would get the same result if we used the actual amounts of money:

   6¢ → 9 → 15¢

   $$\frac{9}{6} = 1.5$$

By using 12% and 30%, we save the trouble of calculating actual amounts. The saving would be greater if the entire budget were something like 87¢. Using the percentages instead would still work, and it would save the trouble of calculating 12% and 30% of 87.

4. **Pudgie has 18% of 50¢, or 9¢, in his comic book budget. If he spends 5¢, he has 4¢ left. He can buy only one comic book, and he will have a penny left over.**

5. **The two possibilities are ice cream, which starts at 30%, and candy, which starts at 12%. The ice cream budget suffers a $33\frac{1}{3}\%$ decrease.**

old 30 → new 20 (10)

$$\frac{\text{difference}}{\text{original}} = \frac{10}{30} = \frac{1}{3}$$

Candy, on the other hand, enjoys a sizeable increase.

old 12 → new 20 (+8)

$$\frac{8}{12} = \frac{2}{3}$$

So candy would undergo the largest percent change, a $66\frac{2}{3}\%$ increase.

While the bar, line, and pie graphs are the three most common types, and many LSAT graphs consist of some variations or combinations of them, they are by no means the only types of graphs used. The makers of the LSAT often use a less familiar looking graph to test your ability to interpret data. A typical section might consist of a chart or table, two or three "basic" graphs, and one or two graphs of an unusual type.

If you come up against a type of graph that you have never seen before, don't panic. The chances are that very few of the other people taking the test have seen it either. Spend a minute or so trying to figure out how it works. When the graph seems very difficult or unusual, the questions will usually not require inferences or calculation but will simply test your understanding of the graph.

A favorite of LSAT testmakers in recent years has been the triangle graph.

THE TRIANGLE GRAPH

Let's see how this graph works. The title tells us the graph is concerned with election returns. As we look at the graph, we see that the votes are to be divided three ways—among Liberals, Conservatives, and Moderates. Five counties appear on the graph (A, B, C, D, and E). The note tells us that the winning candidate in each county will be elected to the state legislature.

ELECTION RETURNS BY COUNTY IN STATE X

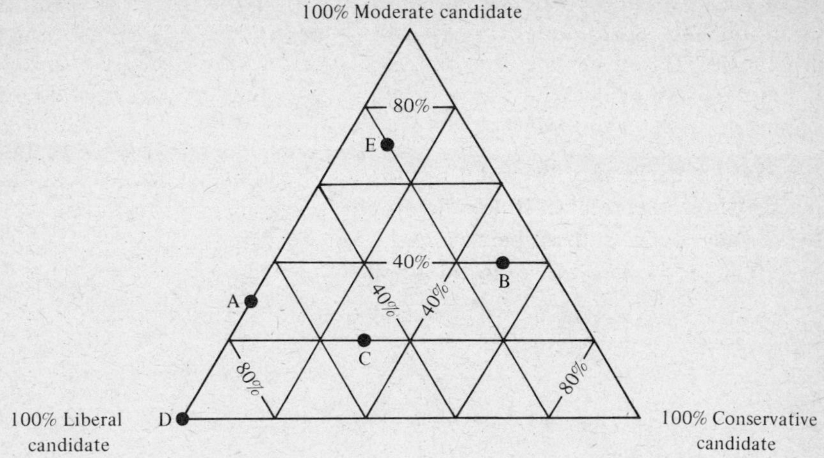

Note: Each lettered dot represents a county. The candidate who gets the most votes in each county becomes that county's representative to the state legislature.

An important thing to look for in any graph is whether the numbers represent actual totals or percentages. In this case, we are dealing with percentages.

Now, how do you read this graph? Let's start by looking only at the Moderate candidates.

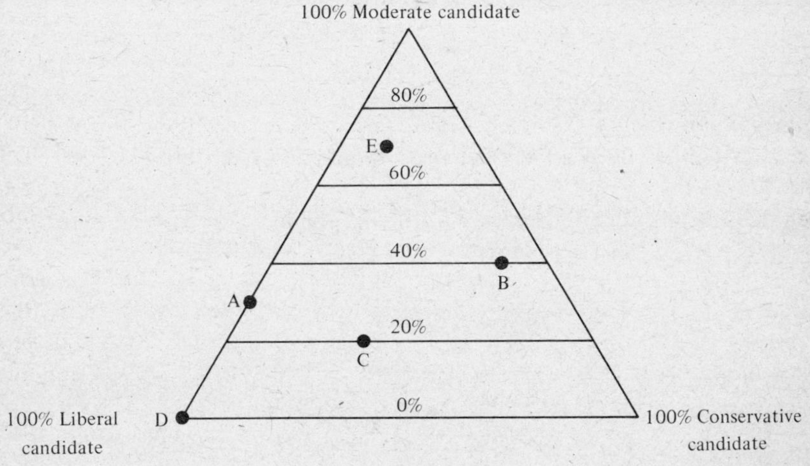

First, we can fill in the rest of the scale. The top of the triangle represents 100% Moderate. If the point representing a county were right on the top vertex (corner) of the triangle, it would mean that everybody in the county voted for the Moderate candidate. On the other hand, if the point falls on the side opposite this vertex (as does the point representing County D), it means that nobody voted for the Moderate candidate. So the Moderate candidates achieved the following results:

County A: 30% of the vote
County B: 40% of the vote
County C: 20% of the vote
County D: 0% of the vote
County E: 70% of the vote

Notice that the position of the point to the left or right makes no difference in the total that the Moderates receive. It does determine, as we shall see, how the remainder of the vote is divided between the Liberals and the Conservatives.

Now, let's add the Conservatives to the graph.

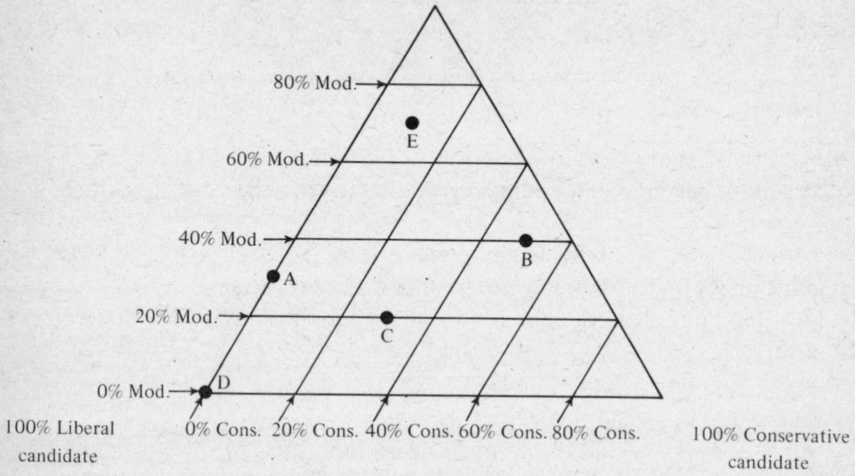

In County A and County D, the Conservative candidates received 0% of the vote. In County E, they polled 10% (halfway between 0% and 20%); in County C, 30%; and in County B, 50%.

Adding the Liberals, we are back to our original graph.

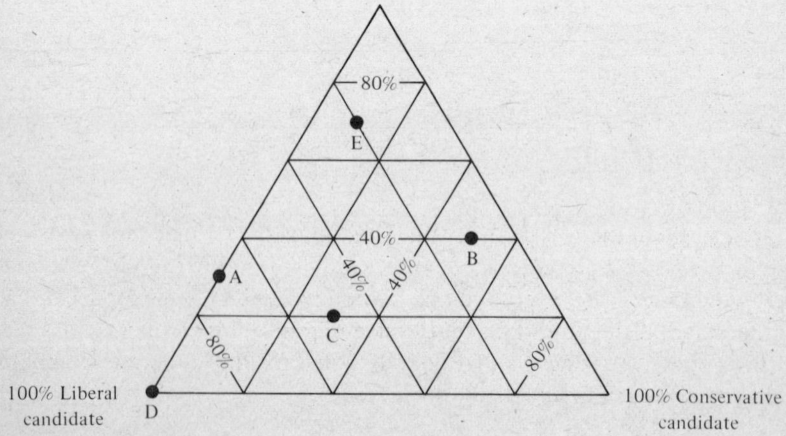

Now, we can make a table of election returns:

County	Liberal	Moderate	Conservative
A	70%	30%	0%
B	10%	40%	50%
C	50%	20%	30%
D	100%	0%	0%
E	20%	70%	10%

Notice that in each county, the votes total 100%. When a county falls in the 100% corner of one part (County D), it is also on the 0% line of the other two parties. Remember also that the center of this triangle is the point where each candidate has $\frac{1}{3}$ of the vote, not the point where one has 50%.

Triangle graphs generally deal in percentages, since the sum of the three items being graphed is always the same. Thus, the graph does not tell how many votes each candidate received. County A may have a population of 50,000 with only 10,000 people in County E. We could not answer a question like "Who received more votes, the Liberal in County B or the Conservative in County C?" The use of the triangle graph is limited to a situation in which something is to be divided among three competitors.

Try this one:

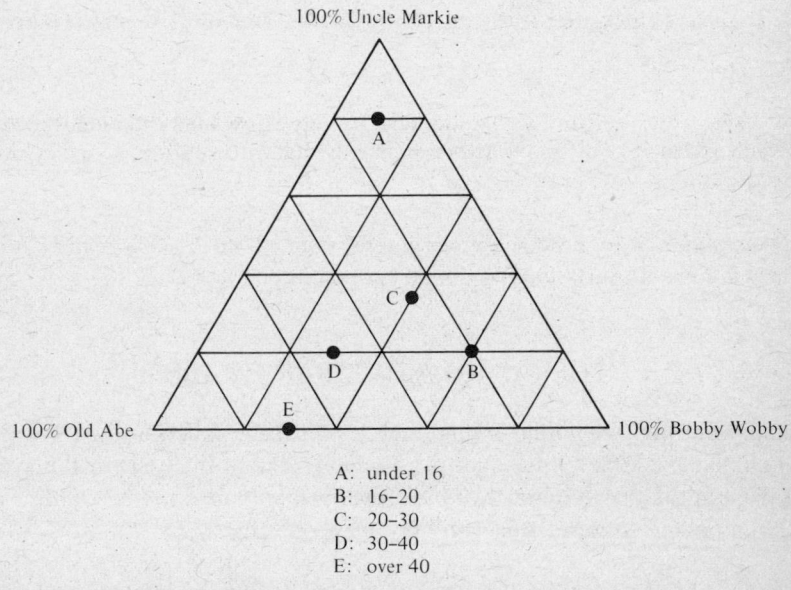

DIVISION OF FUN CITY EVENING RADIO AUDIENCE BY AGE GROUPS

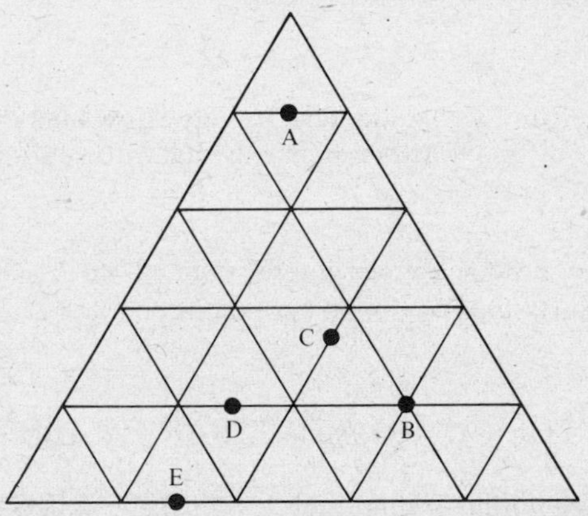

A: under 16
B: 16–20
C: 20–30
D: 30–40
E: over 40

1. Who is most popular with each age group? ______

2. **Assuming that Bobby Wobby's audience in the 30–40 age group is fixed, by what percent does Uncle Markie have to increase his age 30–40 audience in order to equal Bobby Wobby's? ________**

3. **Which age group is most evenly divided in its listening preference? ________**

4. **Which performer has the largest total audience? ________**

– –

1. **Uncle Markie is most popular with the under-16 audience; 80% of that group listens to him. The 16–20 group is dominated by Bobby Wobby (60%). The race for the 20–30 group is close, but Bobby Wobby's 40% is the best total. Old Abe captures the 30–40 (50%) and over-40 groups (70%).**

2. **In order to answer this question, we will assume that the 30–40 age group includes 100 listeners. (How many listeners there actually are does not matter. We choose 100 because it is easy to work with.) Bobby Wobby has 30% of the audience. If the audience is 100, he has 30 listeners, and Uncle Markie (20%) has 20 listeners. Therefore, Uncle Markie needs 10 more listeners to equal Bobby Wobby's share of the audience. This figure represents a 50% increase for Uncle Markie.**

   20 → 30 (10 increase)

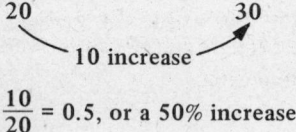

   $\frac{10}{20}$ **= 0.5, or a 50% increase**

3. **The 20–30 age group (group C) is most evenly divided; it is closest to the center of the triangle. (The center is the $33\frac{1}{3}\%$–$33\frac{1}{3}\%$–$33\frac{1}{3}\%$ point.) Group C is divided about 40%–35%–25%.**

4. **To answer this question, we would have to know how many people were actually in each audience. The graph does not give us that information, so we cannot answer this question.**

As you are exposed to more and more graphs, you will notice that many (though not all) of them are merely variations of simple bar graphs and line graphs.

THE CUMULATIVE BAR GRAPH

The important thing to notice in this graph is that the numbers at the left are percentages, not numbers of athletes. In other words, about 20% of the basketball players had A averages. We can't tell what number of basketball players had A averages unless we know how many players there were altogether. Try these questions:

ACADEMIC GRADE AVERAGES OF ATHLETES AT STATE U, 1986

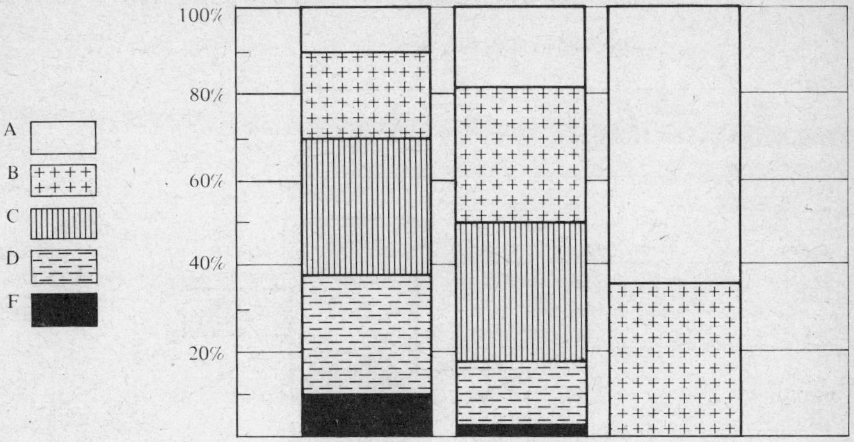

1. Which team had the largest number of F averages? ______________

2. Which team had the smallest number of F averages? ______________

3. What percentage of all athletes on the three teams had A averages? ______________

4. If twice as many players played baseball as played football, which team had more players with B averages? ______________

— — — — — — — — — — — — — — — — — — — —

1. We can't tell. We know that the baseball team had the largest percentage of F averages, but if (for a ridiculous example) 1,000 of the players played basketball and only 10 played baseball, many more F averages would have occurred on the basketball team.

2. We *can* tell, easily. No one on the football team had an F average, so the football team had the smallest number.

3. Let's hope that you didn't spend too much time on this one. Think about it for a minute, and you will see why you can't figure it out—you would have to know *how many people were on each team.*

4. To do this, we will assume that the football team has 100 players. What number we pick does not matter, but, since we are dealing with percentages, 100 is very convenient. Of the 100 team members, 30 had B averages. If twice as many players played baseball, they must have numbered 200, with about 18% of them, or 36, having B averages. So more baseball players than football players would have B averages.

THE THREE-DIMENSIONAL BAR GRAPH

UNEMPLOYMENT BY SEX IN CITY X, 1975–1985

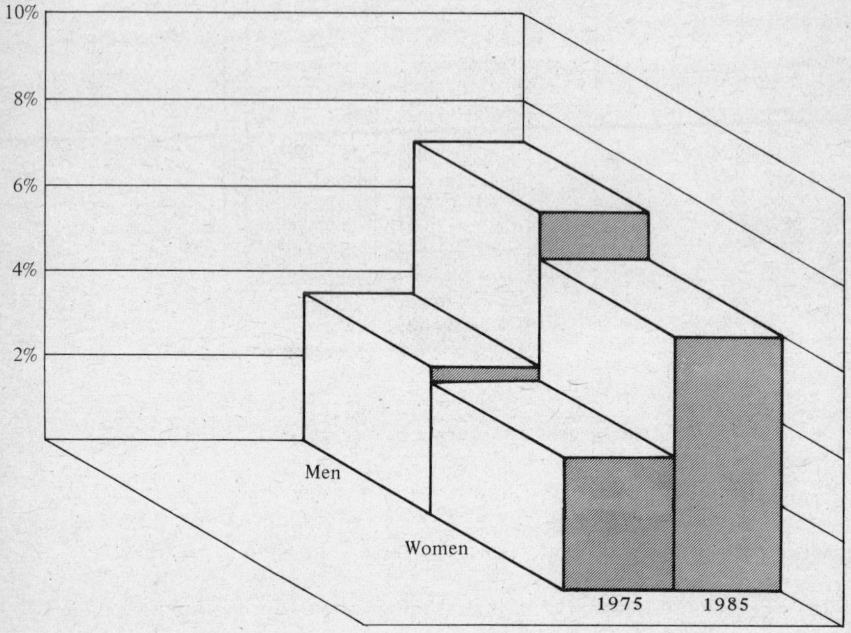

Don't be intimidated by a graph like this. It is simply a collection of ordinary bar graphs. The only problem in reading it is that you must remember that it is three dimensional, not two dimensional.

A three-dimensional graph has three variables instead of two—in this case, sex, the year, and the percentage of unemployment.

What percent of women were unemployed in City X in 1985? It looks like about 6%. Find the bar that represents women and 1985 (the front right) and see how tall it is. That's all there is to it.

Note that this graph could be broken down into ordinary bar graphs:

UNEMPLOYMENT IN CITY X, 1975–1985

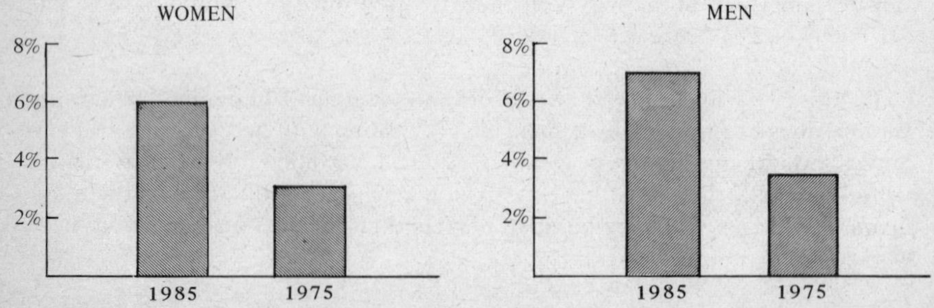

Once you think of a three-dimensional graph in these terms, it becomes very easy to read.

Countless different types of graphs may be used, but most of them involve the same basic principles. In the pages that follow, you will be exposed to a reasonable sampling of graph types that might appear on your LSAT. If you work carefully and understand them all, you should be able to apply what you have learned to anything that you might encounter, even if it seems totally unfamiliar.

Two practice Data Interpretation Self-Tests are given below. Each consists of 28 questions on four graphs. You should set aside 40 uninterrupted minutes to do each self-test. Always try to simulate actual test conditions whenever possible.

On page 317 at the back of the book is an Answer Sheet similar to that used for the LSAT. To best simulate testing conditions, pull out this sheet and record on it your answers to each of the chapter self-tests as you read through this book. (If you prefer, you can circle the best answer from among the choices given.) Answers and explanations are given following each self-test.

We recommend that you take Data Interpretation Self-Test A first. Then study the answers, as soon as possible after taking the test, before you go on to Data Interpretation Self-Test B.

Data Interpretation Self-Test A

Time: 40 minutes

28 questions

Directions: **This section consists of various displays of data. Each display is followed by questions based on its content. After studying the display, select the best answer to each question on the basis of the information presented or implied in the display.**

DISTRIBUTION OF THE CLOWN MARKET AMONG THE THREE CLOWN AGENCIES

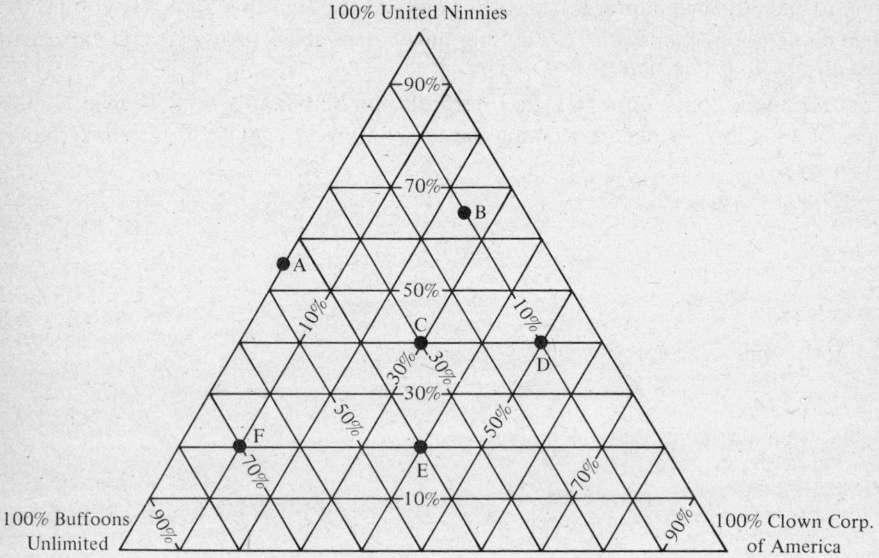

Employers:
A: All-American Asinine Association
B: Barney's Bizarre Bazaar
C: City Clown Convention
D: Danny's Dunces
E: Egbert's Elephant Emporium
F: Fannie's Follies

1. **Which employer hires most evenly from the three agencies?**

   (A) A (B) B (C) C (D) D (E) E

2. **Which of the following statements is true?**

   (A) *A* hires most of its clowns from Buffoons Unlimited.
   (B) Each employer hires clowns from each agency.
   (C) *B* and *D* prefer clowns from Buffoons Unlimited.
   (D) *A* hires all of its clowns from two agencies.
   (E) None of the above

3. **Danny wants to give equal business to United Ninnies and Clown Corp. of America. Assuming that he does not fire anybody, by what percent does he have to increase**

the number of clowns he hires through United Ninnies in order to accomplish this goal?

(A) 10% (B) 20% (C) 25% (D) 40% (E) 50%

4. If Fannie hires eight clowns through United Ninnies, which of the following statements is true?

(A) She hires two clowns through Clown Corp. of America.
(B) She hires 28 clowns through Buffoons Unlimited.
(C) She hires 28 clowns through Clown Corp. of America.
(D) She hires eight clowns through Clown Corp. of America.
(E) None of the above

5. If Buffoons Unlimited sends twice as many clowns to Barney as they send to Danny, then the ratio of United Ninnies' clowns working for Danny: United Ninnies' clowns working for Barney is nearest to:

(A) 1:3 (B) 2:3 (C) 1:1 (D) 3:1 (E) It cannot be determined from the information given.

6. Who hires the largest number of clowns from a single agency?

(A) A (B) B (C) D (D) F (E) It cannot be determined from the information given.

7. Who hires the smallest number of clowns from a single agency?

(A) A (B) B (C) D (D) F (E) It cannot be determined from the information given.

OCCUPATIONS OF STATE U GRADUATES,
CLASS OF 1984

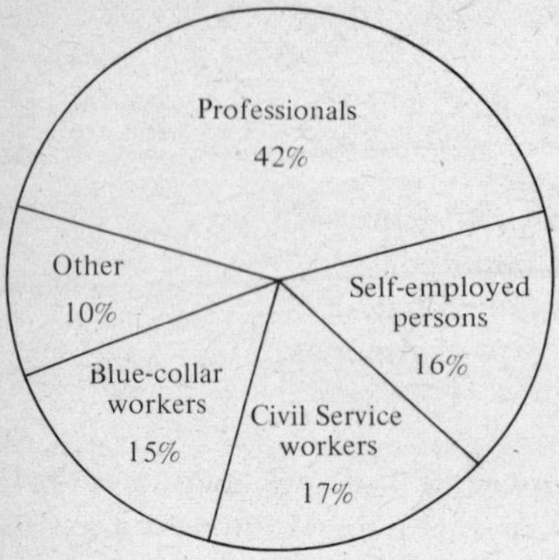

CLASS OF 1984 PROFESSIONALS
BY PROFESSION

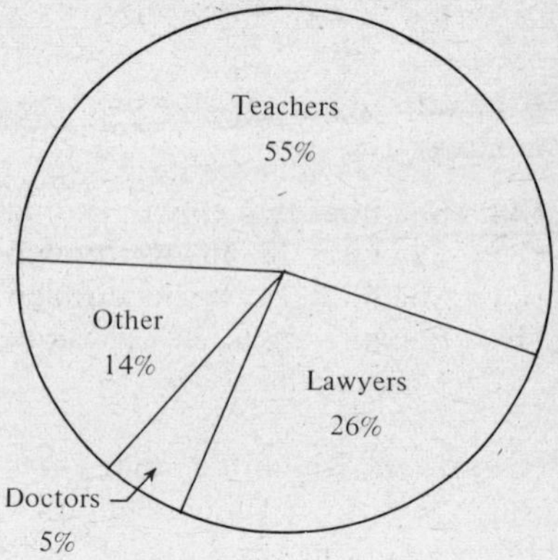

Note: The class of 1984 had 950 graduates.

8. **About how many graduates in the Class of 1984 ended up in Civil Service jobs?**

   (A) 17 (B) 160 (C) 170 (D) 180 (E) It cannot be determined from the information given.

9. **Which group contains the largest number of graduates of the Class of 1984?**

   (A) Lawyers (B) Doctors (C) Self-employed persons (D) Civil Service employees (E) Blue-collar workers

10. **For the class of 1984, by what percent would the number of self-employed persons have to increase in order to equal the number of teachers, assuming that the number of teachers remains the same?**

    (A) 7% (B) 38% (C) 44% (D) 243% (E) It cannot be determined from the information given.

11. **How many graduates from the Class of 1984 are teachers?**

    (A) 187 (B) 220 (C) 231 (D) 523 (E) It cannot be determined from the information given.

12. **In the Class of 1984, what percent of the number of doctors is the number of blue-collar workers?**

    (A) 200% (B) 300% (C) 700% (D) 1,300% (E) It cannot be determined from the information given.

13. **How many more 1984 graduates are lawyers than are doctors?**

    (A) 21 (B) 88 (C) 200 (D) 84 (E) It cannot be determined from the information given.

14. Which of the following statements about the Class of 1984 is false?

(A) More graduates are professionals than any other two categories combined.
(B) Professionals and self-employed persons together made up more than half of the graduates of the Class of 1984.
(C) It is impossible to tell if any graduates were bankers.
(D) If half of all the teachers are English teachers, more graduates are English teachers than are blue-collar workers.
(E) None of the above

UNEMPLOYMENT INSURANCE BENEFITS

Weekly Benefit Amounts				Duration of Benefit Weeks	
State	Average	Legal Minimum	Legal Maximum	Average	Legal Range
Conn.	$63.45	$15–20	$86–129	16.3	22–26
Del.	52.62	10	65	11.4	16–26
Maine	47.28	12	63	12.7	11–26
Mass.	57.00	12–18	74–111	17.8	9–30
N.H.	47.86	14	75	11.1	26
N.J.	58.33	10	76	16.2	12–26
N.Y.	59.01	20	75	16.1	26
Pa.	52.63	12–17	85–93	13.7	30
R.I.	56.32	12–17	79–99	14.0	12–26
Vt.	55.07	15	77	15.8	26

Note: When two figures are given for legal minimum or legal maximum, the larger figure includes dependents' allowances.

15. In the state where benefits have the shortest average duration on the chart, the legal minimum is what percent more than the lowest legal minimum on the chart?

(A) 0% (B) 14% (C) 40% (D) 700% (E) 140%

16. What is the average duration of benefits in the 10 states listed?

(A) 11.2 weeks (B) 12.1 weeks (C) 14.5 weeks (D) 17.3 weeks
(E) It cannot be determined from the information given.

17. Assuming the maximum allowance for dependents, what percent of the minimum benefit is the maximum benefit in Connecticut?

(A) 760% (B) 430% (C) 573% (D) 645% (E) 860%

18. What is the largest total amount that a person with no dependents can collect in Massachusetts?

(A) $1,014.60 (B) $1,317.20 (C) $2,220.00 (D) $3,330.00
(E) It cannot be determined from the information given.

19. What percent more money per week would a person receiving the average weekly benefit in Massachusetts have to receive in order to be receiving the same as a person receiving the legal maximum in New York?

(A) 32% (B) 3.5% (C) 103.5% (D) 132% (E) It cannot be determined from the information given.

20. Which of the following statements is true?

(A) No other state listed allows benefits for as long a period as does Massachusetts.
(B) New Hampshire has the lowest average weekly benefits on the chart.
(C) The state with the lowest legal maximum on the chart is not the state with the lowest legal minimum.
(D) In general, the smaller the legal minimum, the shorter the average duration.
(E) None of the above

21. Which state listed spends the most money on unemployment insurance?

(A) Massachusetts (B) New York (C) Connecticut (D) Pennsylvania (E) It cannot be determined from the information given.

PRODUCTION OF MINERAL, FUEL, AND WATER POWER ENERGY IN U. S. 1920–1985

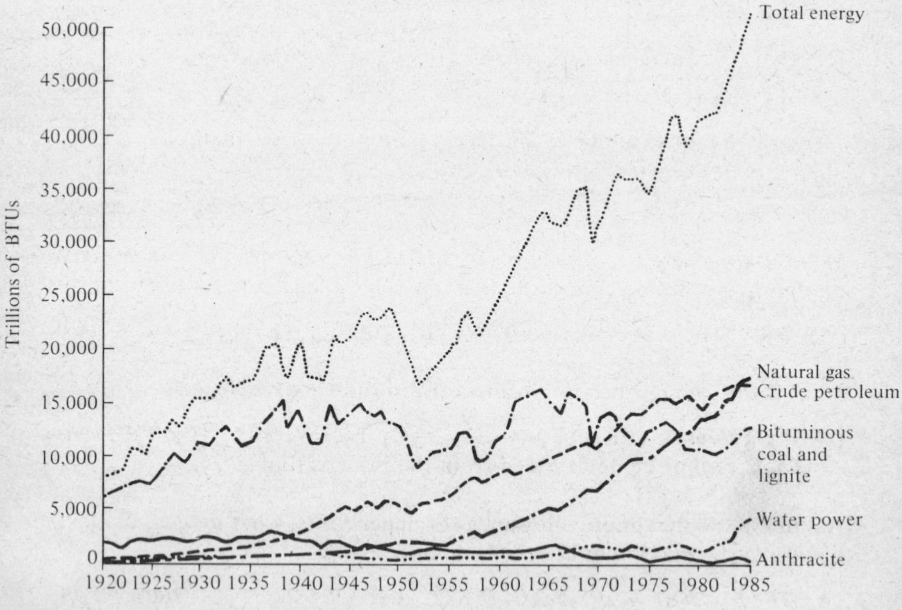

22. Which type of fuel shows a decrease between 1920 and 1985?

(A) Bituminous coal and lignite
(B) Natural gas
(C) Crude petroleum
(D) Water power
(E) Anthracite

23. The major influence in the total energy figures in 1920 was:

(A) natural gas. (B) crude petroleum. (C) bituminous coal and lignite. (D) water power. (E) anthracite.

24. The major influence in the total energy figure in 1985 was:

(A) natural gas. (B) crude petroleum. (C) bituminous coal and lignite. (D) water power. (E) anthracite.

25. From 1920 to 1955, total energy and bituminous coal and lignite run nearly parallel, but from 1955 to 1985, they do not. Why?

(A) Decrease in relative importance of bituminous coal and lignite
(B) Growth of natural gas and crude petroleum
(C) Changing of relative importances of the different types of power
(D) All of the above
(E) It cannot be determined from the information given.

26. What percent of America's energy supply was produced by natural gas in 1970?

(A) 5% (B) 10% (C) 17% (D) 33% (E) 50%

27. Which of the following statements is true?

(A) After 1965, bituminous coal and lignite were never the major influence in the total energy figure.
(B) Crude petroleum was never the major influence in the total energy figure.
(C) Through the years, anthracite has produced a fairly steady percentage of the country's total energy needs.
(D) Total energy fell to an all-time low about 1952.
(E) None of the above

28. The amount of power obtained from anthracite was at one time or another equal to the amount obtained from:

I. natural gas.
II. crude petroleum.
III. bituminous coal and lignite.
IV. water power.

(A) IV only (B) I and IV (C) I, II, and IV (D) II and IV (E) All of the above

STOP

IF YOU FINISH BEFORE THE TIME IS UP,
CHECK YOUR WORK ON THIS SECTION.
WHEN THE TIME IS UP, CHECK YOUR ANSWERS
AGAINST THE ANSWER KEY AND EXPLANATIONS ON THE FOLLOWING PAGE.

Answers to Data Interpretation Self-Test A

1. (C) Point C is closest to the center point $\left(33\frac{1}{3}-33\frac{1}{3}-33\frac{1}{3}\right)$.

2. (D) *A* hires only from Buffoons Unlimited and United Ninnies. Point *A* is on the 0% line of Clown Corp. of America.

3. (C) Danny hires 50% from Clown Corp. of America and 40% from United Ninnies. We can assume that he hires 100 clowns, 50 from Clown Corp. and 40 from United Ninnies. Therefore he needs 10 more from United Ninnies.

   40 → 50 (10)

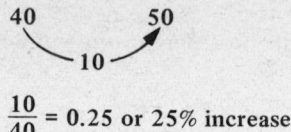

   $\frac{10}{40} = 0.25$ or 25% increase

4. (B) Fannie hires 20% of her clowns through United Ninnies. If 20% of her staff is 8 clowns, then she hires 40 clowns altogether.

   8 = 20% of total

   $8 = \frac{1}{5}x$

   $40 = x$ = total number of clowns

   She hires 10%, or 4 clowns, from Clown Corp. of America, and 70%, or 28 clowns, from Buffoons Unlimited.

5. (A) Barney and Danny each hire 10% of their clowns from Buffoons Unlimited. Therefore, if Buffoons Unlimited sends twice as many clowns to Barney, Barney must hire twice as many clowns as Danny. Let's assume that Barney hires 20 clowns and Danny hires 10. Then Danny hires 40% of 10, or 4 clowns, from United Ninnies, and Barney hires 65% of 20, or 13 clowns, from United Ninnies. The ratio is 4:13, which is closest to 1:3.

6. (E) Since we don't know how many total clowns each employer hires, we cannot determine who hires the most from any agency.

7. (A) All-American hires no clowns at all from Clown Corp. of America. If every employer hired from each agency, the answer would have been (E).

8. (B) Of the 950, 17% worked in Civil Service jobs. Without calculating, we can see that the number will be a little less than 170 (17% of 1,000). The only number that qualifies is 160.

9. (D) More graduates are lawyers than are doctors, and more are civil servants than are self-employed persons or blue-collar workers, so we need consider only lawyers and civil servants. From question 8, we know that the graduates include 160 civil servants. Twenty-six percent of 42% of 950 graduates, or 103, are lawyers.

10. (B) There are 55% of 42% of 950, or 219, teachers, and 152 self-employed persons. There would have to be 57 more self-employed workers. A 38% increase would be required.

152 → 219 (57)

$$\frac{57}{152} = 0.38 \text{ or } 38\% \text{ increase}$$

11. (B) We have already answered this question in question 10 (55% of 42% of 950).

12. (C) The number of blue-collar workers is about 700% of the number of doctors.

Number of doctors = 5% of 42% of total

= 2.1% of total

Number of blue-collar workers = 15% of total

$$\frac{15}{2.1} = 7$$

13. (D) Slightly fewer than 88 (8.8% of 1,000) more graduates are lawyers than are doctors. Alternatively, about 95 of the graduates are lawyers and about 11 are doctors, but more calculation is involved to determine these figures.

Number of lawyers = 26% of 42% of 950
Number of doctors = 5% of 42% of 950

Difference = 21% of 42% of 950
= 8.8% of 950

14. (D) (A) is true. The two largest other categories add up to only 33%. (B) is true; they add up to 58%. (C) is also true; they might be self-employed and they might be "others," but we don't know if there are any. (D), however, is false. The number of English teachers would be 50% of 55% of 42%, or about $\frac{1}{2} \cdot \frac{1}{2} \cdot 42\%$, or $\frac{1}{4}$ of 42%—only about 10% of the class.

15. (C) The state with the shortest average duration is New Hampshire (11.1 weeks). The legal minimum in New Hampshire is $14. The lowest minimum is $10 (Delaware and New Jersey).

$$\frac{\text{difference}}{\text{original}} = \frac{4}{10} = 0.4, \text{ or } 40\%$$

16. (E) Averaging the 10 states is no help unless you know how many people participate in each state and weight the averages accordingly.

17. (D) In order to understand what an "allowance for dependents" is, you have to read the note. Allowing the maximum dependents' allowance, the minimum benefit in Connecticut is $20, and the maximum is $129.

$$\frac{129}{20} = 6.45, \text{ or } 645\%$$

18. (C) Without dependents, the maximum benefit in Massachusetts is $74, and the maximum duration is 30 weeks.

$$30 \cdot \$74 = \$2,220$$

19. (A) The average weekly benefit in Massachusetts is $57, and the maximum in New York is $75.

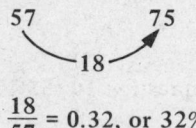

57 → 75 (18)

$$\frac{18}{57} = 0.32, \text{ or } 32\%$$

20. (C) (A) is false; Pennsylvania also allows 30 weeks. (B) is false; Maine has a lower average. (C) is true; the lowest maximum is in Maine ($63), and the lowest minimum, as we have seen, is in Delaware and New Jersey.

21. (E) You cannot determine the money spent unless you know how many people receive the benefits in each state.

22. (E) On this basic line graph, the only line that shows a decrease is the line for anthracite.

23. (C) Looking at the graph, we find that bituminous coal and lignite produced more energy in 1950 than any other source.

24. (A) Again, as in question 23, look at the graph. Natural gas is the major influence.

25. (B) The amount of coal remained fairly constant, but total energy went way up, on the strength of sharp increases in crude petroleum and natural gas.

26. (C) In 1970, about 4,000 out of 30,000 units came from natural gas. You need not convert to British thermal units (BTUs); use the units of the graph.

27. (E) (A) is false. They remained the major influence until about 1970. (B) is also false. Crude petroleum was the major influence for about 10 years from 1970 to 1980. (C) is false. Anthracite has been produced at a steady rate, but the total energy has increased significantly. (D) is also false, since even in 1950 the total energy did not dip below its 1920 levels.

28. (C) Anthracite never produced as much power as bituminous coal and lignite but equalled crude petroleum in about 1940, natural gas in about 1948, and water power in about 1966.

Note: If you had particular trouble with any of these questions, review the appropriate part of the first two chapters before you go on to Data Interpretation Self-Test B.

Data Interpretation Self-Test B

Time: 40 minutes

28 questions

Directions: **This section consists of various displays of data. Each display is followed by questions based on its content. After studying the display, select the best answer to each question on the basis of the information presented or implied in the display.**

GRADUATES FROM ACE MECHANIC SCHOOL (AMS), 1980–1986

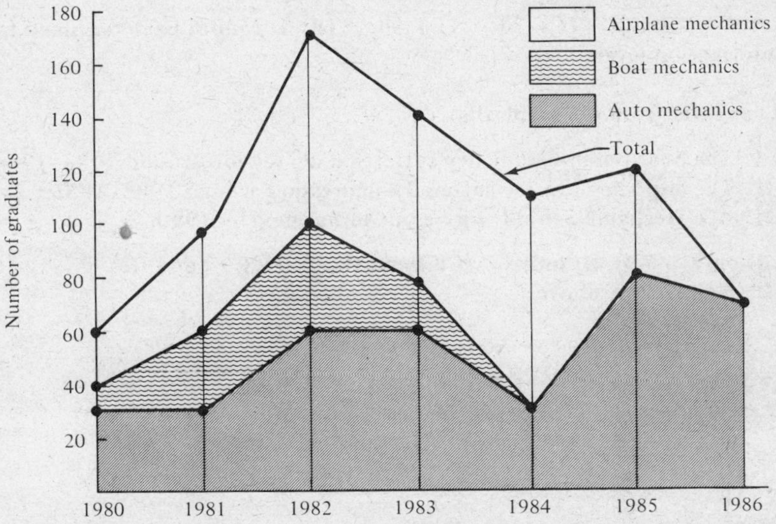

1. **How many airplane mechanics graduated from AMS in 1983?**

   (A) 16 (B) 60 (C) 64 (D) 76 (E) 140

2. **What percent more mechanics graduated in the year in which the largest number graduated than in the year in which the smallest number graduated?**

   (A) 110% (B) 180% (C) 210% (D) 280% (E) It cannot be determined from the information given.

3. **In what year was the percentage of boat mechanics in the graduating class the highest?**

   (A) 1980 (B) 1981 (C) 1982 (D) 1983 (E) 1984

4. **In which years did the graduating class have exactly two different types of mechanics?**

   I. 1983 II. 1984 III. 1985 IV. 1986

   (A) III only (B) II and IV (C) III and IV (D) II and III (E) II, III, and IV

5. Which of the following statements is false?

(A) The graduating class in 1986 represents about a 16% increase over the class of 1980.
(B) In 1986, only auto mechanics were graduated.
(C) Boat mechanics were never the largest group of graduates.
(D) The largest number of consecutive years on the graph in which the graduating class was larger than that of the previous year is two.
(E) None of the above

6. In the year in which the largest number of boat mechanics was graduated, how many airplane mechanics were graduated?

(A) 40 (B) 60 (C) 70 (D) 80 (E) It cannot be determined from the information given.

7. You can infer from the graph that:

I. The boat-building industry suffered a depression around 1983–1984.
II. The airplane industry suffered a depression around 1985–1986.
III. Ace Mechanic School will be out of business by 1990.

(A) II only (B) III only (C) I and II (D) I, II, and III (E) None of the above

AVERAGE INCOME OF VARIOUS OCCUPATIONS
BASED ON NUMBER OF YEARS IN THE FIELD

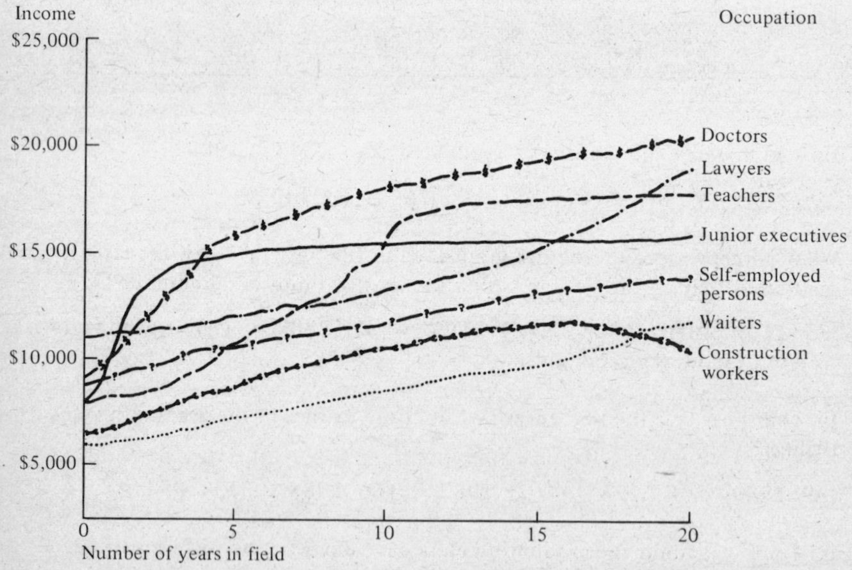

8. Which group is highest paid after three years of work?

(A) Waiters (B) Teachers (C) Doctors (D) Junior executives (E) Lawyers

9. The group with the smallest net increase in salary for the period between 8 and 20 years in the field is:

(A) Teachers (B) Junior executives (C) Self-employed persons (D) Waiters (E) Construction workers

10. During the first 20 years of his or her career, a doctor can expect an average annual increase in income of about:

(A) \$560 (B) \$610 (C) \$700 (D) \$720 (E) \$1,000

11. Which of the following statements is false?

(A) After equal numbers of years in the field, doctors always make more than self-employed persons.
(B) The only group that shows a drop in income for any period is construction workers.
(C) Doctors only make more than junior executives after about $3\frac{1}{2}$ years of service.
(D) Lawyers have the highest starting salary.
(E) None of the above

12. How many years does a teacher have to work in order to have the same salary as a doctor in the fourth year?

(A) 5 (B) 7 (C) 8 (D) 9 (E) 10

13. What percent increase in income would a lawyer in the sixth year of service need in order to be making the same salary as a doctor in the third year?

(A) 8% (B) 14% (C) 17% (D) 20% (E) 22%

14. Which of the following ratios of salaries is the lowest?

(A) 10th-year waiter:11th-year waiter
(B) 1st-year teacher:16th-year waiter
(C) 10th-year waiter: 2nd-year teacher
(D) 19th-year construction worker:11th-year teacher
(E) 4th-year doctor: 20th-year junior executive

TOTAL TONNAGE OF JUNK HANDLED BY SALVAGE COMPANIES AND RETAIL OUTLETS IN 1971

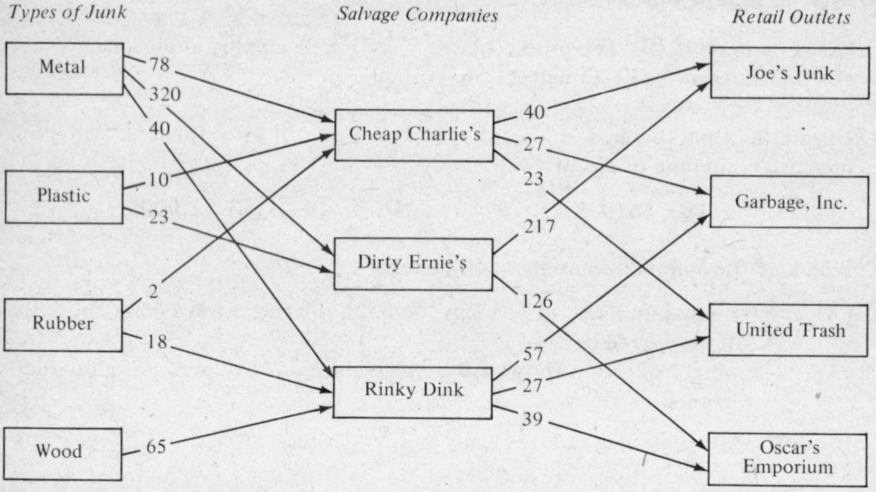

Note: All figures are in tons.

15. **According to the graph, which retailer handles the smallest number of tons of junk?**

(A) Charlie (B) Joe (C) United (D) Oscar (E) Garbage

16. **According to the graph, what percent of all the metal is bought by Rinky Dink?**

(A) 9% (B) 13% (C) 40% (D) 73% (E) It cannot be determined from the information given.

17. **What percent of Rinky Dink's rubber is sold to Garbage, Inc.?**

(A) 15% (B) 21% (C) 32% (D) 46% (E) It cannot be determined from the information given.

18. **What is the minimum number of tons of metal sold by Cheap Charlie's to Garbage, Inc.?**

(A) 0 (B) 15 (C) 19 (D) 27 (E) It cannot be determined from the information given.

19. **Which of the following *could not* have happened?**

(A) Joe bought 257 tons of metal.
(B) United bought 10 tons of plastic.
(C) United bought 19 tons of rubber.
(D) Joe bought 5 tons of wood.
(E) None of the above

20. **Which of the following represents the smallest ratio?**

(A) Charlie's metal purchases: Ernie's plastic purchases
(B) Ernie's plastic purchases: Charlie's United sales
(C) Charlie's plastic purchases: Ernie's Oscar sales
(D) Charlie's rubber purchases: Ernie's plastic purchases
(E) Rinky Dink's metal purchases: Rinky Dink's wood purchases

21. **By what percent must Rinky Dink increase its metal purchases in order to equal Dirty Ernie's, assuming that Ernie's metal purchases remain constant?**

(A) 12.5% (B) 70% (C) 280% (D) 700% (E) 800%

EXPORT COEFFICIENTS RELATED TO ECONOMIC DEVELOPMENT, 1963

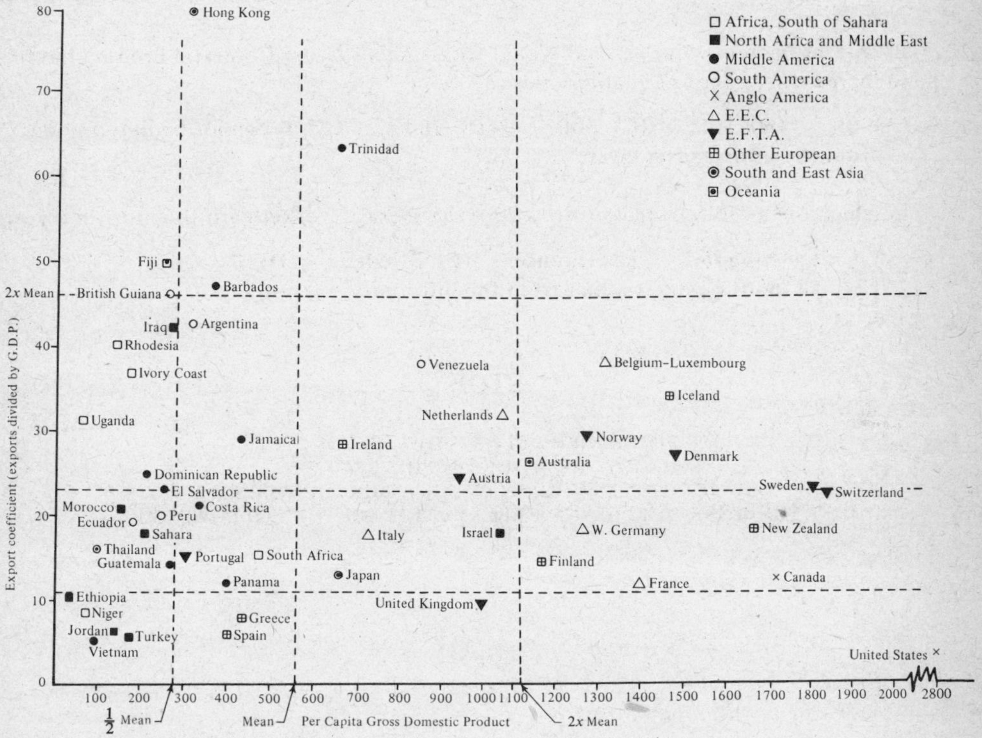

22. **Which nation has the third highest export coefficient of any nation of the graph?**

(A) Trinidad (B) Fiji (C) Switzerland (D) Spain (E) Iceland

23. **Which nation has the highest per capita Gross Domestic Product of any South American nation on the graph?**

(A) British Guiana (B) United States (C) Argentina (D) Ecuador (E) Venezuela

24. **Which of the following statements is (are) supported by the graph?**

I. The nations of the free world tend to have a higher export coefficient than members of the communist bloc.

II. The highest export coefficient in Oceania is higher than the highest in South and East Asia.

III. The United States has the highest export coefficient in North America.

(A) I only (B) II only (C) III only (D) II and III (E) None of the above

25. Which of the following nations had the lowest per capita exports?

(A) Uganda (B) El Salvador (C) Panama (D) Japan (E) Costa Rica

26. By what percent does the United States per capita Gross Domestic Product exceed the mean?

(A) 200% (B) 300% (C) 400% (D) 500% (E) It is less than the mean.

27. By approximately what percent would Guatemala's Gross Domestic Product have to increase in order to equal the mean?

(A) 0% (B) 50% (C) 100% (D) 200% (E) It cannot be determined from the information given.

28. In which of the following countries does the average worker earn the most in a year?

(A) United Kingdom (B) France (C) Sweden (D) Barbados (E) It cannot be determined from the information given.

STOP

IF YOU FINISH BEFORE THE TIME IS UP,
CHECK YOUR WORK ON THIS SECTION.
WHEN THE TIME IS UP, CHECK YOUR ANSWERS
AGAINST THE ANSWER KEY AND EXPLANATION ON THE FOLLOWING PAGE.

Answer to Data Interpretation Self-Test B

MECHANIC SCHOOL GRAPH

This graph is called a *band graph.* The number of each type of mechanic is determined not by the position of the line but by the width of the band. For example, the number of boat mechanics in 1982 is 40, not 100. The dark line at the top indicates the total number of mechanics graduating in each year.

1. (C) The difference between 76 and 140.

2. (B) Only 60 graduated in 1980 (the smallest), and 170 graduated in 1982 (the largest). The difference (110) is not quite twice as much as the original (60), so the percent increase is a little less than 200%.

   60 → 110 → 170

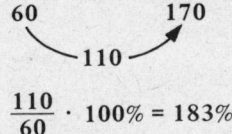

   $$\frac{110}{60} \cdot 100\% = 183\%$$

3. (B) In 1982, 40 boat mechanics were graduated, but they only made up 24% of the class. While only 30 were graduated in 1981, they made up 32% of the class.

4. (D) No boat mechanics were graduated in 1984, 1985, or 1986, but in 1986 no airplane mechanics were graduated either.

5. (E) (A) is true. The class increased from 60 to 70. (B) is true (see question 4). (C) is true. There were always more airplane mechanics. (D) is also true. The largest streak is from 1980–1982.

6. (C) The year is 1982 (when 40 boat mechanics were graduated). Approximately 70 airplane mechanics were graduated that year.

7. (E) Draw no inferences that are not supported by *facts* from the graph.

AVERAGE INCOME GRAPH

In this fairly straightforward line graph, each of seven lines represents one profession.

8. (D) After 3 years, junior executives are earning a little over $14,000.

9. (E) While the junior executives show a very slight increase during the period, note the way the construction workers drop off after the sixteenth year. All told, they show a smaller net increase.

10. (A) During the 20 years, the average doctor's income goes from \$9,000 to a little more than \$20,000—an increase of over \$11,000, or a little more than \$550 per year.

11. (C) (A) is true. Doctors start higher and self-employed persons never catch up. (B) is also true. No other group ever shows a drop. (C) is false. Doctors also make more during the first year. (D) is true. Lawyers start at \$11,000, the highest starting salary on the graph.

12. (E) A doctor earns \$15,000 in the fourth year. A teacher does not reach that level until the tenth year.

13. (A) A lawyer in the sixth year earns a little more than \$12,000. A doctor in the third year earns a little more than \$13,000. The difference is only about \$1,000. This change is equal to less than 10%.

12,000+ → 13,000+ (1,000)

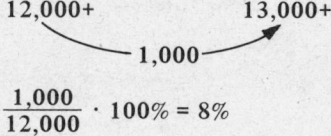

$$\frac{1{,}000}{12{,}000} \cdot 100\% = 8\%$$

14. (D) (A) Nearly 1:1
(B) 8,000:10,000, or 4:5
(C) Nearly 1:1
(D) About 11,000:15,000, or a little more than 2:3
(E) Close to 1:1

THE JUNK DEALER GRAPH

How does this graph work? To read it is really quite simple; let's isolate one of the salvage companies in order to demonstrate.

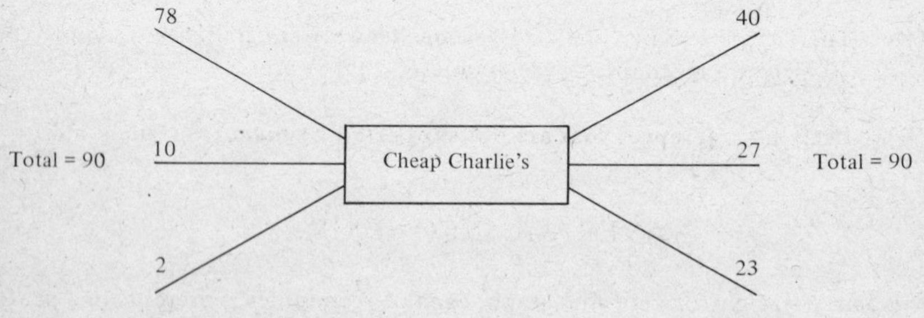

Each salvage company collects junk and sells it to retail outlets. The key is that, for each company, the amount sold is exactly equal to the amount collected; whatever goes into each box must come out the other side. Now, let's look at the questions.

15. (C) First of all, Charlie is not a retailer. Of the retailers, Joe handles 257 tons, Garbage 84 tons, United 50 tons, and Oscar 165 tons. So United handles the smallest number of tons.

16. (A) Rinky Dink buys 40 of the 438 tons of metal. No need to calculate; it is a little less than 10%.

17. (E) We cannot tell what happens to the different *types* of junk handled by Rinky Dink, only what percent of the total is sold to each retailer.

18. (B) We can determine that Cheap Charlie sells 90 tons of junk, 78 of which are metal junk. Thus Charlie sells only 12 tons which are not metal. Altogether, he sells 27 tons to Garbage, Inc., so at least 15 tons must be metal.

19. (D) Joe has no access to wood, since he does not buy from Rinky Dink, the only salvage company to handle wood.

20. (C) Let's look at the ratios:

(A) 78:23, or approximately 3:1
(B) 23:23, or 1:1
(C) 10:126, or approximately 1:12+
(D) 2:23, or approximately 1:12–
(E) 40:65, or approximately 2:3

Without actually calculating, the only two possibilities are (C) and (D). Since (C) is smaller than 1:12 and (D) is a little larger than 1:12, (C) is the answer.

21. (D) At present, Rinky Dink buys 40 tons of metal and Ernie buys 320 tons. Remember, we want $\frac{\text{difference}}{\text{original}}$. It would take a 700% increase.

40 → 280 → 320

$$\frac{280}{40} = 7$$

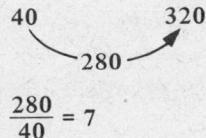

THE EXPORT GRAPH

You can tell three things about each country on the graph. First, by the shape which locates it on the graph, you can tell which geographical or political group it belongs to. Second, by reading the horizontal axis, you can learn the country's per capita Gross Domestic Product (GDP), which is determined by dividing the GDP by the total population. Finally, by reading the vertical axis, you can determine the export coefficient, which is calculated by dividing total exports by GDP.

22. (B) What we want is the point which is third highest on the vertical scale—Fiji.

23. (E) South America is represented by an empty circle. We want the empty circle that is farthest to the right, or Venezuela.

24. (E) *I* is not supported because nothing on the graph reflects the ideology of any of the countries. *II* is wrong because Hong Kong, a southeast Asian country, has the highest export coefficient on the graph. *III* is also false. The United States actually has the lowest export coefficient in North America—only about 5.

25. (A) Conceptually, this question is probably the hardest in the section. We must find total exports per person. The horizontal axis gives us GDP per person, and the vertical axis gives us exports divided by GDP. If we multiply these two, we will get what we want. This figure comes out lowest for Uganda (32 · 80 = 2,560).

$$\frac{\text{GDP}}{\text{person}} \cdot \frac{\text{exports}}{\text{GDP}} = \frac{\text{exports}}{\text{person}}$$

26. (C) The figure for the United States is 2,800. According to the graph, the mean is about 560. The difference divided by the original will give us the percent difference.

560 2800

2240

$$\frac{2{,}240}{560} = 4$$

The United States has a per capita GDP 400% greater than the mean.

27. (C) Guatemala is just about half the mean. It will have to double, for an increase of 100%.

28. (E) All figures on the graph relate to total population. We know nothing about the size of the work force or, consequently, how much the average worker earns.

This chapter should prepare you sufficiently to handle any graph type you might find on the LSAT. However, if you would like to learn more about graphs, you might read Peter H. Selby's *Interpreting Graphs and Tables,* another Wiley Self-Teaching Guide.

CHAPTER THREE

Quantitative Comparison

A recent addition to the LSAT is the quantitative comparison section. When it appears on the test, it usually replaces the data interpretation section. In at least one instance, however, students were given an exam with 15 minutes each of data interpretation and quantitative comparison.

The questions in this section, as you might guess from its name, have to do with the comparison of quantities, one from Column A and one from Column B. If the quantity in Column A is larger, you will answer "A," and if the one in Column B is larger, "B." If the two quantities are the same, you will answer "C," and if the information is not adequate to tell which is larger, you will answer "D." You must be particularly careful, because unless you are told otherwise (as the instructions will remind you), the diagrams are not necessarily drawn to scale.

You should follow these instructions for the quantitative comparison sections:

Directions: **In each question in this section, you are asked to compare two quantities, one in Column A and one in Column B. Choose answer**

(A) if the one in Column A is larger;
(B) if the one in Column B is larger;
(C) if the two are equal;
(D) if the information presented is insufficient to determine the relationship.

General information: **Information centered above the two columns pertains to both. Any symbol appearing in both columns represents the same thing in each. All numbers used in this section are real numbers.**

Diagrams: **Diagrams are not necessarily drawn to scale unless they are so labeled. You are to solve the problems using your knowledge of mathematics, not sight or measurement. Unless you are told otherwise, figures lie in the plane, lines shown as straight are straight, and points, angles, and the like are in the order shown.**

Note that no matter how much an angle looks like a right angle, you cannot assume that it is a right angle unless it is so labeled. Similarly an angle that looks obtuse might actually be acute. Be very careful not to make unwarranted assumptions in this section.

You might also come across the following symbols, which you will be expected to recognize:

$>$ greater than
$<$ less than
$\geqslant$ greater than or equal to
$\leqslant$ less than or equal to
$\neq$ not equal

In other words "$A \geqslant B$" means "A is greater than or equal to B."

The basic math that we reviewed in Chapter 1 will stand you in good stead as you do this section. Most of this chapter will be concerned with geometry.

First, let us say a few more words on the basics, starting with signed numbers. Any negative number will always be a smaller quantity than any positive number. In other words, –124 is much smaller than $+\frac{1}{2}$.

Do you remember how to work with signed numbers? Apply the directions on page 51 to the questions below. (Answers and explanations are given below the line of dashes.)

	Column A	*Column B*	
1.	$(-6)-(-4)$	$(-4)\div(-3)$	Ⓐ Ⓑ Ⓒ Ⓓ
2.	$(-1)^5$	$(-1)^4$	Ⓐ Ⓑ Ⓒ Ⓓ
3.	$(-2)^3$	(-2)	Ⓐ Ⓑ Ⓒ Ⓓ
4.	$(-4)(-3)(+2)$	$(-24)+(+12)$	Ⓐ Ⓑ Ⓒ Ⓓ
5.	y^3	0	Ⓐ Ⓑ Ⓒ Ⓓ

– –

1. (B) The rule, which should sound at least vaguely familiar, is that when you subtract a negative number, the result is the same as adding a positive number.

$$\begin{array}{r} -6 \\ \underline{-(-4)} \end{array} \quad \text{is the same as} \quad \begin{array}{r} -6 \\ \underline{+4} \end{array}$$

The answer is –2.

In Column B, we have $\frac{-4}{-3}$, which is equal to $+\frac{4}{3}$. The rule: *When two negatives are multiplied or divided, the result is positive.* Column B, then, is the larger.

2. (B) $(-1)^5 = (-1)(-1)(-1)(-1)(-1) = -1$

$(-1)^4 = (-1)(-1)(-1)(-1) = +1$

A negative number raised to an even power will be positive; to an odd power, negative.

3. (B) $(-2)^3 = (-2)(-2)(-2) = -8$, which is less than –2.

4. **(A)** $(-4)(-3)(+2) = 24$

$-24 + 12 = -12$

5. **(D)** **We don't know whether y is a positive or a negative number.**

Let's review a few basic algebraic concepts in the context of quantitative comparison. Remember the directions on page 51. Now try these comparisons:

	Column A	*Column B*	
1.	$\frac{1}{3} \div \frac{3}{4}$	$\frac{1}{2}$	Ⓐ Ⓑ Ⓒ Ⓓ
	$a > b > c$		
2.	$\frac{a}{b}$	$\frac{b}{c}$	Ⓐ Ⓑ Ⓒ Ⓓ
3.	$x(y + z)$	$yx + zx$	Ⓐ Ⓑ Ⓒ Ⓓ
	$a > 1, b > 1$		
4.	$(a^2 b^3)^4$	$(a^3 b^4)^3$	Ⓐ Ⓑ Ⓒ Ⓓ
5.	$\frac{2}{3} + \frac{1}{8}$	$\frac{5}{8} + \frac{1}{6}$	Ⓐ Ⓑ Ⓒ Ⓓ

---

1. **(B)** **When dividing by a fraction, the rule is to invert and multiply, so $\frac{1}{3} \div \frac{3}{4}$ becomes $\left(\frac{1}{3}\right)\left(\frac{4}{3}\right)$, or $\frac{4}{9}$, which is less than $\frac{1}{2}$.**

2. **(D)** **Suppose $a = 10$, $b = 2$, $c = 1$. Then suppose $a = 3$, $b = 2$, $c = 1$.**

3. **(C)** **This is called the distributive property. Thus $x(y + z) = xy + xz$, which is, of course, the same as $yx + zx$.**

4. **(B)** **When raising an exponentiated number to a further power, multiply the exponents.**

$$(a^2 b^3)^4 = a^8 b^{12}$$
$$(a^3 b^4)^3 = a^9 b^{12}$$

The latter is the larger, since both a and b are larger than 1.

5. **(C)** **The trick in solving this problem is the "least common denominator." Convert all of the fractions to twenty-fourths. In Column A, we have:**

$$\frac{16}{24} + \frac{3}{24}, \text{ or } \frac{19}{24}$$

In Column B, we have:

$$\frac{15}{24} + \frac{4}{24}, \text{ or } \frac{19}{24}$$

Now, let us go on to geometry. The scope of our review will be limited to the very basic formulas that will be helpful to you in handling this test section. We shall deal with angle measurement, perimeter and area, and the Pythagorean theorem.

The most basic thing to remember about angles is that the sum of the angles on one side of a straight line is always equal to 180°, or half of a circle.

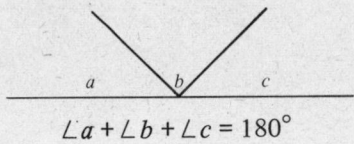

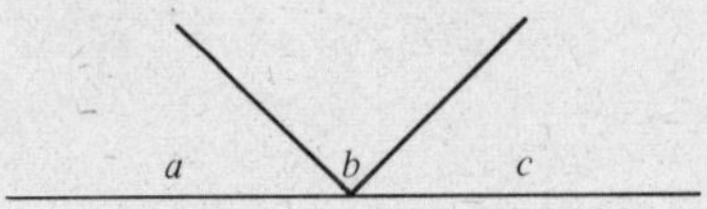

$$\angle a + \angle b + \angle c = 180^\circ$$

The sum of the angles on both sides of the line (or, if you prefer, around a point) is equal to 360°, or a full circle.

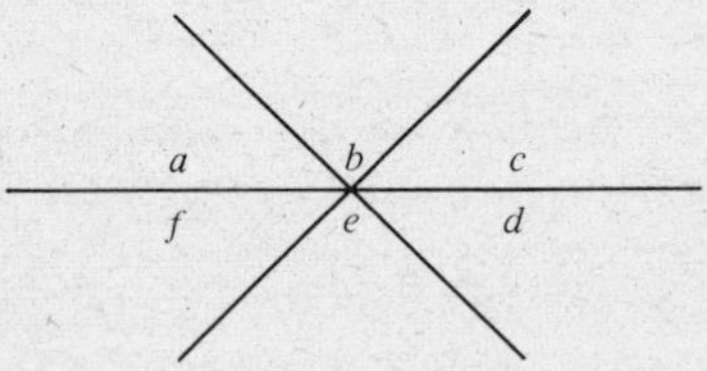

$$\angle a + \angle b + \angle c + \angle d + \angle e + \angle f = 360^\circ$$

Another basic fact that you probably remember from your youth is that the sum of the angles of a triangle is 180°.

Try these questions:

Column A | *Column B*

Questions 1 and 2 **refer to the following diagram:**

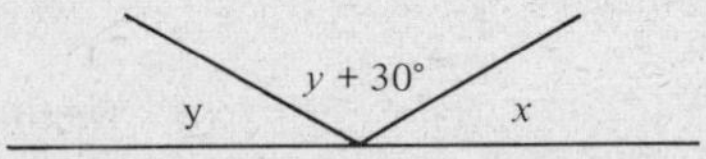

	Column A	Column B	
1.	x	y	Ⓐ Ⓑ Ⓒ Ⓓ
2.	$150^\circ - x$	$2y$	Ⓐ Ⓑ Ⓒ Ⓓ

Column A	Column B	
Questions 3 and 4 refer to the following diagram:		

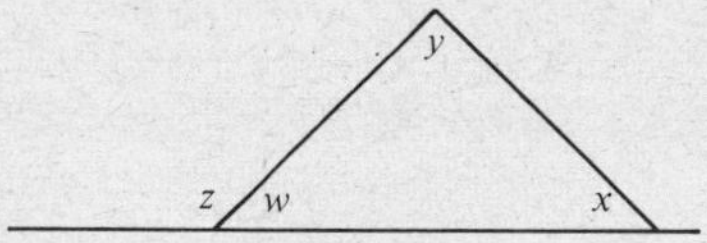

	Column A	Column B	
3.	z	$x + y$	Ⓐ Ⓑ Ⓒ Ⓓ
4.	z	x	Ⓐ Ⓑ Ⓒ Ⓓ

---

1. (D) Remember, this diagram is not necessarily drawn to scale. It's possible, for example, that $\angle x = 100°$ and $\angle y = 25°$, or that $\angle y = 50°$ and $\angle x = 50°$.

2. (C) We do know that $y + y + 30° + x = 180°$.
$$\text{Therefore, } 2y + 30° = 180° - x$$
$$\text{and } 2y = 150° - x$$

3. (C) We know that $z + w = 180°$, and we also know that $x + y + w = 180°$, since they are the three angles of a triangle. It follows, then, that $x + y = z$. In fact, $\angle z$ is called an exterior angle of the triangle, and it is always equal to the sum of the two nonadjacent interior angles.

4. (A) This solution is easy. If $z = x + y$, and y exists, then z must be more than x alone.

Another angle-measurement theorem that you may remember is that when two straight lines intersect, the vertical angles are equal.

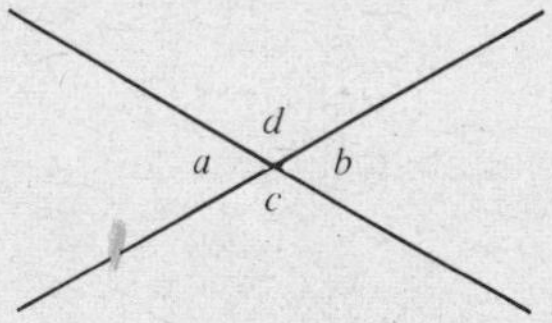

$$\angle a = \angle b; \angle c = \angle d$$

When two parallel lines are cut by a transversal, the alternate interior angles are equal. That rule may sound intimidating, but it is really quite simple as you see from the drawing on the following page. Here, line l is parallel to line m.

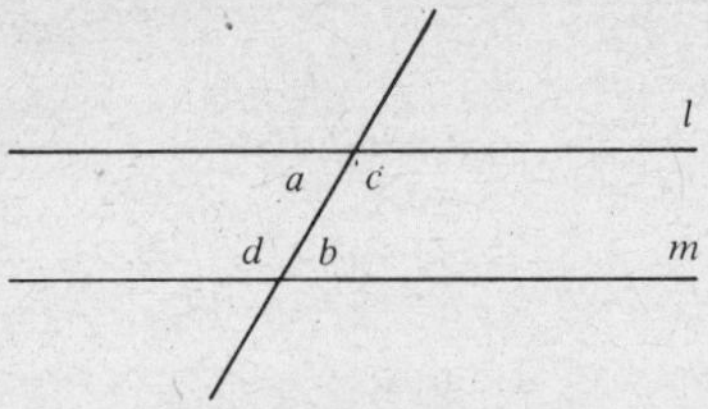

$\angle a = \angle b; \angle c = \angle d$

Note that each pair of alternate interior angles forms a sort of letter Z:

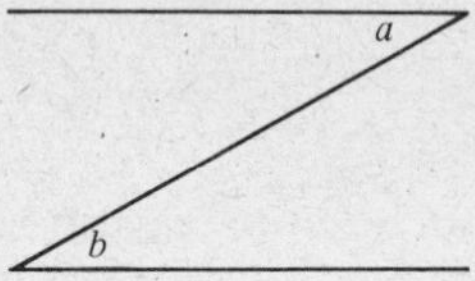

Try these two problems:

Column A	*Column B*	

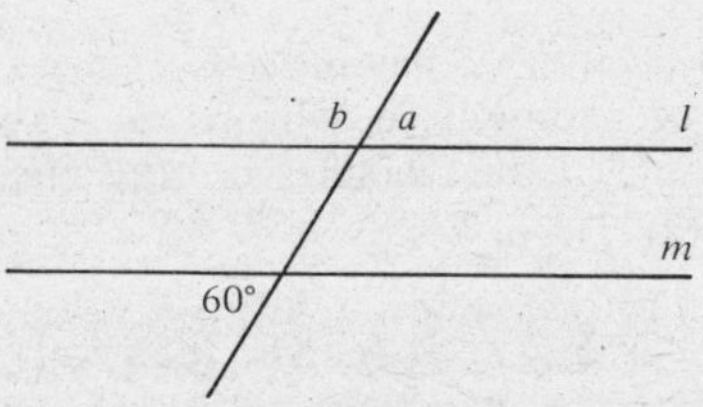

Line *l* is parallel to line *m*

1.	*a*	**60°**	Ⓐ Ⓑ Ⓒ Ⓓ
2.	*b*	**60°**	Ⓐ Ⓑ Ⓒ Ⓓ

Note: If you can't answer these questions, read the first paragraph below the dashed line. Then come back and answer the questions.

– –

Before answering these two questions, let's complete our discussion of parallel lines.

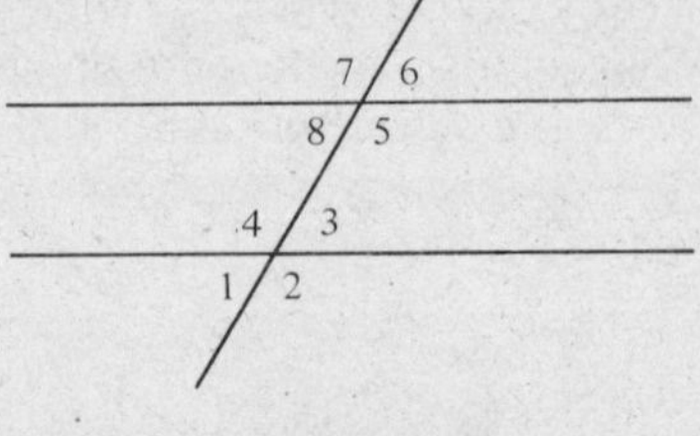

When two parallel lines are cut by a transversal, eight angles are formed. Suppose we know that $\angle 1 - 60°$. Then $\angle 3$ must also be 60°, since $\angle 1$ and $\angle 3$ are vertical angles. But

$\angle 8$ and $\angle 3$ are alternate interior angles, and $\angle 6$ and $\angle 8$ are vertical angles, so $\angle 1 = \angle 3 = \angle 6 = \angle 8 = 60°$. By the same token, $\angle 2 = \angle 4 = \angle 5 = \angle 7$. They are each equal to 120°. (Since $\angle 1$ and $\angle 2$ are the only angles on one side of a straight line, they must add up to 180°.)

While eight angles are formed, then, there are only two distinct measures. Now we can answer the questions.

1. (C) $\angle a = 60°$. It is in the position of $\angle 6$ above.

2. (A) $\angle b = 120°$. It is in the position of $\angle 7$ above.

Before leaving the subject of angle measurement, we should look at two simple theorems involving circles.

The measure of a central angle is equal to the measure of its intercepted arc.

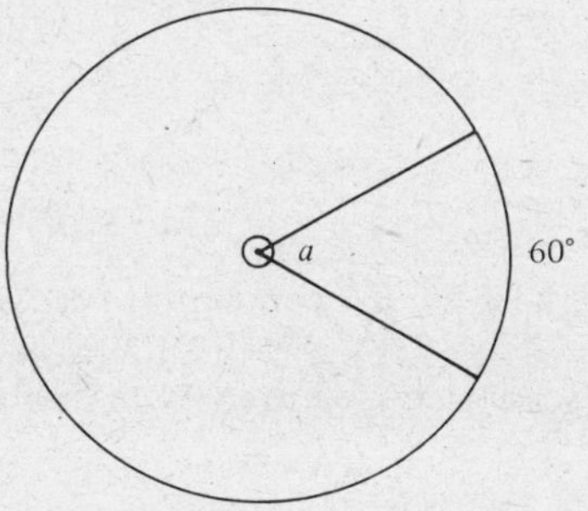

$\angle a = 60°$

The measure of an inscribed angle is equal to half the measure of its intercepted arc.

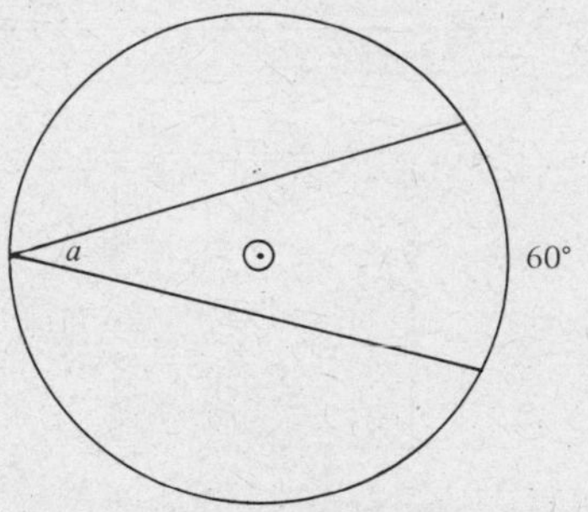

$\angle a = 30°$

Try the following questions:

Column A | *Column B*

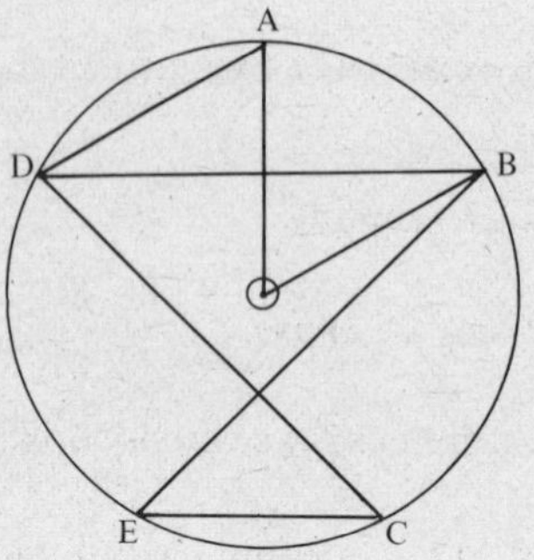

circle O

1. ∠*ADB* — ∠*BDC* (A) (B) (C) (D)

2. ∠*BDC* — ∠*BEC* (A) (B) (C) (D)

---

1. **(D) It all depends on how arc *AB* compares to arc *BC*, which we do not know.**

2. **(C) These two angles are each measured by half of arc *BC*.**

Every geometric figure has a perimeter and an area. The *perimeter* is the total length of the figure's border and the *area* is the size of the enclosed space.

Rectangle:

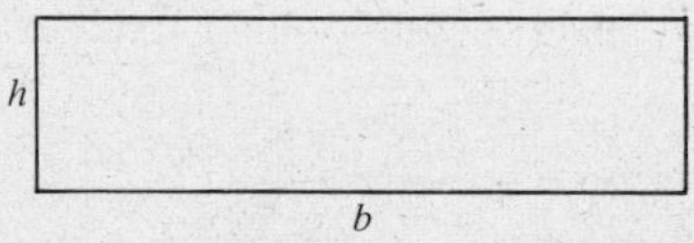

Area = bh
Perimeter = $2b + 2h$

Square (a form of rectangle):

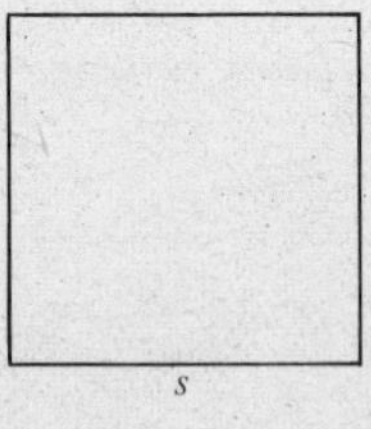

Area = s^2
Perimeter = $4s$

Parallelogram:

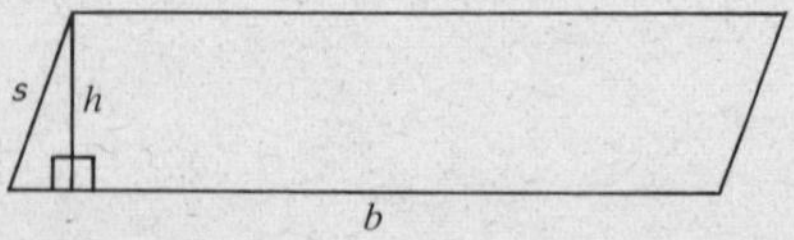

Area = bh
Perimeter = $2b + 2s$

Triangle (half of a parallelogram):

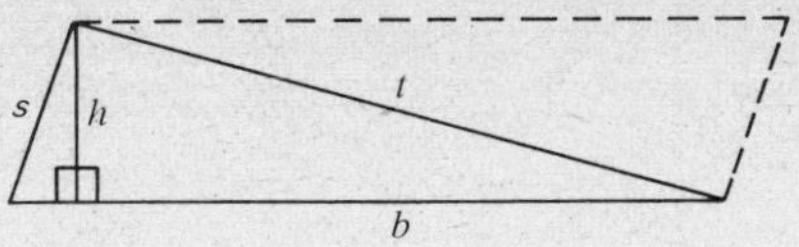

Area = $\frac{1}{2}bh$

Perimeter = $b + s + t$

Trapezoid (bases are parallel):

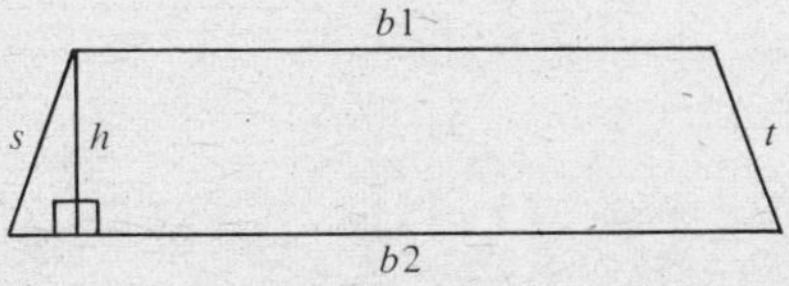

Area = $\frac{1}{2}h\,(b1 + b2)$

Perimeter = $b1 + b2 + s + t$

Circle:

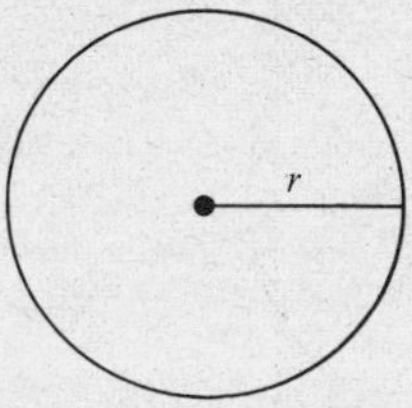

Area = πr^2

Circumference = $2\pi r$ (Perimeter)

$\pi = 3.14$ (approximately)

Try these problems:

Column A	*Column B*	

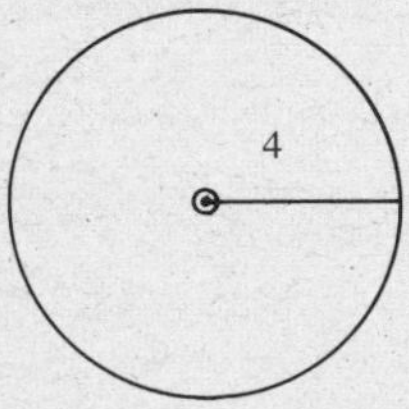

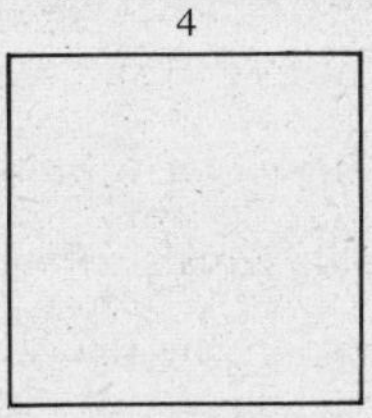

1. **area of the circle** — **area of the square** Ⓐ Ⓑ Ⓒ Ⓓ

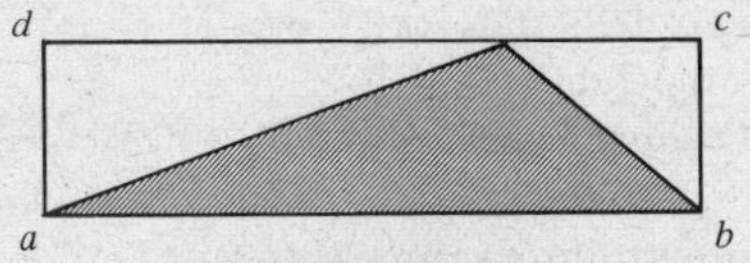

rectangle *abcd*

2. **area of the shaded part** — **area of the unshaded part** Ⓐ Ⓑ Ⓒ Ⓓ

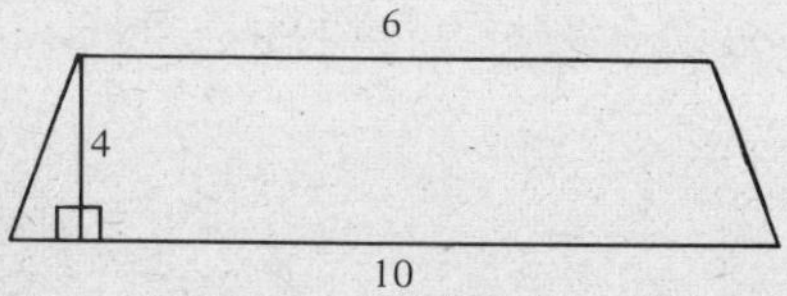

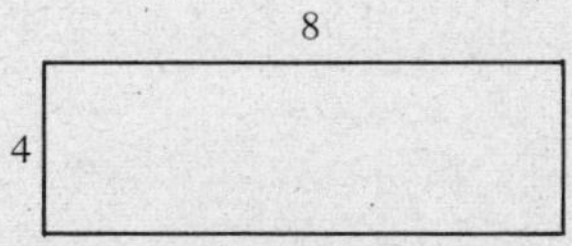

3. **area of trapezoid** — **area of rectangle** Ⓐ Ⓑ Ⓒ Ⓓ

Column A	*Column B*	

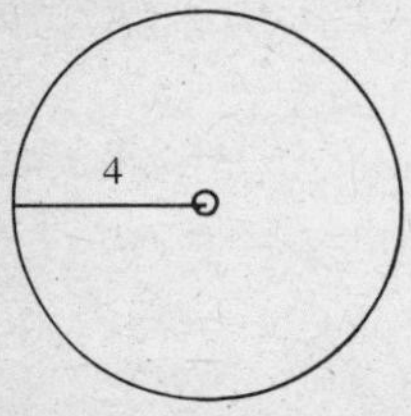

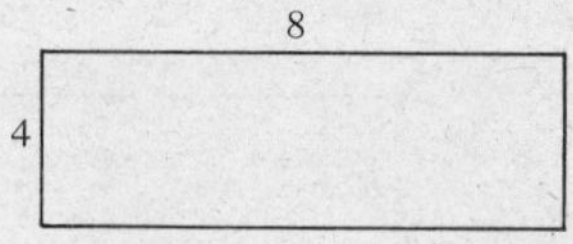

4.	circumference of circle O	perimeter of rectangle	Ⓐ Ⓑ Ⓒ Ⓓ

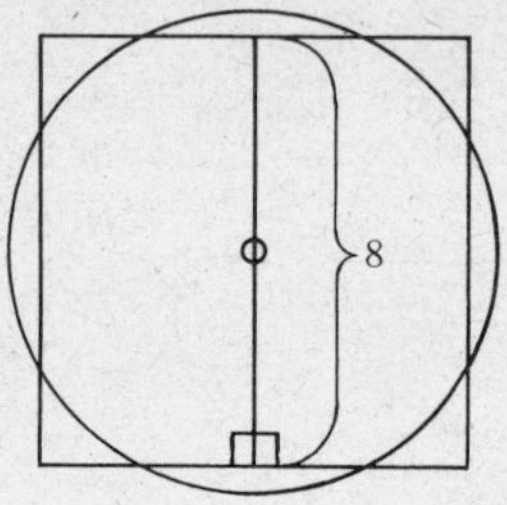

5.	area of square	area of circle O	Ⓐ Ⓑ Ⓒ Ⓓ

– – – – – – – – – – – – – – – – – – – –

1. (A) The area of the circle is $\pi r^2 = 16\pi$.
The area of the square is only 16.

2. (C) The area of the rectangle equals bh.
The area of the triangle equals $\frac{1}{2}bh$.
Therefore, exactly half of the figure is shaded.

3. (C) Area of trapezoid = $\frac{1}{2}(4)(6 + 10) = 32$
Area of rectangle = $(4)(8) = 32$

4. (A) The circumference of the circle equals $2\pi r = 8\pi$.
The perimeter of the rectangle equals 24.
Since π is larger than 3, 8π must be larger than 24, which is $8 \cdot 3$.

5. (D) We would have to know the radius of the circle.

A favorite geometry topic for quantitative comparison questions is the Pythagorean theorem. The theorem itself states that in a right triangle, the square of the length of the hypotenuse is equal to the sum of the square of the lengths of the other two sides.

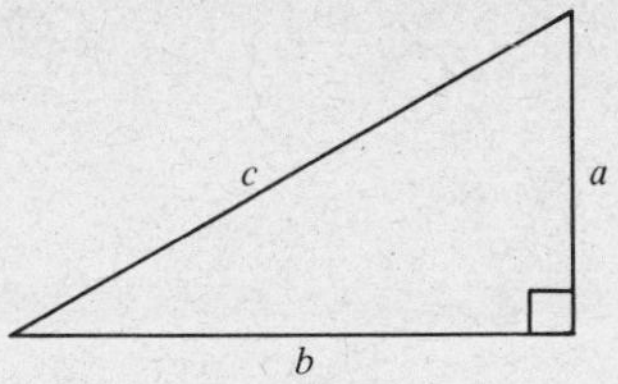

$$a^2 + b^2 = c^2$$

Remember, the hypotenuse is always the longest side (the side opposite the right angle). The theorem applies only to right triangles. It is helpful to remember several sets of what are called *Pythagorean triplets*–sets of integers that can represent the sides of right triangles. The most common set is 3, 4, 5.

$3^2 + 4^2 = 5^2$
$(9 + 16 = 25)$

Any multiple of 3, 4, 5 also works (6, 8, 10, for example). The other common sets, in decreasing order of importance, are:

5, 12, 13
8, 15, 17
7, 24, 25

Now, try these problems:

Column A	*Column B*	

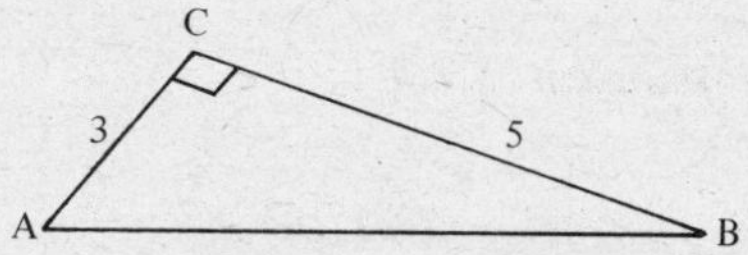

right triangle *ABC*

1.	**length of *AB***	**4**	Ⓐ Ⓑ Ⓒ Ⓓ

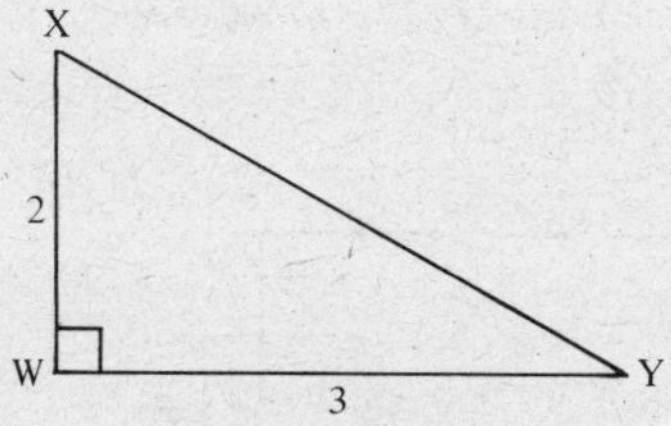

right triangle *WXY*

2.	**length of *XY***	**5**	Ⓐ Ⓑ Ⓒ Ⓓ

Column A	*Column B*	

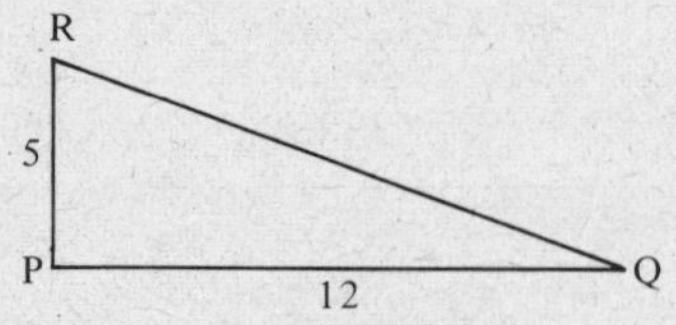

triangle PQR

3.	length of RQ	13	Ⓐ Ⓑ Ⓒ Ⓓ

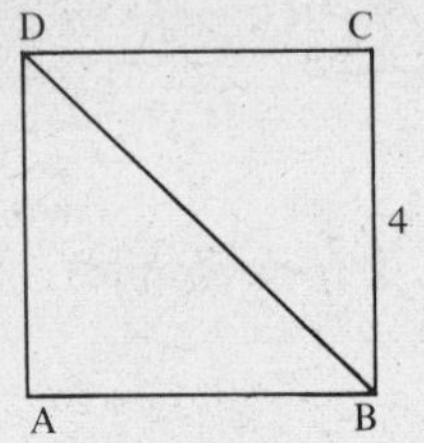

square $ABCD$

4.	length of DB	$4\sqrt{2}$	Ⓐ Ⓑ Ⓒ Ⓓ

---

1. (A) This triangle is not a 3, 4, 5 triangle; remember, the hypotenuse must be the *longest* side. That means, in this case, that it is longer than 5.

2. (B) Let's call the missing hypotenuse h. Then

$$2^2 + 3^2 = h^2$$
$$4 + 9 = h^2$$
$$h = \sqrt{13}$$

which is considerably less than 5.

3. (D) The Pythagorean theorem applies only to right triangles. Without knowing the measure of angle P, we cannot answer the question.

4. (C) We have a right triangle to work with:

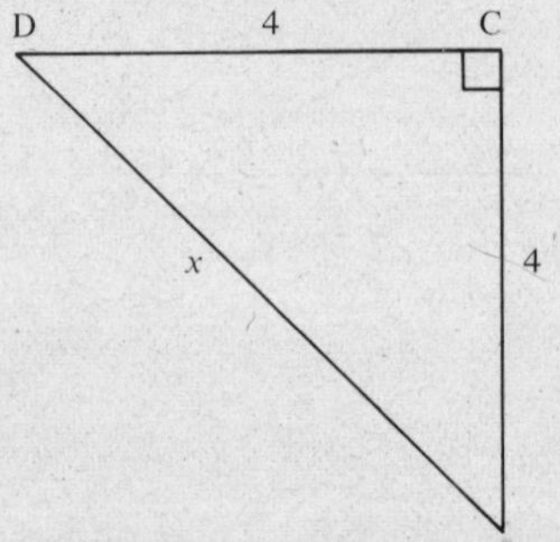

$$4^2 + 4^2 = x^2$$
$$16 + 16 = x^2$$
$$32 = x^2$$
$$x = \sqrt{32} = \sqrt{16} \cdot \sqrt{2} = 4\sqrt{2}$$

The review in this chapter should be sufficient to prepare you for the LSAT sections on quantitative comparison. However, if you want more comprehensive review, you might try two other Self-Teaching Guides, *Practical Algebra* and *Geometry and Trigonometry for Calculus,* both by Peter H. Selby.

Now set aside 10 minutes to do the Quantitative Comparison Self-Test, using the answer sheet from the back of the book.

Quantitative Comparison Self-Test

Time: 10 minutes
15 questions

Directions: In each question in this section, you are asked to compare two quantities, one in Column A and one in Column B. Choose answer

(A) if the one in Column A is larger;
(B) if the one in Column B is larger;
(C) if the two are equal;
(D) if the information presented is insufficient to determine the relationship.

General Information: Information centered above the two columns pertains to both. Any symbol appearing in both columns represents the same thing in each. All numbers used in this section are real numbers.

Diagrams: Diagrams are not necessarily drawn to scale unless they are so labeled. You are to solve the problems using your knowledge of mathematics, not sight or measurement. Unless you are told otherwise, figures lie in the plane, lines shown as straight are straight, and points, angles, and the like are in the order shown.

	Column A	*Column B*	
1.	$\frac{1}{3} \cdot 940 \cdot 210$	$\frac{1}{6} \cdot 470 \cdot 420 \cdot 2$	Ⓐ Ⓑ Ⓒ Ⓓ

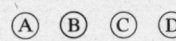

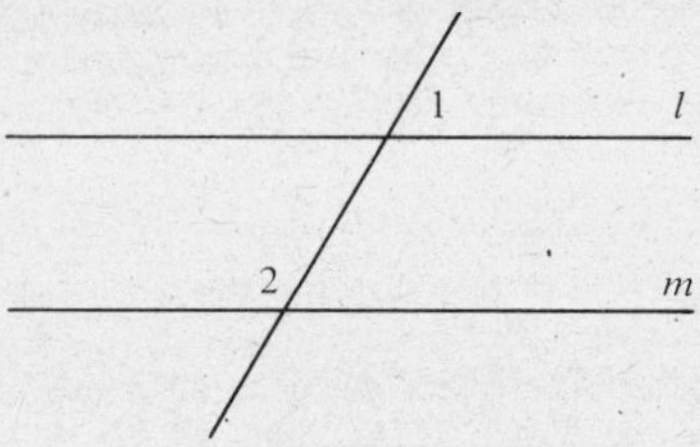

l is parallel to *m*

2.	∠1	∠2	Ⓐ Ⓑ Ⓒ Ⓓ
3.	volume of a cylinder with radius = 2, height = 4	volume of sphere with radius = 2	Ⓐ Ⓑ Ⓒ Ⓓ
4.	% increase in Abe's age from 1950 to 1960	% increase in Mary's age from 1960 to 1970	Ⓐ Ⓑ Ⓒ Ⓓ

Column A	*Column B*	

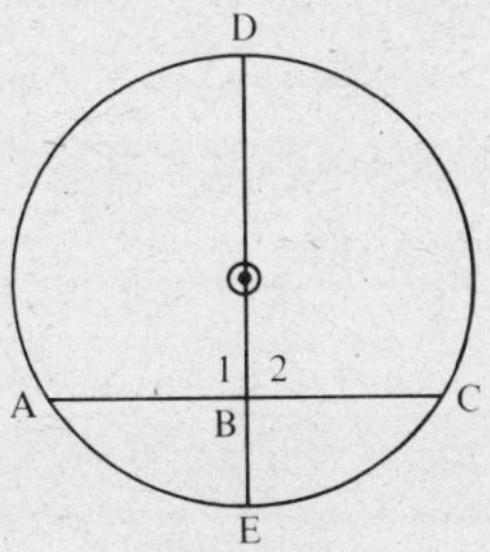

circle O
$AB = BC$
diameter DE

5. $\angle 1$ | $\angle 2$ | (A) (B) (C) (D)

6. Number of numbers between 1 and 99 evenly divisible by 10 | Number of numbers between 1 and 99 evenly divisible by 11 | (A) (B) (C) (D)

$6x = 7y$

7. $\frac{x}{y}$ | $\frac{y}{x}$ | (A) (B) (C) (D)

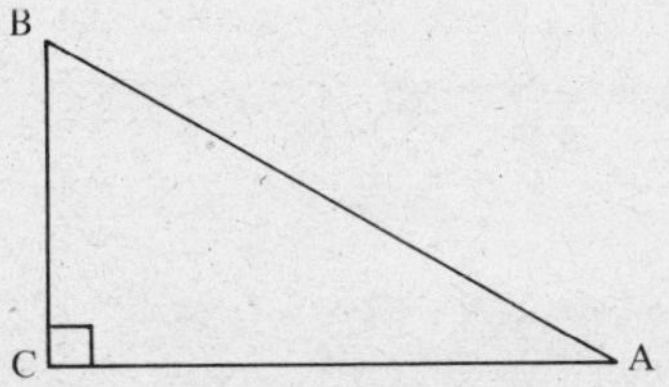

$\angle ACB$ is a right angle

8. length of BA | length of BC + length of AC | (A) (B) (C) (D)

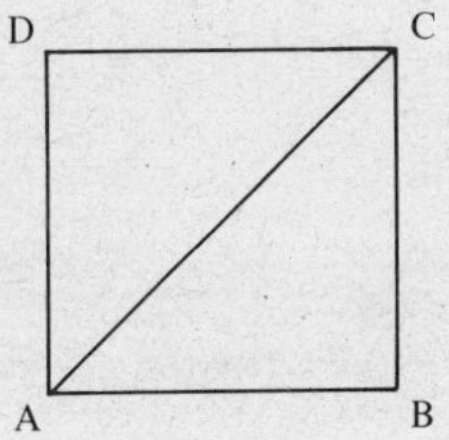

$AC = 3\sqrt{2}$

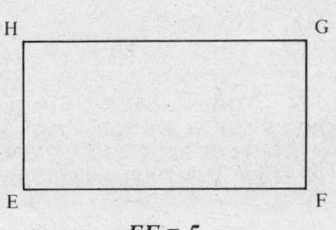

$EF = 5$
$FG = 2$

9. the area of square $ABCD$ | the area of rectangle $EFGH$ | (A) (B) (C) (D)

	Column A	*Column B*	
		$x > y > 0$	
10.	$x^3 - 3x^2y + 3xy^2 + y^3$	$x^3 + 3x^2y - 3xy^2 + y^3$	Ⓐ Ⓑ Ⓒ Ⓓ
11.	the average of 234, 117, 518, and 415	the average of 236, 520, 420, and 109	Ⓐ Ⓑ Ⓒ Ⓓ
12.	x^2	x^3	Ⓐ Ⓑ Ⓒ Ⓓ
13.	50,000,000	$5 \cdot 10^7$	Ⓐ Ⓑ Ⓒ Ⓓ
		$a, b \neq 0$	
14.	$(a + b)^2$	$a^2 + 2ab - b^2$	Ⓐ Ⓑ Ⓒ Ⓓ

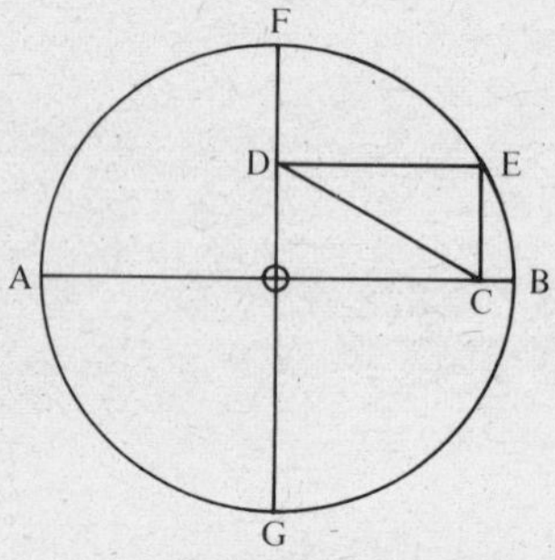

circle O
diameter *BA*
rectangle *OCED*

15.	length of *OA*	length of *CD*	Ⓐ Ⓑ Ⓒ Ⓓ

STOP

IF YOU FINISH BEFORE THE TIME IS UP,
CHECK YOUR WORK ON THIS SECTION.
WHEN THE TIME IS UP, CHECK YOUR ANSWERS
AGAINST THE ANSWER KEY AND EXPLANATION ON THE FOLLOWING PAGE.

Answers to Quantitative Comparison Self-Test

1. (C) You need not multiply these; simply rearrange them slightly.

$$\frac{1}{6} \cdot 470 \cdot 420 \cdot 2 = \frac{1}{3} \cdot 470 \cdot 420$$

If you divide 420 by 2 and multiply 470 by 2, you end up with:

$$\frac{1}{3} \cdot 940 \cdot 210$$

2. (D) Since the lines are parallel, the two angles are supplements, but nothing except appearance indicates which one is larger.

3. (A) For the cylinder, the volume (V) is determined by the formula:

$$V = \pi r^2 h = 16\pi$$

For the sphere:

$$V = \pi r^3 = 8\pi$$

4. (D) It depends on how old they were to begin with.

5. (C) If the diameter bisects the chord, it must be perpendicular to it.

6. (C) There are nine of each.

7. (A) If $6x = 7y$, then $x = \frac{7y}{6}$. That means that x is bigger than y.

8. (B) No matter what kind of triangle ABC is, the shortest distance between A and B is a straight line.

9. (B) The area of the square is 9 $\left(\frac{1}{2}d^2\right.$, where d is the diagonal$\left.\right)$ and the area of the rectangle is 10 (length · width).

10. (B) Since x is larger than y, $3x^2y$ is larger than $3xy^2$, so B, with $+3x^2y$ and $-3xy^2$, is larger than A, which has the reverse.

11. (B) Reorder the numbers and compare (don't actually calculate the averages).

A	117	234	415	518
	8(+)	2(−)	5(−)	2(−)
B	109	236	420	520

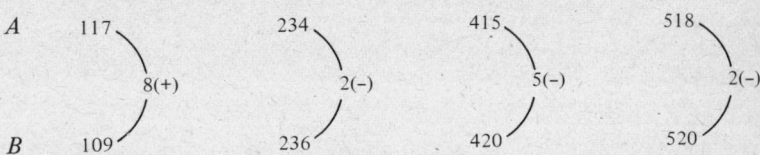

The total in Column B is one higher than the total in Column A.

12. (D) It could go either way, depending on whether x is larger or smaller than 1.

13. (C) $10^7 = 10{,}000{,}000$.

14. (A) $(a + b)^2 = a^2 + 2ab + b^2$. The term "$b^2$" must be positive as long as b is not zero.

15. (C) Draw radius OE. Diagonals of the rectangle are equal, as are radii of the circle.

CHAPTER FOUR

Reading Comprehension and Recall

Reading is tested on the LSAT in two forms. The first form is reading comprehension, or referent reading, with which you are probably familiar. The section usually consists of four passages, each followed by questions, with a total of 25 questions to be answered in 30 minutes; you are allowed to refer back to the passages while answering the questions.

The second form, reading recall, or nonreferent reading, is designed to test your ability to recall what you have read. You are given 15 minutes to read three passages. You then have 15 minutes to answer 30 questions on those passages; you are not allowed to look back at what you have read.

Your basic approach is the same, regardless of whether the passage is referent or nonreferent. The section will contain one passage from each of three basic areas: sciences, social sciences, and the humanities. The science passage may be quite technical, with an emphasis on facts and figures. In each case, you should pay attention to the *central theme* of the passage, as well as specific *details.* Watch also for *inferences* that can be drawn from the text, *unfamiliar words* in the text and clues to their meaning, and the *author's attitude* or point of view (from the "tone" of the passage) where noticeable.

If you understand the passage at all, you should be able to identify the author's central theme, which is most likely to be emphasized in the introduction or conclusion of the passage. On many passages, you will be given a "main idea" question.

Let's try a short sample reading comprehension passage. On the actual exam, the passages will all be longer, but this example will give you an idea of what to expect. Time yourself for $3\frac{1}{2}$ minutes.

Directions: **This section consists of reading passages each followed by questions based on its content. After reading a passage, select the best answer to each question. For each passage, answer the questions on the basis of what is stated or implied in that passage.**

The golden age of the Capetian monarchy occurred in the reign of Philip Augustus' grandson, Louis IX (1226–1270), later made a saint. Louis was a strong, pious king who ruled France wisely and firmly, winning invaluable prestige for the crown through his crusades and charities while his devoted royal officials worked unremittingly to extend the king's power. Capetian officials, unlike their English counterparts, were drawn largely from among ambitious townsmen and university graduates—men lacking strong local roots, utterly devoted to the royal interest. The fusion of local and royal interest, evident in the English administration in general, and the English Parliament in particular, failed to develop in France. Rebellion

became the chief instrument of the French nobility for curbing royal power. Thus the potentialities for both royal absolutism and anarchy were present in thirteenth-century France, although neither threat materialized until after the close of the High Middle Ages.

Medieval culture reached its climax in St. Louis' France. Town life flourished, and in the towns superb Gothic cathedrals were being erected. This was the great age of the medieval universities, and the most distinguished university of the age, the University of Paris, enjoyed the favor and protection of the French crown. The universities produced brilliant and subtle theologians; they also produced learned, ambitious lawyers—men of a more secular cast who devoted their talents to the king and took over the royal bureaucracy. The Capetian government became steadily more complex, more efficient, and from the aristocracy's standpoint, more oppressive.

1. According to the passage, the most important difference between French and English politics in the thirteenth century was:

   (A) the makeup of the aristocracy.
   (B) the attitude of the king.
   (C) the number of rebellions in France.
   (D) the French method of selecting officials.
   (E) the attitude toward universities.

2. The passage supports all of the following statements *except:*

   (A) Medieval culture did not reach a climax in thirteenth-century England.
   (B) Louis IX was well liked by his subjects.
   (C) The Capetian government gained strength during the thirteenth century.
   (D) The French universities produced well-trained officials for the government.
   (E) None of the above

– –

1. (D) See line 5. The Capetian (French) officials are contrasted with their English counterparts. The key difference between them is the French officials' lack of local roots.

2. (A) The passage notes that medieval culture *did* reach a climax in France during the thirteenth century. This statement does not mean that the same thing occurred in England; the passage simply does not say. The other statements are all set forth or strongly implied.

Learning to recognize which details are important is indeed a very valuable skill, and we shall try to help you master it with a special exercise on page 72. As we shall see, one favorite type of detail question asks you to identify the exception to a general rule.

Some ideas may not be spelled out in the passage but can be inferred. Questions seeking this type of information will usually start with the words "the author implies" or "you can infer."

If the passage contains a key word that you don't recognize, that word is likely to be the basis for a question. The passage should contain enough information to help you figure out the meaning of the word from the context in which it was used.

Finally, the "tone" of the passage should leave you with some feeling about the author's point of view toward the subject and his or her likely attitude toward related ideas. Your own reactions to the author should help you answer questions such as "How would the author feel about . . . ?" This chapter will give you practice and pointers for all types of questions.

Time is of the essence in the reading sections of the test. You can't afford to spend 4 minutes reading a passage and then realize that you haven't seen anything since the first paragraph. You must build up your attention span and train yourself to concentrate on what you are reading. Practice reading as fast as you can; if you read too slowly, you will tend to be bored, and your comprehension will be worse than if you pace yourself faster.

Many people find it helpful to preview the passage before reading it in order to increase their reading speed and comprehension. In previewing, you should assess the type of passage you are about to read. What are the topic, the conclusion, and the major subdivisions within the passage?

As you preview and read, you should be making a mental note of how the passage is organized. If you can remember where information is, it will help you to remember what it is; this technique is useful for both referent and nonreferent questions. You *are* allowed to write in your test book, and you should not be at all timid about marking up the reading passages. Underline what you consider to be the important points, topic sentences, conclusions, and key words. Don't underline too much, though, or you defeat the whole purpose. For moderately important material that doesn't rate an underline, you can use a bracket. Develop your own code, but by all means mark the passage. Occasionally you may even find it helpful to make a list in the margin, particularly for the nonreferent passages. One of the best ways to remember something is to write it down.

Remember, you must get what you can out of the passage while you are reading it; even in the referent section you will not have time to do extensive searching and rereading if you plan to answer all of the questions.

Read each question carefully and answer it *based on the information in the passage.* The person who made up the questions is an expert on testing, not on the subject of the passage, and whatever the passage says will be considered true for the purpose of the questions. A nuclear physics expert might get all of the questions in a nuclear physics passage wrong if he tried to answer them based on his own knowledge. The passage itself may be years old. The reading sections test your ability to read, not your ability to keep up with the latest technological advances.

The more complicated the passage is, the simpler the questions are likely to be. The most technical passage will probably have only one question which tests your actual understanding of the technical material. The rest will test your understanding of individual facts. You should be able to answer these questions simply by reading carefully.

The nonreferent section requires some special strategy. You have 15 minutes to read three passages. You should plan to complete your previewing and reading in about $3\frac{1}{2}$ minutes per passage; you should then spend $\frac{1}{2}$ minute reviewing each passage. You may have noticed that you still have 3 minutes left over. They are the most important. If you merely read the three passages one after the other, you would be lucky if you could even remember what the first passage was about by the time you finished reading the third. The extra 3 minutes are for an all-important final review, 1 minute for each passage. You'll be surprised how many facts you can learn in 3 minutes. As you work through this chapter, time yourself and learn to pace yourself in reading the passages.

One of the best ways to study for any test is to try making up a test yourself, and the LSAT is no exception. The best way to learn to spot potential questions in a reading passage is to practice making up your own questions. Study the following passage carefully, and then make up 10 questions. What would you ask about it if you were making up the test? To make up wrong answers might also be good practice—be as tricky as possible. Making up wrong answers is an art, and the best way to understand it is to do it. Some wrong answers are too narrow, some are too broad, some would be right if you could change just one word, and others are merely distortions of what the author said. Learning to apply these tricks yourself will help you to recognize them when someone else tries to play them on you. Remember, the key to doing well on the nonreferent part is to anticipate the questions.

Now, try the passage:

During most of the Classical and Middle Ages, mortality remained very high by modern standards. About one-half of all children died before growing old enough to reproduce. Moreover, the death rate for the entire population was usually between 30–40/thousand/year. Combined with the annual birth rate of between 35–50/thousand, this would have led to a steady growth rate of between 0.5 percent and 1.0 percent/year. This gradual increase did not occur, however. The usual excess of births above the number of deaths was counterbalanced by recurring, severe peaks in the death rate. Usually due to disease, war, or famine, there were occasional periods when mortality stood as high as 150–500/thousand/year.

During most of man's recent history, there can be little doubt that disease was the chief cause of death. Of course, such things as famine and warfare have been important periodic contributors to high death rates, but even their action is not so much one of direct effect but one that indirectly favors the transmission and onset of disease. (For example, more people died during World War I of typhus and influenza than from gunshot wounds.)

It is quite likely that Stone-Age man was no more affected by disease than were the other animal populations with which he shared the natural Paleolithic environment. It was not until men became "civilized" and developed complex cultures in villages, towns, and cities that disease asserted its dominant role in controlling human populations.

Cities developed as men found that they could clear more, grow more, and build more if they pooled their manpower resources. In addition to bringing large numbers of people in contact with one another, villages and towns brought the human inhabitants in contact with other species capable of transmitting disease. Rivers were used for sewers and, as time passed, large cities developed. With the sewers and cities came the black rat, whose flea harbors the bacteria responsible for bubonic plague. The Black Death, as it was called, along with typhus, smallpox, malaria, sleeping sickness, and yellow fever, has been among the greatest killers of mankind throughout history. Some have gone so far as to propose that the fall of Rome was caused by recurring epidemics throughout the Empire culminating with the Plague of Justinian in A.D. 530. These plagues, it is argued, sapped the intellectual and physical strength of the cities of the ancient world, leaving them empty shells that fell before barbarian hordes. During the Middle Ages, an estimated 25 to 33 percent of the European population was lost to bubonic plague between 1348 and 1350. Many cities lost one-half of the inhabitants; indeed, England's population was reduced by almost 50 percent (from 3.8 million to 2.1 million)!

By A.D. 1400, however, the population had begun to increase again. The rate

of growth became more marked by 1650. Explanations of this increase are largely speculative. It began too early for medical advances in public health to have made any inroads on the death rate. So far as is known, there had been no technological changes great enough to make a significant difference in the amount or dependability of food and energy available to man. Too little is known about cultural attitudes of the period, especially outside of Europe, to ascribe the increase to some factor such as average age of marriage or desired number of children.

One possibility that has been advanced is a change in the ecology of these death-dealing diseases. Many disease-causing organisms have very elaborate life histories. Each step in the life cycle requires a very specific coupling with another organism or its physical environment. The rat–flea–bacteria association accompanying human settlement and causing the plague reflects this interdependency of disease-causing organisms. A major change in any link could drastically alter the possibility of the successful transmission of the disease. During the late Middle Ages many personal habits that were not normally regarded as being related to disease at all became widespread. For example, such things as eating from tables instead of from dirt floors, or using footwear, may have limited disease transmission. The decrease in plague that seems to have occurred during this period might have been a result of just such a change. The final disappearance of the plague in Europe in the late 17th century has been attributed to distinct changes in the ecology of rats. The black rat, which established itself in wooden houses, was displaced by the sewer-loving brown rat. This lessened the rat-to-man contact and its subsequent incidence of the plague. To be sure, the rebuilding of London after the great fire of 1666 with brick and stone in place of wood virtually brought an end to the black rat and contributed to a new and sustained period of population growth.

In any event, the gradual increase in the number of people continued, and by 1825 the population reached the 1 billion mark. Along with those unconscious changes that helped to contain outbreaks of disease were several more direct medical developments. With the realization that diseases were caused by specific organisms, not devils and demons, came the first direct attempts at introducing public health measures. The control and monitoring of the community water supply and other public health measures in cities greatly reduced infectious diseases. The beginnings of widespread inoculation and continually improving nutrition enhanced individual health and also substantially cut death rates. These advances, along with the more modern examples of personal health care, have virtually eliminated the misery of infectious diseases and accounted for the most recent period of rapid population growth.

Now try to make up 10 questions on the passage you just read. Then compare your questions with ours, given below the dashed line.

- - - - - - - - - - - - - - - - - - - -

Ten possible questions based on the passage follow:

1. **During the Middle Ages, the death rate was typically about ______ percent.**

2. **The main reason that the population did not grow during this period was that ______.**

3. **Which of the following does not contribute to high death rates?**

4. **The actual cause of bubonic plague was ________.**

5. **In 1348–1350, what percent of the English population was lost to bubonic plague?**

6. **When did the great fire of London occur?**

7. **In what year did the population of the world reach 1 billion?**

8. **Which of the following did not contribute to the control of disease?**

9. **The "Black Death" is another name for ________.**

10. **What were the reasons for the population increase around A.D. 1400?**

(*Note:* The answer to question 10 would be that the author does not tell us the reasons.)

How did your questions compare with our examples? We surely didn't agree on every question, but you should have focused on the same kind of information. Most nonreferent questions come right out of the passage; only a finite number of facts are mentioned, some of which are more important than others. As you read a passage, try to anticipate possible questions. If you anticipate a question, there is no reason why you should not be able to answer it correctly.

Now, set aside 30 minutes and do the referent reading section that follows, which presents four passages with 25 questions to answer. Use the answer sheet provided at the back of the book.

Reading Comprehension Self-Test

Time: 30 minutes

25 questions

Directions: This section consists of reading passages each followed by questions based on its content. After reading a passage, select the best answer to each question. For each passage, answer the questions on the basis of what is stated or implied in that passage.

For Muslims themselves Islam has always been a civilization and an orientation to the world. It is not merely a religion in the usual, limited, modern sense (whatever religion may mean). In the Muslim view, ideally, there are few or no aspects of individual and social life that may not be considered as immediate expressions of Islam or the working out of its implications. Since the Muslim vision of the world—at least for most people and until fairly recent times—has always been integral and whole, with the religious commitment seen as the central point from which all else flows, it is all but impossible to draw the line between those facets of Islamic experience that are religious and those that are not. Indeed, many Muslim thinkers would insist that it is illegitimate even to try to do so. The closer such people stand to the traditional culture of the Islamic world, the more likely they are to be firm in this insistence. A great deal of covert secularism and also some overt espousal of a secularist view have been evident in the Muslim mentality in recent times, to be sure, but the majority of Muslims are uneasy with them. Muslim thinkers adopt a number of devices to escape secularism's more radical implications. There is a deeply ingrained impulse among Muslims to think and to try to live in terms of an Islamic world view. Such an impulse persists along with conscious efforts to change aspects of social life, even when these amount to a veritable transformation of traditional Islamic society. Means are sought, though not always as a conscious process, to bring the changes desired under the perspective of a traditional Islamic outlook. Historically, when one generation of Muslims has departed from modes of behavior or ways of thinking already established in the community (and therefore, because of the Islamic view of history, correct and righteous ways), succeeding generations have usually found the means to extend the cloak of legitimacy over the acceptable parts of these innovations. Among Sunni Muslims what was innovative, and perhaps therefore questionable, for one generation has become authoritative for those who follow by being considered part of the ongoing tradition of the righteously guided community. For Shi'i Muslims the agent of this accommodation to change has been the authority of the living Imam as exercised by the *mujtahidîn* of the community. Whatever the mechanism at work, Muslims have been enabled through the ages to sustain a lively faith in the integrity of their world view and the rightness of their social forms by the continued expansion of a religiously based understanding of life to include the emergent aspects of Islamic experience.

In more recent times when the Islamic world has faced the painful dilemma posed by its relations with the dominant force of modernity and its own failure of dynamic, means have been pursued to enable the borrowing that is essential to survival, means that would at the same time not compromise the Muslim sense of identity, of special destiny, and of living under the law of God. Characteristically the device chosen, in von Grunebaum's words, is to consider the heterogenetic to be orthogenetic (von Grunebaum, 1962). The possibly disruptive effects of the profound impulse to change have in large part been blunted by giving an Islamic coloring to the processes at work. Thus one witnesses the phenomenon among our Muslim contemporaries of radical changes in social life being pursued on the ground that such changes truly represent traditional Islamic values.

1. According to the passage, which of the following statements is most accurate?

   (A) Islam is a religion.
   (B) Islam is an integrated way of life.
   (C) Islam is a set of secular principles.
   (D) Islam is easily adapted to changes in society.
   (E) None of the above

2. The author's attitude toward Muslims is best characterized as:

   (A) approval.
   (B) extreme criticism.
   (C) extreme distaste.
   (D) tolerance.
   (E) The author expresses no attitude at all toward Muslims.

3. When their society changes as a result of secular influences, Muslims are most likely to:

   (A) reject the changes.
   (B) incorporate the change into their religion.
   (C) define the change in terms of a secular counterculture.
   (D) attempt to hide the change.
   (E) convert to a new religion.

4. An Imam (line 30) is probably:

   (A) a deity. (B) a book. (C) a school of Islamic thought. (D) a priest. (E) a tradition.

5. The author's views seem to be closest to those of:

   (A) von Grunebaum. (B) the *mujtahidîn.* (C) the Sunni Muslims. (D) the Koran. (E) None of the above

6. The best title for this passage would be:

   (A) "Islamic Religious Tradition."
   (B) "The Modernization of Islam."
   (C) "The Adaptability of Islamic Culture."
   (D) "Change among the Shi‘i Muslims."
   (E) "Islam: Living by the Book."

Darwin's work had a profound effect on biology in two quite different directions. One was the enormous interest it generated in, and focus it gave to, the study of animal and plant phylogeny. Once the basic concept of evolution itself became accepted in scientific circles, it became possible, and enormously popular, to trace out phylogenetic histories of all sorts of species. So overriding did the aims of phylogeny become during the last 40 years of the nineteenth century that virtually every other biological discipline, except perhaps general physiology and biochemistry, took second place to, or was actually pressed into the service of evolutionary theory. A second direction was the methodology that Darwin's work (principally *The Origin of Species*) set forth. Darwin wrote in *The Origin of Species* that he had proceeded in a basically inductive way, gathering together vast quantities of data—information—which his general theory of natural selection then encompassed like an umbrella. The idea of natural selection was to Darwin an inductive generalization that gave meaning to a whole host of otherwise disparate facts.

Actually, historical study has shown that Darwin proceeded far less inductively than he maintained, or than he chose to present in his writings. Nonetheless, the image that the Darwinian approach presented to the scientific public in the latter years of the century was one based primarily on induction. More and more, the methodological legacy of Darwin came to place a high value on the large-scale comprehensive type of theory, which brought all questions, all types of problems, into its purview. This legacy became of utmost importance in conditioning the development of a large number of grandiose theories that arose toward the end of the century.

Darwin's methodological influence extended in another, related direction. He drew support for the theory of natural selection from many areas of biological research. Systematics, professional plant and animal breeding, biogeography, comparative anatomy, ecology, and embryology were all areas whose findings were incorporated into his arguments in *The Origin of Species.* By so doing, Darwin gained support for his general idea of evolution by natural selection; he also demonstrated the forcefulness of any theory that can, by a single concept, relate evidence from so many diverse areas of biology. Thus, while the broad generalizations that Darwin drew served as an umbrella under which many seemingly diverse areas of biology could be gathered, the use of evidence from so many areas gave further support to the generalizations. There were two sides to the methodological coin in Darwin's legacy, and each supported the other.

At the same time, the Darwinian theory encountered several problems, both substantive and methodological. The major component of the former was Darwin's assertion, without any direct proof, that small, heritable variations arose and persisted in a population. The whole mechanism of evolution by natural selection rested on this idea because, if the small individual variations that exist in a population are not heritable, selection for or against them would produce no change in the makeup of the population, and no evolution would occur. Consequently, the nature of variations—their origin and inheritance—became a topic of considerable concern during the post-Darwinian period. The major methodological problem of Darwin's work was that the mechanism of natural selection was not at the time directly subject to experimental test. While Darwin himself did make reference to experiments in artificial selection (by plant and animal breeders), he used these experiments only as a model (an analogy) for natural selection. It did not prove that selection in nature operates at all in the same way.

7. According to the passage, Darwin's work was most important because of:

I. the interest it generated in phylogeny.
II. its implications for animal breeders.
III. Darwin's methods.

(a) I only (B) I and II (C) II only (D) I and III (E) I, II, and III

8. Which of the following statements is best supported by the passage?

(A) Darwin's methods relied less on induction than Darwin would have liked people to believe.
(B) Darwin's work was profoundly important to the study of biochemistry.
(C) Darwin's legacy was virtually forgotten by the end of the nineteenth century.
(D) Animal breeders were reluctant to accept Darwin's theories.
(E) None of the above

9. Which of the following statements provides evidence of the strength of Darwin's methodology?

(A) It relied largely on generalizations.
(B) It drew on many areas of biological study.
(C) It had practical application to plant and animal breeding.
(D) It related evidence from diverse sources.
(E) All of the above

10. The main substantive problem encountered by Darwin was:

(A) that natural selection was not directly subject to experimental test.
(B) that he was unable to prove that heritable variations arose and persisted.
(C) a lack of understanding about the nature of variations.
(D) his failure to make use of experiments in artificial selection.
(E) that he miscalculated the effect of the variations.

11. According to the passage, Darwin's theories had substantial impact on:

(A) only the study of plant and animal phylogeny.
(B) several related areas of biological study.
(C) most areas of biological study.
(D) all areas of science.
(E) many areas of politics.

12. Which of the following would seriously refute Darwin's work?

I. Discovery that natural selection and artificial selection operated quite differently.
II. A court order making it illegal to teach the theory of evolution.
III. Proof that Darwin's work was not as inductive as he maintained.

(A) I only (B) II only (C) I and II (D) I and III (E) I, II, and III

13. The best title for this passage would be:

(A) "The Methods and Substance of Darwin's Work."
(B) "The Origin of Species: Biological Revolution."
(C) "The Influence of Darwinian Thought on Late Nineteenth-Century Biology."
(D) "Darwinian Induction."
(E) "Problems of Darwinian Theory."

It was the plight of Harry Haller, the brooding protagonist in Hermann Hesse's novel *Steppenwolf,* to live through an age of chaotic change. Surely Haller's predicament is not unfamiliar to Americans living in the postwar era. America's rapid transition from a nineteenth-century rural agrarian state to an urbanized technetronic leviathan has astonished, mesmerized, and numbed recent generations. Our environment alters more each decade than it has in centuries. The accelerating velocity of this change, especially during the last 25 years, has produced a widespread cultural malady that one writer has aptly termed "future shock." At one time or another most thoughtful people can lament with Harry Haller that there seems to be "no standard, no security, no simple acquiescence."

This was not always the case. There was a time in our nation's not too distant past when change seemed gradual and society's norms and institutions meshed rather smoothly with the slowly advancing state of technology. If it can be said that America's traditional norms and institutions were the product of any dominant ethical system it would be that adopted by our seventeenth-century Puritan forefathers. The Puritan ethic was clearly defined and somewhat rigid in matters concerning work, leisure, sexual conduct, child rearing, and the treatment of elders. Although these standards of human conduct led in some instances to blatant repression and hypocrisy, there was little confusion about what constituted deviant behavior. There was a pervading certainty and orderliness about life that seemed natural and assuring. As Calvinist theology went bankrupt during the eighteenth and nineteenth centuries the Puritan ethic was secularized into what became known as the "gospel of success" and "Victorian morality." Nevertheless, the basic Puritan values of a receding agrarian age remained intact and were carried into the twentieth century with the rising tide of moralistic, middle-class Progressivism.

Disillusionment among the "Lost Generation" intellectuals of the 1920s led to a bitter assault on Puritan morality, but the diatribes of Malcolm Cowley and H. L. Mencken were not so damaging to the old moral verities as the emerging mass culture. America's early modern culture, the Jazz Age, was diffused throughout the country by commercial radio, photographs, motion pictures, telephones, and automobiles. By the 1920s American technology had spawned a consumption-oriented society with an insatiable appetite for labor-saving appliances and commercial entertainment. This was a watershed decade that repudiated the values of rural, farm-oriented, Protestant America. The exigencies of depression and war provided impetus for a shift in the national mood. Concern for the country's precarious morale gradually began to eclipse the debate over morality. During the postwar years new technological advances in electrification and biological chemistry raised agonizing questions about the relevance of America's old values. The traditional Puritan ethic, which President Nixon recently trumpeted before a conference of Republican governors at colonial Williamsburg, has encountered automation and the new morality, and Americans are faced with a crucial moral dilemma.

14. Which of the following is not mentioned as incorporating, at least to some degree, the Puritan ethic?

(A) Calvinist theology (B) The "gospel of success" (C) Victorian morality (D) Progressivism (E) None of the above

15. The best title for this passage would be:

(A) "President Nixon and the Puritan Ethic."
(B) "The Puritan Ethic in a Changing America."
(C) "Postwar Puritan Ethic."
(D) "The Puritan Ethic."
(E) "The Puritan Ethic and the Lost Generation."

16. The passage probably goes on to discuss:

(A) the origin and nature of America's ethical predicament.
(B) President Nixon's views on the Puritan ethic.
(C) how *Steppenwolf* relates to modern America.
(D) how the Puritan ethic relates to the new technological advances.
(E) hypocrisy in modern America.

17. Malcolm Cowley probably would have found himself most in agreement with:

I. H. L. Mencken. II. the author of the passage. III. the "Lost Generation" intellectuals. IV. President Nixon.

(A) I only (B) I and II (C) I and III (D) I, II, and III (E) I and II

18. The author probably uses the word "leviathan" (line 5) to signify:

(A) a type of machine.
(B) a sea monster.
(C) a large vessel.
(D) large size in general.
(E) the postwar society's need for large amounts of water.

19. The Puritan ethic was not designed to deal with:

(A) business conduct.
(B) sexual conduct.
(C) how to bring up children.
(D) technological advances.
(E) treatment of old people.

In spite of Okinawa's subtropical geographic position, it has distinct seasonal differences demanding appropriate adjustments in living routine and clothing. Temperatures in the Taira region may reach a minimum of 38 degrees in January and February and a maximum of 96 degrees in July or August. The average daily mean temperature, however, shows much less variation. From the low 50's in early winter it rises to the low 80's in midsummer. The relative humidities, having daily means of 70% in January and February and 82% in July and August, may often reach an uncomfortable 96% preceding or following one of the many rain squalls in the hot season.

From January through March, winds blowing from the northwest to north carry cold, damp air from the Asian continent across the East China Sea. Although many houses in Taira are somewhat protected by bushes separating them from the open valley behind, nevertheless, house doors are often kept shut during this coldest part of the year.

March and April offer a pleasant, balanced climate. Winds are east to southeast, rainfall is low, and temperatures reach the high 60s. The rainy season begins in late May and lasts until late June. During these four weeks it sometimes rains steadily for one or two days, and adults are forced to give up working.

Children take shelter during the worst downpours, but they reappear outside even before the rains are over to play in puddles or little streams running down the streets. During this time floods and landslides occur.

Midsummer is often so hot and humid that villagers frequently comment on their discomfort. This is one of the busiest agricultural seasons, but exhaustion causes many people to take naps during noon hours. Work efficiency decreases, and fewer daily trips are made to the mountains. Children also stay at home in the afternoon. It is believed that the heat causes severe headaches. The hot season gradually gives way to a few weeks in late October, November, and early December which correspond in climate to an early fall in northeastern United States.

Typhoons are known to have hit Okinawa at almost any time of the year. The most dangerous season for these violent storms, however, with wind velocities of over 50 miles per hour, is from late June until October. An extensive warning system exists, and Taira, though remote and without radio, is notified immediately by telephone of storm warnings, sometimes days in advance. Taira people hardly need such warnings. They can sense the oncoming storm and often predict one correctly before the official forecasts confirm that a storm is approaching the island. Since 1955 was one of the rare years in which no major storm hit the island, no firsthand description can be given. The damage is always considerable, not only to crops and trees but also to houses and other property.

20. The average temperature in Taira in January and February is about:

(A) 38°. (B) 48°. (C) 52°. (D) 70°. (E) 82°.

21. Floods and landslides are most likely to occur during:

(A) January. (B) April. (C) June. (D) July. (E) August.

22. According to the author, the weather is most likely to cause physical discomfort in:

(A) January. (B) July. (C) September. (D) November. (E) December.

23. Just after the rainy season comes:

(A) a period corresponding to early fall in northeastern United States.
(B) a period of northwest to north winds, carrying cold, dry air.
(C) a period of pleasant, balanced climate.
(D) a very cold period.
(E) a period when typhoons are most likely to occur.

24. The average daily mean temperature during the year in Taira is about:

(A) 50°. (B) 65°. (C) 67°. (D) 80°. (E) Impossible to determine from the passage

25. The best title for this passage would be:

(A) "The Climate of Taira."
(B) "The Climate of Okinawa."
(C) "Subtropical Climates in the Pacific."
(D) "The Effects of Asian Continental Weather on the Okinawa Region."
(E) "Typhoon Warnings Without Radio."

STOP

IF YOU FINISH BEFORE THE TIME IS UP,
CHECK YOUR WORK ON THIS SECTION.
WHEN THE TIME IS UP, CHECK YOUR ANSWERS
AGAINST THE ANSWER KEY AND EXPLANATION
ON THE FOLLOWING PAGE.

Answers to Reading Comprehension Self-Test

1. (B) In line 2, we are told that Islam is not merely a religion. The first ten lines of the passage expand on this view. Choice (C) is wrong; secularism signifies a lack of religious ideas. Choice (D) is not fully supported in this passage.

2. (E) The author's style is impersonal and analytical; he expresses neither approval nor disapproval.

3. (B) This detail can be found at line 21. The change becomes part of the "ongoing tradition."

4. (D) Since the Imam is "living" and has "authority," (D) seems to be the best choice.

5. (A) Von Grunebaum is cited with apparent approval at line 40, to illustrate one of the author's points. Again, the author gives no indication whether he approves or agrees with any of the other choices.

6. (C) Choice (A) seems a bit too broad; choice (D) is too narrow; and choices (B) and (E) are off the point.

7. (D) In the first sentence, we are told that Darwin's work had a profound effect on biology in two directions. The two are expressed in *I* and *III*.

8. (A) This detail is stated at line 15. No support is given for any of the other choices.

9. (E) The third paragraph (beginning at line 24) deals with the strengths of Darwin's methodology; all the choices are directly mentioned or at least implied.

10. (B) This detail can be found at line 38. (Choice (A) is the main methodological problem.)

11. (C) At line 5 we are told that "virtually every other biological discipline . . . was . . . pressed into the service of evolutionary theory." The impact seems to be substantial. Nothing in the passage indicates that the impact extended to *all* areas of science.

12. (A) Choice *I* would do the trick, since Darwin generalized from his studies of artificial selection. Choices *II* and *III* are irrelevant.

13. (C) Choices (A), (D), and (E) are too narrow; choice (B) is off the point. Choice (C) describes exactly what the passage is about.

14. (E) All are mentioned in the second paragraph beginning on line 11.

15. (B) Choices (A) and (E) are too narrow; choices (C) and (D) are too broad.

16. (A) The portion which we have read ends with the mention of "a crucial moral dilemma" facing Americans. We may logically expect this idea to be expanded upon.

17. (C) Malcolm Cowley is mentioned on line 27 in conjunction with H. L. Mencken; both seem to be "Lost Generation" intellectuals.

18. (D) A leviathan is a huge sea monster. Of the choices, only the size is relevant.

19. (D) This is a detail question. The other choices are all mentioned at lines 16–18.

20. (C) The temperature reaches a minimum of 38° in January and February, but at line 5 we are told that it averages in the low 50s.

21. (C) Floods and landslides occur during the rainy season, which comes in May and June.

22. (B) The heat causes discomfort, including exhaustion and headaches, during midsummer–July and August.

23. (E) Typhoons come from late June to October, just after the rainy season.

24. (E) We know the high and low temperature for the year and the high and low daily mean temperature. We would need much more information in order to calculate the actual average for the year.

25. (A) The entire passage is about the climate of a specific place. That place is Taira.

Now go on and try a section of nonreferent reading. Remember to save 3 minutes for review. You have 15 minutes to read the three passages.

Reading Recall Self-Test

Directions: This section consists of three reading passages. Fifteen minutes will be allocated for reading and studying the passages. Then you will have fifteen minutes to answer questions based on the three passages. Note the key facts and concepts in these passages while you are reading them, because you will not be allowed to refer back to the passages while you are answering the questions. Pace yourself so that you will be able to read all of the material.

At the end of the fifteen minutes of reading, you will be given instructions for answering the questions.

Part A

Time: 15 minutes

Passage 1

By Homer's time, Greek culture was developing throughout the area surrounding the Aegean Sea—in Ionia along the coast of Anatolia, on the Aegean islands, in Athens and its surrounding district of Attica, in the Peloponnesus, and in other regions of mainland Greece. The roughness of the Ionian Coast, the obvious insularity of the islands, and the mountains and inlets that divided Greece itself into a number of semi-isolated districts discouraged the development of a unified pan-Hellenic state, but the existence of the myriad city-states of classical Greece cannot be explained entirely by the environment. There are numerous examples of small independent states separated by no geographical barriers whatever—of several autonomous districts, for example, on a single island. Perhaps the Greeks lived in city-states simply as a matter of choice. Whatever the reason, classical Greek culture without the independent city-state is inconceivable.

We have used the term "city-state" to describe what the Greeks knew as the "polis." Actually, "polis" is untranslatable, and "city-state" fails to convey its full meaning. In classical times the word was packed with emotional and intellectual content. Each polis had its own distinctive customs and its own gods and was an object of intense religious-patriotic devotion. More than a mere region, it was a community of citizens—the inhabitants of both town and surrounding district who enjoyed political rights and played a role in government. Words such as "political," "politics," and "polity" come from the Greek "polis"; to the Greeks, politics without the polis would be impossible. Aristotle is often quoted as saying that man is a political animal; what he really said was that man was a creature who belonged in a polis. In a vast empire like that of Persia, so the Greeks believed, slaves could live—barbarians could live—but not free and civilized men. The polis was the Greeks' answer to the perennial conflict between man and the state, and perhaps no other human institution has succeeded in reconciling these two concepts so satisfactorily. The Greek expressed his intense individualism *through* the polis, not in spite of it. The polis was sufficiently small that its members could behave as individuals rather than mass men. The chief political virtue was participation, not obedience. Accordingly, the polis became the vessel of Greek creativity and the matrix of the Greek spirit. A unified pan-Hellenic state might perhaps have eliminated the intercity warfare that was endemic in classical Greece. It might have brought peace, stability, and power, but at the sacrifice of the very institution that made classical Greece what it was.

Still, the system of independent warring "city-states" was a remarkably inefficient basis for Greek political organization. The Greeks were able to evolve and flourish only because they developed in a political vacuum. The Minoans were only a memory, and Macedonian and Roman imperialism lay in the future. During the formative period of the polis system in the ninth, eighth, and seventh centuries the Assyrians were concerned primarily with maintaining their land empire, and the seafaring Phoenicians were not a dangerous military power. The chief threat to the Greek of the dark age was the violence of his own people. As a matter of security the inhabitants of a small district would often erect a citadel on some central hill which they called an acropolis (high town). The acropolis was the natural assembly place of the district in time of war and its chief religious center. As local commerce developed, an agora or marketplace usually arose at the foot of the acropolis, and many of the farmers whose fields were nearby built houses around the market, for reasons of sociability and defense.

At about the time that the polis was emerging, descendants of the original tribal elders were evolving into a hereditary aristocracy. An occasional polis might be ruled by a king (*basileus*) but, generally speaking, monarchy died out with Mycenae or was reduced to a ceremonial office. By about 700 B.C., or shortly thereafter, virtually every Greek king had been overthrown or shorn of all but his religious functions, leaving the aristocracy in full control. The aristocrats had meanwhile appropriated to themselves the lion's share of the lands that the clan members had formerly held in common. Slowly the polis was replacing the clan as the object of primary allegiance and the focus of political activity, but the aristocracy rode out the waves of change, growing in wealth and power.

Below the aristocracy was a class of small farmers who had managed to acquire fragments of the old clan common lands or who had developed new farms on virgin soil. These Greek farmers had no genuine voice in political affairs, and their economic situation was always hazardous. The Greek soil is the most barren in Europe, and while the large-scale cultivation of vine and olive usually brought a profit to the aristocrat, the small farmer tended to sink gradually into debt. His deplorable condition was portrayed vividly by the eighth-century poet Hesiod, a peasant himself, who wrote in a powerful, down-to-earth style. In his *Works and Days* Hesiod describes a world that had declined from a primitive golden age to the present "age of iron," characterized by a corrupt nobility and a downtrodden peasantry. For the common farmer, life was "bad in winter, cruel in summer—never good." Yet Hesiod insists that righteousness will triumph in the end. In the meantime the peasant must work all the harder: "In the sweat of your face shall you eat bread." Out of an age in which the peasant's lot seemed hopeless indeed, Hesiod proclaimed his faith in the ultimate victory of social justice and the dignity of toil.

Passage 2

We have become so accustomed to running to the tap for water and to the store for our goods that it is easy to forget that we are all drawing on the same limited supply of resources. The water available to man is almost exclusively confined to water that has reached the land and is on its way to the sea. The United States receives approximately 4,300 billion gallons of rainfall a day. Of this total, 3,000 billion gallons evaporate directly from the soil or are transpired by plants, the remainder (a little more than one-fourth—1,300 billion gallons) runs off in rivers and streams or becomes ground water.

A major entry, often overlooked in man's water budget, is the water used in food production. The amount of water passing through crops (used for both food and feed) and transpiring back to the atmosphere must be considered consumption because it is not again available until it is brought back to land by precipitation. Accounting for this transpiration brings man's water budget to staggering heights. The average American's daily food water budget is about 3,500 gallons. Georg Borgstrom has calculated the water costs of some common foods, which will give us an idea of this heavy taxation made on the water cycle.

- an orange: 90–110 gallons
- an egg: 120–150 gallons
- a 16-ounce loaf of bread: 300 gallons
- a quart of milk: 1,000 gallons
- a pound of beef: 3,500 gallons

The figures include the water needed to make the feed going into animal production. Secondary production—raising animals—is extremely costly in water terms because the water must pass first through the plants and then through the livestock. Although the animals themselves consume some water, and some is used in the dairies, factories, and farms, the major water use occurs in raising the crops to be fed to the livestock.

Man's requirements in transpired water exceed those for food alone because much of his clothing and home furnishings also come from living tissue. Borgstrom calculates that one wool suit carries a "water price tag" of 225,000–250,000 gallons. A cotton suit appears to be a bargain day special—10 to 20 times less. (Why do you suppose?)

This type of analysis can be expanded to include the water costs of industrial processes. For instance, the production of an average-size car requires 65,000 gallons of water. If a suit of synthetic fiber is more to your liking than one of wool or cotton, you should count on the manufacturing process using 1,250 gallons of water. For every ton of coal used in an electric power plant, 600 *tons* of water are needed. Nuclear power plants take even more water.

About 270 billion gallons of water per day are directly used in the U.S. (1960 figure), accounting for about 22 percent of the total run-off. Of course, most of this is reused again and again, as downstream cities receive upstream sewage discharges into their water supplies. Only an estimated 5 percent (61 billion gallons) is actually consumed per day. Thus, the U.S. would seem to have sufficient water to meet its needs.

But what of this talk of water shortages and a water crisis? This stems partially from the realities of water distribution—the people are not where the water is. Another factor contributing to shortages in the midst of plenty is the effect of our use on water quality. Our use of fresh water often leaves it unsuitable for reuse without costly treatment. Ninety-five percent of our freshwater run-off is used as a conveyor belt carrying domestic and industrial wastes including heat to the sea. Run-off from irrigated and chemically treated agricultural lands also ends up in that ultimate waste receptacle. In most of our rivers and streams we have now reached the maximum concentration of wastes that the flowing water can handle alone. The main problem then is not having enough water, but having enough that is fit for various human, industrial, agricultural, and recreational uses.

Sediments, foodstuffs, poisons, and heat are constantly and naturally entering waters. The biotic and abiotic elements of the various water ecosystems can handle certain amounts of each of these things during certain periods of time. However, if man puts in large amounts of these substances in a relatively short period of time, the water system is unable to handle the inputs and the system is changed and ultimately destroyed. Normal amounts of sediments, foodstuffs (detritus matter), poisons, or heat are not pollution. However, if they are introduced at a rate exceeding the normal rate, then they constitute pollution.

Passage 3

"Born to lament, to labor and to die . . . ," wrote the poet Matthew Prior about the human condition. Theologians dwelt often on this theme, and elaborated on the ambiguous nature of man—created in God's image yet inclined toward sin, standing midway between angels and beasts in the hierarchy of creation, and drawn in both directions. But many Enlightenment philosophers took issue with the priests and theologians, arguing that man was basically good and had been corrupted only by society. They asserted the cheerful doctrine that Nature was kind and beneficent, that both man and society might progress indefinitely. Alexander Pope incorporated such views in his epic poem *Essay on Man* (1733), declaring optimistically:

> All discord, harmony not understood
> All partial evil, universal Good
> And, spite of Pride, in erring Reason's spite,
> One truth is clear, whatever is is right.

Yet so soothing a notion, which dominated the early Enlightenment, collapsed overnight. In 1755, an earthquake and tidal wave destroyed Lisbon. The kind and bountiful Nature of song and theory had just reached out and obliterated a great Christian city. Why? In an effort to explain the catastrophe, Voltaire (1694–1778), the leading spirit of the Enlightenment, looked again at the philosophy of Optimism, and the problems of evil, sin and unmerited disaster. In a long poem, "The Disaster of Lisbon," Voltaire expressed his disillusionment with Optimism, and argued that evil and disaster had been accounted for no better by Enlightenment philosophers than by theologians; indeed, the new philosophers had denied them altogether. Voltaire followed this poem with his most celebrated work of fiction, *Candide,* a short satirical novel that described a series of unparalleled disasters which befell the hero and his companions, most of which were undeserved and could hardly have occurred in the best of all possible worlds. Voltaire's concluding advice was reminiscent of Job—let us stay home and cultivate our own gardens.

For a while, it appeared as if Voltaire and the Lisbon earthquake had obliterated all notions of optimism, progress, and moral improvement. But optimism is a seductive notion, and it reappeared toward the end of the century under a new name. Now called the doctrine of progress, it found a home in the philosophy of the Marquis de Condorcet (1743–1794), a pathologically cheerful aristocrat who finished his book while hiding from the police. Condorcet argued that the regular operation of natural laws applied to human affairs as well, and he perceived a progression of ages in human history, each marked by greater virtue and enlightenment. The French Revolution was the last age, and the principles of peace, virtue and justice were about to triumph. The tyrants and priests could no longer prevent it. Under the circumstances, Condorcet's arguments were not altogether convincing.

He was imprisoned by the revolutionary government and died in prison while awaiting the guillotine.

If Condorcet's hymn of faith in human perfectibility failed to win converts, it was not merely because of the Revolution. In the two decades before 1789 the Enlightenment climate of opinion had begun to change, away from dependence on the harsh rigor of science and reason toward the more human terrain of emotions. Virtue and justice were still the goals, but the immutable and impersonal laws of science might not lead there. Virtue must come from within. It must be inculcated through education, said the Swiss philosopher Jean-Jacques Rousseau (1712–1778) in *Emile.* A natural education, far from the corruption and artificiality of society, would produce a truly moral man. The novelist Bernardin de Saint-Pierre carried this theme forward to his romantic books, notably *Paul et Virginie.* In this early soap opera, two children were abandoned on an East India isle and grew up living with nature rather than society. They were profoundly virtuous, the product of a beneficent nature and their own innate goodness. This touching tale mirrored the new mythology precisely. People were tired of logic. Feelings were more important.

These various inquiries into the human condition were prompted by a general search for a new system of ethics and morality. Moral strictures had traditionally come from God, but religious morality was distasteful to this secular age with its emphasis on science and man. One of these, or both, must be the foundation of moral virtue, and the moral laws might be as absolute and unshakable as when they were derived from God. No one took this view more seriously than Benjamin Franklin, a rising young man from Philadelphia. In his *Autobiography,* Franklin described his plan to reach moral perfection. He listed 13 salient virtues, and emphasized each one until he mastered it. Alas, it did not work. "I soon found I had undertaken a task of more difficulty than I had imagined," Franklin wrote, "While my care was employ'd in guarding against one fault, I was often surprised by another." His contemporaries, lacking his sturdy realism, kept searching for the origins of virtue in all the disciplines they knew. They, too, failed. The religious explanations of virtue and morality remained intact.

STOP

IF YOU FINISH BEFORE THE TIME IS UP,
REVIEW THIS PART ONLY.
DO NOT LOOK AT ANY OTHER PARTS OF THE BOOK.
WHEN THE TIME IS UP, GO ON TO PART B ON THE FOLLOWING PAGE.

PART B

Time: 15 minutes

30 questions

Directions: The following questions test your memory of main points and important details of the passages you have just read, as well as your ability to draw certain inferences from them. Select the best answer to each question. You may not refer back to the passages.

Questions on Passage 1

1. The district surrounding Athens was called:

   (A) Attica. (B) Anatolia. (C) Aegea. (D) Macedonia. (E) Persia.

2. Which of the following are mentioned as reasons for the existence of city-states?

   I. Geographical considerations
   II. Political considerations
   III. Historical considerations

   (A) I only (B) I and II (C) I and III (D) II and III (E) I, II, and III

3. According to the passage, "polis":

   (A) means "city-state."
   (B) is basically a religious concept.
   (C) is basically an intellectual concept.
   (D) is not actually a Greek institution.
   (E) is untranslatable.

4. Which of the following statements is suggested by the passage?

   (A) The Greeks believed that only barbarians could live in a vast empire like that of Persia.
   (B) The polis was a small unit allowing for individual expression.
   (C) Aristotle said that man is a political animal.
   (D) The Greeks expressed their individualism is spite of the polis.
   (E) All of the above

5. The chief military threat to the Greek city-states came from:

   (A) Minoa. (B) Macedonia. (C) Assyria. (D) other city-states. (E) Phoenicia.

6. Which of the following facts are true of the acropolis?

   I. It was a religious center.
   II. It housed the local marketplace.
   III. It served as an assembly place.

   (A) I only (B) I and II (C) I and III (D) II and III (E) I, II, and III

7. The word *basileus* means:

(A) leader. (B) king. (C) tribal elder. (D) marketplace. (E) high town.

8. All of the following statements are true of Greek farmers *except:*

(A) They sometimes acquired parts of the old clan common lands.
(B) Their soil was quite barren.
(C) They were often in debt.
(D) They had a voice in political affairs.
(E) None of the above

9. The poet Hesiod was:

(A) born in the seventh century B.C.
(B) a peasant.
(C) a religious scholar.
(D) A soldier.
(E) a nobleman.

10. In *Works and Days,* Hesiod speaks of all the following *except:*

(A) an "age of iron."
(B) corrupt nobility.
(C) an ultimate triumph of righteousness.
(D) the dignity of toil.
(E) None of the above

Questions on Passage 2

11. Approximately how much of the daily rainfall in the United States evaporates?

(A) 13% (B) 25% (C) 43% (D) 50% (E) 75%

12. The average American uses how many gallons of water per day?

(A) 1,300 (B) 3,000 (C) 3,500 (D) 4,300 (E) 4,800

13. Approximately how many gallons of water are needed to produce one quart of milk?

(A) 100 (B) 150 (C) 300 (D) 1,000 (E) 2,500

14. "Secondary production" refers to:

(A) raising animals.
(B) the water used in factories.
(C) the water used in dairies.
(D) the water used on farms.
(E) All of the above

15. The passage implies that a cotton suit costs much less water than a wool suit because:

(A) of differences in the manufacturing process.
(B) of the amount of waste involved in making wool.
(C) wool comes from an animal.
(D) cotton is a very dry fabric.
(E) The passage does not offer any explanation.

16. According to the passage; about what part of the total run-off is used directly?

(A) All of it (B) $\frac{1}{2}$ (C) $\frac{1}{3}$ (D) $\frac{1}{5}$ (E) $\frac{1}{10}$

17. Which of the following is *not* mentioned as being a factor that could contribute to a water shortage?

(A) The location of the people who need the water.
(B) The effect of water use on its quality.
(C) The variety of uses that the water must be put to.
(D) The normal amounts of poisons entering the water.
(E) None of the above

18. Georg Borgstrom is mentioned for his work in:

(A) water conservation techniques.
(B) fighting pollution.
(C) calculating water costs of common foods.
(D) cutting the water cost of power production.
(E) All of the above

19. According to the passage, how much of the run-off is actually consumed?

(A) 5% (B) 22% (C) 50% (D) 61% (E) 78%

20. Which of the following is *not* mentioned as entering the water naturally?

(A) Sediments
(B) Foodstuffs
(C) Poisons
(D) Heat
(E) None of the above

Questions on Passage 3

21. "Born to lament, to labor and to die . . ." are the words of:

(A) Prior. (B) Pope. (C) Voltaire. (D) Condorcet. (E) Rousseau.

22. Enlightenment philosophers believed that man was:

(A) inclined to sin.
(B) ambiguous in nature.
(C) midway between angels and beasts.
(D) basically good.
(E) All of the above

23. Which of the following statements is (are) true of *Essay on Man?*

I. It was an epic poem.
II. It was written after the Lisbon earthquake.
III. It was an optimistic work.
IV. It was written by Pope.

(A) I only (B) I and II (C) II and III (D) III and IV (E) I, III, and IV

24. Lisbon was destroyed in:

(A) 1694. (B) 1733. (C) 1743. (D) 1755. (E) 1778.

25. Voltaire's concluding advice was basically:

(A) Progress lends to disaster.
(B) Strive for moral improvement.
(C) Get a job.
(D) Find happiness in your own backyard.
(E) Stay away from earthquakes.

26. The "doctrine of progress":

I. resurrected the idea of optimism.
II. was part of the philosophy of the Marquis de Condorcet.
III. was first expounded by Voltaire.

(A) I only (B) I and II (C) I and III (D) II and III (E) I, II, and III

27. The main reason that Condorcet's arguments were not convincing was that:

(A) he was an aristocrat.
(B) there were too many tyrants and priests.
(C) the police were looking for him.
(D) he died in prison.
(E) All of the above

28. According to Rousseau, virtue:

(A) must be inculcated through education.
(B) cannot be achieved due to the corruption of society.
(C) was no longer the goal.
(D) cannot come from within.
(E) All of the above

29. Enlightenment philosophers searched for a new system of ethics and morality primarily because:

(A) they found religious morality distasteful.
(B) there was no workable religious explanation of virtue and morality.
(C) they felt that feelings were not as important as science.
(D) they were basically atheistic.
(E) All of the above

30. The main problem encountered by Franklin was that:

(A) he needed religion.
(B) he could not correct all of his faults at once.
(C) he was not perfect.
(D) there are actually more than 13 salient virtues.
(E) he was not realistic enough in his approach.

STOP

IF YOU FINISH BEFORE THE TIME IS UP,
CHECK YOUR WORK ON THIS PART ONLY.
DO NOT REFER TO ANY OTHER PART OF THE BOOK.
WHEN THE TIME IS UP, CHECK YOUR ANSWERS
AGAINST THE ANSWER KEY AND EXPLANATIONS ON THE FOLLOWING PAGE.

Answers to Reading Recall Self-Test

Very few nonreferent reading questions require much analysis—most are simply details from the passage. In many cases, a reference to a line number should be sufficient to enable you to look up the answer.

1. (A) Line 3.

2. (A) Environment was one consideration, as we learn in the first paragraph. Apparently other considerations contributed, but the passage does not say what they are.

3. (E) Line 14. Note that "city-state" *fails* to convey the full meaning.

4. (B) Line 28. The other statements are all slight distortions of ideas from the same paragraph.

5. (D) Line 42. The others are all mentioned as *not* providing threats.

6. (C) Lines 44–45. The marketplace was at the foot of the acropolis.

7. (B) Line 51.

8. (D) This statement is the one that does not fit with the others, all of which *are* mentioned; see line 61.

9. (B) Line 65.

10. (E) All are mentioned in the description of *Works and Days* beginning at line 66.

11. (E) Since a little more than one-fourth is left after evaporation (line 7), about three-fourths must evaporate.

12. (C) Line 14.

13. (D) Line 20.

14. (A) Line 23.

15. (C) Remember, it is the secondary production that is so costly.

16. (D) About 22% is used directly (lines 39–40).

17. (D) Normal amounts are not a problem (lines 61–62). The other choices are all mentioned as possible contributors to a water shortage.

18. (C) He gave us the chart at lines 10–13.

19. (A) Line 25.

20. (E) All are mentioned at line 32.

21. (A) First sentence of the passage.

22. (D) Lines 5–6. This point is where the Enlightenment philosophers took issue with priests and theologians.

23. (E) Lines 8–9. It was written in 1733, twenty-two years before the earthquake.

24. (D) Line 15.

25. (D) Line 27.

26. (B) Lines 29–32. Voltaire would not have approved.

27. (D) Lines 38–40. It does shake his argument a bit.

28. (A) Lines 45–46. The others are all distortions.

29. (A) Lines 57–58. That religious ideas were in fact workable is demonstrated by the last sentence of the passage. Choices (C) and (D) are completely off.

30. (B) The quotation which begins at line 63 expresses this problem.

This chapter should have prepared you sufficiently to pace yourself for the type of reading questions asked on the LSAT. However, if you would like additional practice to build up speed and comprehension, you might try *Reading Skills,* by W. Royce Adams, Jr., another Self-Teaching Guide.

CHAPTER FIVE

Principles and Cases

Questions on principles and cases on the LSAT come in five varieties. The typical section contains three types. The first four types are variations on the same basic theme—all of the facts will be given to you in the "case," and all of the applicable law will be given to you in the "principle." Always keep in mind that only two types of issues are presented in any proceeding before a court—issues of fact and issues of law. YOU NEED ONLY TO APPLY THE LAW TO THE FACTS. Remember, we are dealing with *facts,* not merely evidence. Whatever the case says, no matter how unlikely it may seem to you, must be taken to be true. You must then determine how the principle applies to the facts, and it must fit *exactly.* Do not change, omit, or add anything to the case in order to accommodate your answer.

Note also that the principles need not have any relation to the real law. Do not try to decide cases on the basis of what you believe to be the actual law or even the Constitution. You must accept the principle as the valid and controlling law and apply it to the facts of the case as they are given to you.

The questions in this section do not presuppose any legal knowledge on your part. You do not need an extensive legal vocabulary. Some questions may assume that you know things which are considered to be common knowledge. For example, the *plaintiff* is the person who is suing, and the *defendant* is the person who is being sued. If the *defendant* wins, we say that the court "held for" the defendant. Note that a case of criminal prosecution also has two parties—the defendant and the prosecution.

The exam may use words like *felony* which have legal meaning, but they will usually be words which, like felony, are understood by lay persons to have a certain meaning; you will not be expected to know anything more technical than the ordinary meanings of such words.

Throughout this section, only four possible answers are given, as opposed to the five offered on most of the rest of the test.

The first type of question (Principle-Case-Reason) starts with a fairly long principle which is followed by a series of cases, each of which is decided on the basis of some part of the principle. In each case, you are given the facts and told who is seeking legal action against whom as well as the theory behind the action. You must decide who wins and why, on the basis of the principle. Usually, two answers will favor each party. In a variation (Major Factor-Principle) you may be told who wins and asked to choose among four possible reasons why (the major factor).

On this section of the exam, you should use the same basic techniques you used for the reading sections. Read the principle carefully, underlining it and making notes as you go. Note its main idea and important details. In some instances, you may find it helpful to make an outline or flow chart. For example, if the principle defines murder, breaks it down into two degrees, and then mentions several exceptions (like a defense of insanity), your outline might look like this:

MURDER

FIRST DEGREE	SECOND DEGREE
Elements 1.	Elements 1.
2.	2.
3.	

EXCEPTIONS
1.
2.
3.

Now, when you read the cases which follow, check them against the outline. Does the crime fit the elements of first-degree murder? If so, do any of the exceptions apply? Once you have answered these questions, you will know if the defendant should be acquitted or convicted, and, if convicted, of which degree.

Remember, the facts you are given are the truth, the whole truth, and nothing but the truth; don't add or subtract anything. Sometimes a fact may be irrelevant, but make sure no other answer is better before you discount such a fact in order to accommodate your answer.

Now, let's look at the principle on which we based the outline and try a few questions.

Directions: **In this section you will be presented with some legal principles that may or may not be real. You are to accept them as valid. Following each principle will be several short cases. For each case, you will be presented with four possible applications of the principle to that case. Answer each question by selecting the most reasonable application.**

These questions assume no prior legal knowledge on your part; answer them using only ordinary logical reasoning.

Time: 4 minutes

Principle

Murder is the wilful killing of another human being. An attack can constitute first-degree murder only if it was intended to kill, rather than simply to injure, and if it was premeditated. Unpremeditated murder is murder in the second degree.

If the defendant is adjudged insane or temporarily insane, or is a minor under the age of 18, the killing cannot constitute murder.

Cases

1. **Seventeen-year-old Chuck Boyson failed science last term and hates Mr. Wizard, his**

science teacher. When no one is around, he rigs Mr. Wizard's Bunsen burner to explode the next time it is lit. Late that day, Mr. Wizard lights his burner and is killed by the ensuing explosion. When Chuck is tried for first-degree murder, he will be:

(A) convicted, because the murder was premeditated.
(B) acquitted, because he is insane.
(C) convicted, because he succeeded in killing Mr. Wizard.
(D) acquitted, because he is a minor.

2. Frank Wilson has been visiting Dr. Pate, his psychiatrist, every week for 31 years. One day they have an argument about Frank's bill, and Frank, in the heat of the moment, takes out a gun and shoots Dr. Pate. When Frank is tried for first-degree murder, he will be:

(A) convicted, because he killed Dr. Pate and none of the exceptions apply.
(B) acquitted, because he is insane.
(C) convicted, because he intended to kill Dr. Pate.
(D) acquitted, because the killing was not premeditated.

3. Milt Donner lends money to Mr. Oz. When Mr. Oz fails to repay the loan, Donner decides to beat him up. While Donner does not intend to kill Mr. Oz, he hits him a bit too hard, because the beating proves fatal. When Donner is tried for second-degree murder, he will be:

(A) convicted, because the attack was wilful, and Mr. Oz died.
(B) convicted, because the attack was premeditated.
(C) acquitted, because he did not intend to kill Mr. Oz.
(D) acquitted, because the killing was premeditated.

— — — — — — — — — — — — — — — — — — — —

First, let's fill in our outline.

MURDER

FIRST DEGREE	SECOND DEGREE
1. Killing	1. Killing
2. Wilful (intended to kill)	2. Wilful (not intended to kill)
3. Premeditated	

EXCEPTIONS

1. Adjudged insane
2. Adjudged temporarily insane
3. Minor

1. (D) The fact that Chuck is a minor overrides the fact that he met all of the requirements for first-degree murder.

2. (D) None of the exceptions apply; nothing in the case indicates that Frank has ever been adjudged insane. He can't, however, be convicted of first-degree murder because no evidence of premeditation exists. Had he been tried for second-degree murder, he would have been convicted.

3. (A) **Both requirements of second-degree murder have been met; premeditation is unnecessary.**

The third type of question (Case–Principle–Reason) works along the same lines as the first. The only difference is that you are given a long case at the beginning, followed by a series of principles with questions, each relating to a different part of the original case. Each question refers only to one principle, but wrong answers will sometimes play on earlier principles in order to confuse you. In a variation (Major Factor–Case), you are told who wins and asked to choose the major factor.

The techniques are basically the same as for those we have discussed. You should read the case carefully and highlight it. You might wish to skim the principles first, in order to give yourself an idea about what to look for in the case, but this step is not essential.

Now, let us try a few questions of this type. As the directions indicate, this is the Major Factor–Case variation.

Directions: **Each case in this part is followed by several principles, which may or may not be real principles of law. You are to accept them as valid. Each principle is followed by a question with four possible answers, each a potential factor in the application of the principle to the case. In each question, you are to select the choice which is the major factor. Your answer should be based on what is stated or implied in the principle and the case. Each of these questions is independent of all of the others.**

These questions assume no prior legal knowledge on your part; answer them using only ordinary logical reasoning.

Time: 3 minutes

Case

Misty Limmer, an aspiring actress, meets Monty Video, a TV personality, at a party. Video says that he can make her a star and takes her back to his apartment for a screen test. When he is unable to seduce her, he calls upon his friend Ned, who dons a fake minister's costume and declares them man and wife. They live as man and wife for a long time, but Misty never becomes a star, and she finally leaves Video after 10 years.

1. **A suit for desertion brought by Monty Video against Misty is held for Monty on the following principle:**

   Desertion takes place when one party to a legal marriage deserts the other. A legal marriage can be created in either of the following two ways:

   1. *The parties take part in a valid legal ceremony.*
   2. *The parties live together for a period of 7 years during which time they hold themselves out to be man and wife.*

   Which of the following was the major factor in the disposition of this case?

   (A) **Misty deserted Monty.**
   (B) **Misty and Monty took part in a ceremony.**
   (C) **Misty and Monty lived together as man and wife for 7 years.**
   (D) **Misty never became a star.**

2. **A suit for breach of nuptial promise brought by Misty against Monty is held for Monty on the following principle:**

   A nuptial promise is one which induces a party to engage in a valid ceremonial marriage with the promising party.

   Which of the following was the major factor in the disposition of the case?

   (A) Monty did not make Misty a star.
   (B) Ned was not a real minister.
   (C) Monty and Misty lived together as man and wife for 10 years.
   (D) Misty cannot prove that the promise of stardom was her real reason for marrying Monty.

– –

1. **(C) Two elements are needed for a successful suit for desertion. One is the fact of the desertion itself. Without question, in this case Misty left Monty. The major factor, therefore, will be the establishment of the second necessary element—the existence of a valid marriage. Choice (B) cannot be correct, because the ceremony was not valid; the minister was not really a minister.**

2. **(B) The principle from the last question does not apply in this instance. Choice (C) has nothing to do with this question. Under this principle, a valid ceremonial marriage is required and, as we have noted, Misty and Monty never had one.**

The fifth type of question (Related Cases) presents a slightly different problem. You are given a case and told who wins. Each of the answers is a principle. You are asked to select the *narrowest principle* that *reasonably explains* the holding of the case. By "narrowest," we mean the principle which conforms most closely to the case at hand. More specifically, we want the principle which best covers the *legal* issues in the case. For example, in a case where a teacher is convicted of punching one of his female students during class, the four choices might be as follows:

(A) No person shall punch another person in school.
(B) No male shall punch any female in school.
(C) No teacher shall punch any of his students in school.
(D) Teachers may punch their students when they feel it is necessary in order to maintain discipline in class.

– –

First of all, (D) is obviously wrong, because it holds the wrong way. We need a principle that convicts the teacher.

Of the first three, we can eliminate (A) for being broader than (B) or (C). It works, and it could be the right answer, but (B) and (C) are both narrower.

The better answer is (C). It deals with the legal relationship between the people involved—teacher and student. Answer (B), on the other hand, deals only with the essentially irrelevant factor of gender, which gives us additional *factual* narrowness but no real *legal* narrowness.

An added complication occurs in Related Cases. Later principles in a series must not contradict earlier decisions, and earlier principles must not make later decisions impossible. Now, suppose another case arises later in the same series in which a teacher slaps a student who is in the process of causing a major disturbance in the classroom. The court this time holds for the teacher. Which of the principles below would you select as best supporting the holding of the case? Before you answer, read the directions you should follow for this section:

Directions: **This section consists of several groups of cases. Each case ends with a judicial holding and a set of four legal principles. You must select the *narrowest* principle that reasonably explains the judicial decision but is *not inconsistent* with any previous holdings in that group of cases.**

For the first case in each group, eliminate any principles that do not conform to the facts of the case and do not provide a reasonable explanation of the holding. Then select the narrowest of the reasonable principles.

In the remaining cases in that group, the basic procedure is the same, but you must also eliminate any principles that contradict earlier answers in the group before you select the narrowest principle.

These questions assume no prior legal knowledge on your part; answer them using only ordinary logical reasoning.

(A) When a student is causing a major disturbance, a teacher may use whatever physical force is necessary to preserve order.
(B) Teachers may slap students whenever they feel it is necessary.
(C) Teachers may not use physical force on their students except in self-defense.
(D) Teachers may slap students in order to prevent immediate harm to other students.

— — — — — — — — — — — — — — — — — — —

This question demonstrates three reasons for rejecting possible answers. Answer (A) contradicts the principle in the first question, which says that teachers may *never* punch students. Answer (A) seems to allow punching a student who causes a major disturbance. It is also very broad, referring to "whatever physical force is necessary." Answer (C) holds against the teacher, who was not defending himself in this case, and answer (D) has no basis in the facts of the case—we are given no indication that any other student was in danger.

The correct answer, by default, is (B), which holds for the teacher and does not contradict either the facts of this case or the principle in the previous case.

Always look first for answers that can be eliminated as contrary to the holding, the facts, or an earlier principle. Getting them out of the way will help to avoid confusion in seeking the narrowest of the principles that work.

If you get an early answer wrong, your incorrect choice usually should not prevent you from answering the later questions correctly, but it sometimes can. If you feel that the best answer to a question contradicts one of your earlier answers, it might be wise to go back and check the earlier answer.

Now, set aside 40 uninterrupted minutes to try this Principles and Cases Self-Test. Like most principles and cases sections on the LSAT, this self-test is divided into three parts, each with a different type of question. Be sure you read the directions for each part carefully, so you are sure you know what is required; question types are not labeled. Use your answer sheet from the back of the book.

Principles and Cases Self-Test

Time: 40 minutes

30 questions

Part A

Directions: In this section you will be presented with some legal principles that may or may not be real. You are to accept them as valid. Following each principle will be several short cases. For each case, you will be presented with four possible applications of the principle to that case. Answer each question by selecting the most reasonable application.

These questions assume no prior legal knowledge on your part; answer them using only ordinary logical reasoning.

Principle 1

Kidnapping occurs when one person forcibly moves another, against his will, to another country or to another part of his own country, state, or county. If the victim is moved in order to facilitate the commission of another crime against the same victim, the criminal can be charged with kidnapping only if the movement of the victim was substantial and not merely incidental to the commission of the second crime. Even very slight movement will be sufficient to constitute kidnapping if the danger to the victim is substantially increased by the movement.

1. Spikes picks up Jennifer, a hitchhiker, on Interstate 66 one night. Interstate 66 is unlighted. Midway between exits 17 and 18, about 55 miles later, Jennifer says, "You can let me out here, thanks." Spikes immediately pulls the car over and parks it behind a bush, hidden from the road. He then rapes Jennifer. When Spikes is tried for kidnapping, he will be:

   (A) convicted, because he transported Jennifer 55 miles.
   (B) acquitted, because the movement against her will was only incidental to the commission of the rape.
   (C) convicted, because his sole purpose in picking up Jennifer was to rape her.
   (D) acquitted, because he did not transport her against her will.

2. As Mr. and Mrs. Plush are returning to their Park Avenue apartment one night, Frankie and Johnny jump into their car and order Mr. Plush at gunpoint to drive around the city while they collect all of the cash and jewelry that the couple is carrying. The drive takes about 20 minutes, covers about $2\frac{1}{2}$ miles, and ends back at the Plush home. When Frankie and Johnny are tried for kidnapping, they will be:

   (A) acquitted, because the movement was merely incidental to the robbery.
   (B) convicted, because they transported the Plushes against their will.
   (C) acquitted, because they had no intention of kidnapping the Plushes.
   (D) convicted, because they moved the Plushes at gunpoint.

3. Steve Pill sees Loretta's camper parked at a rest area near Boston, and he decides to steal it. He drives it to New York where he parks it in another rest area and leaves it. Unknown to him, Loretta is asleep in the back of the camper and wakes up just after they park in New York. She calls a policeman who arrests Steve. When Steve is tried for kidnapping, he will be:

(A) acquitted, because he did not know that Loretta was in the camper.
(B) convicted, because Loretta did not want to go to New York.
(C) acquitted, because moving Loretta was strictly incidental to stealing the camper..
(D) acquitted, because Loretta was in no real danger.

4. Saxon and Jordan hide in Nell's car so that they can rob her. When she gets in, Saxon takes the wheel while Jordan tells Nell to hand over all of her money. When Saxon, who is a terrible driver, crashes the car into a tree, Jordan is thrown through the front windshield and killed, and Nell escapes. When Saxon is tried for kidnapping, he will be:

(A) acquitted, because the movement was merely incidental to the robbery.
(B) convicted, because Nell did not want to go where Saxon and Jordan took her.
(C) acquitted, because they had only gone a few blocks when they crashed.
(D) convicted, because the ride was extremely dangerous.

5. As 12-year-old Petunia is walking home from school, Morlock sneaks up behind her and throws her into his truck. He then drives 20 miles to his hideout, where he realizes that he wanted to kidnap Violet, whose father is a millionaire, so he returns Petunia, unharmed, to where he picked her up. When Morlock is tried for kidnapping, he will be:

(A) acquitted, because the movement of Petunia was merely incidental to the commission of the crime.
(B) acquitted, because he brought Petunia back unharmed.
(C) convicted, because Petunia did not want to be taken to Morlock's hideout.
(D) acquitted, because no second crime was involved.

Principle 2

In general, a landowner may not intentionally harm a trespasser. A landowner owes no duty, however, to an unknown trespasser except for a duty to refrain from setting traps for him. If he has reason to suspect that trespassers are using his land, he has a duty to warn them about any dangerous aspects of the land about which he has prior knowledge. The landowner, however, has no duty to look for such dangers. Should the landowner see a trespasser on his land, he is obliged to warn the trespasser if he knows him to be in danger.

6. Mr. Greenjeans owns a farm upstate, but he spends all of his time in the city, so he never gets upstate to inspect his land. His children, however, use the cabin every summer, so Mr. Greenjeans has them set bear traps around the property. Every fall, as Mr. Greenjeans knows, the hunters swarm all over the county in search of deer. Mr. Hunter is injured by one of the bear traps. When Hunter sues Greenjeans for damages, he will:

(A) win, because one may not set traps for trespassers.
(B) win, because no warning about the traps was posted.
(C) lose, because the trap was set for bears, not hunters.
(D) lose, because Mr. Greenjeans was in the city and had no way of knowing that Hunter was on the property.

7. Mr. Cross has a corner house near a nursery school. Every day, the children cut across his land and wear out his lawn. Cross decides to dig a deep hole in the spot that shows the worst wear. He intends to turn the hole into a beautiful well. He posts signs on the edge of his property saying, CAUTION–EXCAVATION IN PROGRESS. The next day, 4-year-old Billy falls into the hole and is injured. When Billy sues Cross for damages, he will:

(A) win, because Cross was not allowed to set a trap for the children.
(B) win, because Cross did not adequately warn the children.
(C) lose, because Cross is allowed to dig a well on his property if he wants to.
(D) lose, because Cross posted the necessary warning.

8. One night, Mr. Farmer wakes up and finds Tom Young walking on his carrot beds. He brandishes his shotgun, which is loaded with salt, and warns Young to get off his land. Young curses and sticks out his tongue at Farmer, who then shoots him. Young sustains a few minor scratches and bruises. When Young sues Farmer for damages, he will:

(A) win, because no signs were posted on the land.
(B) lose, because Farmer warned him to get off.
(C) win, because Farmer had no right to shoot him.
(D) lose, because Farmer owed him no duty.

9. Wilson owns a farm upstate. Unknown to him, his two children dig a hole and cover it with leaves and branches as a trap for bears, which have been seen in the neighborhood lately. That night, Wilson hears a vandal on his land. He goes out to investigate and yells, "Get off my land or I'll shoot!" He then sees the vandal fall into the bear trap. When the vandal sues Wilson, he will:

(A) win, because no warning about the trap was posted.
(B) win, because Wilson was there and failed to warn him.
(C) win, because a parent is responsible for the acts of his children.
(D) lose, because Wilson did not know about the trap.

10. Smith's swimming pool is empty for the winter. Signs posted around it say, CAUTION–EMPTY SWIMMING POOL. Smith's neighbor, Jones, comes over to argue about the property line. Jones knows that the pool is empty. Smith orders him to get off the land, reminding Jones that Smith had told him a week ago never to come back. Jones backs away, and Smith watches him fall into the pool. When Jones sues Smith for damages, he will:

(A) lose, because the signs clearly warned of the danger.
(B) win, because Smith knew that he would fall in and failed to warn him.
(C) lose, because he knew the pool was empty.
(D) win, because Smith set a trap for him.

Part B

Directions: In this section you will be presented with some cases, each of which is followed by several legal principles. These may or may not be real principles of law, but you are to accept them as valid. Following each principle are four possible applications of the principle to the case. Answer each question by selecting the most reasonable application.

These questions assume no prior legal knowledge on your part; answer them using only ordinary logical reasoning.

Case 1

Shahnon calls the *Daily Planet* in order to place an advertisement. He intends the copy to read, "$20,000 deductible insurance—only $25 per year premium," but he actually says "$20,000 coverage." He has been running the same ad on and off for about 5 years, but the *Daily Planet* prints it as Shahnon dictated it, and Shahnon, who reads the paper daily, does not notice the mistake.

Jones sees the ad and immediately goes to Shahnon's office, asks for "the $25 special from today's paper," and signs the contract without reading it. Smith also asks for the special, but he notices that it does not correspond to the ad. When he points this out to Shahnon, he is told that the ad was a mistake. He is furious. Meanwhile, when Jones suffers $200 worth of damage and tries to collect, he learns that his policy is not what he thought it was, and he becomes livid. Both report Shahnon to the Better Business Bureau.

11. *If the parties to a contract make a mutual mistake which alters the purpose or scope of the contract, the contract is a nullity. If one party to a contract knowingly takes advantage of the other party's mistake, the contract is a nullity.*

    When Jones sues Shahnon to get his $25 back, he will:

    (A) win, because he was mistaken as to what the contract said.
    (B) lose, because Shahnon knew what the contract said.
    (C) win, because Shahnon took advantage of the mistake.
    (D) lose, because he wanted to take advantage of Shahnon's mistake.

12. *An advertiser is bound to the terms of his advertisement unless there is a mistake in the advertisement which is solely the fault of the publisher, in which case he may refuse to agree to the terms of the advertisement, providing he does so immediately on discovering the mistake.*

    When Smith sues Shahnon to force him to honor the ad, he will:

    (A) win, because the ad was published.
    (B) win, because Shahnon read the paper and did not notice the mistake.
    (C) win, because Shahnon himself made the mistake.
    (D) lose, because the paper should have noticed the mistake.

13. *When a contract is signed with one of the parties laboring under a misapprehension as to the terms of the contract, the party who is mistaken may sue to void the contract if he does so immediately on discovery of the mistake.*

When Jones sues Shahnon for payment of his $200 claim, he will:

(A) win, because he sued as soon as he realized the mistake.
(B) lose, because he made the mistake.
(C) win, because Shahnon is bound by the terms of the advertisement.
(D) lose, because he is not entitled to recover $200.

14. *When a newspaper makes a mistake in an advertisement and the mistake causes damage to the reputation of the advertiser, the paper is liable for all such damages.*

When Shahnon sues the *Daily Planet* for the damage to his reputation, he will:

(A) win, because the mistake in the ad caused damage to his reputation.
(B) lose, because no damage was caused.
(C) win, because the paper should have known the ad was a mistake.
(D) lose, because the paper made no mistake.

15. *The intentional substitution of a less desirable insurance contract for an advertised contract constitutes fraud. The perpetrator of such fraud must honor his advertised policy.*

When Jones sues Shahnon for insurance fraud, he will:

(A) win, because Shahnon never intended to sell Jones the advertised policy.
(B) lose, because Shahnon did not realize what the ad actually said.
(C) win, because his policy is not what he expected from the advertisement.
(D) lose, because he should have read his policy.

Case 2

Dr. Salt hires 15-year-old Nit to clean up his office at night. Among his duties is the sterilization of the doctor's instruments. Nit is not a good worker, and Mrs. Jenkins suffers an infection from a dirty instrument.

Nit is a compulsive gambler; he owes over $800 to a bookie, who has threatened to kill him if he does not pay soon. Since he earns only $95 per week, Nit steals $1,500 worth of Drew Co. drugs from Dr. Salt's sample chest, and sells them to Brown for $1,200. Brown dies of impurities in the drugs. With his extra $400, Nit puts a $300 down payment on a car, which is to be delivered in a month, and puts $100 down on $400 worth of food which he begins to eat immediately. Two weeks later he sues to get out of both contracts, because he needs money to pay another gambling debt.

16. *A drug company is held liable for any and all damages resulting from the use of any impure drug it manufactures, so long as the user obtains the drugs from a licensed druggist or physician.*

When Brown's Estate sues Drew Co. for damages, it will:

(A) win, because the drugs were distributed through Dr. Salt.
(B) win, because the drugs were impure.
(C) lose, because he bought the drugs from Nit.
(D) lose, because he did not pay value for the drugs.

17. *A minor is not liable for any contracts he enters into while a minor unless the other party has substantially performed.*

When Nit sues the car dealer for release from the contract, he will:

(A) win, because the car had not been delivered.
(B) lose, because he has made a substantial down payment.
(C) lose, because gambling is illegal and cannot take precedence over a legal contract.
(D) lose, because a deposit is not refundable.

18. *A doctor is absolutely liable to his patients for any damage which results from the use of unsterile instruments. If another party can be held legally responsible for the condition of the instruments, the doctor can sue that party for indemnity. A minor cannot be held liable for damages resulting from unsterile instruments.*

When Mrs. Jenkins sues Nit, she will:

(A) win, because the instruments were unsterile.
(B) lose, because Nit is a minor.
(C) win, because the doctor is absolutely liable.
(D) lose, because she sued Nit.

19. *A minor cannot be held liable for any contracts he enters into while a minor.*

When Nit sues the food company to get his $100 back, he will:

(A) win, because he was a minor when he agreed to the deal.
(B) lose, because the food had been delivered.
(C) lose, because he had already eaten some food.
(D) lose, because food is a necessity.

20. *Any unlicensed person who sells drugs at a profit is guilty of the crime of drug pushing.*

When Nit is tried for drug pushing, he will:

(A) win, because the drugs were worth $1,500 and he sold them for $1,200.
(B) lose, because he made a $1,200 profit on the drugs.
(C) win, because he was guilty of selling stolen goods, not drug pushing.
(D) lose, because he had a $400 profit after paying his debt.

Part C

Directions: This section consists of several groups of cases. Each case ends with a judicial holding and a set of four legal principles. You must select the *narrowest* principle that reasonably explains the judicial decision but is *not inconsistent* with any previous holdings in that group of cases.

For the first case in each group, eliminate any principles that do not conform to the facts of the case and do not provide a reasonable explanation of the holding. Then select the narrowest of the reasonable principles.

In the remaining cases in that group, the basic procedure is the same, but you must also eliminate any principles that contradict earlier answers in the group before you select the narrowest principle.

These questions assume no prior legal knowledge on your part; answer them using only ordinary logical reasoning.

Group 1

21. The two main products of the Gerald Drug Company are sleeping pills and antacid tablets. The two pills look almost identical, but they are kept in wholly separate areas in the warehouse, and the employees usually work with only one type of pill at a time. One day, however, Ted Scuttle, the foreman, trying to save time, brings out 1,000 of each type to fill an order. He accidentally mixes them up, and some of the sleeping pills get into a bottle marked "Antacid." The bottle is bought by Needham, who swallows 10 pills (despite the directions on the bottle, which indicate a dosage of one or two) in an effort to cure his upset stomach. The hospital bill for pumping Needham's stomach is $500, and he sues the Gerald Drug Company. *Held,* for Needham.

    The *narrowest principle* that *reasonably explains* the action is:

    (A) A drug company is liable for all damages resulting from use of its products as long as the directions are followed.
    (B) A manufacturer of consumable goods is liable for any damage resulting from the mislabelling of such goods.
    (C) A drug company which mislabels its goods is liable for any damages that may result from the mislabelling.
    (D) A drug company which fails to label a poison properly is liable for any damage that results.

22. The Good Food Company (GFC) sells all types of meats. One night, L. Nomen, the meat labeller on the night shift, puts a "beefsteak" label on a package of pork chops. A. Petite buys the package, which he leaves unrefrigerated for 3 days. He then cooks it and gets a severe case of ptomaine poisoning. Petite sues GFC for his medical expenses. *Held,* for GFC.

    The *narrowest principle* that *reasonably explains* this action, and is *not inconsistent with the ruling given in the first case,* is:

    (A) A seller of goods intended for human consumption is liable for damages caused by mislabelling only if the mislabelling is the prime cause of the damage.

(B) A seller of mislabelled goods is strictly responsible for any damage resulting from the use of the goods.
(C) A seller of food is liable for damage resulting from the use of mislabelled food only if the mislabelling was so deceptive that the reasonably prudent man could not see that the food was mislabelled.
(D) A seller of food is liable for damage resulting from the use of mislabelled food only if the mislabelling was the prime cause of the damage.

23. Handee buys a can of what be believes to be drain cleaner from the Carbon Chemical Company. It is actually a mismarked can of a more corrosive liquid, but the can bears many warnings against contact with the skin. Handee spills some of the liquid on his arm and suffers more severe burns that he would have from normal drain cleaner. He sues Carbon Chemical for his medical expenses. *Held,* for Carbon Chemical.

The *narrowest principle* that *reasonably explains* this action, and is *not inconsistent with the rulings given in the cases already cited,* is:

(A) A manufacturer who mislabels goods is liable for damages only if the goods are meant for consumption by human beings.
(B) A manufacturer who mislabels goods which are not intended for human consumption is liable only for those damages which are caused solely by the mislabelling.
(C) A manufacturer of mislabelled goods which are not intended for human consumption is liable for any damages which result from the mislabelling.
(D) A manufacturer of mislabelled goods which are not intended for human consumption is liable for damages only if the goods are used for their intended purpose.

24. For his Fourth of July party, Ben Bliss purchases an item marked "Roman Candle" and manufactured by the All-American Fireworks Company. Unfortunately, it turns out to be a stick of dynamite. When Ben lights it, it explodes, killing him. His widow sues All-American. *Held,* for Mrs. Bliss.

The *narrowest principle* that *reasonably explains* this action, and is *not inconsistent with the rulings given in the cases already cited,* is:

(A) A manufacturer of mislabelled goods which are not intended for human consumption is automatically liable for damages if death results from the use of the goods.
(B) A manufacturer of mislabelled goods which are not intended for human consumption is liable for all damages which are a result of the mislabelling.
(C) A manufacturer of mislabelled fireworks is liable for all damages resulting from the mislabelling of the fireworks.
(D) A manufacturer of mislabelled fireworks is liable for all damages resulting from the use of such fireworks.

25. The Salve Drug Company makes a skin ointment which is a deadly poison if taken internally. All tubes containing dangerous substances are carefully marked, but the tube purchased by Mr. Roth contains instead a rat poison which is also manufactured by Salve. Before Mr. Roth uses any of his ointment, it is eaten by his son Brad. Mr. Roth sues the Salve Company for the death of his son. *Held,* for Salve.

The *narrowest principle* that *reasonably explains* this action, and is *not inconsistent with the rulings given in the cases already cited,* is:

(A) A drug company which fails to label a poison properly is liable for any damage that results.
(B) A drug company which mislabels its goods is liable only for damage which results from the mislabelling.
(C) A drug company is not liable for damages resulting from the use of a product labelled "dangerous."
(D) A drug company can only be held liable for mislabelling which is a result of gross negligence.

Group 2

26. Ed Ploy is driving to Philadelphia to sell insurance for the South Orange Insurance Company. The sole purpose of his trip is to sell the insurance. He is driving his own car, but the company pays for his gas and other expenses. Ploy is very tired, having stayed up all night preparing his sales pitch, and he carelessly hits Ms. Fort with the car. Ploy has only minimal insurance and no money of his own, so Fort sues South Orange Insurance. *Held,* for Fort.

The *narrowest principle* that *reasonably explains* this action is:

(A) An employer is liable for any act committed by his employee in furtherance of his employment.
(B) An employer is liable for any act of his employee which involves negligence on the part of the employer.
(C) An employer is liable for any act committed by his employee.
(D) An employer is liable for any damage caused by his employee if the employee is not at fault.

27. Mr. Bloom, the owner of Bloom's Florist Shop, sends his 17-year-old assistant, Mort Neil, out in the company truck to deliver some flowers to Mrs. Rife who lives 10 blocks away. Unknown to Mr. Bloom, Mort has no driver's license. When Mort is halfway to Mrs. Rife's house, he spots Amy Moore hitching and stops to pick her up. They drive 6 miles past Mrs. Rife's house and then Mort, not noticing Win Burnes asleep on the sidewalk, hits him with the car. Burnes sues Bloom's Florist Shop. *Held,* for Bloom.

The *narrowest principle* that *reasonably explains* this action and is *not inconsistent with the ruling given in the first case,* is:

(A) An employer is not liable for damages caused by an unlicensed driver in his employ if he did not know that the driver was not licensed.
(B) An employer is not liable for damage from traffic accidents caused by his employee if the employee is not acting in furtherance of his employment.
(C) An employer is not liable for damages caused by his employee if the employee is a minor.
(D) An employer is liable for any act committed by his employee in furtherance of his employment.

28. Barry Rille owns a tavern in the bad part of town. He hires two professional fighters, Roger and Waxwing, as bouncers. One night they see Roger's former manager, Shirke, quietly sipping a drink and decide to beat him to a bloody pulp, right there in the tavern. Rille tries to stop them, but they won't listen. Shirke is severely injured, and sues Rille. *Held,* for Shirke.

The *narrowest principle* that *reasonably explains* this action, and is *not inconsistent with the rulings given in the cases already cited,* is:

(A) An employer is liable for all acts of his employees.
(B) An employer is liable for any act committed by his employees in furtherance of their employment.
(C) An employer is liable for any act of his employees committed in his presence if he fails to make a reasonable effort to prevent the act.
(D) An employer is liable for all acts committed in his place of business by his employees.

29. Pop Riddle, owner of the Riddle Messenger Service, sends his 15-year-old son, Nick, out in the company truck to deliver a message. Nick has no driver's license. He decides to take a detour to buy a pack of baseball cards, and he accidentally drives the truck through the window of Mr. Vincent's Beauty Shop. Mr. Vincent sues Pop for the damage to his store. *Held,* for Mr. Vincent.

The *narrowest principle* that *reasonably explains* this action, and is *not inconsistent with the rulings given in the cases already cited,* is:

(A) An employer is responsible for any damage caused by an unlicensed driver who is driving in his employ.
(B) An employer is responsible for any damage caused by an employee driving a vehicle owned by the company.
(C) A parent is responsible for any damage caused by his child provided the child is a minor.
(D) An employer is responsible for any acts of his employee committed in furtherance of his employment.

30. Larry Antwerp, the owner of Speedy Messenger Service, hires his son Robinson, age 22, as a messenger. Robinson has been in the Army for the last 3 years, and his driver's license has expired, unknown to Larry. One day, when Robinson is faithfully performing an errand on which Larry has sent him, he accidentally hits Mr. Flatte with the car. Mr. Flatte sues the Speedy Messenger Service. *Held,* for Mr. Flatte.

The *narrowest principle* that *reasonably explains* this action, and is *not inconsistent with the rulings given in the cases already cited,* is:

(A) A parent is responsible for any damage caused by his child.
(B) An employer is liable for any damage caused by an unlicensed driver in his employ.
(C) An employer is responsible for any acts of his employees committed in furtherance of his employment.
(D) An employer is responsible for any damage caused by an employee driving a vehicle owned by the company.

Answers to Principles and Cases Self-Test

Part A

1. (B) Remember, the distance of 55 miles was covered with Jennifer's consent. She was not moved against her will until she asked to be let out. At that point, the movement was only incidental to the rape.

2. (A) Again, the movement had no significance of its own; its only purpose was to facilitate the robbery.

3. (B) The movement is far too substantial to be considered incidental. Nothing in the principle says that the movement must be *intentional.* As long as it was against Loretta's will, it was kidnapping.

4. (D) The last clause of the principle governs in this case; the ride was so dangerous the Jordan was killed. Obviously, the danger to Nell was increased.

5. (C) The movement involved was certainly substantial and cannot be thought of as incidental to a second crime, since the only crime being attempted was kidnapping. The fact that Petunia was moved against her will, then, should be determinative.

6. (B) Mr. Greenjeans knows that the hunters come every year, so he has "reason to suspect" that they will be on his land. Therefore, he must warn them.

7. (B) Again, Cross knows that the children will cut across his lawn. He must also know that nursery school children will not be able to read his sign.

8. (C) The first sentence of the principle covers this case completely.

9. (D) Wilson could not actually have shot the vandal, but since he had no duty of inspection and had no actual knowledge of the trap, he cannot be held liable for what happened.

10. (B) The last clause of the principle covers this—the duty to warn a trespasser known to be in danger.

Part B

11. (A) The mutual mistake is the parties' belief that the ad was accurate. Remember, Shahnon knew what the *contract* said.

12. (C) The mistake was not solely the fault of the publisher. Shahnon could have corrected it when he read the ad.

13. (D) This principle allows Jones to void the contract, not collect on what he thought were its terms.

14. (D) The *Daily Planet* printed the ad as it was dictated to them.

15. (B) The key word is "intentional." Since Shahnon did not know what the ad said, the substitution cannot be considered intentional.

16. (C) Brown obtained the drugs from Nit, not a licensed druggist or physician.

17. (A) Nit was a minor when he contracted for the car; the dealer has not yet performed.

18. (D) Mrs. Jenkins has an action against the doctor, not against Nit. Only Dr. Salt can sue Nit, so the fact that Nit is a minor does not matter to Mrs. Jenkins.

19. (A) This principle is absolute, unlike the one in question 17. Remember, you must answer each question of this type independently.

20. (B) He paid nothing for the drugs and sold them for $1,200.

Part C

21. (C) (C) is narrower than (A) or (B), since it specifies both the mislabelling and the fact that drugs are the product. (D) is off the point; the pills are not poisonous.

22. (D) (D) is narrower than (A) and (B) because it specifies food. (C) might lose for the food company; we don't have enough information to choose it as the answer.

23. (B) (C) would lose for Carbon. We can't be sure about whether (D) applies, but it seems broader than (B) anyway. (A) is much too broad.

24. (C) (A) and (B) contradict the answer to question 23 which would allow liability only if the death were a result of the mislabelling. (D) is not as narrow as (C).

25. (B) This principle is the other side of the coin; this limit on liability does not contradict anything in the earlier answers. (A) contradicts the principle in question 23; (C) and (D) contradict the principle in question 21.

26. (A) (A) is narrower than (C), since it specifies "in furtherance of his employment." (B) and (D) depart from the facts of the case.

27. (B) This principle carves out an allowable exception to the last principle. (A) would contradict the last principle if the unlicensed driver were acting in furtherance of his employment, as would (C). (D) would hold the wrong way and does not fit the facts.

28. (D) (D) is the only possibility. (A) contradicts the principle in question 27, and (B) and (C) are contrary to the facts of the case.

29. (C) Note that Pop, and not the Riddle Messenger Service, is being sued. (A), (B), and (D) would contradict the principle in question 27, anyway.

30. (C) This time the messenger service (not the parent) is being sued. (B) and (D) would contradict the principle in question 27.

CHAPTER SIX

Practical Judgment

The practical judgment section is also a recent innovation on the LSAT. When it appears, it generally replaces the LSAT reading recall section. The section tests your ability to analyze business situations.

Each passage is normally between 1,000 and 1,500 words long and describes a situation in which a decision must be made. The decision-maker is faced with a series of alternatives, each of which is discussed thoroughly in the passage; you may or may not be told which one he or she finally selects. In a typical practical judgment section, you will be given one each of two types of passages. In the first type, the decision-maker is usually an individual who is planning to make a large purchase, choose a career, or select a location for a business. The individual usually has five options open to him. In the second type, the decision-maker is more likely to be a group, such as the board of directors of a large business. The group is likely to be faced with a problem which it is under pressure to solve as quickly and as economically as possible; any number of options may be open to it. In either case, the passage will contain many facts and figures, and you should read it carefully and highlight it as you would any reading selection on the LSAT. Two types of questions will generally follow each passage—19 data evaluations and 6 data applications. The evaluation questions will ask you to classify certain items as objectives, major or minor factors, assumptions, or unimportant issues. The application questions often test reading comprehension; they may sometimes involve some calculation based on the facts and figures in the passage, or they may ask you to select the best alternative for the decision-maker.

Let us look first at the data evaluation questions. The instructions for the data evaluation questions are as follows:

Directions: **Each of the items below relates to the passage you just read. Select answer**

(A) if the item is a *Major Objective* in the decision—the result desired by the decision-maker.

(B) if the item is a *Major Factor* in the decision—something specifically mentioned and important in reaching the decision relating to a Major Objective.

(C) if the item is a *Minor Factor* in the decision—something specifically mentioned that affects a Major Factor but relates only indirectly to a Major Objective.

(D) if the item is a *Major Assumption* underlying the decision—an expectation or projection taken for granted by the decision-maker before the alternatives are examined.

(E) if the item is an *Unimportant Issue* in the decision—something neither relevant nor significant.

Suppose that the passage concerns a man who wishes to quit his job as a bus driver and buy his own taxicab, because he wants to be his own boss. He must earn at least $15,000 each year to support himself and his family. He examines five cabs, both new and used.

What are his *objectives?* Each passage will have several (typically three) items that can properly be classified as major objectives. One is always the goal of the decision itself—the situation as the decision-maker hopes it will be after the decision is made. In our example, that would be the purchase of a taxicab. The others will usually be byproducts of the accomplishment of the first. They relate to the personal wishes of the decision-maker. One might reflect some condition which is necessary if the venture is to be successful; another might relate directly to personal happiness. In this case, the decision-maker *needs* a certain minimum income and *wants* to be his own boss. The two choices might be phrased "maintenance of minimum income of $15,000" and "establishment of own business," or "being self-employed." By their very nature, since objectives represent the achievement of certain goals, they will generally be depicted by nouns formed from *verbs.* Look at the ones we just mentioned—*purchase* of a taxicab, *maintenance* of a minimum income, *establishment* of own business, *being* self-employed. If you think about it, the objectives really can be expressed in no other way. The objectives will be set out in the expository part of the passage.

The most important characteristic of all *factors* is that they exert some influence on the decision process. The extent of their influence determines whether they are major or minor factors. Some examples of such factors are cost, financial conditions, and relevant laws.

Each passage will include approximately three *major factors.* Unlike minor factors, they usually exert a *direct* influence on the decision. In other words, a major factor may afford you the means to compare all of the alternatives. In our example, the cost of each taxi might be a major factor. If the need for the decision is triggered by a problem, the problem itself may be a major factor. For example, if the need for a decision is brought about by the fact that the company in question is going bankrupt, the financial condition of the company would be a major factor. You will usually be able to see a direct relationship between a major factor and at least one of the objectives.

Minor factors, on the other hand, exert direct influence only on major factors—they may, in some cases, even be component parts of major factors. In our example, total cost of the cab for the first year might be a major factor, and down payment, maintenance costs, and license fees might be minor factors. The more general and comprehensive the factor, the more likely it is to be considered major. More specific factors and factors which do not relate to all of the alternatives will probably be minor. For example, if one of the taxicab manufacturers has a special financing plan that makes purchase of its cab easier, the existence of that plan will be a minor factor—it has no bearing on the other four taxis. Any number of minor factors may be mentioned in a passage.

Factors, in order to exert an actual influence on the decision, must be tangible. Their first words, then, will most likely be tangible nouns like "cost," "amount," or the like. While some factors may be mentioned in the exposition, most will become apparent as the alternatives are discussed.

The *major assumptions,* like the objectives, will usually be set out in the first couple of expository paragraphs, since the decision-maker will make them in advance of evaluating the various alternatives. In our example, if a consumer organization publishes a report on the reliability of various taxicab models, our protagonist may assume the *validity* of the report. The results of the report might then become a factor in the decision, while the validity of the report, itself, is an assumption. Again, an assumption, by its nature, gives itself away. It will usually start with a word abstract enough to indicate something that is assumed rather than certain. Some examples are "validity," "ability," and "likelihood." An item that may or may not be true, based on the facts of the passage, is usually an *assumption.* An item, the truth of which can be ascertained factually, will usually be a *factor.* Any number of assumptions may be suggested in a given situation.

The final category is *unimportant issues.* Any item that is not an objective, factor, or assumption *relating to the decision at hand* is an unimportant issue. Any item relating to the future of bus drivers would be unimportant, since our decision-maker does not plan to be a bus driver in the future. Anything which was not mentioned in the passage would also fit into this category. Unimportant issues can be phrased to sound like any of the other categories, so be careful. Examples in this case might be expansion of the taxicab company (if not mentioned in the passage), a new bus driver contract to go into effect after our driver left the company, or a special licensing law not mentioned in the passage. No set number of unimportant issues will be mentioned in a given situation.

For practice with data evaluation questions, read the condensed passage below and answer the questions that follow.

> **Mr. Shannon is president of the Bigger Widget Company, which is in precarious financial condition. It has just spent a great deal of money developing a new Wonder Widget and has suffered a sudden reversal on its substantial holdings in the securities market. A competitor, Green Stallion Electronic Widgets, has made a bail-out offer, but Mr. Shannon wants Bigger to remain independent. In order to justify refusal of the bail-out offer, Bigger will have to generate in the next 4 months about $60,000 worth of sales over and above the income received from the sales of the company's Standard Simple Widget. Mr. Shannon believes that the new Wonder Widget will do the trick if only he can get it out on the market within 2 months. [The passage then goes on to discuss the various plans offered by the officers of the corporation—paying overtime to the current staff, hiring additional help, contracting out some of the work. The officers must decide whether to adopt one of the plans, and if so, which one.]**

Directions: **Each of the items below relates to the passage you just read. Select answer**

- **(A) if the item is a *Major Objective* in the decision—the result desired by the decision-maker.**
- **(B) if the item is a *Major Factor* in the decision—something specifically mentioned and important in reaching the decision relating to a Major Objective.**
- **(C) if the item is a *Major Factor* in the decision—something specifically mentioned that affects a Major Factor but relates only indirectly to a Major Objective.**
- **(D) if the item is a *Major Assumption* underlying the decision—an expectation or projection taken for granted by the decision-maker before the alternatives are examined.**
- **(E) if the item is an *Unimportant Issue* in the decision—something neither relevant nor significant.**

1. Financial reversals in securities market suffered by Bigger Ⓐ Ⓑ Ⓒ Ⓓ Ⓔ

2. Cost of each plan Ⓐ Ⓑ Ⓒ Ⓓ Ⓔ

3. Ability of Wonder Widgets to generate enough sales Ⓐ Ⓑ Ⓒ Ⓓ Ⓔ

4. Expansion of line to include Super Widgets Ⓐ Ⓑ Ⓒ Ⓓ Ⓔ

5. Maintaining Bigger as an independent business Ⓐ Ⓑ Ⓒ Ⓓ Ⓔ

6. Cost of overtime Ⓐ Ⓑ Ⓒ Ⓓ Ⓔ

7. Continuation of demand for Simple Widget Ⓐ Ⓑ Ⓒ Ⓓ Ⓔ

8. Financial condition of Bigger Widget Company Ⓐ Ⓑ Ⓒ Ⓓ Ⓔ

9. Existence of substantial market for Wonder Widget Ⓐ Ⓑ Ⓒ Ⓓ Ⓔ

10. Selection of a plan to get the Widgets to the market Ⓐ Ⓑ Ⓒ Ⓓ Ⓔ

11. Personal feelings of other officers towards Mr. Shannon Ⓐ Ⓑ Ⓒ Ⓓ Ⓔ

12. Time required to complete each plan Ⓐ Ⓑ Ⓒ Ⓓ Ⓔ

13. Location of Green Stallion plant Ⓐ Ⓑ Ⓒ Ⓓ Ⓔ

14. Keeping Bigger from going bankrupt Ⓐ Ⓑ Ⓒ Ⓓ Ⓔ

15. Time needed to train new employees Ⓐ Ⓑ Ⓒ Ⓓ Ⓔ

16. Availability of new laborers Ⓐ Ⓑ Ⓒ Ⓓ Ⓔ

17. Cost of special equipment for manufacture of Wonder Widgets Ⓐ Ⓑ Ⓒ Ⓓ Ⓔ

18. Bail-out offer by Green Stallion Ⓐ Ⓑ Ⓒ Ⓓ Ⓔ

19. Cost of research on Simple Widgets Ⓐ Ⓑ Ⓒ Ⓓ Ⓔ

– –

For purposes of going over the answers, let's first pick out the objectives. They are numbers 5, 10, and 14. The event that the decision will result in is the selection of a plan (10). The decision is necessary to prevent Bigger's bankruptcy (14), and the decision-maker personally wants to keep Bigger independent (5). With these objectives in mind, let's go through the answers in order. Note the first word (or words) of the answer in each case.

1. (C) **These reversals are but one factor causing the current financial crisis in the Bigger Company. The crisis itself will be a major factor. First words: financial reversals.**

2. (B) This important way to compare all of the plans will be a major factor in the decision. First word: cost.

3. (D) Note the language in the passage: "Mr. Shannon *believes* the Wonder Widget will do the trick." First word: ability.

4. (E) Nobody at all mentioned Super Widgets. Whether any further expansion is contemplated at present is doubtful.

5. (A) As we noted above, this item is a major objective. First word: maintaining.

6. (C) This item is a contributing factor to the cost of the plan involving overtime work. It can be considered a component part of 2.

7. (D) Whether the demand will continue remains to be seen. Mr. Shannon *assumes* that it will.

8. (B) This problem touched off the need for the decision in the first place. It must be considered a major factor.

9. (D) This item is very similar to 3.

10. (A) Another major objective.

11. (E) This item is totally irrelevant to the decision and was not mentioned in the passage.

12. (B) Time must be considered with regard to all plans; remember, they need the money within 4 months.

13. (E) This item is also totally irrelevant to the decision, even if the location had been mentioned, since Bigger plans to stay independent.

14. (A) The third major objective.

15. (C) This minor factor relates to just one plan. The major factor relating to time is 12.

16. (D) This decision is difficult. Based on what we have been told in the passage, we could only consider the item an assumption. The passage gives no indication that the number of workers available might be a minor factor.

17. (E) No special equipment was mentioned. If it were mentioned, it might be a minor factor, assuming it affected the decision in some way.

18. (C) The offer must be considered a minor factor, since it exists; but since the decision-maker is not anxious to accept it, it will not exert a major influence on the decision.

19. (E) The research cost is so far in the past that it has no relevance to the current decision. The cost of research on Wonder Widgets would be a minor factor (component part of the financial condition of the company–8). You must watch out for this type of trick.

The data application questions will be more familiar to you. Some will be standard reading comprehension questions; others will be reminiscent of the data interpretation section. You will have to find certain figures in the passage and then do some sort of calculation based on them. If the passage does not tell you what final decision was reached, that is likely to be the subject of a question. You will then have to take into account all of the data and choose the best alternative.

Just for practice, read the following condensed passage and answer the data application questions which follow it.

Lenny McCoy, an unmarried biology major, is about to graduate from State University, and he must decide what to do with his life. He wants to enjoy his career, but he also must consider his invalid mother, whose savings amount to $30,000 and whose maintenance costs $10,000 per year. Mrs. McCoy receives $4,000 each year from the government.

By the time his mother's savings run out, Lenny would like to be earning enough to keep his mother out of a state-run nursing home.

Lenny would like most to become a doctor. To go through medical school would cost him $3,000 per year for 3 years, including his support. He has no savings and would have no income for those 3 years, but his mother would be willing to lend him any funds that she could spare. In the fourth year, Lenny would be an intern with an income of about $8,000; of that, he would need $5,000 to support himself. In his fifth year, he would earn about $16,000, and his income would increase steadily after that.

Lenny has been offered a partial fellowship by City College for graduate study in biology. He would get free tuition and a stipend of $2,000 per year for the 3 years of study. During his third year, he would be able to earn an additional $5,000 in the work-study program which the college operates in cooperation with Local Laboratory. When he graduates, he would be assured of a job at Local, earning $10,000 the first year, $12,000 the second year, and $17,000 each year after that. The union at Local expects to have negotiated a starting salary of $11,000 by the time Lenny graduates, with equivalent raises across the board. The main problem with this plan is that Lenny is afraid that biological research may be boring. Dr. Stern, Lenny's advisor, has assured him that this is not the case, however, and Lenny has a great deal of respect for Dr. Stern.

Lenny's third option is that he has been offered a job as a respiration therapist. Breath, Inc., would pay him $5,000 for his year of training, and would place him after that in Nearby Hospital at a $10,000 annual starting salary, with the understanding that his salary would be raised to $15,000 when he has completed 3 years of service in the hospital. Unfortunately, Lenny feels that the job offers no chance for advancement and is extremely boring.

Lenny is in love with Ms. Jensen and would like to marry her as soon as possible. Unfortunately, she will probably be undergoing occasional traction for the next 5 years and will be unable to generate any income. In fact, her addition to the McCoy family would cost Lenny an extra $4,000 per year. As much as Lenny wishes to get married, he recognizes that his first responsibility is to provide for his mother's security.

***Directions:* Each of the questions below relates to the passage you have just read. Select the best of the five choices.**

1. Which alternative(s) is (are) financially possible for Lenny if he does not get married?

I. Medical school II. Fellowship III. Respiration therapy

(A) II only (B) III only (C) I and III (D) II and III (E) All

2. For how many years could Mrs. McCoy support herself if she neither gave money to nor received money from Lenny?

(A) 3 (B) 4 (C) 5 (D) 6 (E) It cannot be determined from the information given.

3. Under which option is Lenny financially able to get married the earliest?

(A) Medical school (B) Fellowship (C) Respiration therapist (D) He cannot get married. (E) It cannot be determined from the information given.

4. The main reason for not accepting the job as a respiration therapist is:

(A) the low starting salary.
(B) the objection of Dr. Stern.
(C) the size of the raise at the end of 3 years.
(D) the nature of the job itself.
(E) None of the above

5. Which of the following statements is not true?

(A) The job with the quickest immediate return will pay the least in the long run.
(B) The job with the least chance for advancement is the most boring.
(C) Lenny would like to be a doctor.
(D) Lenny's advisor is not opposed to his accepting the fellowship.
(E) None of the above

6. If Lenny accepts the fellowship, how many years will it be before he has grossed as much as if he had worked for Breath, Inc. (assuming maximum salaries of $17,000 and $15,000)?

(A) 5 (B) 10 (C) 14 (D) 18 (E) It cannot be determined from the information given.

- - - - - - - - - - - - - - - - - - - -

These questions were particularly difficult, with a fairly heavy emphasis on calculation.

1. (E) If Lenny goes to medical school, he will be earning enough by the fifth year to support his mother and himself. The question is whether they can get through the first 4 years, and the answer is that they would just make it, as the following analysis shows:

	1st year	*2nd year*	*3rd year*	*4th year*
Savings:	$30,000	$21,000	$12,000	$ 3,000
Government:	4,000	4,000	4,000	4,000
Income:	—	—	—	8,000
	$34,000	$25,000	$16,000	$15,000
Expenses:	13,000	13,000	13,000	15,000
Balance at end of year:	$21,000	$12,000	$ 3,000	$00,000

Medical school, then, is possible if no unforeseen expenses arise. Next, find out whether accepting the fellowship is possible. If it is, the answer must be (E) because no choice lists just I and II. If not, the answer must be (C), since no choice gives I alone. No financial problem is presented with acceptance of the fellowship even if Lenny's personal expenses are $5,000 per year all the way through. Respiration therapy also offers no financial bar.

2. (C) Don't forget her government checks. She starts with $30,000; by the end of the fifth year, she will have received $20,000 from the government, a total of the $50,000 she needs to support herself for 5 years.

3. (C) If he goes to work immediately, he can get married immediately. Enough money is available to support the family until the time that Lenny starts making $15,000, at which time the family income ($19,000) would be sufficient for support.

4. (D) The job is boring and offers little chance for advancement.

5. (E) All of the statements are true. Remember, Dr. Stern assured Lenny that the research would not be boring.

6. (C) In the first 5 years, Lenny would earn $17,000 more with Breath, Inc. After that, he could earn $2,000 more per year having taken the fellowship, so it will take 9 more years to make up the difference, a total of 14 years in all, as the following chart demonstrates:

	Breath, Inc.	*Fellowship*
1st year	$ 5,000	$ 2,000
2nd year	10,000	2,000
3rd year	10,000	7,000
4th year	10,000	10,000
5th year	15,000	12,000
5-year totals	$50,000	$33,000
6th year on	15,000	17,000

Now, set aside 20 minutes to do a full-scale practical judgment passage. Use the answer sheet from the back of the book.

Practical Judgment Self-Test

Time: 20 minutes
25 questions

Directions: In this section you will be presented with long passages followed by two sets of questions: data evaluation and data application. Both sets of questions focus on the relative importance of various facts and issues in the passage. Specific instructions will follow each passage.

Jim Sink is the first mate on the *Bob–Harris,* a passenger fishing boat at the Monticello Marina on Monticello Bay. He has always wanted a boat of his own and has finally saved up what he figures is enough money to buy one. While he is very eager to fulfill his life-long ambition, his concern for his family causes him some hesitation. He feels that they can live on $8,000 per year if they are not extravagant. He currently has $12,000 in the bank.

Mr. Sink believes that fishing is going to continue to rise in popularity even during a recession, because it is economical for individuals to catch their own fish. He has a fine reputation at the marina and is sure that it will enable him to build up a sizable clientele in a very short time. He is currently considering several boats.

The first is the *Marco,* which is in dry dock at the Monticello Marina. Its location means that no transportation cost would be added to the purchase price, and the *Marco* is already equipped for fishing, but it needs extensive renovation. It would not last the entire season in its current condition. The boat itself is being offered at $6,000, but the repairs will cost about another $8,000, if Mr. Sink pays to have them done. The parts cost only $1,000, but if Mr. Sink is to do the work himself and be finished in time for the opening of the season, which is only 30 weeks long, he will need the help of his cousin, Saul, who wishes to be his partner. This partnership would be tolerable to Mr. Sink, but he would really prefer to be the sole owner. Once renovated, the *Marco* would hold about 40 customers; based on a poll by the *Marina Gazette,* it should average 80% of capacity at $5 a head. Besides the captain, the *Marco* needs a crew of two at $20 per day each, and would cost about $40 per day to run. Mr. Sink would plan to work 6 days per week for the entire season.

The second boat, the *Carolina,* is in beautiful condition and would require no work. Mr. Sink heard about it from a friend who sailed on it during a vacation. The problem with the *Carolina* is that it is docked at Lake Emerson, 900 miles from Monticello Bay. The *Carolina* would hold 30 people and, according to the *Marina Gazette* report, would probably go out full every day at $6 a head. Operating costs would be the same as for the *Marco.* The boat, which Mr. Sink figures is worth $12,000, is being offered for $10,000, but transportation of the boat would cost a minimum of $6 per mile. The alternative to transporting the boat would be to move to Lake Emerson (which would cost about $1,000), but the Sink family does not wish to move.

The New Englander Boat Company has just come out with a model called the *Sprite.* It would cost $15,000, counting delivery charges, if Mr. Sink could pay cash; otherwise, the company would allow him to finance it in four payments of $4,000 at 3-month intervals. The *Sprite* seats 24, requires only one crew member besides the captain, and costs only $25 per day to run. Furthermore, it comes with a one-year guarantee on all parts and labor. The model is still too new to have been included in the *Marina Gazette*'s report, but Mr. Sink believes that he could fill it at $6 per person.

The fourth boat that Mr. Sink is considering is the *Sasha,* which is currently docked 100 miles down the coast at Port Elizabeth. The *Sasha* is a large old boat, capable of holding 50 fishermen, and is particularly attractive because of its price—only $5,000. To bring it to Monticello Bay would cost only about $100, since it could definitely make the trip under its own power. Unfortunately, its engine has seen better days. A new one, installed, would cost $4,000, but even if Mr. Sink ordered it now, it would not be ready in time for the season. The installation job itself takes from 10 to 12 weeks. As long as the *Sasha* survived the fishing season, the job could be done easily during the winter. According to the *Marina Gazette*, the *Sasha* should be able to average going out at 80% of capacity at $5 a head. It requires three crewmen besides the captain and can be run for $45 per day.

Mr. Sink is also interested in the *Gunder*, another Monticello Marina boat, currently owned by Captain Michaels who has been thinking about retirement. The *Gunder* currently earns an average net total of $90 per day, and Captain Michaels would want $9,000 for it if he decides to sell. The boat is in fairly good condition, but Mr. Sink would like to make improvements that will cost about $1,500. The problem is that Captain Michaels cannot seem to decide whether or not he wants to sell. Mr. Sink likes the idea of buying a boat that is already popular at the Marina, but Captain Michaels has refused to commit himself, and if Mr. Sink waits much longer, he may be too late to act on any of his other options. The captain has promised him an answer by the first week of the fishing season.

Mr. Sink's main concern is to be sure of his ability to support his family. If he cannot do that, he will have to abandon the idea of owning his own boat.

Directions: Each of the items below relates to the passage you just read. Select answer

(A) if the item is a *Major Objective* in the decision—the result desired by the decision-maker.

(B) if the item is a *Major Factor* in the decision—something specifically mentioned and important in reaching the decision relating to a Major Objective.

(C) if the item is a *Minor Factor* in the decision—something specifically mentioned that affects a Major Factor but relates only indirectly to a Major Objective.

(D) if the item is a *Major Assumption* underlying the decision—an expectation or projection taken for granted by the decision-maker before the alternatives are examined.

(E) if the item is an *Unimportant Issue* in the decision—something neither relevant nor significant.

1. Proximity of New Englander Boat Company

2. Total cost of each boat

3. Accuracy of *Marina Gazette* report

4. Mr. Sink's reputation

5. Number of boats currently serving Monticello Marina

6. Selection of a boat

7. Number of customers each boat would attract daily

8. Attitude of the captain of the *Bob–Harris*

9. Condition of each boat

10. Ability of Mr. Sink to attract customers

11. Amount of income each boat would generate

12. Purchase of own boat

13. Cost of making each boat seaworthy

14. Availability of qualified crewmen

15. Cost to Mr. Sink of transportation of each boat

16. Continuation of popularity of fishing

17. Ability of Sink family to live on $8,000 per year

18. Maintenance of minimum income level

19. Cost of equipment for each boat

Directions: Each of the questions below relates to the passage you just read. Select the best of the five choices.

20. Which boat or boats can Mr. Sink absolutely count on to be able to sail out of Monticello Marina at the beginning of the fishing season?

    I. *Marco* II. *Carolina* III. *Sprite* IV. *Sasha* V. *Gunder*

    (A) I only (B) I and III (C) I and II (D) III and IV (E) I, III, and IV

21. Which of the following statements is (are) true;

    (A) Mr. Sink will be satisfied to enter a partnership as long as he can be part owner of a boat.
    (B) The *Marina Gazette* report indicates that the *Sprite* could fill up at $6 per person.
    (C) The *Gunder* needs no improvements.
    (D) The only boat which would present a transport problem is the *Carolina.*
    (E) None of the above

22. The only aspect of the *Sprite* which might cause difficulty is:

    (A) obtaining financing. (B) Mr. Sink's estimates. (C) delivery. (D) renovation. (E) operating costs.

23. Which of the boats can Mr. Sink afford to buy if he is to be the sole proprietor and remain in Monticello?

    I. *Marco* II. *Carolina* III. *Sprite* IV. *Sasha* V. *Gunder*

    (A) III only (B) III or IV (C) III or V (D) III, IV, or V (E) II, III, IV, or V

24. If Mr. Sink buys the *Sasha,* and it survives the fishing season, how much money will he have in the bank at the end of the year, if the Sink family spends exactly $8,000 on living expenses?

(A) None (B) $10,000 (C) $12,000 (D) $13,900 (E) $14,900

25. All things considered, which boat is the best choice for Mr. Sink?

(A) *Marco* (B) *Carolina* (C) *Sprite* (D) *Sasha* (E) *Gunder*

STOP

IF YOU FINISH BEFORE THE TIME IS UP,
CHECK YOUR WORK ON THIS SECTION.
WHEN THE TIME IS UP, CHECK YOUR ANSWERS
AGAINST THE ANSWER KEY AND EXPLANATION ON THE FOLLOWING PAGE.

Answers to Practical Judgment Self-Test

First, let's isolate the objectives. The result of the decision is to be the selection of a boat (6). Maintenance of a minimum income level (18) is a necessity, and the purchase of his own boat (12) is what Mr. Sink wants to accomplish. Now, let's go through the answers in order:

1. (E) This item is totally irrelevant to Mr. Sink, since the company is going to pay for delivery.

2. (B) A cost comparison is a major means of comparing boats, since Mr. Sink is limited as to how much he can afford.

3. (D) Is the report accurate? Mr. Sink assumes so when he uses it in making his decision. Note the first word: accuracy, an abstract noun.

4. (C) This item is a contributing factor to 11, the amount of income each boat can generate. The existence of the reputation is a fact, not an assumption, and it will help create income. The effect of the reputation may be an assumption (see 10), but once assumed, Mr. Sink's reputation must be considered a factor.

5. (E) No indication is given that this item will have any effect on the decision.

6. (A) We have already indicated that this item is to be the result of the decision. Note the verbal noun "selection."

7. (C) Another contributor to 11. "Number" is a classic first word for a factor.

8. (E) Who cares? Certainly not Mr. Sink.

9. (B) This item is important. Mr. Sink can't afford an unreliable boat, since he needs a steady source of income.

10. (D) Can he attract customers? He assumes he can. While his reputation is a fact, his ability to attract customers is pure assumption. "Ability" is a classic abstract noun and almost always indicates an assumption.

11. (B) This item relates directly to 18; Mr. Sink needs a certain amount of income, and must consider this factor with regard to all choices.

12. (A) A major objective, as noted above.

13. (C) A contributing factor to 2, the total cost of each boat.

14. (D) An underlying assumption is that Mr. Sink can get all the crewmen he needs. (We cannot tell whether or not he can.)

15. (C) Another contributing factor to 2.

16. (D) Will it continue? Mr. Sink obviously believes it will, or he would not be buying a boat.

17. (D) Can they do it? Mr. Sink thinks so, because he based his calculations on their ability to live on $8,000 per year. Note the presence of "ability" again.

18. (A) Another major objective.

19. (C) Still another contributing factor to 2. "Cost" is another favorite word for factors.

20. (B) The *Marco* is there and ready to go, but noticing that eliminates only Choice (D). If Mr. Sink buys the *Carolina,* he may have to sail from Emerson Lake, and the question asks about boats that are ready to sail from Monticello Marina. That eliminates only Choice (C). The *Sprite* can be ready to go with no problems. That narrows the choice to either (B) or (E)—the only difference between them is the *Sasha,* which is by no means a safe bet.

21. (D) Mr. Sink does not want a partnership if he can possibly avoid it; the *Marina Gazette* did not mention the *Sprite,* and Mr. Sink feels that the *Gunder* needs $1,500 worth of improvements. The only boat besides the *Carolina* that Mr. Sink has to transport himself is the *Sasha;* its transportation presents no problem—the total cost will be only $100.

22. (B) The passage does not indicate why Mr. Sink believes that he can fill this boat at $6 per person. None of the other choices have any potential to cause difficulty.

23. (D) In order to buy the *Marco,* he would need his cousin as a partner; in order to buy the *Carolina,* he would have to move. The rest are within his budget.

24. (C) Mr. Sink starts with $12,000 and will net $95 per day ($200 take, less $60 for the crew and $45 for expenses) 6 days a week for 30 weeks—a total of $17,100. His expenses would be $8,000 for the family, $5,000 for the boat, $100 for transportation, and $4,000 for the new motor, or a total of $17,100 expenses. He would end up with the same bank balance he started with.

25. (C) As long as his estimates are close, the *Sprite* is safe. As we have noted, he does not want to take a partner or to move, so (A) and (B) are poor choices. The *Sasha* is unreliable, and the *Gunder,* unless Captain Michaels makes up his mind ahead of schedule, is uncertain.

CHAPTER SEVEN
Logical Reasoning

The logical reasoning section is another recent innovation on the LSAT. When it appears, it generally replaces the reading comprehension section and tests basically the same skills. Instead of long reading passages followed by a series of questions, you are presented with single paragraphs followed by one or two questions each.

To look at a set of directions for the logical reasoning section might be helpful at this point:

Directions: **This section consists of a series of short passages and statements. In each case you should evaluate the reasoning in the passage or draw a conclusion and then select the *best* of the five alternatives. The best answer will neither require unsupported assumptions nor violate common sense.**

Sometimes the questions are simply reading comprehension questions. In other instances, you may be asked something about the reasoning in the passage. For example, you might be asked what is wrong with Amy's reasoning in the following argument between two classmates:

Bob: Mrs. Dearie is a lousy teacher. She knows nothing at all about economics.
Amy: That's not true—you failed history last term as well.

The problem is that Amy never refutes Bob's argument. She offers no assertion that Mrs. Dearie does, in fact, know something about economics. She simply flails out at Bob but never answers his point.

In another standard question type, you are asked to find a parallel to the reasoning in the original statement. Look at the example below.

1. **Since 9 out of 10 heroin addicts start out on pot, we can conclude that smoking pot leads to heroin addiction.**

   In terms of its logical features, the statement above most closely resembles which of the following?

   (A) Since most men who are arrested for pickpocketing wear underwear, wearing underwear leads to pickpocketing.
   (B) Since most wealthy men smoke pipes, pipe-smoking is a sign of affluence.
   (C) Since many children who grow up to be doctors start out wanting to be firemen, wanting to be a fireman leads to becoming a doctor.

(D) Since many high school teachers had good grades in college, they probably also had good grades in high school.
(E) Since most people who are good in math are also good in physics, being good in math probably leads to being good in chemistry.

– –

The best answer to this question is Choice (A). The basic structure of the original statement is that since most *Q*'s started as *P*'s, being a *P* leads to becoming a *Q*. Choice (A) follows this model, but each of the others deviates from it. Choice (B) would be close, if it concluded that pipe-smoking *led to* wealth. Choice (C) speaks of "many" children (a far cry from "most"). Choices (D) and (E) bring in conclusions that aren't even mentioned in the original premise.

Along basically the same lines are questions which ask you to extend the reasoning that you have just read, either by selecting the best conclusion for the passage or by telling how the speaker would feel about something related to his or her previous statements.

Still others resemble syllogisms. A *syllogism* is a series of premises which lead to a conclusion. A classic is:

All cows are animals.
All animals are alive.
Therefore, all cows are alive.

The first two statements are premises; the third is the conclusion. You might be given a series of premises and a set of conclusions and then be asked which conclusions can validly be drawn from the premises. For example:

All boys play basketball.
Some girls dance.
No one who dances plays basketball.

Which of the following is (are) valid?

(A) No girls play basketball.
(B) Some girls play basketball.
(C) No boys dance.

The first two conclusions might or might not be true, depending upon whether any of the nondancing girls play basketball. (Nothing says that a person must either dance or play basketball; quite possibly, some do neither.) The third conclusion must be true, since all boys play basketball, and no one can do both.

As you will see when you work the practice section that follows, you need not make a formal study of logic. Your reading skills and common sense are all you need. While we have just mentioned a few of the more common question types, the possibilities are limitless. By its very nature, this section lends itself less to preparation than any of the others. The best thing to do is to work through some questions and get a feel for them. The section that follows should give you good practice. Use your answer sheet from the back of the book.

Logical Reasoning Self-Test

Time: 30 minutes
25 questions

Directions: This section consists of a series of short passages and statements. In each case you should evaluate the reasoning in the passage or draw a conclusion and then select the *best* of the five alternatives. The best answer will neither require unsupported assumptions nor violate common sense.

1. The rank of the cards in poker is as follows: A, K, Q, J, 10, 9, 8, 7, 6, 5, 4, 3, 2. A is the highest and 2 the lowest. There are four cards of each rank (one in each suit). A full house consists of three cards of one rank and two of another. If more than one player holds a full house, the one with the highest ranking three-of-a-kind wins (for example, 77722 beats 666QQ). If there are four players in the game, and each of them has a full house, which of the following hands must be a winning hand?

   I. AAAKK II. KKKAA III. AAA66

   (A) I only (B) I and III (C) I and II (D) III only (E) I, II, and III

Questions 2–3

So much attention is paid to criminals and prison inmates that we are losing sight of those who really are in need—the victims. I believe in ___(3)___ but society should direct its efforts toward assisting those upon whom felons prey.

2. Which of the following assumptions does the author seem to make?

   I. Assistance for criminals and assistance for victims are mutually exclusive.
   II. Criminals need rehabilitation.
   III. Some prison inmates are not actually guilty.

   (A) I only (B) I and II (C) I and III (D) I, II, and III (E) None of the above

3. Which of the following phrases best fills in the blank in the passage?

   (A) punishing criminals
   (B) being sympathetic to victims
   (C) a harsher correctional system
   (D) fair and just treatment for law breakers
   (E) social work for criminals and victims alike

4. Since all of my pets are cats, anything which is not a cat is not my pet.

   Which of the following statements most closely parallels the kind of reasoning used in the sentence above?

   (A) Since all men are animals, no man is a plant.
   (B) Since all girls are beautiful, anyone who is not a girl is not beautiful.
   (C) Sincc all buffoons are fools, anyone who is not a fool is not a buffoon.
   (D) Since no dogs are cats, all cats are not dogs.
   (E) Since all monkeys are not men, all men are not monkeys.

5. All cakes are fattening.
Everything fattening tastes good.
Nothing nutritious tastes good.

Which of the following statements must be false?

I. Some cakes are nutritious.
II. All cakes taste good.
III. Potatoes are fattening and nutritious.

(A) I only (B) II only (C) II and III (D) I and III (E) I, II, and III

6. Perhaps the expression "youth will be served" should be amended to "youth will be served, probably well done." Our society is a rich gold mine for the innovative, and many of us are destined to be Klondikes at one time or another.

The author most likely uses the word "Klondike" to mean a:

(A) mineral. (B) food. (C) particular person. (D) easy mark.
(E) exploiter of the meek.

7. Which of the following people appears to be the most reasonable and trustworthy?

(A) Mayor: "These are the best years the city has ever seen."
(B) Brother: "My sister is an idiot."
(C) Teacher for 20 years: "This is the worst class I have ever taught."
(D) Typist: "This typewriter needs a new ribbon."
(E) Auto mechanic: "Your car needs a new transmission."

Questions 8–9

Persons without education certainly do not want either acuteness or strength of mind in what concerns themselves, or in things immediately within their observation; but they have ___(8)___, no general standard of taste, or scale of opinion. They see their objects always near, and never in the horizon. Hence arises that ___(9)___ which has been remarked as the characteristic of self-taught men.

8. The words which best fill the blank are:

(A) no power of abstraction
(B) a serious phychological impairment
(C) the situation backwards
(D) no appreciation of the finer things
(E) not realized the truth

9. The word which best fills the blank is:

(A) foolishness
(B) delight
(C) egotism
(D) apprehension
(E) generosity

10. The president should no longer be considered to be above the law.

In terms of its logical features, the sentence above most closely resembles which of the following?

(A) The governor should pay taxes.
(B) Firemen should never be allowed to strike again.
(C) The emperor should be put in jail.
(D) All men should be considered equal.
(E) The police should not use brutality.

11. The red team and the green team have a traditional rivalry. The red team has won 11 of the last 12 games between the teams. All the players on the red team cheat.

Which of the following is a valid conclusion based on what is given?

(A) The players on the green team do not cheat.
(B) The red team wins because the red players cheat.
(C) The red team will win the next game between the two teams.
(D) The players on the red team are more talented than those on the green team.
(E) None of the above

12. Valto Batteries are used in most airplanes. Therefore, you can be sure that a Valto Battery will be right for your car. Remember, Johnny Thunder, ace racing driver, uses a Valto Battery.

Which of the following statements does the advertiser not intend the listener to "assume"?

(A) Johnny Thunder thinks Valto Batteries are the best.
(B) Some correlation exists between the ability to make good airplane batteries and good car batteries.
(C) Johnny Thunder is an expert on car batteries.
(D) Airlines select good batteries for their airplanes.
(E) None of the above

13. As much as anything, our futile efforts to curb or even understand the dramatic and continuing rise in crime have been frustrated by our optimistic and unrealistic assumptions about human nature. Considering that our society is in the grip of a decade-old crime wave despite a decade-long period of prosperity, it is strange that we should persist in the view that we can find and alleviate the "causes" of crime, that serious criminals can be rehabilitated, that the police can somehow be made to catch more criminals faster, and that prosecutors and judges have the wisdom to tailor sentences to fit the "needs" of the individual offender.

The author criticizes society's view of crime control by pointing out that:

(A) It depends too heavily on human nature.
(B) It rests on invalid assumptions.
(C) It does not work.
(D) It does not meet the needs of society.
(E) All of the above

14. All clowns are funny.
Some clowns are sad.
Girls cannot be funny and sad at the same time.

Which of the following statements must be true?

I. No girls are clowns.
II. No sad clowns are girls.
III. No girls are sad.

(A) I only (B) II only (C) I and II (D) II and III (E) I, II, and III

Questions 15–16

In times of economic hardship, Americans characteristically respond in two ways. ___(15)___ Radical causes of the left and the right win adherents they ordinarily cannot attract. Demagogues with dark dreams and simple answers gain a hearing they do not deserve. The last depression brought Adolf Hitler to power in Germany and led to a terrible war. Americans, ___(16)___, pondered Sinclair Lewis's novel *It Can't Happen Here.*

15. Select the answer which best fills blank (15) above:

(A) Socially, they do a complete about-face.
(B) Politically, their perspective shifts.
(C) They become distinctly more anarchistic.
(D) They lose sight of their primary objectives.
(E) They stop functioning independently.

16. Select the answer which best fills blank (16) above:

(A) hoping to avoid another depression
(B) turning their energies to literature
(C) attempting to mitigate the results of the depression
(D) spawning several less fearsome demagogues of their own
(E) in the effort to defeat Hitler

17. Mr. H.: Many men are fine cooks.
Mr. M.: That's not really true—I know quite a few who aren't.

Mr. M's answer shows that:

(A) Mr. H. is incorrect.
(B) He interpreted Mr. H.'s remark to mean that more men are fine cooks than not.
(C) He is not a fine cook.
(D) He interpreted Mr. H.'s remark to mean that all men are fine cooks.
(E) None of the above

18. It is long since Mr. Carlyle expressed his opinion that if any poet or other literary creature could really be "killed off by one critique" or many, the sooner he was so despondent the better; a sentiment in which I, for one, humbly but heartily concur.

Which of the following would the author of this statement be most likely to agree with?

(A) A poet should be particularly vulnerable to criticism from a man like Mr. Carlyle.
(B) Critics reflect the prevailing word of the public.
(C) Literary criticism is an important art in its own right.
(D) It is about time that Mr. Carlyle received some of the ridicule he so richly deserved.
(E) Poets should not take destructive criticism to heart.

19. My friend and I have built a wall
Between us thick and wide;
The stones of it are laid in scorn,

The best ending for this verse would be:

(A) And plastered high with pride.
(B) And painted on each side.
(C) Behind our wall we hide.
(D) The Burgermeister cried.
(E) Because my puppy died.

20. Still one thing more, fellow citizens—a wise and frugal government which shall restrain men from injuring one another, which shall leave them otherwise free to regulate their own pursuits of industry and improvement, and shall not take from the mouth of labor the bread it has earned. This is the sum of good government, and this is necessary to close the circle of our felicities.

The author of this statement would be most likely to approve of:

(A) anti-trust legislation.
(B) taxicab licensing.
(C) suspension of all criminal laws.
(D) enforced segregated schools.
(E) None of the above

21. An unusual shape will help me control altitude. Most imitate an orange or a pear, but mine will copy the carrot, with a point on top to streamline it against drafts.

The speaker is describing a:

(A) glider. (B) bathysphere. (C) salad. (D) balloon. (E) satellite.

22. If anything is a widget, then it is grundled.

Assuming that the above statement is true, which of the following must be true?

I. All grundled things are widgets.
II. If a thing is not a widget, it is not grundled.
III. If a thing is not grundled, it's not a widget.

(A) I only (B) I and III (C) II and III (D) I and II (E) III only

23. You have put your head inside a wolf's mouth and taken it out again in safety. That ought to be reward enough for you.

This remark would have been made most appropriately to:

(A) a lion tamer. (B) a parachute jumper. (C) a commuter. (D) a sky diver. (E) a deep-sea treasure hunter.

Questions 24–25

Equity is a roguish thing. For Law we have a measure, know what to trust to; Equity is according to the conscience of him that is Chancellor, and as that is larger or narrower, so is Equity. 'Tis all one as if they should make the standard for the measure we call a "foot" a Chancellor's foot; what an uncertain measure would this be! One Chancellor has a long foot, another a short foot, a third an indifferent foot.

24. "Equity" probably refers to:

(A) a rule of law.
(B) an invention of the current Chancellor.
(C) a doctrine under which the Chancellor has wide discretion.
(D) an illegal practice of Chancellors.
(E) a system of criminal regulations.

25. The most appropriate ending for this paragraph would be:

(A) 'Tis the same thing in the Chancellor's conscience.
(B) 'Tis the same thing with the hand of the Law.
(C) 'Tis hardly fair when you stop to think of it.
(D) A standard foot is an absolute necessity.
(E) 'Tis the same thing with Law and Equity.

STOP

IF YOU FINISH BEFORE THE TIME IS UP,
CHECK YOUR WORK ON THIS SECTION.
WHEN THE TIME IS UP, CHECK YOUR ANSWERS
AGAINST THE ANSWER KEY AND EXPLANATION ON THE FOLLOWING PAGE.

Answers to Logical Reasoning Self-Test

1. (E) *I* and *III* must win, since no other player can have three aces. *II* wins for the same reason—no other player can have three aces if you have two, since there are only four in the deck; therefore, the kings must win.

2. (A) *I* seems to be assumed by the author. The suggestion is that victims should be attended to instead of criminals. Nothing in the paragraph indicates that the author believes in either *II* or *III*.

3. (D) The key to this question is the contrast that the author has set up. What is missing is something positive for the criminals, while not inconsistent with the first sentence.

4. (C) This should have been an easy one; the structures are identical.

5. (D) *I* must be false. Since cakes are fattening, they taste good, and therefore cannot be nutritious. *II* is true, by a combination of the first two premises. *III* must be false for the same reason that cakes cannot be nutritious if they are fattening.

6. (D) The paragraph is about the exploitation of the unsuspecting by the enterprising. Klondike, the site of a gold rush in the Yukon, is used to denote a rich mineral deposit.

7. (D) The typist is qualified to judge and has no reason at all to lie. The mayor and the mechanic have vested interests; the teacher and brother may have slightly jaundiced views.

8. (A) We need something that fits in with the series that follows, all of which involve abstraction.

9. (C) The seeing of their objects as "always near" and acuteness "in what concerns themselves" both sound like egotism.

10. (B) The key element is the assumption that the president has in the past been considered above the law. Only choice (B) contains that element.

11. (E) None of these statements follow from the given facts, unless you make unwarranted assumptions.

12. (E) The advertiser would like you to believe all of these statements: (A) because Thunder uses them, he thinks that they are the best; (B) because they are used in planes, they should be good in cars; (C) because Thunder is a driver, he is an expert (and his advice has meaning for you); and (D) because airlines are professionals, they make a good selection.

13. (E) In a question like this, once you are *sure* that two answers are right, you know that all of them must be. (A) and (B) are similar, and (C) and (D) are similar; they are all correct.

14. (B) Girls can be sad or girls can be funny—they cannot be both at the same time. Since clowns are always funny, only *II* can be true.

15. (B) Immediately after the missing sentence, the paragraph deals with the political shift. This sentence is the logical connection.

16. (D) Contemplation of a novel called *It Can't Happen Here* (after mention of Hitler) is most significant in the light of spawning our own demagogues.

17. (D) Mr. M.'s remark does not answer Mr. H.'s statement as it stands. The only way it makes sense is as a response to the interpretation in choice (D).

18. (E) The statement says, basically, any poet who gets discouraged by critics doesn't deserve to be a poet. Choice (E) reflects this attitude.

19. (A) (A) is the only choice which carries both the mood and the meaning of the poem. Choices (D) and (E) are silly, and (B) makes no sense after the third line. Choice (C) is possible, but (A) is a better follow-up to "laid in scorn."

20. (E) Choices (A) and (B) represent the types of regulation that the author disapproves of; choice (C) does not provide restraint against injury, and choice (D) interferes with freedom to regulate one's own pursuits.

21. (D) "Altitude" refers to something in the air, and the shape (along with the fact that it can be affected by wind) indicates a balloon.

22. (E) If you have ever taken a course in logic, you will recognize the choices as the converse, inverse, and contrapositive of the original statement. Only the contrapositive is true. If you haven't taken such a course, your common sense will serve you—if *all* widgets are grundled, something which is not grundled could not be a widget; if it were, it would be grundled. Right?

23. (E) The second sentence implies that whatever danger was risked was in pursuit of some reward (like a treasure). This question is a hard one.

24. (C) The whole point of the passage is that the relief available under Equity depends upon the discretion of the Chancellor.

25. (A) The Chancellor's conscience, in other words, is subject to as much variation as his foot—and, with it, the possible remedy available to the person who goes to the Chancellor for help.

CHAPTER EIGHT

Writing Ability

The writing ability part of the LSAT has nothing to do with writing and very little to do with ability. It is scored separately from the rest of the exam. In addition to the three-digit score you receive for the main part of the LSAT, you will be given a two-digit writing ability score, which can range from 20 to 80. While most admissions officers will probably not place nearly as much importance on the writing ability score as on the three-digit LSAT score, they might question any substantial discrepancy. Therefore, to spend some time preparing in this area seems worthwhile.

Two types of questions are asked: error recognition and sentence correction. In the error recognition section, you are asked to label sentences according to what type of errors they contain (if any). In the sentence correction section, you are asked to correct sentences (or leave them unchanged if they are already correct).

In error recognition, one of four answers is possible:

(A) Poor diction: Usage that is incorrect either because a word's meaning is inappropriate in the sentence or because the word is not acceptable in standard written English.
Examples: I am waiting for the medicine to take *affect.*
The new symphony is *out of sight.*

(B) Verbosity: Repetitious elements which do not add meaning to the sentence, and which are not justified for special emphasis.
Examples: All of the judges were in *agreement* and there was no *dissent.*
With *great speed,* he *quickly* ran home.

(C) Faulty grammar: Grammatical or structural word forms and expressions that are improper in standard written English, such as errors in case, number, or parallelism.
Examples: Each of the boys must bring *their* own baseball equipment.
My sister is studying reading, writing and *how to do arithmetic.*

(D) Correct sentence.

Be sure to use these definitions of the errors, rather than your own ideas. No sentence contains more than one type of error.

To see how this type of question works, classify the following sentences according to the definitions above:

1. **Almost every player on the team have scored a touchdown this year.** Ⓐ Ⓑ Ⓒ Ⓓ

2. **At the same time, Mike and Bob were unemployed simultaneously.** Ⓐ Ⓑ Ⓒ Ⓓ

3. **Richard, who was losing his hair, wanted to eat bran flakes.** Ⓐ Ⓑ Ⓒ Ⓓ

4. **You go first and I'll precede you.** Ⓐ Ⓑ Ⓒ Ⓓ

– –

The answers are:

1. (C) **In this case, the subject and the verb do not agree, which is a grammar error. "Every player *has* scored" would be correct.**

2. (B) **"Simultaneously" means the same thing as "at the same time," so this sentence fits the definition of verbosity.**

3. (D) **The sentence contains no error.**

4. (A) **The speaker couldn't have meant to "precede" his companion, since "preceding" and "going first" are the same. He probably meant to "follow." The use of the wrong word is a diction error.**

The most important thing you can do to prepare for this section is to familiarize yourself with the LSAT definitions of the different types of errors, which may not be exactly the same as the definitions to which you are accustomed.

Diction errors are of two types. The first is the use of a word which is improper because its meaning does not fit the sentence. Examples would be the use of "affect" for "effect" or "ingenuous" for "ingenious." Such a question is designed to test your vocabulary. The second type of diction error is the use of a word or expression that is not acceptable in standard written English. In other words, the use of slang is a diction error. Examples would be the use of "far out" or "groovy."

Verbosity errors are usually the easiest to spot, because most verbose sentences contain at least two instances of unnecessary repetition, and the repetition is clearly not used for emphasis. An example is a phrase such as "the whole, complete test."

Faulty grammar, according to the test directions, deals with the structure and form of sentences rather than the dictionary definitions of the words in the sentences. Either the forms of the words will be incorrect or the parts of the sentence will not fit together properly. Examples would be dangling modifiers and errors in case, number, or parallelism.

The sentence correction exercises have a slightly different focus. They test correctness and effectiveness of expression, paying attention to grammar, choice of words, and sentence construction. Each question consists of a sentence, part of which is underlined. Following that are five choices, each of which is a possible replacement for the underlined part. Choice (A) is always the same as the original, and you should select it if the original is the best. Try this example:

When one has to feed the baby, you must first sit him in his chair.

(A) you must first sit him
(B) one must first sit him
(C) he must first be sat
(D) one must first seat him
(E) you must first seat him

The answer is (D). The first error involves the switch of pronouns from "one" to "you." Choices (A) and (E) are wrong for this reason. Second, the verb "to sit" does not take an object and is the wrong word to use in this situation. Choices (A), (B), and (C) are wrong for this reason. Choice (C) also contains an unwarranted change from the active to the passive voice. Choice (D), then, is the correct answer.

The emphasis of the sentence correction exercises will be on general clarity, economy of language, and appropriate diction.

We shall now provide a general review which should be helpful for both writing ability sections. The exercises on the pages which follow are not actual LSAT questions but rather are designed to provide you with a solid background in grammar and diction. At the end of the chapter we have included full self-tests of error recognition and sentence correction.

Let us begin with grammar. A comprehensive review of grammar would be totally unnecessary; we shall not attempt it. Instead, we will point out the particular items that will be most helpful for this portion of the LSAT.

Punctuation is virtually never at issue in the error recognition part, and rarely in the sentence correction part. When it does come up, the most likely problem is correcting a run-on sentence. For example:

The game was fun, the home team won.

This sentence can be corrected in any number of ways. The most effective would probably be to change the comma to a semicolon.

The game was fun; the home team won.

These sentences are also grammatically correct:

The game was fun because the home team won. (The use of a connecting word.)
The game was fun. The home team won. (Split into two sentences.)

Another elementary grammatical error that is just as bad as the run-on sentence is the incomplete sentence. For example:

Having started the sentence in order to illustrate his point.

This phrase has no subject and no verb. That is the key to fixing it; add a subject and verb.

He started the sentence in order to illustrate his point.

Let's take another easy rule. Equally important items in a sentence should be expressed in parallel form.

For example:

I like *to go home* and *visiting* my parents.

The two verbs carry equal weight, so they should be in parallel form–either:

I like *going home* and *visiting* my parents.

or:

I like *to go home* and *to visit* my parents.

Here's another one:

You should practice floating, swimming, and how to dive.

It should read:

You should practice floating, swimming, and diving.

The writing-ability part will always include some parallelism questions.

Now let's look at a particularly important rule. The subject and verb must agree, but when they are separated by other parts of the sentence it is easy to make mistakes. If the subject is singular, then the verb must also be singular; if the subject is plural, then the verb must also be plural. Sometimes, making a slight mental substitution in the sentence will be helpful. For example, consider this sentence:

Professor Reid said that either Gary or Seth are going to fail English History.

We can substitute "either one" for "either Gary or Seth." "Either one" is singular and requires a singular verb ("Either one *is* going to fail"). So the sentence should read as follows:

Professor Reid said that either Gary or Seth is going to fail English History.

Now make the necessary corrections in the following sentences (be careful):

1. **Neither Bob nor Mike are capable of bowling a 300 game.**

2. **An army of 6,000 men are marching down Broadway.**

3. **Partridge is one of the men who have been declared incompetent.**

4. **Keith is the only one of the men who have been living in the women's tent.**

5. **Mutt and Jeff is my favorite comic strip.**

6. **Mutt and Jeff is going to the ballgame today.**

7. **The admissions officer said that his favorite reason for rejecting candidates are their failure to include their zip codes.**

8. **A member of one of the teams have to pay the umpire.**

– – – – – – – – – – – – – – – – – – – –

The answers are:

1. **"Neither," like "either," always takes a singular verb. Substitute: "Neither *one* are capable. ...." Now it is easier to see that it is wrong. It should read "Neither one *is* capable. . . ."**

   Neither Bob nor Mike is capable of bowling a 300 game.

2. **Leave out the phrase "of 6,000 men." An army, no matter how many men are in it, *is* singular.**

   An army of 6,000 men *is* marching down Broadway.

3. **In this case, a number of men have been declared incompetent, and they need a plural verb. The sentence is correct.**

4. **Only one man *has* been living in the women's tent. Drop the phrase "of the men," and you get "Keith is the only one who has been . . ."**

   Keith is the only one of the men who has been living in the women's tent.

5. **This one is correct. If the two subjects joined by "and" form a unit, treat them as a singular subject . . .**

6. **. . . but if they are two *separate* people, treat them as a plural subject.**

   Mutt and Jeff are going to the ballgame today.

7. **Drop the phrase "for rejecting candidates" for a moment, and then "his favorite reason *is* their failure. . . ."**

   The admissions officer said that his favorite reason for rejecting candidates is their failure to include their zip codes.

8. **Same idea again. "A member *has* to pay . . ."**

   A member of one of the teams has to pay the umpire.

A pronoun must agree not only with its verb, but with what we call its antecedent as well. You may remember that the antecedent is simply the noun or pronoun to which the pronoun refers. Once again, substitution may be helpful. Consider this sentence:

Either the champ or the challenger will bring their stopwatch.

The word "either" is still singular, and it requires a singular antecedent, just as it requires a singular verb. (Either *one* will bring *his* watch). The sentence should read:

Either the champ or the challenger will bring his stopwatch.

Now try to correct these sentences, applying what you have already learned about agreement of subject and verb. The rules are similar for making the antecedents agree with their subjects:

1. **Each of the children brought their own beer and pretzels to the birthday party.**

2. **Neither Tom nor Keith brought their guitars.**

3. **Tom and Keith brought their kazoos.**

4. **The band brought their equipment.**

5. **The band brought their instruments.**

– –

1. **Change the structure slightly: "Each *one* brought *his* own. . . ."**

2. **Neither *one* brought *his* . . . , so:**

   Neither Tom nor Keith brought *his* guitars.

   Remember, "either" and "neither" always take a singular verb and pronoun.

3. **This one is correct. Just as the compound subject took a plural verb, it takes a plural pronoun.**

4. **The band is acting as a unit, and it needs a singular pronoun. The band brought *its* equipment. (Note that the possessive pronoun "its" has no apostrophe; the word "it's" means "it is.")**

5. **This one is correct. The members are acting individually, each bringing his own instrument. Therefore, they take a plural verb.**

One last word on pronouns. Make sure that you have the right case (nominative, which is the case of subjects and predicate nominatives, or objective). Subjects and predicate nominatives are *he, she, who, we,* and so on, and objects are *him, her, whom, us,* and the like.

The best way to handle these questions is to move the pronouns (mentally) next to the verb. When dealing with "who" or "whom," rewrite the sentence with "he" or "him"; if "he" fits, you need "who"; if "him" is correct, use "whom." For example, consider this:

Who do you trust?

You would say "I trust him," rather than "I trust he." Therefore, the correct sentence reads:

Whom do you trust?

Now, correct the following sentences wherever it is necessary:

1. **Us smart stinkweed smokers would rather die than stop.**

2. **Did you bring a present for us boys?**

3. **Who did Ted paint this time?**

4. **Mr. Statelmoose is the person being painted by Ted.**

5. Keith is going to allow you and I to see his famous doll collection.

6. Everyone on the team, except for Richard and him, was slender.

7. Whomever wants my car can have it.

8. I will sell it to whomever offers the most money.

9. It was her.

10. It seemed to be her.

The answers are:

1. Remember, put the pronoun right next to the verb. "Us would rather . . ." doesn't work. We need a subject: "We would rather. . . ."

   We smart stinkweed smokers would rather die than stop.

2. This one is correct. If in doubt, read it without "boys." Then, "us," not "we," is clearly needed (the objective case).

3. Remember, whenever you have "who" or "whom," turn the sentence around and substitute "he" or "him" to find out if you need a subject or an object. In this case "Ted painted *him.*" Therefore, we need "whom."

   Whom did Ted paint this time?

4. This one is correct. *He* is being painted by Ted. So:

   Mr. Statelmoose is the person being painted by Ted.

5. In a sentence like this, drop the "you and." Now it is definitely wrong; "Keith is going to allow I. . . ."

   Keith is going to allow you and *me* to see his famous doll collection.

6. This one is correct. "Except for him" is fine as it is.

7. The rule is the same as for "who" and "whom." In this sentence, "he" fits in—"he wants my car"—so "whoever" is correct.

   Whoever wants my car can have it.

8. "Whoever" is the subject of the clause "whoever offers the most money." ("He offers the most money.")

9. The verb "to be" takes the nominative case . . .

   It was she. (It is I, and so on.)

10. . . . except for the infinitive, which takes the objective case. This one is correct.

That brings us to the subject of misplaced modifiers and dangling words. You must be able to recognize them. You should know that they are grammar errors, and be aware of how to correct them. For example, consider the following sentence:

Jumping over 14 barrels, Mark photographed the ice skater.

The problem with this sentence is that it sounds as if Mark, rather than the skater, was jumping over the barrels. The way to correct this type of sentence is to bring the dangling words as close as possible to what they refer to.

Try to correct these sentences:

1. **Climbing up the side of the Empire State Building, we saw King Kong.**

2. **Obviously designed by an incompetent, Paul thought that the airplane should have landing gear.**

3. **Reading the biographies of presidents that my aunt gave me cheered me up.**

4. **When just a baby, his great-grandmother taught him to play pinochle.**

5. **Keith agreed that evening to lend his dolls to the museum.**

– –

1. **The way this is written, it sounds as if we are climbing the building.**

   We saw King Kong climbing up the side of the Empire State Building.

2. **In this sentence, it sounds as if Paul, rather than the plane, was designed by an incompetent.**

   Paul thought that the airplane, obviously designed by an incompetent, should have landing gear.

3. **In this sentence, it sounds as if the presidents themselves were a gift.**

   Reading the presidential biographies that my aunt gave me cheered me up.

4. **Who was just a baby? Not the great-grandmother, as the sentence implies.**

   When *he* was just a baby, his great-grandmother taught him to play pinochle.

5. **Two possibilities exist; either one could be right. What must be determined is what happened that evening. The way the sentence is structured, it could be either the agreement or the actual loan. If this appeared in the error recognition section, it would be a grammar error; if in the sentence correction section, either of the following would be correct:**

   That evening, Keith agreed to lend his dolls to the museum.

   or

   Keith agreed to lend his dolls to the museum that evening.

Our last topic in this brief overview of LSAT grammar will be a few points about verb tenses.

First, let us consider the subjunctive tense, which is used in conditional sentences such as the following:

In the present:

If Richard *were* a young man, he *would* have more hair.

In the past:

If Richard *had been* smarter, he *would have* known what to do.

Remember, for the subjunctive tense:

Present:	were	would
Past:	had been	would have

When two actions both took place in the past, the one that happened earlier can be distinguished by the use of the past perfect tense. For example, consider the following sentence:

Mr. Budapest invited me to the Mul Divit concert, but I had already seen him play on Thursday.

The use of "had seen" in this sentence places the concert that the speaker attended earlier in time than the invitation from Mr. Budapest. Correct any incorrect tenses in the sentences below.

1. If I were ill-tempered, Pongo would have been dead.

2. If Pongo had been polite, I would not have gotten angry.

3. He was already killed when Morlock shot him.

– –

The first two sentences deal with the subjunctive tense.

1. If I *were* ill-tempered, Pongo *would* be dead.

2. This one is correct.

3. Remember, when two actions take place at two different times in the past, the one that happened earlier can be distinguished with the use of the past perfect.

He *had* already *been* killed when Morlock shot him.

Let us now consider the subject of diction, or usage. Any colloquialism in a sentence should be regarded as a diction error. For example:

I really dug the opera last night.

Most diction errors you will see on the LSAT, however, will involve pairs of words that are commonly confused. The following is a list of some of the most common problem pairs:

accept (verb): to receive. Keith *accepted* the new doll as a gift.
except (verb): to leave out. In computing your average, we will *except* your lowest score.
except (preposition): excluding. Everyone *except* Karla knew that Richard was incompetent.

affect (verb): to influence. Did the earthquake *affect* the chess game?
effect (verb): to bring about. Lynne *effected* some changes which improved her standard of living.

affect (noun): an inclination of disposition. His *affect* amused the boys.
effect (noun): result. The fact that all of her students passed had a marvelous *effect* on Jacqueline.

beside (preposition): next to. The dresser is *beside* the bed.
besides: in addition to. *Besides* the LSAT, I hate the GMAT.

bring (verb): convey to the speaker. *Bring* the tools to me.
take (verb): convey away from the speaker. *Take* the medicine *to* Dr. Chin.

could of: This usage is incorrect. People often say "could've" as a contraction of "could have," and some people mistakenly write "could of" where they say "could've." "Could have" is correct. I *could have* told you that.

healthy (adjective): having health. Herb is quite a *healthy* person.
healthful (adjective): producing health. That is a *healthful* herb.

imply (verb): to suggest. He *implied* that Steve had sent him.
infer (verb): to interpret. I *inferred* from his outburst that Steve had sent him. The speaker *implies;* the listener *infers.*

irregardless is not a word. *Regardless* is the correct word. *Irrespective* is also correct usage.

woken is not a word. Rather than saying "I was *woken* up," you should say "I was *awakened.*"

The following sentences will illustrate a few more common errors. See if you can recognize the diction errors and correct them.

1. **What kind of a painting is that?**

2. **This here is one of Ted's originals.**

3. **We have a large amount of them in stock.**

4. **Being that they are so bizarre, I am not surprised.**

5. **We actually have less of them than we did before.**

6. **Just between the three of us, I think that these two are the only good ones.**

7. The one on the right is the nicest of the two.

8. I can't hardly decide between the two.

9. Perhaps you should leave your wife decide.

10. No, I'll take the one on the left. It looks like an optical allusion.

– –

That was quite a conversation. Each sentence contained one error.

1. The word "a" is superfluous. This usage is a diction error.

   What kind *of painting* is that?

2. The word "here" is superfluous.

   This is one of Ted's originals.

3. "Amount" refers to a quantity which is expressed as a unit (such as water or time). "Number" refers to a collection of individual things (such as paintings or minutes).

   We have a large *number* of them in stock.

4. "Being that" and "being as" are incorrect substitutes for "because" and "since."

   Since they are so bizarre, I am not surprised.

5. "Less" refers to quantities that would be described as "amounts"; "fewer" refers to "numbers" (see question 3 above).

   We have *fewer* of them than we did before.

6. "Between" is fine if only two people are involved, but for three or more we need "among."

   Just *among* the three of us, I think that these two are the only good ones.

7. This usage is really a grammar error. Where only two items are involved, the superlative is inappropriate and the comparative should be used.

   The one on the right is the *nicer* of the two.

8. This is a double negative. ("Hardly" is a negative word.)

   I *can hardly* decide between the two. (Or I can't decide . . .)

9. "Leave" is a verb which means "to go away." The verb "let," which means "to allow," is required in this case.

   Perhaps you should *let* your wife decide.

10. An "allusion" is a reference. What the speaker in this sentence means is "illusion"–a false perception.

    It looks like an optical *illusion*.

Verbosity will usually be the easiest error to spot. A verbose sentence will usually be verbose in at least two clear ways. For example:

The huge man, who was very large, was isolated by himself in the corner of the room.
All at once, the minister suddenly began to pound on his pulpit.

As we have already noted, the key to recognizing a verbose sentence is to spot repetition which is not necessary for emphasis. In the sentences above:

huge . . . very large
isolated . . . by himself
all at once . . . suddenly

As we have noted earlier, the sentence correction questions will involve not only the correction of actual errors, but also some emphasis on clarity and economy of language.

Correct the following sentences, making them clearer and more effective wherever possible:

1. Connie took five tests, and all five were passed by her.

2. Behind the first door is a lion. The second door has a beautiful woman behind it.

– –

1. This sentence contains a change in the voice of the verb, which is a grammar error. The sentence begins in the active voice (the subject—Connie—is performing the action) and ends in the passive voice (the action is being done to the subject—the tests). Correcting the error and economizing ("five" need not be repeated), the sentence should read:

Connie took five tests and passed them all.

2. This pair of sentences can be consolidated and made more parallel:

Behind the first door is a lion; behind the second, a beautiful woman.

Remember also that you should not change the meaning of the original sentence.

You are now ready to try a full section. Set aside 20 minutes to do the following error recognition section. Use the answer sheet from the back of the book.

Error Recognition Self-Test

Time: 20 minutes
35 questions

Directions: This section consists of individual sentences. Some of the sentences are correct, but some are incorrect in standard written English for one of the following reasons.

Poor diction: Usage that is incorrect either because a word's meaning is inappropriate in the sentence or because the word is not acceptable in standard written English.
Examples: I am waiting for the medicine to take *affect.*
The new symphony is *out of sight.*

Verbosity: Repetitious elements which do not add meaning to the sentence, and which are not justified for special emphasis.
Examples: All of the judges were in *agreement* and there was no *dissent.*
With *great speed,* he *quickly* ran home.

Faulty grammar: Grammatical or structural word forms and expressions that are improper in standard written English, such as errors in case, number, or parallelism.
Examples: Each of the boys must bring *their* own baseball equipment.
My sister is studying reading, writing and *how to do arithmetic.*

Be sure to use these definitions of the errors, rather than your own ideas. No sentence contains more than one type of error. Select choice

(A) if the sentence contains a *diction* error.
(B) if the sentence contains a *verbosity* error.
(C) if the sentence contains a *grammar* error.
(D) if the sentence contains *no* error.

1. Driving 90 miles per hour, the red light was passed by John. Ⓐ Ⓑ Ⓒ Ⓓ

2. Since the suit did not fit perfectly, Igor brought it back for altercation. Ⓐ Ⓑ Ⓒ Ⓓ

3. Everybody should raise their hand at least once during the hour. Ⓐ Ⓑ Ⓒ Ⓓ

4. The shoes, which had been destroyed by the rain, and the toys, which had been discarded by the children, should have been thrown away. Ⓐ Ⓑ Ⓒ Ⓓ

5. The politician, who was an honest man before he ran for office. Ⓐ Ⓑ Ⓒ Ⓓ

6. That sentence is repetitively redundant. Ⓐ Ⓑ Ⓒ Ⓓ

7. My car needs brakes, tires, shock absorbers, and having the oil changed. Ⓐ Ⓑ Ⓒ Ⓓ

8. When confronted with what he had done, he became contrite. Ⓐ Ⓑ Ⓒ Ⓓ

9. When will that take effect? Ⓐ Ⓑ Ⓒ Ⓓ

10. I will do better if I had studied. Ⓐ Ⓑ Ⓒ Ⓓ

11. It was he who had won the event every year. Ⓐ Ⓑ Ⓒ Ⓓ

12. Danny entered all five contests, and the last three were won by him. Ⓐ Ⓑ Ⓒ Ⓓ

13. Of the three boys who came to dinner, Charles is the more friendly. Ⓐ Ⓑ Ⓒ Ⓓ

14. He is wearing the same identical outfit that he wore yesterday. Ⓐ Ⓑ Ⓒ Ⓓ

15. Who will the winner be? Ⓐ Ⓑ Ⓒ Ⓓ

16. Are you one of those girls who takes a long time getting dressed? Ⓐ Ⓑ Ⓒ Ⓓ

17. Joe ran happily to first base, he had driven in the winning run. Ⓐ Ⓑ Ⓒ Ⓓ

18. That wound should heel quite quickly. Ⓐ Ⓑ Ⓒ Ⓓ

19. I was woken up by Jim at 9:30 in the morning. Ⓐ Ⓑ Ⓒ Ⓓ

20. It might have been assumed that this small woman had actually dyed her eyes, as women in the neighborhood dyed their toes and fingernails and even their hair, had it not been that the year-old infant with her had eyes of exactly the same shade. Ⓐ Ⓑ Ⓒ Ⓓ

21. Algernon was gauche, ignorant, and wore an ill-fitting suit. Ⓐ Ⓑ Ⓒ Ⓓ

22. That group of horses are running around the track. Ⓐ Ⓑ Ⓒ Ⓓ

23. Each aspect was considered. Ⓐ Ⓑ Ⓒ Ⓓ

24. More often than not, he usually paid his workers promptly. Ⓐ Ⓑ Ⓒ Ⓓ

25. The invention of integrated circuits is one of the most important advances in modern electronics. Ⓐ Ⓑ Ⓒ Ⓓ

26. Flying across the city, we saw the airplane go into a dive. Ⓐ Ⓑ Ⓒ Ⓓ

27. Bill showed the charity records to Frank because he felt so strongly about them. Ⓐ Ⓑ Ⓒ Ⓓ

28. The only real problem was the corporation's refusal to comply with the order. Ⓐ Ⓑ Ⓒ Ⓓ

29. The unique vase was the only one of its kind. Ⓐ Ⓑ Ⓒ Ⓓ

30. First Sammy took the exam, then he goes back to his room. Ⓐ Ⓑ Ⓒ Ⓓ

31. I cannot drive somebody else's car. Ⓐ Ⓑ Ⓒ Ⓓ

32. He would not accept of my hospitality. Ⓐ Ⓑ Ⓒ Ⓓ

33. When she graduates college, she will be 21. Ⓐ Ⓑ Ⓒ Ⓓ

34. The noise of the trains frighten many people, including me. Ⓐ Ⓑ Ⓒ Ⓓ

35. Everything would have been all right if she had waited. Ⓐ Ⓑ Ⓒ Ⓓ

STOP

IF YOU FINISH BEFORE THE TIME IS UP,
CHECK YOUR WORK ON THIS SECTION.
WHEN THE TIME IS UP, CHECK YOUR ANSWERS
AGAINST THE ANSWER KEY AND EXPLANATION ON THE FOLLOWING PAGE.

Answers to Error Recognition Self-Test

1. (C) It sounds as if the light was driving 90 miles per hour.

2. (A) Wrong word. He brought it back for *alteration.*

3. (C) "Everybody" is singular and requires a singular pronoun. Everybody should raise *his* hand at least once.

4. (D) Nothing is wrong with this sentence.

5. (C) This is not a sentence. (Without the word "who," it would be.)

6. (B) Redundant means repetitious.

7. (C) Parallelism. It needs brakes, tires, shock absorbers, and an oil change.

8. (D) This sentence is correct; "contrite" means "remorseful."

9. (D) This use of "effect" is correct.

10. (C) I *would have* done better if I *had* studied, or I *will* do better if I *study.*

11. (D) Quite right. Remember, "to be" takes the nominative case.

12. (C) This sentence shifts from the active voice to the passive voice. In other words, Danny is the actor in the first half of the sentence and the object of the action in the second half. The sentence should keep the same voice all the way through, following the principle of parallelism discussed earlier.

    Danny entered all five contests and won the last three.

13. (C) Since three boys (not just two) are being compared, we use the superlative. Charles is the *most* friendly.

14. (B) "Same" and "identical" are too similar.

15. (D) "To be" takes the nominative case. (The winner will be *he.*)

16. (C) All of those girls *take* a long time.

17. (C) This is a run-on sentence. It needs a semicolon or the like.

18. (A) Heel is the back part of a foot; the wound should *heal.*

19. (A) Oh, what a terrible thing to say! I was *awakened!*

20. (D) This sentence is beautiful.

21. (C) Parallelism again.

22. (C) The group *is* running.

23. (D) Nothing is wrong.

24. (B) More often than not . . . usually.

25. (D) Nothing is wrong.

26. (C) The airplane was flying, not us. Something is misplaced.

27. (C) Who felt strongly, Bill or Frank? "Because he . . ." is misplaced, so we don't know who is meant.

28. (D) No problem in this sentence.

29. (B) "Unique" means one of a kind.

30. (C) Then he *went* back to his room. (Or first he *goes. . . .*)

31. (D) This sentence is correct.

32. (A) The word "of" is superfluous.

33. (A) She *will be graduated from* college.

34. (C) The word "noise" is singular. It needs a singular verb. The noise *frightens* people.

35. (D) Everything is all right.

Now, set aside 20 minutes for the Sentence Correction Self-Test.

Sentence Correction Self-Test

Time: 20 minutes

25 questions

Directions: Each sentence in this section is either partially or totally underlined. For each sentence, you are given five possible phrasings of the underlined part. Choice (A) is always the same as the original, but choices (B) through (E) all offer alternative versions of the underlined part. You are to choose the best phrasing.

Sometimes the original sentence is most effective; sometimes another phrasing will be preferable in standard written English. In selecting your answer, consider grammar, diction, sentence construction, and punctuation. The best choice should be clear and exact, not awkward or ambiguous. Do not change the meaning of the original sentence.

1. Sailing along New England's craggy coastline, a bygone era of far-roving whalers and graceful clipper ships can be relived.

   (A) New England's craggy coastline, a bygone era of far-roving whalers and graceful clipper ships can be relived.
   (B) New Englands craggy coastline, a bygone era of far-roving whalers and graceful clipper ships can be relived.
   (C) New Englands craggy coastline, you can relive a bygone era of far-roving whalers and graceful clipper ships.
   (D) New England's craggy coastline. A bygone era of far-roving whalers and graceful clipper ships can be relived.
   (E) New England's craggy coastline, you can relive a bygone era of far-roving whalers and graceful clipper ships.

2. Just between you and I, the supervisor has given you and me difficult assignments.

   (A) you and I, the supervisor has given you and me
   (B) you and me, the supervisor has given you and I
   (C) you and me, the supervisor has given us
   (D) you and I. The supervisor has given you and I
   (E) you and I, the supervisor has given us

3. His knowledge of methods and procedures enable him to assist the director in many ways.

   (A) His knowledge of methods and procedures enable him
   (B) His knowledge of method and procedure enables him
   (C) His knowledge of methods and procedures, enable him
   (D) His knowledge of methods and procedures enables him
   (E) His knowledge of methods and procedures. Enables him

4. Who does he think he is? Who does he consider in making his decision?

   (A) Who does he think he is? Who
   (B) Whom does he think he is? Whom
   (C) Who does he think he is, whom
   (D) Whom does he think he is. Who
   (E) Who does he think he is? Whom

5. Everyone of the salesmen must supply their own car.

(A) Everyone of the salesmen must supply their own car.
(B) Every one of the salesmen must supply his own car.
(C) Everyone of the salesmen must supply his own car.
(D) Every one of the salesman must supply his own car.
(E) Every one of the salesmen must supply their own car.

6. Her going away is a loss to our community.

(A) Her going away is a loss to our community.
(B) Her going away is a loss to our Community.
(C) She going away is a loss to our Community.
(D) She going away is a loss to our community.
(E) Her going away, is a loss to our community.

7. Entering the room, a strange mark on the floor attracted my attention.

(A) Entering the room, a strange mark on the floor attracted my attention.
(B) While entering the room, a strange mark on the floor attracted my attention.
(C) While entering the room, my attention was attracted by a strange mark on the floor.
(D) While I was entering the room, a strange mark on the floor attracted my attention.
(E) Entering the room, my attention was attracted by a strange mark on the floor.

8. A crate of oranges were sent from Florida for all the children in Cabin Six.

(A) were sent from Florida for all the children in Cabin Six.
(B) was sent from Florida for all the children in cabin six.
(C) was sent from Florida for all the children in Cabin Six.
(D) were sent from Florida for all the children in cabin six.
(E) was sent from Florida for all the children in cabin Six.

9. It will leave for Cape Town on Friday and arrive on Sunday.

(A) Friday and arrive
(B) Friday, and will arrive
(C) Friday. And arrive
(D) Friday; and arrive
(E) Friday: and will arrive

10. Being that your manners are so objectionable, you are not invited to the party.

(A) Being that your manners are so objectionable, you
(B) Being that your manners are so objectionable you
(C) Since your manners are so objectionable you
(D) Since your manners are so objectionable, you
(E) Being your manners are so objectionable, you

11. Chris said, 'I will come to see you in New York next week."

(A) said, 'I will
(B) said 'I will
(C) said "I will
(D) said, I will
(E) said, "I will

12. It is so dark that I can't hardly see.

(A) dark that I can't hardly see.
(B) dark, that I can't hardly see.
(C) dark, that I can hardly see.
(D) dark that I can hardly see.
(E) dark; that I can hardly see.

13. Neither his words nor his actions were justified.

(A) Neither his words nor his actions were
(B) Neither his words or his actions were
(C) Neither his words or his actions was
(D) Neither his words nor his actions was
(E) Either his words nor his actions was

14. The childrens' determination to find their dog almost resulted in tragedy.

(A) childrens' determination
(B) childrens determination
(C) childrens's determination
(D) children's determination
(E) Children's Determination

15. She is a Barnard alumnus.

~~(A) alumnus.~~ (B) alumna. (C) alumni. (D) alumnae. (E) alumnie.

16. Everybody who reads this book will think themselves knights errant on missions of heroism.

(A) Everybody who reads this book will think themselves knights errant
(B) Every body who reads this book will think themselves knights errant
(C) Everybody who reads this book will think himself a knight errant
(D) Every body who reads this book will think himself a knight errant
(E) Everybody who reads this book will think themself a knight errant

17. The three thieves divided the money between themselves.

(A) thieves divided the money between themselves.
(B) thieves divided the money among themselves.
(C) thieves, divided the money among themselves.
(D) thiefs divided the money between themselves.
(E) thiefs divided the money among themselves.

18. Irregardless of their fields of study, some students are not very studious.

(A) Irregardless of their fields of study, some
(B) Irregardless of their fields of study some
(C) Regardless of their fields of study some
(D) Regardless of their fields of study. Some
(E) Regardless of their fields of study, some

19. He coughed continually last winter.

(A) continually last winter.
(B) continuously last winter.
(C) continuously, last winter.
(D) continually, last winter.
(E) continually; last winter.

20. The development of heart transplants are a major medical advance.

(A) heart transplants are
(B) heart transplants is
(C) heart transplant's is
(D) heart-transplants are
(E) hearttransplants are

21. I have never read "Les Miserables."

(A) read "Les Miserables."
(B) read, "Les Miserables."
(C) read *Les Miserables.*
(D) read, *Les Miserables.*
(E) read, "*Les Miserables.*"

22. People which are always idle can never be happy.

(A) which are (B) whom are (C) that are (D) who are (E) who is

23. That book is your's; this one is ours.

(A) your's; this one is ours.
(B) yours; this one is ours.
(C) yours, this one is ours.
(D) your's; this one is our's.
(E) yours; this one is our's.

24. Returning to the room, the book was missing.

(A) Returning to the room, the book
(B) Returning to the room, they found that the book
(C) When returning to the room, the book
(D) Returning to the room. They found that the book
(E) Returning to the room they found that the book

25. The spectators agreed that the winner was a remarkable fine swimmer.

(A) agreed that the winner was a remarkable
(B) agreed, that the winner was a remarkable
(C) agreed; that the winner was a remarkable
(D) agreed that the winner was a remarkably
(E) agreed, that the winner was a remarkably

STOP

IF YOU FINISH BEFORE THE TIME IS UP,
CHECK YOUR WORK ON THIS SECTION.
WHEN THE TIME IS UP, CHECK YOUR ANSWERS
AGAINST THE ANSWER KEY AND EXPLANATION ON THE FOLLOWING PAGE.

Answers to Sentence Correction Self-Test

1. (E) Keep the apostrophe to show the possessive case and correct the sentence so that the era does not seem to be sailing.

2. (C) "Between" takes the objective case, as does "given," but "us" makes the sentence more effective.

3. (D) His knowledge . . . enables him—singular subject, singular verb. Choice (B) changes the meaning of the sentence slightly.

4. (E) "Is" takes the nominative case, and "consider" takes an object (he is *he,* he considers *him*).

5. (B) "Every one" is two words when used in this sense but is singular nonetheless.

6. (A) This is not the objective case, but rather the possessive, and it is perfectly correct. "Community" need not be capitalized.

7. (D) (D) is the only choice in which the speaker, rather than his attention or a strange mark, enters the room.

8. (C) "A crate" is singular. Cabin Six is the name of a place, and should be capitalized.

9. (A) Nothing is wrong with the punctuation, and choice (B) is bulkier and less effective. The others are incorrect.

10. (D) The comma is necessary. The use of "being that" is a diction error.

11. (E) A comma and a pair of quotation marks are needed in order to begin the quotation.

12. (D) "Hardly" is a negative word. This sentence contains a double negative as it stands. No punctuation is needed.

13. (A) This sentence is perfect. "Neither" takes "nor" (not or), and "actions" requires a plural verb.

14. (D) "Children" is already a plural. The " 's" makes it possessive as well. Capitalization is unnecessary.

15. (B) A male is an alumnus; several are alumni. A female is an alumna; several are alumnae.

16. (C) "Everybody," unlike "every one," is only one word. Like "every one," it is singular.

17. (B) The plural is correct, but three people need "among."

18. (E) "Irregardless" is not a word. The comma is correct.

19. (A) "Continually" means "regular or frequent occurrence over a period of time." "Continuously" means "without any interruption at all."

20. (B) Singular subject (development), singular verb.

21. (C) Book titles are set in italic (or underscored, in typewritten copy).

22. (D) We need a plural pronoun, so the verb must be "are." Since we are referring to people, "which" and "that" are incorrect. Since "they are" fits better than "them are," we need the nominative case "who."

23. (B) "Yours" is possessive already—so no apostrophe is needed. The semicolon is the correct way to link the ideas.

24. (B) They, not the book, were returning.

25. (D) An adverb is needed to modify "fine."

For additional review of grammar and usage, you may wish to refer to *The Little English Handbook: Choices and Conventions,* second edition, by Edward P. J. Corbett (Wiley, 1977) or *The Elements of Style,* second edition, by William Strunk, Jr., and E. B. White (Macmillan, 1972).

Final Self-Test A

The following test is similar to the Law School Admission Test. You should set aside at least 180 uninterrupted minutes to take Final Self-Test A. Keep a clock or watch handy to time yourself for each section. Before you start the test, review "Special Tips on Taking the LSAT," on page xiii. Remember, you'll find this self-test most useful if you try to simulate actual test conditions. At the end of Section III, you may wish to take a 5-minute break, as provided in the actual LSAT.

A full LSAT test will include one additional section–an experimental one. This experimental section, which is not counted in your score, can appear anywhere in the test but is often found at the end (Section VII). The content of these sections cannot be predicted, and people taking the LSAT on the same test date may be given different experimental sections, appearing in different parts of the test. The appendix on page 279 gives examples and practice problems for some recent experimental sections.

The answer sheets for Final Self-Test A are on page 321, perforated so that you can easily pull them out. These answer sheets are specifically tailored for this test. (On the actual LSAT, space may be given for many more answers than there are questions for each section, since people may be given different forms of the test, in different order. So be sure you put your answers in the right place.) Answers to Final Self-Test A are provided following the test. We recommend that you check the answers as soon as possible, to get the most benefit out of this practice.

Now pull out the answer sheets, get your watch ready, and begin. Good luck!

Section I: Reading Comprehension

Time: 30 minutes
25 questions

Directions: This section consists of reading passages each followed by questions based on their content. After reading a passage, select the best answer to each question. For each passage, answer the questions on the basis of what is stated or implied in that passage.

The distribution and nature of Irish mumming has been made fairly well known in recent years, and the continuity of the custom is traceable back at least to the 1780s, and perhaps to the late seventeenth century if the somewhat enigmatic Cork reference can be accepted. Both Chambers and Tiddy had very limited access to Irish examples of mummers' plays. The first systematic attempt to analyze the Irish plays was published only in 1946 by Green, who knew of eighteen play texts from oral tradition; he also listed various printings of late ninteenth-century chapbook texts published in Belfast. Helm's recent analysis of chapbook mummers' plays included comment on the Belfast printed version. Some material that became available since Helm wrote has made clarification of the sequence of Belfast printings possible, and has slightly revised his dating.

In October 1973 a copy of a hitherto unknown Belfast printing on the mummers' plays was acquired by the Ulster Folk and Transport Museum. It was published by the Belfast printers Smythe and Lyons, who were in partnership between 1803 and 1810. Comparison with Helm's listing of other chapbook versions shows it to be the third earliest known chapbook play in these islands, only two of the Alexander group of texts being older, published at Newcastle in 1771 and 1788. Plays of the latter kind are totally unrepresented in Ireland.

Green recently reiterated his view, stated first in 1946, that the east Ulster versions of the mummer's play "are much more likely to have been established by chapbook versions and are probably quite late in date," than that they have developed from textual prototypes introduced from seventeenth-century (or perhaps early eighteenth-century) English oral tradition. The present writer recently took issue on this point with Green, in discussing Helm's listing of a missing Belfast chapbook version which he had dated to as early as about 1806.

In the absence of certainty about the textual content of this missing version, and because of the late printing (about 1890) of the known chapbook plays from Belfast, all printed by Nicholson, extended analysis of the relationships between the printed and oral plays was unjustified. Indeed, it seemed reasonable to assume that this earlier missing version might well have been the text transcribed by Patterson in 1872, which is very close to the later Nicholson texts. However, Tiddy's reprinting of a transcription of a Belfast chapbook version, sent to him by a correspondent, had been overlooked; nobody has ever commented on some differences between it and the Nicholson texts. Perhaps this was due to Tiddy's own confusing the two. Discovery of the Smyth and Lyons chapbook version now proves the accuracy of Tiddy's informant. A chronological sequence of the known chapbook versions printed in Belfast is now established from which it seems fairly clear that if Helm's information was correct, the missing version he listed falls between the Smyth and Lyons chapbook and the Patterson transcription, and as suggested above, these two may be the same.

The certainty that now exists as to the nature of an early nineteenth-century chapbook play text permits an attempt to assess the connections between oral and printed plays in Ireland. Questions of textual origins are not at issue here. Some conclusions will be possible, however, of wider application than simply to Ireland, mainly on account of the very "modern" aspect of the Smyth and Lyons text.

The Smyth and Lyons chapbook measures approximately 8 cm by 5.3 cm, and consists of thirty-two pages, including the covers. The paper is of poor quality, slightly yellowish in color, and the chapbook is thread stitched. Apart from the centrally placed words CHRISTMAS RHIME, the front and back covers are decorated all over with repeat leaf patterns of the kind frequently used for borders in nineteenth-century chapbooks. It is illustrated by a series of woodcuts, obviously all prepared specifically for this chapbook, and some of them show details of clothing consistent with the date of printing during Smyth and Lyons's partnership. It should be noted that the illustrations differ from those used in the 1890s by Nicholson. The chapbook includes other rhymes, for children, also illustrated by cuts of the same character. The mummers' play text occupies sixteen pages, including the title page which reads: "THE CHRISTMAS RHIME OR; THE [Mum]er's own Book. [L]ittle Master Doubt [who] with his broom, [w]ill sweep them out. ALSO, THE Children's Pretty Rhimes, OF *Swing-swang, Peg-top,* &c. BELFAST: Printed and sold, wholesale by Smyth & Lyons."

1. The author believes that Ulster versions of the mummer's play:

   I. have never been established by chapbook versions.
   II. are quite late in date.
   III. have developed from textual prototypes.
   IV. were introduced from English oral tradition.
   V. The author expresses no opinion of his own on this point.

   (A) V only (B) I, II, III, and IV (C) III and IV (D) I only (E) II only

2. The first systematic analysis of Irish mumming was published in:

   (A) 1771 (B) 1806 (C) 1872 (D) 1890 (E) 1946

3. The author believes that the Belfast chapbook listed by Helm as missing:

   (A) probably never existed.
   (B) was discovered by Tiddy.
   (C) might have been transcribed by Patterson.
   (D) was probably the forerunner of the Smyth and Lyons chapbook.
   (E) was printed by Nicholson.

4. Which of the following statements about the Smythe and Lyons chapbook is false?

   (A) It is illustrated with woodcuts.
   (B) The mummer's play text fills about half of it.
   (C) The illustrations are more modern than those used in the Nicholson printing.
   (D) The covers are characteristic of chapbooks printed in the 1800s.
   (E) None of the above

5. The person who we can infer had access to the most complete collection of Irish mummer's plays was:

   (A) Helm. (B) Green. (C) Cork. (D) Chambers. (E) Tiddy.

6. A chapbook is:

(A) a small volume containing popular tales, plays, or nursery rhymes.
(B) an analysis of Irish mumming.
(C) a book of mummer's plays.
(D) strictly an Irish institution.
(E) All of the above

Comet Kohoutek, like other comets, is a celestial fountain spouting from a large dirty snowball floating through space. The fountain is activated and illuminated by the sun. It is greatly enhanced because it is spouting in a vacuum and essentially in the absence of gravity. We see the fountain as the comet's head and tail. The tail can extend for tens of millions of miles, but we never see the snowball, whose diameter is only a few miles.

The word "comet" comes from the Greek *aster kometes,* meaning long-haired star. The tail of the comet is of course the hair; the head, or coma, of the comet could be considered the star. Within the coma is the snowball: an icy nucleus that moves in a huge orbit under the gravitational control of the sun. The nucleus spends almost all its lifetime at great distances from the sun, hibernating in the deep freeze of space. When its orbit swings it in toward the sun, its surface begins to sublime, or evaporate, and the sublimated gas flows into space. Pushing against the weak gravity of the relatively small nucleus, the outflowing molecules and atoms carry with them solid particles. Thus does the nucleus give rise to the gaseous and dusty cloud of the coma.

The sun floodlights the dust and gas of the coma, making the comet visible. Some comets are very dusty. Most of their observed light is simply sunlight scattered by the dust and is slightly reddish. Other comets contain little dust. Since molecules and atoms in a gas scatter light feebly, such gaseous comets become bright only through a double process. First the ultraviolet radiation from the sun tears the molecules apart; water, for example, is dissociated into hydrogen (H) and the hydroxyl radical (OH). Then the atom or the broken molecule can fluoresce, that is, absorb solar light at one wavelength and radiate it at the same wavelength or (more usually) at a series of longer wavelengths.

Almost all the light from gaseous comets comes from such bands of wavelengths, which are mostly emitted by broken molecules of carbon, nitrogen, oxygen, and hydrogen such as CH, NH, NH_2, CN, and OH, and also C_2 and C_3. What are the parent molecules that split up to produce these unstable radicals? Ammonia (NH_3) and methane (CH_4) are prime suspects, but the suspicion has not yet been confirmed. There is much doubt about the parent molecule for CN. Could it be cyanogen gas (C_2N_2)? Or hydrogen cyanide (HCN)? Or possibly some even more exotic molecule?

Regardless of the answers to such questions, it is now understood that the coma of a comet shines with sunlight scattered by dust or with sunlight reradiated by fluorescent gas, usually with both. The tail of a comet is created by another action of the sun. Comet tails, like comet heads, have a gaseous component and a dusty one. For dust tails the action of the sun is uncomplicated: the radiation pressure of sunlight pushes the dust particles out of the coma. Following the laws of motion for orbiting bodies, the dust particles lag behind the coma as they stream away from it; therefore they form a curved tail that can be rich in detail.

Most comets, particularly the brightest, display a huge tail that is only slightly curved. Like the gas in the coma, these tails shine by fluorescence. The molecules responsible for the radiation, however, are ionized, that is, electrons have been removed to leave molecules with a positive electric charge. In such ion tails we find ionized carbon monoxide (CO^+), carbon dioxide (CO_2^+), nitrogen (N_2^+) and the radicals OH^+ and CH^+, but no un-ionized molecules or radicals. Sunlight can ionize some of the molecules, but what pressure can be responsible for pushing them back into space with forces sometimes greater than 1,000 times the gravity of the sun?

The question of how the ion tails are made was long a mystery and has been solved only in the era of space exploration. Space probes have sent back data showing that the sun continuously ejects a million tons of gas per second moving at a radial speed of 250 miles per second. This solar wind, which has a temperature of a million degrees, drags with it chaotic magnetic fields. The fields are carried by currents of electrons in the gas, which is almost completely ionized. Nearly a decade before the first space probe, Ludwig F. Biermann of the Max Planck Institute for Physics in Göttingen demonstrated that something like the solar wind was needed to account for the ion tails of comets. Although the solar-wind theory of ion tails is not yet very precise, it indicates that two processes couple the solar wind to the cometary gas.

First, the high-energy electrons in the solar wind ionize the molecules in the coma (along with the solar radiation). Second, the solar wind gives rise to a bow wave around the coma. The chaotic magnetic fields now act as a magnetic rake that selectively carries the ions away from the coma, leaving the un-ionized molecules and atoms unaffected. The force of the solar wind on the ions can accelerate them to velocities of several tens of miles per second, so that changes in an ion tail can be seen at distances of many millions of miles on a time scale as short as half an hour.

John C. Brandt of the Goddard Space Flight Center of the National Aeronautics and Space Administration has explained the beautiful curvature of these great tails. It results from the transverse motion of the comet at some tens of miles per second across the movement of the solar wind blowing radially from the sun. The ion tails interact with the high-velocity solar wind in the same way that the smoke rising from a smokestack interacts with moving air to produce a graceful billowy arch on the earth.

7. The best title for this passage would be:

(A) "Kohoutek—Celestial Snowball."
(B) "The Nature of Comets."
(C) "Comet Tails—A Mixture of Gas and Dust."
(D) "Cometary Debris."
(E) "Comet Kohoutek—Astronomical Disappointment."

8. Which of the following statements is false?

(A) A comet has a very small nucleus.
(B) The coma shines with sunlight reradiated with fluorescent gas.
(C) As they near the sun, comets become self-illuminating.
(D) The coma is a cloud of dust and gas.
(E) None of the above

9. Which of the following is most important in order for a gaseous comet to become bright?

(A) Water (B) The hydroxyl radical (C) Ultraviolet light
(D) Infrared light (E) NH_3 and CH_4

10. The solar-wind theory:

(A) is not supported by enough evidence to gain general acceptance.
(B) has been perfected only in the era of space exploration.
(C) explains how the comet glows.
(D) explains how comets move.
(E) explains the magnetic pull on ionized molecules in the tail.

11. Which of the following statements is true?

(A) Comets sometimes have gravity 1,000 times that of the sun.
(B) The high-energy electrons in the solar wind are entirely responsible for ionizing the molecules in the coma.
(C) The solar wind causes the ionized molecules to move.
(D) The solar wind is extremely hot.
(E) None of the above

12. The ionic tail of a comet might contain:

I. CH   II. NH   III. OH^- IV. CO^+ V. C_2 VI. NH_3

(A) I, II, and V   (B) III and IV   (C) I, II, IV, and V   (D) IV only
(E) All of the above

One likes to think that one's attitudes, beliefs, and related behavior form a consistent pattern. Incongruity that is detected results in a sense of imbalance or dissonance, which the person then seeks to correct. The motivating effects of the need to correct incongruity, imbalance, or dissonance has been the occasion for several theories. We may select for consideration the theory proposed by Festinger which treats *cognitive dissonance* and its reduction. The kind of disagreement or disharmony with which Festinger has been chiefly concerned is that which occurs after a decision has been made, after one is committed to a course of action; under such circumstances there is often some lack of harmony between what one does and what one believes, and there is pressure to change either one's behavior or one's beliefs. For example, if a regular smoker reads about the relationship between smoking and lung cancer, the habitual action and the new information are dissonant. If the decision is made to continue smoking, the dissonance will be reduced by disbelieving the information about the relationship between smoking and lung cancer; if the decision is made to give up smoking, the information on the linkage between smoking and lung cancer will be accepted. The fact that this information also affected the decision is not important here. As Festinger and others have shown, the weighing of alternatives is more realistic prior to the decision; after the decision the pressure is great to bring belief and action into balance.

The theory goes on to make some nonobvious predictions: for example, in some cases failure of expectations instead of destroying belief may strengthen it. This was illustrated by the study of a group of people who expected to be saved from a prophesied disastrous flood by the intervention of a heavenly being. The theory predicted that when the long-awaited day arrived and the prophecy failed (no flood), those who had the social support of the other believers would indeed proselyte for their beliefs with new enthusiasm; while those who had to face the crisis alone would have their faith weakened. These predicted results did indeed occur, the rationalization for the group of disappointed believers who faced failure together being that God had postponed his vengeance because of their faith.

The tendency to be consistent is but one aspect of how self-perception influences motivation. Earlier illustrations of human motivation might also be reinterpreted in these terms. For example, the success motivation and the avoidance of failure are also concerned with how a person sees himself. R. W. White, for example, reinterprets many motives concerned with curiosity, and desire for knowledge and for achievement as though they are all concerned with one's sense of *competence* as a person who is effective in relation to the environment. In another sense, the person likes to develop his potentials to the full, to be as complete a person as he can. For such a pervasive type of motive, the expression *self-actualization* was coined, originally by Carl Jung, one of Freud's followers who later developed a system of his own. By self-actualization he meant the development of full individuality, with all parts somehow in harmony. The term and closely related ones (productive orientation, creative becoming, etc.), have been used by many psychologists who criticize contemporary motivational theory as being too narrow, concerned with short episodes of choice and behavior rather than with the more profound and pervasive aspects of individual hopes and aspirations.

13. Which of the following situations is most likely to give rise to cognitive dissonance?

    (A) Baseball fans watching their team lose
    (B) An antique collector being told by an expert that the vase he has just paid $75 for is worth only $25
    (C) A student failing an exam
    (D) A man cutting himself shaving
    (E) None of the above

14. In the case that one's expectations fail, belief:

    (A) will be destroyed.
    (B) will be shaken, but not destroyed.
    (C) will be strengthened.
    (D) may be destroyed or strengthened.
    (E) will be neither destroyed nor strengthened.

15. With which of the following statements would Jung be most likely to agree?

    (A) Parents should not allow their children to smoke.
    (B) Parents should force their children to study piano.
    (C) Parents should give their children complete freedom.
    (D) Parents should encourage their children to pursue any interests they might have.
    (E) Parents should encourage their children to express all of their aggressions.

16. Consistency is most important in the theories of:

    (A) Festinger. (B) White. (C) Jung. (D) Freud. (E) All of the above

17. This passage probably comes from:

    (A) the introduction to a book.
    (B) the first chapter of a book.
    (C) the middle of a textbook.
    (D) an article in a news weekly.
    (E) the middle of a popular book.

18. The best title for this passage would be:

(A) "Self-actualization."
(B) "Self-reference in Human Motivation."
(C) "The Reduction of Cognitive Dissonance."
(D) "Cognitive Dissonance and the Self."
(E) "The Self."

The earliest English Puritans were devout members of the Church of England and had no desire to produce a schism. By the time of Elizabeth's reign the Church of England was clearly Protestant in respect to its separation from Rome. The Puritans wished the reform to be carried much further, in order to simplify or "purify" the creeds and rituals and to diminish the authority of the bishops, but still no official break was intended. In 1633, however, the elevation of Archbishop Laud put the Church of England in the control of a tyrant who was determined to root out "Calvinist" dissenters, Presbyterian or Puritan, by legal persecution. The consequent soul-searching among Puritans, who were never a "sect" in the sense that the Presbyterians were, carried them closer to certain fundamental tenets of John Calvin (1509–1564); and the most powerful and radical of them, unwilling to submit to the abusive and cruel laws against them, soon formed the core of the New England clergy. It should be emphasized, however, that the Puritans did not regard the word of Calvin as the word of authority. They agreed with him when they thought him reasonable, but there were many aspects of his theology that they found unreasonable and so disregarded.

The ideas of Martin Luther (1483–1546), the earlier leader of the great Reformation, likewise became a permanent influence on both religious and civil institutions of American democracy. Concepts of authority, both civil and ecclesiastical, had been everywhere slowly weakening; they were shattered, wherever Luther's words were received, by his doctrine of the "priesthood of believers." "Neither Pope nor Bishop nor any other man," he said, "has a right to impose a single syllable of law upon a Christian man without his consent."

Calvin's *Institutes,* on the other hand, authorized a theological system in certain respects as rigid as that of the Church of Rome, but its ultimate official authority was the consensus of its constituents, and not a hierarchy. In this system the New England "congregational meeting" was inherent from the beginning. In earlier stages of the Reformation it was held that the religion of the ruler should be the religion of the country he dominated, but Calvin, like Catholic thinkers, insisted that the church should be independent. The state should, in fact, be its servant. The result, in early New England during the Puritan period, was that the leading clergymen, powerful and well trained, were for a time the dominating temporal as well as spiritual authority; but by 1700 their civil powers began to crumble under the weight of new secular influence.

In common with all advocates of strict Christian orthodoxy, American Puritans subscribed to Calvin's insistence that the omnipotent God had created the first man, Adam, in his own perfect image, that Adam in his willfulness had broken God's covenant, and that, as *The New England Primer* put it, "In Adam's fall we sinned all." It was Calvin's dogmas of predestination and grace that set him sharply apart from Luther on the one hand and the Roman Catholic Church on the other. The redemption of the individual came only by regeneration, the work of the spirit of God "in the souls of the elect and of them alone." Calvin and the Puritans put a special emphasis on the doctrine of original depravity. Adam's children were not mere automatons of evil impulse, since they possessed, as Adam had, a limited freedom of the will to make the good or evil choice. Still, nothing in man's personal power could mitigate the original sinfulness of his nature. Hence, redemption must be a free gift of God's saving grace, made to those predestined to receive it. No person could earn grace by good works, since good works, in themselves, could only be the result and fruition of grace. These doctrines were characteristically reflected in the interpretation of Christ the Redeemer as representing God's New Covenant with mankind, as Adam represented the Old Covenant.

These doctrines, to which Jonathan Edwards gave the classic recapitulation when Puritanism was already waning, have been interpreted by many modern critics as excessively grim and gloomy. A stereotype of the Puritan has been created, depicting him as a dour, thinly ascetic fellow employing censorship and blue laws to impose his prudish standards on others. Most of the Puritans would have voted to put him in the stocks. It is true that extreme zealots among them, overinterpreting their dogmas, despised this mortal life in contrast to the next. The same zealots, during an outbreak of hysterical superstition, persecuted the "witches." Yet the Puritans in general were lovers of life, their clergy were well-educated scholars in whom the Renaissance lamp of humanism still burned. They did not forbid gaily colored clothes if they could get them; they developed a pleasing domestic architecture and good arts and crafts on American soil; they liked the drink even if they despised the drunkard; they feared both ignorance and emotional evangelism, and made of their religious thought a rigorous intellectual discipline. They were the earliest colonists to insist on common schools; they had the first college (Harvard, 1636) and the first printing press in the colonies (Cambridge, 1638); and they were responsible for the most abundant and memorable literature created in the colonies before 1740. In their influence on American life, there is much more to bless them for than to condemn.

19. Which of the following statements is true of Calvin?

(A) The New England clergy relied almost exclusively on him.
(B) The Archbishop Laud popularized his views.
(C) His views were popularized by both Presbyterians and Puritans.
(D) His ideas were not adopted until about 70 years after his death.
(E) He predeceased Martin Luther.

20. Which of the following statements is false?

(A) Calvin's rules were almost as rigid as those of the Roman Catholics.
(B) Luther died at a later date than Calvin.
(C) Luther proposed a new set of ecclesiastical rules and regulations.
(D) The "congregational meeting" was inherent among the New England Calvinists.
(E) None of the above

21. The idea that man has complete freedom of choice in his life would have been least favored by:

(A) Calvin.
(B) Luther.
(C) the Roman Catholic Church.
(D) early English Puritans.
(E) Archbishop Laud.

22. Under Calvinist theory, redemption was:

 (A) earned by good deeds.
 (B) earned by the fruition of grace.
 (C) impossible to achieve.
 (D) possible for all of Adam's children.
 (E) a free gift for those lucky enough to be predestined for it.

23. Jonathan Edwards was:

 (A) a dour, truly ascetic fellow.
 (B) not representative of the Puritans.
 (C) popular among the Puritans.
 (D) persecuted as a "witch."
 (E) a lover of life.

24. Which of the following statements is true of the Puritans?

 (A) They despised the mortal life.
 (B) They refused to wear brightly colored clothes.
 (C) They did not drink intoxicating beverages.
 (D) They had an unhealthy effect on early American life.
 (E) None of the above

25. Which of the following terms best describes the author's feeling about the philosophy of the Renaissance?

 (A) Approval (B) Indifference (C) Mild disapproval
 (D) Strong disapproval (E) It cannot be determined from the information given

STOP

IF YOU FINISH BEFORE THE TIME IS UP,
CHECK YOUR WORK ON THIS SECTION ONLY.
DO NOT LOOK AT ANY OTHER SECTION IN THE TEST.
WHEN THE TIME IS UP, GO ON TO THE NEXT SECTION.

Section II: Data Interpretation

Time: 40 minutes
28 questions

Directions: **This section consists of various displays of data. Each display is followed by questions based on its content. After studying the display select the best answer to each question on the basis of what is presented or implied in the display.**

NUT CONSUMPTION IN MEXICO AND CANADA, 1983

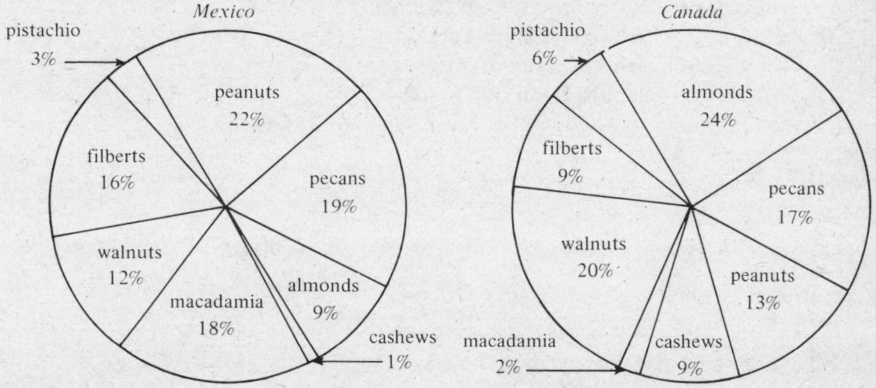

Total amount of nuts consumed = 500,028,000 pounds.
The population of Mexico is 39.8 million.

Total amount of nuts consumed = 300,296,000 pounds.
The population of Canada is 20 million.

1. **What is the approximate angle formed by the section of the graph representing walnuts consumed in Canada?**

(A) 12° (B) 72° (C) 20° (D) 60° (E) 43°

2. **Approximately how many pounds of almonds were eaten by the average Canadian?**

(A) 1.6 (B) 1.2 (C) 3.6 (D) 6.2 (E) 7.2

3. **Which kind of nut was eaten more than any other in both countries combined?**

(A) Almonds (B) Macadamia (C) Peanuts (D) Pecans (E) Cashews

4. **Which kind of nut was eaten less than any other in both countries combined?**

(A) Cashews (B) Pistachio (C) Filberts (D) Peanuts (E) Walnuts

5. **How many pounds of filberts were eaten in Mexico?**

(A) 40,000 (B) 20,000,000 (C) 40,000,000 (D) 80,000,000 (E) 21,000

6. Which of the following statements is (are) true?

I. Twice as many pistachio nuts were eaten in Canada as in Mexico.
II. The amount of peanuts eaten in Canada is greater than the amount of almonds eaten in Mexico.
III. A greater difference exists between the total amount of macadamia nuts consumed in the two countries than between amounts of any other kind of nut.

(A) I (B) II (C) III (D) II and III (E) I, II, and III

7. The amount of macadamia nuts eaten in Mexico is equivalent to the amount of:

(A) filberts and pistachios eaten in Canada.
(B) filberts and cashews eaten in Canada.
(C) filberts and cashews eaten in Mexico.
(D) pecans and peanuts eaten in Canada.
(E) pecans eaten in Mexico plus cashews eaten in Canada.

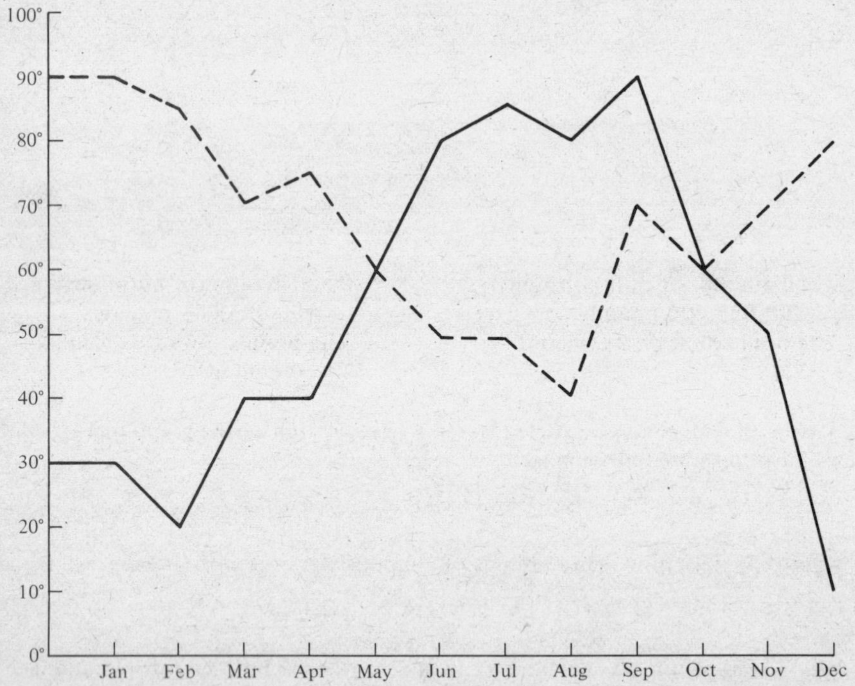

Note: This graph shows the average temperatures in New York City and Melbourne, Australia, for each month of 1973. The solid line represents New York and the broken line represents Melbourne.

8. The greatest increase in temperature in Melbourne occurred between what months?

(A) January and February
(B) April and May
(C) August and September
(D) September and October
(E) November and December

9. In March, the average of the temperatures of the two cities was:

(A) 65° (B) 70° (C) 60° (D) 40° (E) 55°

10. The greatest total decrease in temperature for the two cities occurred between which two months?

(A) January and February
(B) April and May
(C) August and September
(D) September and October
(E) November and December

11. The difference between the highest New York temperature and the lowest Melbourne temperature is:

(A) 35° (B) 50° (C) 80° (D) 70° (E) 40°

12. Which of the following is (are) true?

I. New York had a lower average temperature than Melbourne for 6 months of the year.
II. Melbourne had a lower average temperature than New York for 6 months of the year.
III. Between the months of May and October, the average temperature of the two cities combined was 60°.

(A) I (B) II (C) III (D) I and II (E) I, II, and III

13. In which two months was the difference in temperature between the two cities the same?

(A) March and June
(B) January and February
(C) June and August
(D) April and October
(E) February and December

14. Between April and June, the approximate average difference in temperature between the two cities:

(A) remained the same.
(B) increased by 2°.
(C) increased by 8°.
(D) increased by 10°.
(E) cannot be determined from the information given.

UNITED STATES ENERGY FLOW, 1980

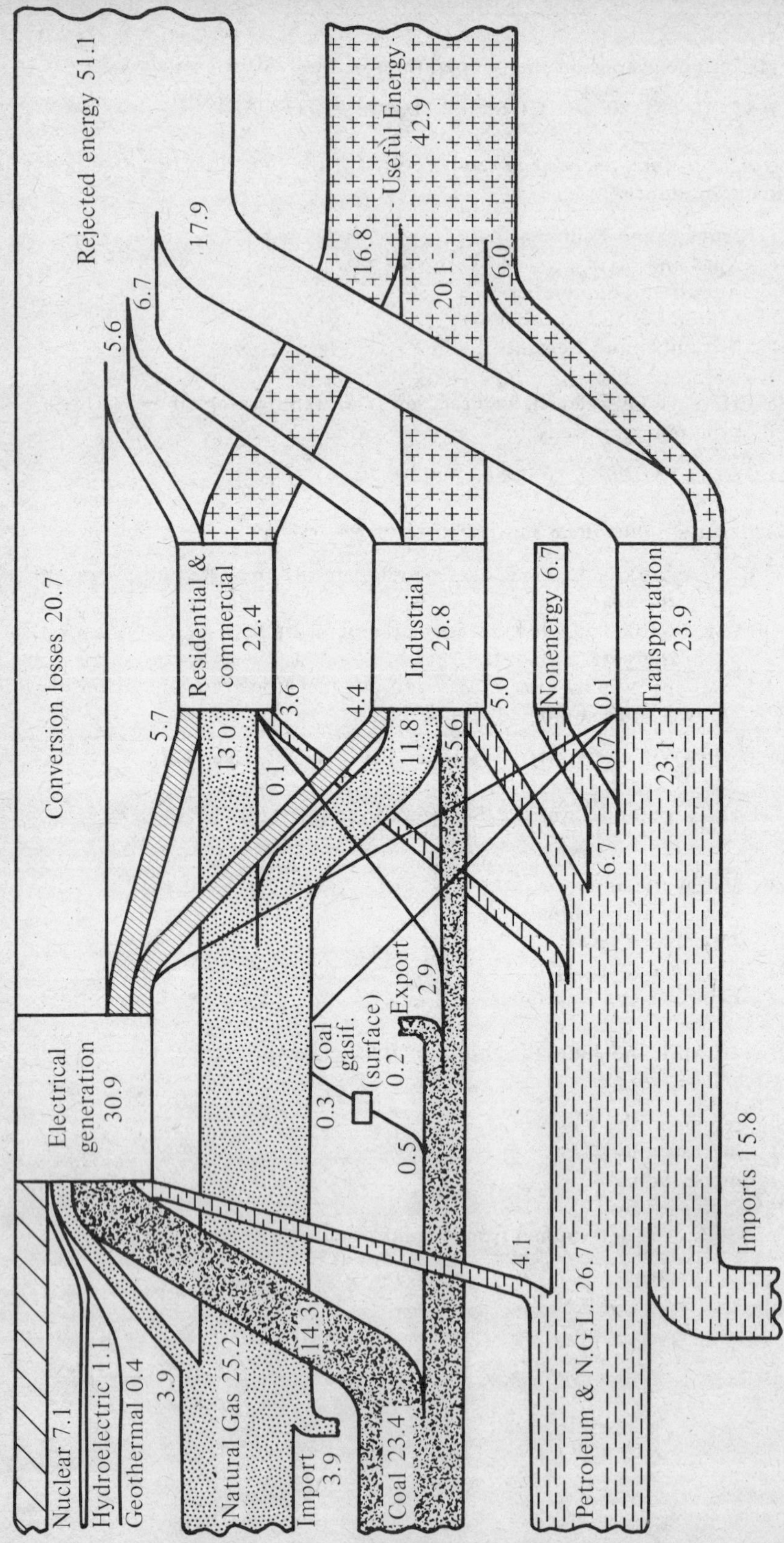

15. How many units of the energy used in industry were classified as useful energy?

    (A) 6.7 (B) 14.0 (C) 20.1 (D) 42.9 (E) It cannot be determined from the information given.

16. Approximately what percent of the energy used in electrical generation came from natural gas?

    (A) 4% (B) 13% (C) 31% (D) 50% (E) It cannot be determined from the infomation given

17. How many units of energy went to residential and commercial uses?

    (A) 13.0 (B) 16.8 (C) 19.0 (D) 22.4 (E) 25.2

18. What is the minimum number of units of natural gas that could have been used (as opposed to rejected) by industry?

    (A) 5.1 (B) 5.6 (C) 6.4 (D) 11.8 (E) It cannot be determined from the information given.

19. Approximately what percent of all natural gas went to industry?

    (A) 12% (B) 25% (C) 29% (D) 40% (E) 47%

20. What percent of all coal used in electrical generation was lost in conversion?

    (A) 14% (B) 46% (C) 61% (D) 67% (E) It cannot be determined from the information given.

21. What percent of all coal was exported?

    (A) 12% (B) 20% (C) 24% (D) 34% (E) 52%

THE SUMMER OLYMPIC GAMES

	Sites	Year	Men's Sports	Male Athletes	Women's Sports	Female Athletes	Total Athletes	Total Nations	Total Events
I	Athens	1896	10	285	0	0	285	13	42
II	Paris	1900	12	1,060	1	6	1,066	20	60
III	St. Louis	1904	10	496	0	0	496	11	67
IV	London	1908	17	2,023	3	36	2,059	22	104
V	Stockholm	1912	15	2,484	3	57	2,541	28	106
VII	Antwerp	1920	19	2,543	3	63	2,606	29	154
VIII	Paris	1924	18	2,956	3	136	3,092	44	137
IX	Amsterdam	1928	16	2,725	4	290	3,015	46	120
X	Los Angeles	1932	17	1,281	3	127	1,408	37	124
XI	Berlin	1936	19	3,741	4	328	4,069	49	142
XIV	London	1948	19	4,030	5	438	4,468	59	138
XV	Helsinki	1952	19	5,294	5	573	5,867	69	149
XVI	Melbourne	1956	19	2,813	5	371	3,184	67	145
XVI	Stockholm*	1956	1	132	1	13	145	29	3
XVII	Rome	1960	18	4,859	5	537	5,396	84	150
XVIII	Tokyo	1964	20	4,833	8	732	5,565	94	163
XIX	Mexico City	1968	19	5,238	8	844	6,082	109	172
XX	Munich	1972	24		6		8,500	121	194

*Equestrian games only

22. In the year in which the fewest nations participated, how many men's sports were presented?

(A) 0 (B) 10 (C) 11 (D) 67 (E) 496

23. What was the largest number of successive Olympics in which the number of male athletes increased?

(A) 2 (B) 3 (C) 4 (D) 5 (E) 6

24. In which of the following years did female athletes make up the largest percentage of total athletes?

(A) 1896 (B) 1928 (C) 1948 (D) 1964 (E) 1968

25. If the ratio of females to males in 1972 was twice as high as in 1928, approximately how many female athletes participated in 1972?

(A) 580 (B) 700 (C) 980 (D) 1,600 (E) 1,800

26. In how many years were equestrian games part of the Olympics?

(A) 0 (B) 1 (C) 17 (D) 18 (E) It cannot be determined from the information given.

27. In the first city which hosted the Olympics twice, what was the percent increase in total athletes from the first time to the second time?

(A) 190% (B) 290% (C) 90% (D) 240% (E) 140%

28. **In how many years on the graph did women participate in fewer than four Olympic sports?**

(A) 6 (B) 7 (C) 8 (D) 9 (E) 10

STOP

IF YOU FINISH BEFORE THE TIME IS UP,
CHECK YOUR WORK ON THIS SECTION ONLY.
DO NOT LOOK AT ANY OTHER SECTION IN THE TEST.
WHEN THE TIME IS UP, GO ON TO THE NEXT SECTION.

Section III: Reading Recall

Time: 30 minutes for whole section

Directions: This section consists of three reading passages. Fifteen minutes will be allocated for reading and studying the passages. Then you will have 15 minutes to answer questions based on the three passages. Note the key facts and concepts in these passages while you are reading them, because you will not be allowed to refer back to the passages while you are answering the questions. Pace yourself so that you will be able to read all of the material.

At the end of the 15 minutes of reading, you will be given instructions for answering the questions.

Part A

Time: 15 minutes

Passage 1

An essential requirement for any kind of nuclear fission technology, explosive or otherwise, is the provision of enriched uranium fuel. Uranium comes in two isotopes, the common nonfissioning uranium 238 and the fissioning uranium 235. For reactor purposes a fuel must be provided that has at least three percent U-235 rather than the 0.7 percent found in a sample of natural uranium.

To make the enrichment requires separating the two isotopes. Chemical means do not generally work in such cases since different isotopes of the same element react the same way chemically. Physical means have to be used. The present technology, gaseous diffusion, in which hot gas diffuses up and down a stack so that the upper layers become richer in the lighter U-235, is cumbersome, expensive and slow. Therefore there is great interest in experiments that attempt to use laser light as a means of separating the uranium isotopes.

At the 8th International Quantum Electronics Conference in San Francisco last week Benjamin R. Snavely of the Lawrence Livermore Laboratory gave for the first time some technical details of an experiment that has succeeded in separating "microscopic" quantities of the uranium isotope. In those microscopic amounts the proportion of U-235 went higher than 60 percent.

The basic method of laser separation is in fact applicable to many elements besides uranium, but the heavy interest is on uranium because the demand for it runs into tons a year and is rising, whereas the demand for other isotopes for medical or chemical purposes may be measured in grams or even fractions of a gram. Snavely estimates that successful commercial applications of laser separation of uranium could save upwards of $100 billion in capital investment.

Ironically, information is given more freely about experiments involving other elements than uranium because uranium is caught up in national defense, and information gets classified. In addition to Livermore, uranium work is known to be going on by a collaboration of Exxon and the Avco Corp., in Israel and in West Germany. What may be going on in the Soviet Union is not public knowledge, but Soviet scientists have worked on laser separation of other elements and published accounts of their experiments.

Laser separation of isotopes depends basically on the way in which atoms and molecules absorb energy from incident light. Each species absorbs a particular pattern of specific resonant wavelengths that correspond to the different ways in which it can become energetically excited. It happens that because of the difference in atomic weight between two isotopes of the same element, the resonance pattern for one isotope will be shifted slightly from that of the other. If the shift is large enough it may be possible to tune a laser so that one isotope of the given element will absorb the light and become excited while the other is not affected.

In the uranium case, a stream of uranium vapor at 2,500 degrees K. is irradiated by light of 5,900 angstroms wavelength. This excites one of the isotopes. Then a second beam of light (3,000 angstroms from a mercury-arc source) is passed through the vapor stream. This second light beam ionizes the already excited isotope but does not affect the other. The vapor stream now contains one isotope that is electrically neutral and one that is charged (ionized). The charged can be separated from the uncharged by a combination of electric and magnetic fields. Severe difficulties must be overcome before the method becomes commercial, if indeed it ever does. Nevertheless, success in the basic method is an important and essential first step.

Other experiments on other isotopes tend to use photochemistry rather than photoionization in making the separation. In these cases use is made of the fact that energetically exicted atoms or molecules are chemically more reactive than unexcited ones and thus a chemical reaction can be used to separate the excited species. Work being done at the University of California at Berkeley and described by Stephen R. Leone preferentially excites bromine molecules containing bromine-81, then induces them to react with hydrogen iodide. This produces hydrogen bromide containing bromine-81. The hydrogen bromide can then be precipitated out by passing the gas over chilled baffles. Another photochemical method uses natural formaldehyde that is a mixture of the hydrogenated variety (H_2CO) and the deuterated variety (D_2CO). Laser light selectively excites the deuterated variety, and the molecule is then induced to break up into D_2 and CO, thus accomplishing the separation of deuterium from hydrogen. A photochemical method for recovering uranium isotopes might seem attractive from a raw-materials point of view since one could start with the common substance uranium hexafluoride rather than having to refine out pure uranium first, but Snavely is very pessimistic about such a development because of difficulties with uranium chemistry and because the absorption frequencies of uranium hexafluoride overlap so much that laser tuning seems impossible.

Passage 2

For the Jie and Turkana, marriage is not just a single legal act of making a girl the wife of a man, but it is a long ceremonial process which begins with the preparations for the wedding and whose explicit object is the ritual, spiritual and social creation and establishment of the marital union, and to ensure the fertility of the woman and the welfare of her children. In Turkanaland the process is completed between two and three years after the actual wedding (i.e. the formal acceptance of bridewealth) when the first child of the union has been reared to the walking stage. In Jieland the process is completed not less than five years after the wedding, for at least two children have to be similarly reared. In both societies the total process culminates in the ritual incorporation of the woman into her husband's house, family and clan, at which time she finally abandons her natal affiliations.

The marriage process consists of a number and variety of events which take place in a strict order such that the completion of one allows preparations to go forward for the next. Each event is consciously related to a further stage in the process. Some of them are of vital ritual significance, some are of importance in establishing and cementing affinal relationships, and some appear almost trivial, scarcely to be raised to the level of a stage of this process. An example of the latter is the naming of the first child and the ceremonial provision of the baby-carrying sling of sheepskin—a common enough event in primitive societies. But even such an event is performed with due ceremony at the relevant time and by conventionally determined people from either side of the union. It is regarded as a new stage in the development, that is, the birth of the child is a further step in the woman becoming a "full-wife" and in uniting her with her husband and his house. It also marks a further step in the linking together of the new affines.

In fact, there are two interwoven processes; one is the development from unmarried girl, to bride, to "bride-wife" (*nateran*), to mother, to "full-wife" (*aberu*); the other is the gradual binding together of the husband with his wife's father and full-brothers, and to a lesser degree the houses and even the families of each. By the time the process is completed, the marriage union and the surrounding affinal bonds have been firmly established, emotional adjustments settled, and the woman has an assured status and role in her new house and family. Only when the wife and her children are incorporated into the man's group is marriage completed; then, the natives say "*Adowun akotan daang*" (the whole marriage is finished).

Among the Jie there are some 15 successive stages, beginning with the formal request of the girl in marriage and ending with her ritual incorporation. Most stages require the slaughter of animals for ceremonial feasts, and many of them necessitate the cooperation of clan elders on both sides. As usual, Turkana ritual is neither so rich in detail nor so frequent in occurrence, but the basic pattern is the same. In both societies, the exact pattern of the process is defined by clan membership. In general the process is essentially similar, in each tribe, for all clans; but many clans differ in the actual details of ritual prescription, and a few clans call for one or two extra stages. Some of the stages are determined by the man's clan and some by the bride's father's clan.

Strictly legally, it is the transfer of bridewealth (literally, "stock of marriage") in the name of the groom to the relatives of the bride which causes a girl to become a wife, although not, as we have seen, a full-wife. As one Jie put it, "You know a woman is married if stock have been given. How do you know a wife if there are no cattle? Other men go away when they know about the stock." Occasionally when recording genealogies I have been unsure whether some woman is married or not, and invariably my query was answered in the form: "Stock have been given. She is a wife."

The prime, extrinsic features of legal marriage are the man's sexual monopoly over his wife and authority over her children. On the reverse side, the wife gains the opportunity to bear legitimate children and the rights of support and protection from her husband, and she and her children obtain rights in his herds. The norm of domestic union is of course provided within the framework of marriage, which is conceived of as establishing such cooperation. Nevertheless, it must be emphasized that the transfer of bridewealth and its formal, public acceptance is but one stage of the total marriage process, though a critical stage in the eyes of all people. The marriage can only be completely established by the due performance of the ritual and ceremonial acts already mentioned.

Passage 3

Early man, as long as he merely hunted, fished and wandered from one place to another, was satisfied to find shelter under protruding rocks or at the tops of large trees. The lucky ones found natural caves. It was only in the Neolithic period (New Stone Age, which began perhaps in 8000 B.C.) that man actually began building. The glaciers had receded; tools in stone and bone implements had already developed to a certain perfection; agriculture and breeding of cattle began to develop; pottery was formed and at times decorated with primitive designs.

Now man first began to dig deep holes—so-called round-pit dwellings—into the soil and to cover them with twigs, weeds and probably skins of animals. Next, man started to construct real huts over a scaffold of lumber and to fill in the walls with clay or interwoven twigs and weeds. When possible, these huts were erected at the banks of lakes, anchored on poles in the shallow water for protection against enemies. Later on, man began to use stones, which he put together and covered with earth—thus constructing an artificial cave.

This kind of building cannot be called architecture. Only when men tried to bring a certain order into their structures and consciously began to give them a distinct shape can we speak of architecture. This started—perhaps around 4000 B.C.—with the first great historic civilizations: the Egyptian, the Mesopotamian, the Cretan and those of the Far East.

The most striking thing about Egyptian architecture is that it was shaped in geometrical forms, as regular as possible. The pyramids are a good example. The hard stone with which everything in the Nile Valley was built increased still more the massive severity of these angular structures.

We are compelled to admire the skill of those ancient Egyptians who erected the huge pyramids and the enormous temples with their heroic columns, for the builders had none of the technical aids that we consider necessary. They had only brain and brawn. The work of machines was substituted for by tens of thousands of people working millions of hours. It took generally a lifetime to complete one of the large pyramids in which the kings from the Third to the Fifth Dynasties (2900–2500 B.C.) were buried. Later, the kings were buried in tombs hewn into the rocks that confined the Nile Valley. Gigantic statues of gods, superhuman in scale, were sculptured to guard the entrances as custodians. Large temples were constructed in connection with these rock tombs. From about 1800 B.C. on we encounter temples, or rather groups of temples, that were sometimes erected in connection with the palace of a king. These temples consisted of large halls with statues of gods in the interior, courtyards, alleys of sphinxes and storerooms. The largest among them were built at Karnak and Luxor (1400?–1180 B.C.) and at Thebes, once the capital of Egypt. It is astonishing that the Egyptians who developed such a monumental type of strict and strong architecture in their temples and tombs had relatively little interest in what we would call today "housing." The majority of houses were exceedingly primitive, put together from clay, reeds and sun-dried bricks, even in the larger cities.

In Mesopotamia, the fertile area between the rivers Euphrates and Tigris, one empire followed the other from 4000 to 600 B.C. The empire of the ancient Sumerians gave way to that of the Babylonians; then followed the Assyrians, the second Babylonian Empire, and finally the Persians. The capitals—Ur, Babylon, Kish, Assur, Nineveh, Persepolis—changed with the reigns of these successive empires. The types of buildings, however, changed very little. Stone and wood were equally rare in these regions, so that bricks, sun-baked and oven-baked, became the building materials. One sort of building became a type. It was called "ziggurat." This was a rather large fortified terrace on which a tremendous tower arose in receding steps, crowned by a structure similar to a modern penthouse. This tower contained the palace of the ruler, the quarters of the highest officers and officials; and on the top was the temple. From excavations we are able to judge that these towers were very high. The whole area was about the size of a small town. The description of the Tower of Babel in the Old Testament refers to such a ziggurat.

The Babylonians and Assyrians first made use of the arch. Neither the Egyptians nor the Cretans and Greeks who came later employed it. The decoration of the Mesopotamian buildings consisted first of glazed bricks. Later, when stone came into use, reliefs were carved on stone.

STOP

YOU MAY CONTINUE STUDYING PART A OF THIS SECTION UNTIL YOUR TIME IS UP.
DO NOT LOOK AT ANY OTHER SECTION IN THE TEST.
WHEN THE TIME IS UP, GO ON TO PART B.

Part B

Time: 15 minutes

30 questions

Directions: The following questions test your memory of main points and important details of the passages you have just read, as well as your ability to draw certain inferences from them. Select the best answer to each question. You may not refer back to the passages.

Questions on Passage 1

1. Enriched uranium fuel must contain at least:

   (A) 0.7% U-235. (B) 3% U-235. (C) 0.7% U-238. (D) 3% U-238. (E) 7% U-238.

2. Which of the following statements is false?

   (A) U-235 is lighter than U-238.
   (B) Laser separation works for elements other than uranium.
   (C) Russian scientists have worked on laser separation.
   (D) The present technology involves gaseous diffusion.
   (E) None of the above

3. Chemical means of separation:

   (A) work, but are too slow and expensive to be practical.
   (B) work well, but laser separation works better.
   (C) work but yield too low a percentage of the desired isotope.
   (D) work only at extremely high temperatures.
   (E) do not work.

4. Laser separation works because:

   (A) the two isotopes are actually the same element.
   (B) the difference in atomic weight causes a difference in resonance pattern.
   (C) the difference in weight allows a filtration process to take place.
   (D) uranium is radioactive.
   (E) one isotope is more sensitive to light than is the other.

5. The laser is used on uranium vapor at a temperature of:

   (A) 2,500° K. (B) 5,900° K. (C) 3,000° K. (D) 5,900 angstroms. (D) 3,000 angstroms.

6. Which of the following statements is correct?

   (A) The first beam ionizes the isotope and the second excites it.
   (B) The first beam vaporizes the isotope and the second ionizes it.
   (C) The first beam excites the isotope and the second vaporizes it.
   (D) The first beam excites the isotope and the second ionizes it.
   (E) The first beam ionizes the isotope and the second vaporizes it.

7. The method of separating the uranium using two successive laser beams could be best characterized as:

(A) photoelectricity. (B) photochemistry. (C) photoionization. (D) photovaporization. (E) None of the above

8. The photochemical method is:

(A) inferior from a raw materials point of view.
(B) useful only with pure uranium.
(C) not regarded optimistically by Snavely.
(D) favored by the author.
(E) None of the above

9. A charged isotope is said to be:

(A) ionized. (B) deuterated. (C) hydrogenated. (D) electrified. (E) negative.

10. Enriched uranium is necessary for:

(A) separation of bromine-81. (B) nuclear fission. (C) separation of D_2CO. (D) production of uranium hexafluoride. (E) nuclear fusion.

Questions on Passage 2

11. Which of the following statements is (are) true?

I. A Jie woman must rear one child before she is considered married.
II. A Turkana woman must rear one child before she is considered married.
III. A Jie woman must rear two children before she is considered married.
IV. A Turkana woman must rear two children before she is considered married.
V. Both Jie and Turkana women must rear two children before they are considered married.

(A) V only (B) II and III (C) I and IV (D) I and II (E) None of the above

12. Which of the following sequences is correct?

(A) Unmarried girl, bride, bride-wife, mother, full-wife
(B) Unmarried girl, bride, bride-wife, full-wife, mother
(C) Unmarried girl, bride-wife, bride, mother, full-wife
(D) Unmarried girl, bride, full-wife, bride-wife, mother
(E) Unmarried girl, bride-wife, bride, full-wife, mother

13. *Aberu* is a(n):

(A) unmarried girl. (B) bride. (C) bride-wife. (D) full-wife. (E) mother.

14. The first step in the Jie marriage ritual is:

(A) ritual incorporation.
(B) agreement between the groom and the bride's father. (C) formal request.
(D) transfer of the bridewealth. (E) evaluation of the bridewealth.

15. *Adowun akotan daang* means:

(A) Stock has been given. She is a wife.
(B) The whole marriage is finished.
(C) You know a woman is married if stock has been given.
(D) The whole marriage is terminated.
(E) The family is incorporated.

16. The main difference between Jie and Turkana marriage ceremonies is that:

(A) The Jie ritual is more simple.
(B) The Turkana ritual varies more with individual clans.
(C) The Jie ritual has only five stages.
(D) The Jie ritual is more complicated.
(E) The Jie ritual varies more with individual clans.

17. You can infer that the author is a(an):

(A) Jie. (B) Turkana. (C) historian. (D) anthropologist. (E) psychologist.

18. One can infer that the author:

(A) thinks that the Jie ritual is superior.
(B) thinks that the Turkana ritual is superior.
(C) disapproves of both rituals.
(D) approves of both rituals.
(E) None of the above

19. The stages of the ritual are determined by:

I. the bride's father's clan.
II. the groom.
III. the groom's father's clan.
IV. the chief of the tribe.
V. the grooms' mother's clan.

(A) IV only (B) I, III, and IV (C) I and V (D) I and III (E) I, IV, and V

20. Authority over the children is held by:

(A) the mother. (B) the father. (C) the mother and father. (D) the chief. (E) the bride's father.

Questions on Passage 3

21. The first architecture took place:

(A) during the Neolithic era.
(B) around 4000 B.C.
(C) around 8000 B.C.
(D) around 2900 B.C.
(E) during the New Stone Age.

22. Which of the following is *not* listed in the passage as one of the first great historic civilizations?

(A) Egyptian (B) Mesopotamian (C) Babylonian (D) Cretan
(E) Far Eastern

23. Which of the following statements is *not* true of Egyptian architecture?

(A) Simple machines were used. (B) It took a lifetime to build one structure.
(C) It was geometrically regular. (D) It was angular.
(E) It included enormous temples.

24. The Third Dynasty took place around:

(A) 1180 B.C. (B) 2500 B.C. (C) 2900 B.C. (D) 1400 B.C.
(E) 4000 B.C.

25. Which of the following was a capital of Egypt?

(A) Karnack (B) Luxor (C) Thebes (D) Nile (E) Babylon

26. Which of the following was *not* a Mesopotamian capital?

(A) Tigris (B) Ur (C) Kish (D) Babylon (E) Persepolis

27. The arch was used by:

I. Babylonians. II. Egyptians. III. Cretans. IV. Greeks.
V. Assyrians.

(A) I only (B) I and V (C) I and III (D) I, III, and V (E) II, IV, and V

28. The ziggurat was characteristic of the architecture of:

(A) Egypt. (B) Babel. (C) the Old Testament. (D) the New Testament.
(E) Mesopotamia.

29. The best title for this passage would be:

(A) "Ancient Egyptian Architecture."
(B) "Stone Age Architecture."
(C) "Neolithic Architecture."
(D) "Shelter in the Nile Valley."
(E) "Early Architecture."

30. Which of the following are Mesopotamian rivers?

I. Nile II. Tigris III. Euphrates IV Ur V. Assur

(A) II and III (B) I, II, and III (C) II, III, IV, and V (D) IV and V
(E) I, IV, and V

STOP

IF YOU FINISH BEFORE THE TIME IS UP,
CHECK YOUR WORK ON PART B ONLY.
DO NOT LOOK AT ANY OTHER PART OF THE TEST.
WHEN THE TIME IS UP, GO ON TO THE NEXT SECTION.

Section IV: Principles and Cases

Time: 40 minutes

30 questions

Part A

Directions: In this section you will be presented with some cases, each of which is followed by several legal principles. These may or may not be real principles of law, but you are to accept them as valid. Following each principle are four possible applications of the principle to the case. Answer each question by selecting the most reasonable application.

These questions assume no prior legal knowledge on your part; answer them using only ordinary logical reasoning.

Case 1

Alice went to Robert's automobile showroom to buy a car for her camping trip in the Rocky Mountains. She told Robert she needed a car which could ride smoothly over rugged terrain and steep mountain roads. Robert showed her a sample car, and said that he believed that model was "unbeatable" and real "tough." He told her he had never had a dissatisfied customer and that this was the car he would buy if he were in Alice's position. Alice agreed to buy the car, arranging to pay Robert half the price down and the rest in 20 monthly installments.

When she reached the foothills of the Rockies, Alice discovered that the car could not go up even the gentlest of inclines. Since there was no other way she could get all her equipment to the campground, she started driving home. While she was on her way back to Robert's to return the car, the engine died. The mechanic who attended to it said the car was worthless and could not be repaired. When Alice spoke to Robert, he told her he could not return her money because "that's not the way the auto industry operates."

1. *A sale occurs when one party agrees to transfer ownership of property in return for money or other consideration. When full payment is not made by the time ownership in the property is transferred, the seller at any time may demand that half the unpaid price be paid within 30 days. Upon exercising this option, the seller renounces all right to the other half of the unpaid amount.*

   When Robert sues Alice for half of the unpaid purchase price, he will:

   (A) win, because a valid sale agreement exists.
   (B) win, because Alice still owed him money.
   (C) lose, because Alice already paid half the purchase price.
   (D) lose, because the car was worthless.

2. *A seller creates an express guarantee for his goods by any of the following means:*

   1. An affirmation of fact or a promise made to the buyer, which relates to the goods sold and which is taken into account by the buyer in purchasing the goods, creates an express guarantee that the goods shall conform to the affirmation or promise.

2. A description of the goods which is taken into account by the buyer in purchasing the goods creates an express guarantee that the goods shall conform to the description.

3. A sample taken into account by the buyer in purchasing the goods creates an express guarantee that the goods shall conform to the sample.

However, an affirmation of the value of the goods, or a statement purporting to be the seller's opinion or commendation of the goods, does not create an express guarantee.

When Alice sues Robert for breach of express guarantee, she will:

(A) win, because Robert described the car as "tough."
(B) win, because Robert showed her a sample of the model car she bought.
(C) lose, because Robert did not specifically affirm that the car could go up hills.
(D) lose, because Robert was only affirming the value of the car and expressing his opinion about it.

3. *An implied guarantee that goods sold are merchantable is created whenever the seller is a merchant of goods of that kind. To be merchantable, goods must be of fair average quality, and must be fit for the ordinary purpose for which such goods are intended. Implied guarantees may also arise from the normal practice of the trade or industry.*

When Alice sues Robert for breach of an implied guarantee of merchantability, she will:

(A) win, because Robert is a dealer in cars.
(B) win, because the car was unfit even for ordinary purposes.
(C) lose, because implied guarantees of merchantability are not the normal practice of the automobile trade.
(D) lose, because she did not buy the car for the ordinary purpose for which it was intended.

4. *If, at the time of sale, the seller has reason to know of any particular purpose for which the goods are required, and that the buyer is depending on the seller's skill or judgment to furnish suitable goods, an implied guarantee that the goods will be fit for such purpose is created.*

When Alice sues Robert for breach of implied guarantee of fitness for a particular purpose, she will:

(A) win, because Robert knew she was relying on him to select a car adequate for climbing steep hills.
(B) win, because Robert said the car was what he would buy in her situation.
(C) lose, because she actually used the car only for its ordinary purpose.
(D) lose, because she did not expressly inform Robert that she knew nothing about cars.

5. *When a seller breaches a guarantee, he is responsible for any loss resulting from the buyer's needs which the seller had reason to know, and which the buyer could not reasonably have prevented. The seller is also responsible for injuries to the buyer's person or property resulting from the breach.*

Assume Robert has breached a guarantee. When Alice sues him for the money she lost on her reservation at the campgrounds, she will:

(A) win, because Robert had reason to know she was going to the mountains.
(B) win, because she could not reasonably have prevented her loss.
(C) lose, because Robert did not know she was going on vacation.
(D) lose, because her person and property were not damaged.

Case 2

Andrew and Barbara are married. It is Andrew's birthday, and a costume party is being held for him. Carl, a plainclothes policeman, knocks on the door to tell Andrew the neighbors are complaining about the noise. Andrew lets him in. At that point, Dan, who is in a bad mood, enters the room. He sees Carl and shoots him in a sudden rage. Carl is killed. Ed takes advantage of the confusion to snatch Fran's purse. Fran screams and Dan, now totally out of control, turns and kills her. Andrew wrests the gun from Dan. Dan, still angry, pushes Andrew's 10-year-old son Gary around. Then he crosses the ballroom toward Gary's twin brother Harry, who is cowering in the corner with the rest of the crowd. When he is in the middle of the room, Andrew, who is an expert shot fires at Dan, barely missing his heart. Andrew calls the police and everyone is taken down to the station house. Meanwhile, Barbara, who had been detained at work, approaches the house with her 15-year-old daughter Ida. In front of the house she sees Jack tossing lit torches into her open window. She tells Jack to stop but he doesn't. Barbara takes out the gun she is licensed to carry and shoots Jack, who dies as a result. Then a malicious neighbor, Ken, tells them that Andrew has been killed. When they see the blood in the house, Ida becomes hysterical, grabs Barbara's gun, and kills herself.

Questions 6 and 7

Second-degree murder can be established in three ways:
1. *intent to kill someone, whether or not the actual victim is the intended one;*
2. *highly reckless behavior evincing a depraved indifference to human life, which creates a grave risk of death and results in someone's death;*
3. *any death arising during the commission of one of the following felonies: another murder, armed robbery, rape, or arson. If someone dies during the transaction, the felon is guilty of second-degree murder.*

Defenses to second-degree murder exist if there is an extreme emotional distress for which there is a reasonable explanation or cause, if the accused allegedly caused or helped a suicide without engaging in duress or deception, or if the accused acted in defense of an attack upon himself.

6. When Dan is prosecuted for second-degree murder regarding Fran's death, he will be:

(A) convicted, because Fran was killed in the course of the commission of a felony.
(B) convicted, because Fran was killed while Dan was in the course of committing a felony.
(C) acquitted, because Dan was not engaged in a felony.
(D) acquitted, because Dan did not intend to kill Fran.

7. When Ken is prosecuted for second-degree murder regarding the death of Ida, he will be:

(A) convicted, because he showed a depraved indifference to human life.
(B) convicted, because he deceived Ida.
(C) acquitted, because he was lying.
(D) acquitted, because he had no way to forsee that anyone would die.

8. *An adult is guilty of first-degree murder if he causes the death of:*

1. a police officer in the course of his duty, and the killer knew or should have known that the victim was such a person, or
2. an employee of a prison in the course of his duty, and the killer knew or should have known that the victim was such a person.

Further, one is guilty of first-degree murder if one kills anyone while one is serving a life sentence in prison.

When Dan is prosecuted for first-degree murder regarding the death of Carl, he will be:

(A) convicted, because Carl was a police officer in the course of fulfilling his duty.
(B) convicted, because there was no reasonable explanation or excuse for Dan's behavior.
(C) acquitted, because Dan could not have been expected to know Carl was a police officer.
(D) acquitted, because Dan was not serving a life sentence.

Questions 9 and 10

Self-defense is a defense to criminal homicide. One may use whatever force is necessary, short of deadly force, to avoid an attack upon one's property or upon a person in one's care. One may use deadly force if necessary to prevent an attack upon one's own person or to prevent an arsonist from destroying one's property. A person is guilty of attempted second-degree murder if he intentionally did all he could to commit the crime, and was prevented from succeeding only by accident or the intervention of others.

9. When Barbara is prosecuted for criminal homicide regarding the death of Jack, she will be:

(A) convicted, because she used deadly force.
(B) convicted, because she did not act in self-defense since she was not in the house.
(C) acquitted, because she was protecting her property.
(D) acquitted, because Jack was trying to burn her home.

10. When Andrew is prosecuted for attempted criminal homicide concerning the shooting of Dan, he will be:

(A) convicted, because he was entitled to use only nondeadly force.
(B) convicted, because he suffered from an extreme mental disturbance.
(C) acquitted, because he acted in self-defense.
(D) acquitted, because he acted under the influence of extreme mental disturbance for which there was a reasonable explanation.

Part B

Directions: This section consists of several groups of cases. Each case ends with a judicial holding and a set of four legal principles. You must select the *narrowest* principle that reasonably explains the judicial decision but is *not inconsistent* with any previous holdings in that group of cases.

For the first case in each group, eliminate any principles that do not conform to the facts of the case and do not provide a reasonable explanation of the holding. Then select the narrowest of the reasonable principles.

In the remaining cases in that group, the basic procedure is the same, but you must also eliminate any principles that contradict earlier answers in the group before you select the narrowest principle.

These questions assume no prior legal knowledge on your part; answer them using only ordinary logical reasoning.

Group 1

11. Bill, a shy young man, married Betty, who was an outgoing woman and something of a flirt. After they had been married several years, Bill heard Betty talking in her sleep, describing several affairs she had had with other men since she and Bill were married. Bill sues for a divorce, claiming Betty is guilty of adultery. Betty denies everything and opposes the suit. *Held,* for Betty.

    The *narrowest principle* that *reasonably explains* this action is:

    (A) A divorce will not be granted because of conduct which the suing spouse should reasonably have anticipated.
    (B) Adultery is not a ground for divorce.
    (C) An uncorroborated charge of adultery is not a ground for divorce.
    (D) A husband may not testify against his wife.

12. George and Sue had been married for several years. George had a habit of coming home late several times each week, when he would tell Sue he had to work late at the office. Sue became suspicious and hired a detective to follow George. The detective observed George take his secretary to her house, where George remained for several hours before going home. The detective found several witnesses to testify that George had remained in her house for several hours that night with the lights out. Sue sues for divorce on adultery grounds. George denies everything and opposes the suit, but presents no explanation. *Held,* for Sue.

    The *narrowest principle* that *reasonably explains* this action, and is *not inconsistent with the ruling given in the first case,* is:

    (A) Proof of adultery constitutes a ground for divorce.
    (B) Evidence of circumstances conducive to little else than adultery presented by an innocent spouse constitutes grounds for divorce.
    (C) Lying to one's spouse is a ground for divorce.
    (D) A person need not remain married if he suspects his spouse of adultery.

13. Jim and Jane have been married for 10 years. Jim had been having an affair with Marge for several months, but they had a fight and Marge told Jane everything, and gave her proof of her story. Jane sues Jim for divorce on adultery grounds. Jim responds with proof that Jane had a brief affair with Henry 4 years ago, which Jane thought Jim had never found out about. *Held,* for Jim.

The *narrowest principle* that *reasonably explains* this action, and is *not inconsistent with the rulings given in the cases already cited,* is:

(A) A divorce will not be granted if the suing spouse is as guilty of the alleged marital offense as the other spouse.
(B) If two spouses are both guilty of the same crime, a divorce will not be granted.
(C) A party who is guilty of a marital offense may not sue for divorce.
(D) Evidence of circumstances conducive to little else than adultery presented by an innocent spouse constitutes grounds for divorce.

14. John and Mary have been married for 5 years. During the last few months, and for no apparent reason, John has often beaten Mary severely and has refused to let her leave the house. Mary sues for a divorce, which John opposes. *Held,* for Mary.

The *narrowest principle* that *reasonably explains* this action, and is *not inconsistent with the rulings given in the cases already cited,* is:

(A) One who has suffered extreme cruelty at the hands of one's spouse will be granted a divorce.
(B) A marriage is to be terminated when evidence shows the parties are incompatible, even if one of the parties opposes the divorce.
(C) An innocent spouse is entitled to a divorce if treated cruelly by the other spouse.
(D) A cruel and inhuman spouse may not oppose a divorce action.

15. Martin and Cathy have been married for many years. Shortly after their marriage, Cathy had had a brief affair with Larry. Martin has just learned of this, when he accidentally discovered an old letter from Larry. However, Martin has been guilty of countless extramarital affairs throughout the period of their marriage, and Cathy has just learned of these, and has acquired proof of them. Cathy sues for divorce on the grounds of adultery, and Martin opposes the suit. *Held,* for Cathy.

The *narrowest principle* that *reasonably explains* this action, and is *not inconsistent with the rulings given in the cases already cited,* is:

(A) When two spouses are guilty of the same marital offense but one is guilty to a greater degree than the other, the less guilty party is entitled to a divorce.
(B) A habitually adulterous spouse may not successfully oppose a divorce action.
(C) One spouse's guilt of a marital offense will not preclude a suit for divorce if the other spouse is also guilty thereof.
(D) Repeated marital offenses are a ground for divorce.

Group 2

16. John died, leaving a wife and three children. His will directed that his estate be divided into four equal parts, one for each child and the fourth to go to the Red Cross. His wife objects to the will, demanding a share in the estate. *Held,* for the wife.

The *narrowest principle* that *reasonably explains* this action is:

(A) A will may not exclude members of the testator's immediate family from sharing in the estate.
(B) A will may not exclude innocent members of the testator's immediate family from sharing in the estate.
(C) A will may not exclude the testator's spouse from sharing in the estate.
(D) A person is entitled to half the estate of a deceased spouse, because the partners in the marriage share their property equally.

17. Elaine died, leaving a will dividing her estate equally between her husband and her older child, Fred. Her younger child, Frank, who was born after the execution of the will, sues for a share in the estate. *Held,* for Frank.

The *narrowest principle* that *reasonably explains* this action, and is *not inconsistent with the ruling given in the first case,* is:

(A) A will may not exclude members of the testator's immediate household from sharing in the estate.
(B) When one child is left a share in an estate, the other children of the testator are also entitled to a share unless the will specifically says otherwise.
(C) When a will does not explain why a child was excluded from sharing in the estate, it is presumed the exclusion was an oversight.
(D) When a child is born after the execution of a will, it is assumed the testator wanted that child to share in the estate, if the testator's children born before execution were included.

18. William died, leaving a will dividing his estate equally between his wife Joan and younger daughter Nancy. His older daughter, Mary, was not mentioned in the will. Mary sues the estate, claiming a share of William's fortune. *Held,* for the estate.

The *narrowest principle* that *reasonably explains* this action, and is *not inconsistent with the rulings given in the cases already cited,* is:

(A) A testator may exclude whomever he wishes from sharing in his will.
(B) A testator's child not referred to in the will may be excluded from sharing in the estate even if another child receives a share.
(C) A testator may never exclude his child from his will.
(D) When a child born before the execution of a will is excluded from sharing in the estate although another child does receive a share, the omission is valid.

19. Peter was a millionaire whose wife had been dead for many years. He executed a will leaving his entire fortune to his son Jim. Later Jim murdered Peter and sued the estate for Peter's fortune. *Held,* for the estate.

The *narrowest principle* that *reasonably explains* this action, and is *not inconsistent with the rulings given in the cases already cited,* is:

(A) A murderer may not inherit from his victim.
(B) A child may be excluded from sharing in an estate if he is a criminal.
(C) When a wrongdoing child is excluded from sharing an estate, it is assumed the omission was intentional.
(D) The murder of a testator by someone left a share of the estate in the will voids the will.

20. George, a rich man, had three sons–Arthur, Bertram, and Charles–born in 1950, 1952, and 1955, respectively. In 1953 he executed a will leaving ten thousand dollars each to Arthur and Bertram. In 1975 he gave Charles a surprise gift of ten thousand dollars, although neither Arthur nor Bertram had ever received such a gift. When George died, Charles sued for a share in the estate. *Held,* for the estate.

The *narrowest principle* that *reasonably explains* this action, and is *not inconsistent with the rulings given in the cases already cited,* is:

(A) When a child is born after the execution of a will, it is presumed that the testator intended to exclude him from sharing in the estate if there was ample time to execute another will.

(B) When a child of a testator is given a large gift, without further explanation, it is presumed that the testator does not intend for that child to share in the estate.

(C) Without explanation to the contrary, a large gift to one who would otherwise inherit part of the estate is taken to constitute an advance payment of all or part of that person's share in the estate.

(D) A person may preclude anyone from inheriting part of his estate by making him a substantial gift during his lifetime.

Part C

Directions: Each principle in this part is followed by several short cases. The principles may or may not be real. You are to accept them as valid. Each of the cases is followed by a question with four possible answers, each a potential factor in the application of the principle to the case. In each question, you are to select the choice which is the major factor. Answer based on what is stated or implied in the case and principle. Each of these questions is independent of all of the others.

These questions assume no prior legal knowledge on your part; answer them using only ordinary logical reasoning.

Principle 1

The federal police have only a limited right to search private residences. For federal police to make a legal search of a private residence, and to seize evidence of crime found therein, they must have either a valid warrant issued by a magistrate, or probable cause to believe either that a crime is being committed within the residence or that evidence of a crime located within the residence may be destroyed or removed if it is not seized immediately. A valid warrant is one issued upon a showing of probable cause to believe that evidence of a crime exists within the residence, and which describes the precise area to be searched and the exact things to be seized.

Statements made by any residents of the premises during an illegal search are inadmissible in court, and anyone legitimately on the premises may object to the admission of illegally seized evidence. If in the course of a legal search, police find evidence of another crime in plain view, it is admissible in court.

21. John is a dealer in heroin. James, one of his customers, was arrested during an illegal search of his neighbor William's house, where a large supply of heroin was discovered. James made a full confession of his heroin dealings, implicating John. On this evidence the state police obtained a warrant to search John's bedroom for heroin. The search disclosed a large supply of heroin, and John was arrested. At the trial, he objected to the admission of the heroin into evidence. *Held,* for the prosecution.

    Which of the following statements was the major factor in the disposition of this case?

    (A) James was not a resident of William's house.
    (B) The warrant described the precise area to be searched and the exact things to be seized.
    (C) The search was conducted by state police.
    (D) James' confession constituted probable cause to believe John's house contained evidence of a crime.

22. Federal agents learned through a legitimate wiretap that Linda had stolen some jewelry and was keeping it in her apartment. They broke into the apartment and discovered the jewelry hidden in the closet. At trial, Linda moves to suppress the evidence. *Held,* for Linda.

Which of the following statements was the major factor in the disposition of this case?

(A) The police did not have a search warrant.
(B) The jewelry was not in plain view.
(C) There was no probable cause to believe a crime was being committed in Linda's apartment.
(D) There was no probable cause to believe evidence of a crime, located in Linda's apartment, would be destroyed or removed if not seized immediately.

23. George gave a party for his friend Max. George, who had a large amount of marijuana in his possession, was sharing it with his guests, although Max and Jim did not smoke any. A neighbor called the police to complain of the noise from the party. When the federal police arrived they could hear no noise, but knocked on George's door anyway, to inform him of his neighbor's complaint. No one answered the door, so the police opened it and entered the house to see what was going on. Upon entering the house they smelled the marijuana and arrested Max, thinking he was the host. Max said, "It isn't my dope, it's George's." At the trial, George objected to the admission of the evidence obtained by the police. *Held,* for George.

Which of the following statements was the major factor in the disposition of this case?

(A) George was a resident of the house.
(B) Max was not a resident of the house.
(C) There was no evidence of any crime when the police entered the house.
(D) George's house was a private residence.

24. Jerome was overheard saying he had a collection of stolen paintings in his apartment. Upon this information federal agents obtained a warrant to search Jerome's apartment for stolen paintings. During the search they discovered that Jerome only had cheap reproductions of some famous paintings which had recently been stolen. However, the police smelled burning hashish in Jerome's bedroom. They searched the room and found a bag of hashish under Jerome's bed. Jerome was arrested. At trial, Jerome moved to exclude the evidence. *Held,* for the prosecution.

Which of the following was the major factor in the disposition of this case?

(A) The smell of hashish was "in plain view."
(B) There was probable cause to believe evidence of a crime would be destroyed if not seized immediately.
(C) The police had a valid search warrant.
(D) There was probable cause to believe a crime was being committed.

25. The federal police have obtained a valid search warrant to search Dr. Curry's entire house for a rifle they believe he used to murder six people. The doctor is not home, but the police ask his wife if she knows where the rifle is. She tells them that it might be in the laundry room, so they go to the laundry room and find 10 pounds of heroin in plain view on the floor. At trial, the court rules that the heroin can be admitted in evidence.

Which of the following statements was the major factor in the court's decision?

(A) Mrs. Curry was a resident of the house.
(B) The original search warrant was based on probable cause.
(C) Mrs. Curry's statement is not offered as evidence.
(D) The heroin was found in the course of a legal search.

Principle 2

A marriage is created when an unmarried man and an unmarried woman of sufficient age, and with a license, participate in a marital ceremony officiated by a clergyman or a justice of the peace. A marriage may be annulled if it is considered voidable. A voidable marriage is one which either had an irregularity in its formal requirements (such as age of the parties, lack of a license, or an unqualified officiant) or which was entered into because of duress, fraud, or insanity. A voidable marriage is valid until it is annulled. A marriage is void if it involves parties who may not marry because of their relationship with each other or with other people (e.g., bigamy, incest). A void marriage, also known as a null marriage, is considered never to have existed. A marriage is declared void by a decree of nullity. However, the marriage is void even without such a decree. A valid marriage may be terminated by divorce. A divorce may be obtained immediately either by showing that the relationship of the parties has suffered an irretrievable breakdown, or by filing a petition for divorce after the parties have been living separately for a period of 2 years.

A common-law marriage is created in one of two ways. The parties may affirm in the present tense that they are husband and wife and then cohabit and hold themselves out as married, or they may agree to become husband and wife in the future and then begin cohabitation. A common-law marriage is subject to the same restrictions as any other marriage regarding who may marry, and may be dissolved or declared a nullity by the same procedures.

26. Arthur participated in a marital ceremony with Betty, who was at that time married to Calvin. When Arthur found out that Betty was already married, he left her. Several years later, Arthur fell in love with Dora and a marital ceremony was performed. When their relationship did not work out, Dora sought to have the marriage declared a nullity. Her petition was denied.

    Which of the following statements was the major factor in the disposition of this case?

    (A) The relationship between Arthur and Dora did not suffer an irretrievable breakdown.
    (B) They were not married because Arthur was already married to Betty.
    (C) The marriage between Arthur and Betty was a nullity.
    (D) Dora was not a party to Betty's bigamy.

27. Mr. and Mrs. Thane had been fighting for years. Finally things got so bad they could not look at each other without coming to blows. Mr. Thane moved out of the house. A year later he proposed to Brandy, and they promised to marry each other as soon as they could. They immediately began cohabiting without discussing their relationship with anyone. Mr. Thane then filed for divorce. Immediately upon filing his petition, Mr. Thane went to the welfare office to apply for benefits to

which all married men in his circumstances who live with their wives are entitled. The welfare department denied him the benefits.

Which of the following was the major factor in the disposition of this case?

(A) Mr. Thane was not capable of entering into a common-law marriage before he filed for divorce.
(B) Mr. Thane was still married to Mrs. Thane because they had not been separated for 2 years.
(C) Mr. Thane and Brandy did not hold themselves out as husband and wife.
(D) Cohabitation is immoral.

28. Arlene was invited to attend a meeting of an exotic religious sect. When her hosts noticed how intrigued she was by the rituals performed, they invited her to participate in a "tea ceremony." During the ceremony she was told to repeat certain phrases in a foreign language. After the ceremony, she was told that she had been married to the man sitting next to her by the high priest of the cult. No license is required in her state. Arlene brings an annulment action, which is granted.

Which of the following statements was the major factor in the disposition of this case?

(A) The high priest was not qualified to marry the parties.
(B) Arlene was deceived as to the nature of the ceremony.
(C) Cohabitation did not occur.
(D) Arlene was not a member of this religion.

29. Dee and Dum were only 16 years old. They participated in a marital ceremony, although parties in their state must be 18 years old to marry. Many years later, Dum ran off with another woman, and Dee never saw him again. After 3 years, Dee sought to have their marriage annulled. Her request was granted.

Which of the following statements was the major factor in the disposition of this case?

(A) The relationship had suffered an irretrievable breakdown.
(B) The parties had been separated for more than 2 years.
(C) The parties were too young at the time of their marriage.
(D) The parties could not marry because of their relationship with each other.

30. In 1965, Abe and Karen swear they are husband and wife, and live together until 1970, telling everyone they know they are married. However, Abe did not tell Karen that before they met he was married to Cindy. This marriage, which took place in 1960, occurred when Abe was 14 years old. The marriage broke up in 1963, and Abe met Karen in 1964. In 1966, Cindy had the marriage annulled. She then participated in a marital ceremony with Donald, but they had no license and the minister who officiated at the ceremony had been defrocked the month before. In 1970, Abe told Karen of his past. Infuriated, Karen left Abe and ran off with Donald, who had left Cindy in 1969. Karen and Donald marry, but the marriage is later declared a nullity.

Which of the following statements was the major factor in the disposition of this case?

(A) Abe and Karen had a valid common-law marriage which could only be ended by divorce.
(B) Abe and Karen had a voidable common-law marriage.
(C) The marriage between Cindy and Donald was voidable.
(D) No decree of nullity had been granted.

STOP

IF YOU FINISH BEFORE THE TIME IS UP,
CHECK YOUR WORK ON THIS SECTION ONLY.
DO NOT LOOK AT ANY OTHER SECTION IN THE TEST.
WHEN THE TIME IS UP, GO ON TO THE NEXT SECTION.

Section V: Error Recognition

Time: 20 minutes
35 questions

Directions: This section consists of individual sentences. Some of the sentences are correct, but some are incorrect in standard written English for one of the following reasons.

Poor Diction: Usage that is incorrect either because a word's meaning is inappropriate in the sentence or because the word is not acceptable in standard written English.
Examples: I am waiting for the medicine to take *affect.*
The new symphony is *out of sight.*

Verbosity: Repetitious elements which do not add meaning to the sentence, and which are not justified for special emphasis.
Examples: All of the judges were in *agreement* and there was no *dissent.*
With *great speed,* he *quickly* ran home.

Faulty Grammar: Grammatical or structural word forms and expressions that are improper in standard written English, such as errors in case, number or parallelism.
Examples: Each of the boys must bring *their* own baseball equipment.
My sister is studying reading, writing and *how to do arithmetic.*

Be sure to use these definitions of the errors, rather than your own ideas. No sentence contains more than one type of error. Select choice

(A) if the sentence contains a *diction* error.
(B) if the sentence contains a *verbosity* error.
(C) if the sentence contains a *grammar* error.
(D) if the sentence contains *no* error.

1. After a while I was able, although not very consistently, to distinguish the correct answers from the dubious ones.

2. I cannot even think of instituting the new procedure if you will not ascent to its implementation.

3. The best-known professor at the college is Dr. Rawkins, who's novel recently reached first place in the best-sellers list.

4. Since we had arrived late, and it was 6 miles further to town, we decided to spend the night in the country inn.

5. We must endeavor to combine our resources together if we wish to be successful.

6. He knew that there was no danger of the fluid causing a fire, since it was inflammable.

7. Anne invited Andy and myself to the concert at Philharmonic Hall, but I was unable to attend.

8. He made a list of all the writers who he thought were important in that century.

9. Although I took lessons for years and he's completely self-taught, John dances better than me.

10. Anyone of the students whom you suggested can complete the assignment successfully.

11. If you want to finish before Tom does, you will have to be plenty fast.

12. A large amount of impressive medical journals lined the walls of his luxurious office.

13. When it began to grow dark, we lit the lanterns.

14. We were told to arrive at the meeting place early, that we should remove our coats, find seats, and await further instructions.

15. The job of typing the orders and dispatching them to the proper departments is one of her most unpleasant jobs.

16. Everyone but John and me failed the examination.

17. The length of the road is about 14 miles long.

18. Although she didn't really believe that she was ill, she faithfully swallowed the pills which the doctor had proscribed for her.

19. After all, those men are human beings, like you and I.

20. Like many singers, the songs of Jagger are criticized by the press.

21. I am afraid that, in spite of your justifications, I must heartily censor your actions.

22. As he defended the goal flawlessly, the omnipresent goalie seemed to be everywhere, blocking all of our shots.

23. We arrived early in the morning at the cite of the excavation, but the study group had already departed.

24. I got up so the lady could have my seat.

25. The students, remembering their workshop in consumer frauds, were concerned about being ripped off.

26. There is a prize for whoever gets there first.

27. After studying the subject carefully, the problem is still as mystifying as ever.

28. The committee has already held their first meeting of the year.

29. The treasurer as well as the president were held responsible for the management of the company.

30. The counsel are arguing among themselves about the trade issue currently before them.

31. His hair was red in color, so it was very hard to avoid noticing him as he entered the room.

32. If I was in your position, I would accept his offer.

33. Stop aggravating me with your foolish questions!

34. The same is no doubt true of what European and Asiatic nations have heard about we Americans.

35. One should be cautious if you wish to avoid offending your friends.

STOP

IF YOU FINISH BEFORE THE TIME IS UP,
CHECK YOUR WORK ON THIS SECTION ONLY.
DO NOT LOOK AT ANY OTHER SECTION IN THE TEST.
WHEN THE TIME IS UP, GO ON TO THE NEXT SECTION.

Section VI: Sentence Correction

Time: 20 minutes

25 questions

Directions: Each sentence in this section is either partially or totally underlined. For each sentence, you are given five possible phrasings of the underlined part. Choice (A) is always the same as the original, but choices (B) through (E) all offer alternative versions of the underlined part. You are to choose the best phrasing.

Sometimes the original sentence is most effective; sometimes another phrasing will be preferable in standard written English. In selecting your answer, consider grammar, diction, sentence construction, and punctuation. The best choice should be clear and exact, not awkward or ambiguous. Do not change the meaning of the original sentence.

1. Are oranges in Italy somewhat like California?

   (A) somewhat like California?
   (B) somewhat similar to California?
   (C) somewhat like those in California?
   (D) something like California?
   (E) somewhat similar to California's?

2. When we were young, our nurse would tell Mary and me scary stories.

   (A) Mary and me
   (B) Mary and I
   (C) me and Mary
   (D) I and Mary
   (E) Mary together with me

3. Let's you and me go to the scene of the accident at once.

   (A) Let's you and me
   (B) Let's both of us
   (C) Let you and me
   (D) Let us both
   (E) Let's you and I

4. Being that you know more about films than I do, I suggest that you give your opinion first.

   (A) Being that
   (B) Since
   (C) On account of
   (D) In view of
   (E) In that

5. However much we tried the solution to the puzzle eluded us.

   (A) However much we tried the solution to the puzzle
   (B) However, much that we tried the solution to the puzzle
   (C) However much we tried, the solution to the puzzle
   (D) However much we tried the solution, the answer
   (E) However we tried the solution, the answer

6. With six exams this week, I neither have time nor energy to help you move.

(A) neither have time nor
(B) have neither time nor the
(C) have neither the time nor the
(D) neither have the time nor
(E) neither have time or

7. When the principal told him about Mary's success, Professor Williams was as happy if not happier than, his student.

(A) about Mary's success, Professor Williams was as happy if not happier than, his student.
(B) about Mary's success, Professor Williams was as happy as, if not happier than, his student.
(C) about Mary's success, Professor Williams was as happy, if not happier, as his student.
(D) about Mary's success, Professor Williams was as happy if not happier than his student.
(E) of Mary's success, Professor Williams was as happy as, if not happier than his student.

8. Only she could have completed the task so well.

(A) Only she
(B) Only her
(C) None other than her
(D) No one else
(E) None but she

9. There has been as far as I can remember, no 2 minutes in my life as a sailor which were identical.

(A) There has been as far as I can remember,
(B) There have been, as far as I can remember,
(C) There have never been, as far as I can remember,
(D) There has never been, as far as I can remember
(E) There has been, as far as I can remember

10. The lieutenant told me when I arrived to report to you immediately.

(A) when I arrived to report to you immediately.
(B) I was to report to you immediately upon my arrival.
(C) no sooner was I to arrive that I should report to you.
(D) "When I arrived, I was to report to you immediately."
(E) to report to you as soon as I arrived.

11. To carry out this project is really to subject ourselves to intense criticism.

(A) To carry out this project is really to subject ourselves to intense criticism.
(B) To carry out this project is really subjecting ourselves to intense criticism.
(C) Carrying out this project is really to subject ourselves to intense criticism.
(D) Carrying out this project is really going to subject us to intense criticism.
(E) Carrying out this project is really going to subject ourselves to intense criticism.

12. Not only Rocco, but his brother as well, have volunteered to join us in this most unique experiment.

(A) have volunteered to join us in this most unique experiment.
(B) has volunteered to join us in this most unique experiment.
(C) has volunteered to join us in this unique experiment.
(D) has volunteered to join us in this very unique experiment.
(E) have volunteered to join us in this unique experiment.

13. He was angry on her for talking too much.

(A) He was angry on her for talking too much.
(B) He was angry on her at talking too much.
(C) He was angry with her for talking too much.
(D) He was angry with her at talking too much.
(E) He was angry with her talking too much.

14. Although his knowledge of building and construction techniques is exceptional, he never built himself.

(A) Although his knowledge of building and construction techniques is exceptional, he never built himself.
(B) Although his knowledge of building and construction techniques are exceptional, he never built anything himself.
(C) Although he is very knowledgeable of building and construction techniques, he himself has never been a construction worker.
(D) An expert on building and construction, he himself has never engaged in building.
(E) Although his knowledge of building and construction techniques is exceptional, he, himself, has never built anything.

15. Is he one of those scientists who has been using humans in their experiments?

(A) who has been using humans in their experiments?
(B) who has been using human beings in their experiments?
(C) who has been using humans in his experiments?
(D) who have been using human beings in their experiments?
(E) who have been using humans in his experiments?

16. Eating starchy food, working long hours, and without recreation was the reason that workers in the nineteenth-century factories were very inefficient.

(A) hours, and without recreation was the reason that
(B) hours and without recreation were the reasons that
(C) hours and without recreation were the reasons why
(D) hours, and missing recreation was the reason that
(E) hours, and missing recreation were the reasons why

17. After being told he had ruined the magazine's prestige, the reporter burst out of the room.

(A) After being told he had ruined the magazine's prestige,
(B) Upon the magazine telling him he had ruined it's prestige,
(C) After the magazine's accusations,

(D) Since he was told he had ruined the magazine's prestige,
(E) Once he heard the magazine's charges,

18. The books here are as bad as any other firm, except they are costlier.

(A) The books here are as bad as any other firm, except they are costlier.
(B) The books here are as bad as those published by any other firm, but they are more expensive.
(C) The books here are as bad as any other firm's—except their cost is more.
(D) The books here as as bad as any others, except as regards to cost.
(E) The books here are as bad as others', except that they are costlier.

19. I am not certain in respect to which movies to see.

(A) in respect to which movies
(B) on which movies
(C) which movies
(D) as to the choice of which movies
(E) for which movies I am

20. In spite of his asking for your help, you decided to watch television.

(A) In spite of his asking for your help, you decided to watch television.
(B) In spite of his being asked by you to help him, you decided to watch television.
(C) In spite of him asking you to help him, you decided to watch television.
(D) Disregarding his pleas for help, your decision was to watch television.
(E) Even though he asked you to help him, you decided to watch television.

21. The pages were proofread, and the manuscript was sent back to the printer's.

(A) The pages were proofread, and the manuscript was sent back
(B) The pages and the manuscript were proofread and sent back
(C) The pages and the manuscript was proofread and sent back
(D) The pages proofread and the manuscript sent back
(E) The pages and the manuscript were respectively proofread and sent back

22. As it was raining, the woman took her bicycle to be repaired with her car.

(A) the woman took her bicycle to be repaired with her car.
(B) the woman took her bicycle to be repaired, in her car.
(C) the woman took her car when she went to have her bicycle repaired.
(D) the woman who took her bicycle to be repaired was driving her car.
(E) the woman took her bicycle, by car, to be repaired.

23. In the Exam Center, the girl was deep in thought with a sheer blouse.

(A) In the Exam Center, the girl was deep in thought with a sheer blouse.
(B) The girl in the Exam Center was deep in thought with a sheer blouse.
(C) The girl was deep in thought in the Exam Center with a sheer blouse.
(D) With a sheer blouse in the Exam Center, the girl was deep in thought.
(E) The girl with a sheer blouse was deep in thought in the Exam Center.

24. I told him that either I would drop by today or tomorrow morning to discuss the problem.

(A) that either I would drop by today or tomorrow morning
(B) that I would drop by either today or tomorrow morning
(C) either that I would drop by today or if not by tomorrow morning
(D) that I would either drop by today or tomorrow morning
(E) that I would drop by today and if not, tomorrow morning

25. The reason I did poor work in French was because I didn't like the subject.

(A) The reason I did poor work in French was because
(B) The reason I did poorly in French was because
(C) I did poor work in French because
(D) The reason why I did poor work in French was because
(E) The reason for poorly working in French was that

STOP

IF YOU FINISH BEFORE THE TIME IS UP,
CHECK YOUR WORK ON THIS SECTION ONLY.
DO NOT LOOK AT ANY OTHER SECTION IN THE TEST.
WHEN THE TIME IS UP, CHECK YOUR ANSWERS FOR THE WHOLE TEST
AGAINST THE ANSWER KEY AND EXPLANATIONS BEGINNING ON THE FOLLOWING PAGE.

Answers to Final Self-Test A

Section I Answers

Mummers

1. (C) The answer can be found in the third paragraph of the passage. While Green would have agreed with *I* and *II* as well, "the present writer . . . took issue on this point."

2. (E) A detail from line 5. The book referred to is by Green.

3. (C) Another detail, to be found at line 29.

4. (C) The illustrations show clothing from 1803–1810 (the period of the Smith–Lyons partnership). The Nicholson book was published in 1890.

5. (A) Chambers and Tiddy had very limited materials (line 4). The Cork reference, which may be a person or the county, was in either case too early (line 3). Green wrote in 1946 (line 6), but Helm's "recent" analysis (line 8) is probably more recent still.

6. (A) Choices (B) and (D) [and therefore (E)] are absolutely wrong. Choice (C) is too narrow.

Comets

7. (B) The others are all too narrow.

8. (C) The comet depends on the sun for illumination—"The sun floodlights the dust . . ." (line 17).

9. (C) A detail question—at line 21, "*First* the ultraviolet radiation. . . ."

10. (E) A somewhat technical detail, which you can find at lines 56–58.

11. (D) The solar wind, line 53, has a temperature of a million degrees. That sounds hot enough to be called extreme. (C) is not quite right; the ions are moved by magnetic fields, not solar winds.

12. (D) A detail from the sixth paragraph—lines 44–48. Note, positive ions only.

Cognitive Dissonance

13. (B) The key factors are a decision and a related belief. Note the first paragraph.

14. (D) A detail of sorts—see lines 13–16.

15. (D) This is Jung's theory of self-actualization—lines 40 to 41. The theory has nothing to do with aggression and advocates neither complete lack of supervision nor any kind of coercion.

16. (A) It is the basis of his theory of cognitive dissonance reduction (as well as the hobgoblin of little minds).

17. (C) It is too detailed to come from (A) or (B), and too technical to come from (D) or (E). It also refers to "earlier illustrations of human motivation," at line 31.

18. (B) Choices (A), (C), and (D) are too narrow; (E) is too broad.

Puritans

19. (C) A detail at line 8; " 'Calvinist' dissenters, Presbyterian or Puritan. . . ." We can't choose (D), since we are not told in this discussion what was the fate of his ideas.

20. (C) Luther's whole point was that nobody could impose laws (line 22): "Neither Pope nor Bishop. . . ."

21. (A) Calvin believed strongly in predestination—line 39.

22. (E) A detail. See line 46.

23. (B) The average Puritan might fit the description in (A), but note line 56: "Most of the Puritans would have voted to put him in the stocks." We can therefore conclude that he was different from the rest of the Puritans.

24. (E) See lines 59–70. All of these choices are false.

25. (A) See, for example, lines 59–61: "[They] were lovers of life . . . in whom the Renaissance lamp of humanism still burned."

Section II Answers

Nut Graph

1. (B) 20% $\left(\text{or } \frac{1}{5}\right)$ of 360° = 72°

2. (C) Canadians ate 72,000,000 pounds of almonds (24% of 300,000,000 pounds). If the Canadians numbered 20,000,000, each ate 3.6 pounds of almonds on the average.

3. (C) A good shortcut would be to note that Mexico consumes many more nuts than Canada; whatever is eaten most in Mexico is a likely candidate. Then you must remember to deal with each country separately. For example:

Peanuts 22% of 500,000 lbs.	= 110,000,000 lbs.
+ 13% of 300,000,000 lbs. =	39,000,000 lbs.
total	149,000,000 lbs.

4. (A) This question is similar to question 3. Again, what happens in Mexico is most significant.

5. (D) Filberts = 16% of 500,000,000 lbs. = 80,000,000 lbs.

6. (C) Choice *I* would be true only if the total amount of nuts consumed in each country were the same. Choice *II* is also wrong, since 9% of 500,000,000 is more than 13% of 300,000,000. Choice *III* is correct.

7. (D) Mexico eats 90,000,000 pounds of macadamia nuts (18% of 500,000,000). We need an answer that is the equivalent of 90,000,000 pounds–either 18% of Mexico or 30% of Canada.

Temperature Graph

8. (C) The temperature in Melbourne rose 30% during that period.

9. (E) New York was 40°, Melbourne 70°. The average was 55°.

10. (D) New York dropped 30° and Melbourne 10° for a total of 40°.

11. (B) New York reached a high of 90° and Melbourne a low of 40°.

12. (A) Choice *I* is true. The months are January, February, March, April, November, and December. For May and October, they were equal. Choice *II*, then, can't be correct (only four months are left). Finally, you should be able to tell visually that the average for May to October is higher than 60° (if not, you can work it out).

13. (A) In March and June, the two cities are 30° apart.

14. (C) The average in April was $57\frac{1}{2}^{\circ}$; in June, 65°.

Energy Graph

15. (C) Of the 26.8 units used in industry, 6.7 units were rejected. That means 20.1 were used.

16. (B) Of the 30.9 units used in electric energy generation, 3.9 came from natural gas. We can estimate as follows: $\frac{4}{30}$ = approximately 13%.

17. (D) The residential and commercial box indicates the total number of units used; you can read this directly from the graph.

18. (A) A total of 6.7 units are rejected. If they all came from the 11.8 units of natural gas, then the minimum amount of natural gas used would be 5.1 units.

19. (D) Of a total of 29.1 units of natural gas, 11.8 went to industry. (Note that 3.9 units of natural gas are imported and must be added to the original 25.2 units.) This total works out to about 40%.

20. (E) We can't tell here. We know that 20.7 units out of 30.9 are wasted, but we do not know whether or not that ratio applies exactly to coal. For all we know, all or none of the coal might be lost in conversion.

21. (A) Of the total of 23.4 units of coal, 2.9 units were exported. That's about 12%.

Olympic Graph

22. (B) The year was 1904 (eleven nations).

23. (C) The period from 1904 to 1924.

24. (E) Females made up 13.8% in 1968 and only 13.2% in 1964. No other year is close.

25. (C) The ratio in 1928 was 290:2,725, or a little more than 1:10. It should be about 2:10 in 1972. About $\frac{1}{5}$ of the athletes, then, are female. One-fifth of 8,500 is 1,700. If you calculate exactly, you will find that the answer is actually closer to 1,600, but our estimation was much faster, and no other answer came close enough to cause problems.

26. (E) A separate listing was noted in the year 1956, but we have no way to tell (from the graph) how many other years had equestrian events.

27. (A) The city was Paris in 1900 (1,066 athletes) and 1924 (3,092 athletes).

$$\text{Percent increase} = \frac{\text{difference}}{\text{original}} = \frac{2{,}026}{1{,}066} = 190\%$$

28. (C) Just count them (and don't count 1956, when six women's sport events were held—five in Melbourne and one in Stockholm).

Section III Answers

Passage 1: Lasers

1. (B) Line 6.

2. (E) (A) is true (line 10).
(B) is true (line 18).
(C) is true (line 29).
(D) is true (line 9).

3. (E) Line 6.

4. (B) Line 32.

5. (A) Line 39.

6. (D) Lines 39–43.

7. (C) Line 50.

8. (C) Line 64.

9. (A) Line 44.

10. (B) Line 1.

Passage 2: Jie and Turkana

11. (B) Lines 5–9. (The Jie require the rearing of at least two children.)

12. (A) Lines 25–26.

13. (D) Line 26.

14. (C) Line 34.

15. (B) Line 33.

16. (D) Line 37.

17. (D) Probably a social anthropologist, to be precise.

18. (E) The passage is an objective report of facts. The author expresses no opinion at all.

19. (D) Line 42.

20. (B) Line 52.

Passage 3: Architecture

21. (B) Line 17. (Mere building is not architecture.)

22. (C) The others are listed at lines 18–19.

23. (A) Lines 27–28.

24. (C) Line 30.

25. (C) Line 37.

26. (A) Lines 46–47. The Tigris is a river (line 43).

27. (B) Line 57.

28. (E) The ziggurat is mentioned at line 50, in the middle of the paragraph about Mesopotamia.

29. (E) The others are all too narrow.

30. (A) Line 44.

Section IV Answers

Part A

1. (A) As unjust as it may seem, the principle is quite clear on this point. Choice (B) simply restates the question.

2. (D) This alternative fits right into the "however" at the end of the principle. Robert said that he *believed* that the model was unbeatable, and so on. Presumably, the car that Alice bought was no worse than the sample. No express guarantee was given.

3. (B) Choice (A) is also true, but the fact that Robert is a dealer merely activates the guarantee. The reason that Alice can recover is that the guarantee was broken, and that is expressed by Choice (B).

4. (A) Alice told Robert why she wanted the car. What Robert said is irrelevant; he *knew* of her particular reason for wanting the car, and that is enough.

5. (C) The loss of her deposit is too remote. Robert could not have foreseen this, and in order for a loss to be covered, the seller had to have "reason to know."

6. (C) The issue is whether Dan was committing one of the enumerated felonies, and he was not.

7. (D) No intent or even recklessness existed with regard to the death. Despite the fact that Ken did not behave nicely, he cannot be found guilty under this principle. Note that the defense of aiding a suicide does not apply at all in this case.

8. (C) The only relevant part of the principle is Point 1, and the only issue is whether Dan knew or should have known that Carl was a policeman.

9. (D) The use of deadly force is allowed, if necessary, to stop an arsonist.

10. (D) By the time he shot Dan, Andrew was quite upset. The defense would seem to apply.

Part B

11. (C) (C) is the best choice. (B) goes against the holding, (A) is unreasonable, and (D) is far too broad.

12. (B) Choices (A) and (C) are off the facts of the case, and Choice (D) contradicts the preceding decision.

13. (A) No crime is involved, (C) is unreasonable, and the evidence in this case is more than circumstantial.

14. (C) Choice (A) is too broad and also contradicts the answer to question 13. Choice (B) is not as narrow as Choice (C).

15. (A) This choice does not contradict the answer to question 13, which specifies that the two spouses must be equally guilty.

16. (C) Only (C) and (D) mention the word spouse, and (D) seems less reasonable.

17. (D) This choice is the only answer that mentions the crucial factor—the fact that the child was born after the will was drawn.

18. (D) Choice (A) contradicts the answer to question 16, and Choice (B) contradicts the answer to question 17.

19. (A) The murder is clearly the most significant factor, and Choice (A) handles it much more reasonably than Choice (D).

20. (C) Choice (A) contradicts the answer to question 17. Choices (B) and (D) are not particularly reasonable.

Part C

21. (C) This principle limits only the activities of the federal police. Read carefully.

22. (A) Choices (C) and (D) together are reasons why the police needed a search warrant. The fact that they did not have one is the key factor in the decision.

23. (C) While (D) is true, (C) is more crucial. The police simply had no reason to conduct a search.

24. (B) The warrant allowed the police to search only for stolen paintings, but if they did not seize the hashish immediately, it would certainly be destroyed. They were in the apartment legally because of the warrant.

25. (D) As long as the heroin was in plain view (as the case specifies), it is admissible if the search was legal. Mrs. Curry's statement is irrelevant.

26. (C) Since Arthur and Betty were never really married, Arthur was actually single when he married Dora.

27. (A) By applying for the benefits in question, Mr. Thane and Brandy were essentially holding themselves out as married. The key problem is that they can't actually be married until after Mr. Thane's divorce becomes final.

28. (B) She entered into the marriage only because of a fraud—the principle covers this clearly.

29. (C) The fact that both were under age is one of the possible reasons for voiding a marriage. Note that a 2-year separation is grounds for divorce, not annulment.

30. (A) Since Abe's marriage to Cindy had been annulled, he was able to marry Karen. This marriage fits all of the requirements of a common-law marriage.

Section V Answers

1. (D) This sentence is fine.

2. (A) *Ascent* means "upward movement." The implementation will have to be *assented* (agreed) to.

3. (C) "Whose" is the possessive, not *who's* (who is).

4. (A) It was 6 miles *farther* to town (not *further*). *Farther* refers to distance, *further* to any other continuation.

5. (B) "Combine . . . together" is redundant.

6. (A) "Inflammable" means the same thing as flammable. "Not flammable" would be correct in this instance.

7. (C) Drop "Andy and." Then "Anne invited . . . *me* to the concert."

8. (D) "Who" is correct. We need a subject. (If you reorganize the sentence you get: "He thought *they* were important").

9. (C) John dances better than *I* do. Once again, a slight change in the structure of the sentence makes it easier to tell which choice is correct.

10. (A) "Any one" is two words. "Whom" is perfectly correct.

11. (A) This use of "plenty" is not acceptable in standard written English. "Very fast" would be correct.

12. (A) Journals can be counted individually, so there are a large *number* of them.

13. (D) Nothing wrong with this sentence.

14. (C) A parallelism problem exists. For parallel structure, we should have "to arrive," "to remove," "to find," and "to await."

15. (B) The repetition of "jobs" is verbose.

16. (D) "John and me" is the object of the preposition "but."

17. (B) "Lengths" and "long" are repetitious.

18. (A) To *proscribe* is to prohibit. The doctor *prescribed* the pills.

19. (C) "Like" is a preposition, and takes an object. Substituting, we get "like us" or "like you and me."

20. (C) Something is dangling, which makes this a grammar error–it sounds as if we are comparing singers to songs. It should read: "Like *those of* many singers."

21. (A) To *censor* means to monitor or repress. We want to *censure,* or condemn the actions.

22. (B) The fact that the goalie was "omnipresent" means that he was everywhere, and the perfection of his play seems to be mentioned too often for ordinary emphasis.

23. (A) Wrong word. *To cite* is a verb meaning "to allude to." A location is a *site.*

24. (D) This sentence is correct as it stands. "So that" would also be correct.

25. (A) "Ripped off" is a colloquial expression, not appropriate in standard written English.

26. (D) *Whoever* is the subject of the clause "whoever gets there first." If you substitute, you get "he gets there first."

27. (C) Something is dangling. The sentence reads as though the problem studied the subject carefully.

28. (C) The committee can be considered either singular or plural, but we must be consistent. Either "the committee has . . . held its . . ." or "the committee have held their. . . ," but not a mixture.

29. (C) "The treasurer . . . *was*. . . ." The singular verb is needed again.

30. (A) The noun *counsel,* meaning "advice," is totally out of place. Either the *counsellors* or the *council* may be arguing among themselves.

31. (B) "In color" is superfluous.

32. (C) We need the subjunctive tense—"If I *were* in your position. . . ."

33. (A) "To aggravate," which means "to make worse," is improper in this usage. "Annoying" would be better.

34. (C) They have heard it about *us,* not *we.*

35. (C) Lack of agreement between "one" and "you."

Section VI Answers

1. (C) For the sentence to be correct, a pronoun must replace "oranges" in the second part of the sentence. Also, the two parts should be in parallel structure, which is why (C) is better than (E).

2. (A) Mary should be placed before the pronoun, and the correct pronoun is *me,* not *I,* for it is a direct object, not a subject. Substituting, you would get ". . . would tell *us*. . . ."

3. (D) Although (A), (B), and (E) are often used idiomatically, they are grammatically incorrect. (C) makes no sense; the only correct structure is (D).

4. (B) (A) is an idiomatic sentence, used colloquially, but incorrect. The other selections make no sense, and are incorrect as given; the correct answer is (B).

5. (C) (A) and (B) are incorrectly punctuated, which makes the sentence meaningless. (D) and (E) are grammatically correct, but leave out an important part of the sentence—"to the puzzle."

6. (C) (A), (D), and (E) are incorrect because of the adverb "neither." (It modifies "time and energy," not "have," and should therefore be placed after the verb.) (B) is incorrect because "time," without an article, should be followed by "energy," and not "the energy" in order to create the parallel structure necessary with "and."

7. (B) (E) is incorrect, because the sentence should begin with "about," not with "of." (A), (C), and (D) are incorrect because, in a comparison, "as" must appear twice, and "if not happier" must be followed by "than."

8. (A) (B) and (C) are incorrect, because the pronoun is in the wrong case. The pronoun should be the subject; therefore, *she* is required. (D) and (E) are both grammatically correct but change the original sentence slightly.

9. (B) (A), (D), and (E) are incorrect, because the verb should be plural, since the subject is "no 2 minutes." (C) is incorrect because the "never" makes a double negative with the "no" in the second part of the sentence.

10. (E) (C) is grammatically incorrect (it should read "than" rather than "that"), as well as clumsy. (D) is an incorrect use of quotation marks. (A) is ambiguous (what does "when I arrived" refer to?). (B) is a clumsy structure.

11. (A) (B) and (C) are incorrect, because the parallel structure is not followed; if the sentence starts with an infinitive, the parallel clause should also start with the infinitive. (E) uses "ourselves" incorrectly; (C) is grammatically correct, but alters the meaning of the sentence by implying that they are already carrying it out—the original sentence is more hypothetical.

12. (C) (A), (B), and (D) are incorrect, because "unique" is already a superlative and doesn't need an adverb like "most" or "very." (E) is incorrect, because the subject of the verb is "Rocco," not the "brother as well" clause.

13. (C) (A) and (B) are incorrect, because you would be angry *with,* not *on* someone. (D) and (E) are incorrect, because the dependent clause is introduced incorrectly.

14. (E) (B) is incorrect, because the verb of the first clause should be singular (the subject is knowledge, not techniques). (C) and (D) are incorrect in meaning. (A) is incorrect, because, in the main clause, "he never built himself" is ambiguous.

15. (D) (A), (B), and (C) are incorrect, because the verb "has" refers to the scientists, and should be plural. (The verb referring to "he" is the first word, "is.") (E) is incorrect, because, although the verb is plural, the pronoun in front of experiments is singular.

16. (E) (A), (B), and (C) are incorrect, because they violate the parallel structure rule. (E) is preferable to (D), because, with several reasons given, the plural verb is needed.

17. (A) (B) is incorrect, because "it's" is incorrect, and this choice has a clumsy structure; (C) and (E) are interpretations of the original clause and are therefore incorrect. (D) is grammatically correct but adds a meaning of causality which wasn't present in the original sentence.

18. (B) (A) is incorrect, because books and firm are not equivalent (it should read "those of any other firm," or some variant thereof). (C) is incorrect, because it leaves ambiguous which noun is replaced by "their" (is it "firms" or "books"?); it is also a clumsy structure. (D) is incorrect, because it alters the meaning of the original sentence (the books aren't as bad as any others, but as those published by certain other firms). (E) uses "others" incorrectly.

19. (C) (A) and (E) are obviously incorrect. (The sentence has no meaning.) (D) is correct but clumsy. (B) uses "on" incorrectly.

20. (A) (B) is meaningless. (C) is incorrect, because the first pronoun should be "his" and not "him." (It is a possessive case, referring to "asking. . . .") (D) is a totally different sentence. (E) is grammatically correct but changes the meaning slightly.

21. (A) (B) and (C) are incorrect, for the verbs are not placed near their subjects, leading to confusion. (D) has incomplete verbs. (E) is too clumsy and awkward to be acceptable.

22. (E) (A), (B), (C), and (D) are all incorrect, since they lead to confusing interpretations of the situation.

23. (E) All the other choices offer confusing interpretations of the situation (the modifiers are misplaced; in this case, the modifiers are "in the Exam Center," "with a sheer blouse," and "deep in thought").

24. (B) (A), (C), and (D) are incorrect, because of the incorrect position of the adverb "either." Since the adverb modifies "today or tomorrow," it should be placed next to those words. (E) is clumsy and therefore not acceptable.

25. (C) The original sentence, and choices (B) and (D) as well, suffer from double causality ("reason" and "because"). Choice (E) is a total disaster.

Final Self-Test B

Another test similar to the Law School Admission Test follows. Notice that this test has different sections and many more questions than Final Self-Test A; as we've noted throughout this book, LSAT tests vary widely in format. Again, you should set aside at least 180 minutes to do this test. You may wish to take a 5-minute break after you complete Section III. The answer sheets are on page 325, answers follow the test.

Ready? Begin.

Section I: Logical Reasoning

Time: 30 minutes

25 questions

Directions: This section consists of a series of short passages and statements. In each case you should evaluate the reasoning in the passage or draw a conclusion and then select the *best* of the five alternatives.

1. He who plants thorns must never expect to gather roses.

   Which of the following most nearly expresses the same thought as this proverb?

   (A) Cast not your pearls before swine.
   (B) Cast thy bread upon the waters; for thou shalt find it after many days.
   (C) Do unto others as you would have others do unto you.
   (D) It is better to go to the house of mourning than to the house of feasting.
   (E) There is no gathering the rose without being pricked by the thorns.

2. All skinny men wear blue shirts.
   No fat men wear green ties.
   All men are fat or skinny.
   All men wear shirts and ties.

   Which of the following must be false?

   I. Keith wears a blue shirt and/or green tie.
   II. Richard wears neither a blue shirt nor a green tie.
   III. Mark wears a green tie but no blue shirt.

   (A) I only (B) III only (C) II and III (D) I and III (E) None of these

3. The bridge is crowded during rush hour. Since it is not rush hour now, the bridge is not crowded.

Which of the following most closely parallels the reasoning of the preceding statement?

(A) Karla is happy only when she is with Richard. Since Richard just left to go to school, Karla is unhappy.
(B) Richard is happiest when he is eating. He is therefore sad when he is not eating.
(C) Bob loses weight during final exams. He has no exams now, so he is fat.
(D) Time passes quickly for Susan when she is happy. She is unhappy now, so time is passing slowly.
(E) Harris loses money when he goes to the race track. If he stays away from the race track, he will get rich.

4. Generally speaking, men are too cowardly to be willing to undergo severe suffering, since they fear death and pain, but they highly prize being mentioned as having suffered.

Which of the following is least consistent with the preceding generalization?

(A) John's pride in showing off his war medal
(B) The fact that firemen risk their lives to save others
(C) A man who anonymously donates one of his kidneys to save the life of another person
(D) An American Indian who refuses to hunt deer because he believes killing is wrong
(E) A conscientious objector to military service

Questions 5 and 6

Men, steered by popular applause, though they bear the name of governors, are in reality the mere underlings of the __(5)__. The man who is completely __(6)__ has no need at all of glory, except so far as it disposes and eases his way of action by the greater trust that it procures him.

5. The word that best fills the blank, taking into account the rest of the paragraph, is:

(A) multitude. (B) king. (C) legislature. (D) women. (E) foolish.

6. The word or phrase that best fills the blank is:

(A) stupid (B) oppressed (C) generous and talented (D) docile and gentle (E) wise and virtuous

Questions 7 and 8

Why may not a goose say thus: "All the parts of the universe I have an interest in: the earth serves me to walk upon, the sun to light me; the stars have their influence upon me; I have such an advantage by the winds and such by the waters, there is nothing that yon heavenly roof looks upon so favorably as me. I am the darling of Nature! Is it not man that keeps, lodges and serves me?"

7. The argument of the goose would be shaken most by which of the following facts?

(A) Many other animals can make exactly the same claims.
(B) Sometimes Nature is not kind to the goose; for example, when it rains.
(C) Man could stop taking care of the goose at any time.
(D) Man will take care of the goose only until he is ready for goose dinner.
(E) None of the above

8. The author's point is most pertinent to:

(A) animal lovers.
(B) those who believe they can get something for nothing.
(C) national rulers.
(D) children.
(E) people who make a living as entertainers.

9. There are six blue nerdles and four green nerdles.
A trifle cannot be left in a box with a blue nerdle.
There are four trifles.

Which of the following must be false?

I. There are 11 items in the box.
II. There are 10 nerdles in the box.
III. For every trifle in the box, there is at least one nerdle.

(A) I only (B) I and II (C) I and III (D) I, II, and III (E) None of the above

10. Sir Roger made several reflections on the greatness of the British Nation as: that one Englishman could beat three Frenchmen; that we could never be in danger of Popery so long as we took care of our fleet; that the Thames was the noblest river in Europe, with many other honest prejudices which naturally cleave to the heart of a true Englishman.

Judging by the tone of this statement, its author is most likely to be:

(A) a French journalist.
(B) an English statesman.
(C) an English journalist.
(D) a French admiral.
(E) a French statesman.

11. New Skunk Spray Deodorant is not an aerosol. Most aerosols contain ingredients that destroy the ozone layer, cause cancer, and kill flowers, but new Skunk Spray is not an aerosol. It is even more effective than Skunk Roll-on. Buy new Skunk Spray today.

Which of the following claims (which the advertiser does not actually make), would he apparently intend the reader to infer?

I. Skunk Spray is safer than Skunk Roll-on.
II. Aerosols are dangerous.
III. Skunk Spray is safer than aerosols.
IV. Skunk Spray is new.
V. Skunk Roll-on is effective.

(A) II and III (B) II, III, and V (C) II, III, IV, and V (D) III and V (E) II, IV, and V

12. The atrocious crime of being a young man, which the honorable gentleman has charged upon me, I shall neither attempt to palliate nor deny, but content myself with wishing that I may be one of those whose follies may cease with their youth, and not of that number who are ignorant in spite of experiences.

Which of the following is most likely to be true?

(A) The speaker has great respect for the honorable gentleman.
(B) The speaker is about to challenge the honorable gentleman to a duel.
(C) The speaker is the apprentice of the honorable gentleman.
(D) The speaker is embarrassed by his lack of experience.
(E) The speaker does not believe that wisdom necessarily follows age.

Questions 13 and 14

Dreams are the first casualty of __(13)__. The daydream may be of some idle extravagance such as a color television set instead of black-and-white or a trip to Acapulco instead of the Catskills. Or it may be of something much more substantial, much harder to lay aside, such as a a college education or __(14)__. Or it may be a noble public vision of abolishing slums forever or ending poverty within a decade.

13. The phrase that best fills the blank is:

(A) an inflation
(B) a depression
(C) a personal financial tragedy
(D) a serious injury
(E) a poor night's sleep

14. The phrase that best fills the blank is:

(A) a new car
(B) a charitable contribution
(C) a home of one's own
(D) a stereo system
(E) an original Picasso

15. Radio advertisement: Join in celebrating our great nation's 200th birthday. Purchase this "I Love America" T-shirt for only $20. Send cash or money order to Buy-Centennial Sales, Inc.

This advertisement deliberately plays on the listener's:

(A) moral views.
(B) patriotism.
(C) sarcasm.
(D) desire to get a bargain.
(E) enthusiasm.

16. Politician: My opponent suggests socialized medicine. What a ridiculous idea: Even a child can see that only a dangerous communist would suggest such a thing. Why, the very thought of it frightens me severely.

The most serious problem with the politican's "reasoning" is that:

(A) He never deals with his opponent's suggestion.
(B) He does not describe fully enough the child he mentions.
(C) He does not explain his own views on communism.
(D) He fails to define socialized medicine.
(E) He confuses Socialism with Communism.

17. We are living in an epoch of great disillusionment. We are beginning to suspect that to fulfill a hope is to defeat it, and to make a dream come true . . .

The best conclusion to this statement would be:

(A) is to turn it into a nightmare.
(B) is impossible.
(C) is to destroy its beauty.
(D) is not desirable.
(E) is the straw that broke the camel's back.

18. Rocky Goldstein is the greatest player the Bimbos have ever had. Now that he has been hired to manage the Bimbos, they are bound to do well.

What assumption does the speaker make?

I. Good players make good managers.
II. Goldstein was a good player.
III. Teams with good managers win.

(A) I only (B) I and II (C) I and III (D) II only (E) I, II, and III

19. Since the Silly Party took office in Middletown, unemployment has gone down by 4%. Therefore, the Silly Party is obviously the best–vote Silly this year.

Which of the following would cast the most serious doubt on the wisdom of voting Silly?

(A) The candidate of the rival Sensible Party has a much higher I.Q.
(B) The Silly Party accomplished very little in nearby Humpville.
(C) Unemployment is not the only issue this year.
(D) The Silly Party is not running the same candidate this year as they ran in the last election.
(E) The average decrease in unemployment in the rest of the state was 9%.

Questions 20 and 21

'Twas thine own genius gave the final blow,
And help'd to plant the wound that laid thee low:
So the struck eagle, stretch'd upon the plain,
No more through rolling clouds to soar again,

20. The most likely ending to this poem would be:

(A) View'd his own feather on the fatal dust,
And wing'd the shaft that quiver'd in his heart.
(B) Tried to fly up in the sky,
But did not know he was to die.
(C) Thought nature's pointer, yet the best,
Had liv'd to try another test.
(D) Between the morn and evening light,
Would try his best to flee the night.
(E) Play'd sadly on his song of woe,
Before he flew away so slow.

21. The poet's tone is:

(A) sarcastic. (B) soulful. (C) condescending. (D) ironic. (E) allegorical.

22. Man makes the circumstances, and spiritually as well as economically is the artificer of his own fortune. Man's circumstances are the element he is appointed to live and work in; so that in another no less genuine sense, it can be said that circumstances make the man.

The speaker would probably be least sympathetic toward:

(A) a poor man stealing a loaf of bread.
(B) a wealthy man behaving snobbishly.
(C) a wealthy man embezzling funds from his company.
(D) a man who kills in the heat of passion.
(E) a prostitute.

Questions 23 and 24

Industry in art is a necessity—not a virtue—and any evidence of the same, in the production, is a blemish, not a quality; a proof, not of achievement, but of absolutely insufficient work, for work alone will expose the footsteps of work.

23. This statement is best described as:

(A) ironical. (B) sarcastic. (C) a paradox. (D) plaintive. (E) iconoclastic.

24. Which of the following statements is a reasonable paraphrase of the author's point?

(A) Artists should not work hard at art—it should come naturally.
(B) Too many cooks spoil the broth.
(C) The harder an artist works, the less his work is appreciated.
(D) Many hands make light work.
(E) None of these

25. Since we have tested 500 dogs, and all of them drink water, probably all dogs drink water.

    The reasoning used in this statement is an example of:

    (A) inductive reasoning.
    (B) deductive reasoning.
    (C) circumstantial evidence.
    (D) documentary evidence.
    (E) circular reasoning.

STOP

IF YOU FINISH BEFORE THE TIME IS UP,
CHECK YOUR WORK ON THIS SECTION ONLY.
DO NOT LOOK AT ANY OTHER SECTION IN THE TEST.
WHEN THE TIME IS UP, GO ON TO THE NEXT SECTION.

Section II

Time: 30 minutes

Part A: Quantitative Comparison

Time: 15 minutes

25 questions

Directions: In each question in this section, you are asked to compare two quantities, one in Column A and one in Column B. Choose answer

- (A) if the one in Column A is larger;
- (B) if the one in Column B is larger;
- (C) if the two are equal;
- (D) if the information is insufficient to determine the relationship.

General Information: Information centered above the two columns pertains to both. Any symbol appearing in both columns represents the same thing in each. All numbers used in this section are real numbers.

Diagrams: Diagrams are not necessarily drawn to scale unless they are so labeled. You are to solve the problems using your knowledge of mathematics, not sight or measurement. Unless you are told otherwise, figures lie in the plane, lines shown as straight are straight, and points, angles, and the like are in the order shown.

	Column A	*Column B*

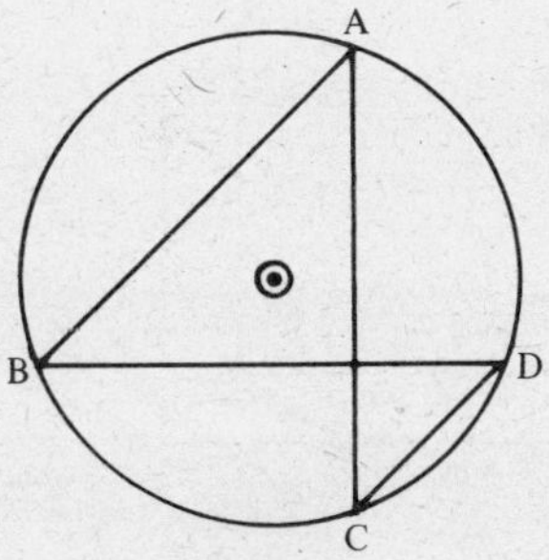

Circle O
Inscribed ∠s ABD, ACD

1.	measure of $\angle ABD$	measure of $\angle ACD$
2.	6 feet	Shadow of 6-foot-tall man if sun is at 45° angle
3.	$\frac{11}{21}$	$\frac{27}{53}$

Four coins are tossed.

4.	probability of four heads	probability of no heads

	Column A	*Column B*
5.	$(x + 2)^2$	$(x - 3)^2$

Bob is older than Mike.

6.	% that Bob's age is greater than Mike's	% that Mike's age is smaller than Bob's
7.	$(16x)^0$	1^{16x}

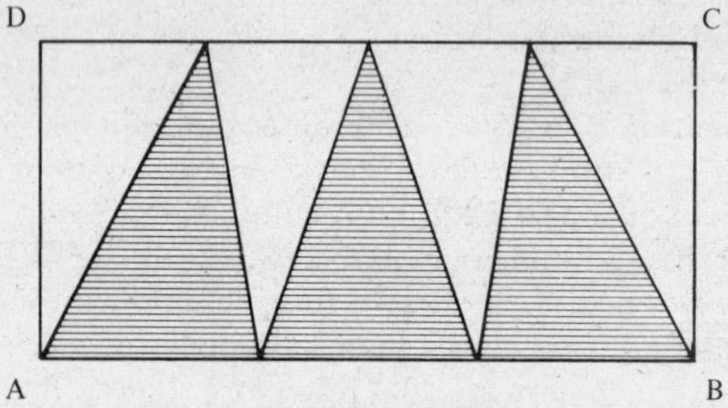

Rectangle *ABCD*

8.	area of shaded part	area of unshaded part

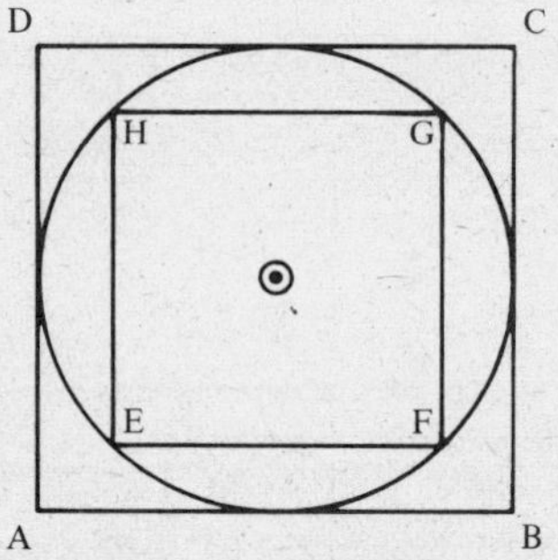

Circle O
Circumscribed and inscribed squares *ABCD*, *EFGH*

9.	area of *ABCD*	twice area of *EFGH*

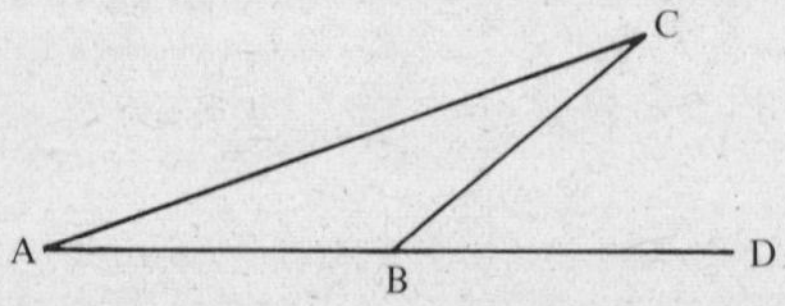

10.	$\angle ACB$	$\angle CBD$
11.	$-(3x - 6)$	$-(4x - 12)$

	Column A	*Column B*
12.	$37\frac{1}{2}\%$ of $33\frac{1}{3}\%$ of 8,000	$14\frac{2}{7}\%$ of $87\frac{1}{2}\%$ of 7,000

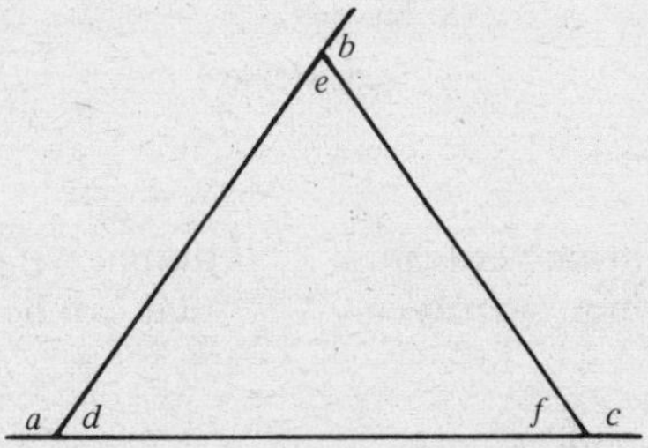

13.	$2(\angle d + \angle e + \angle f)$	$\angle a + \angle b + \angle c$
14.	$(+1)^{40}(-2)^{13}(-3)^{12}$	$(-1)^{51}(-2)^{-13}(+3)^{12}$
15.	area of circle with radius of 4 inches	area of square with side of 7 inches

Questions 16 to 18 refer to following diagram

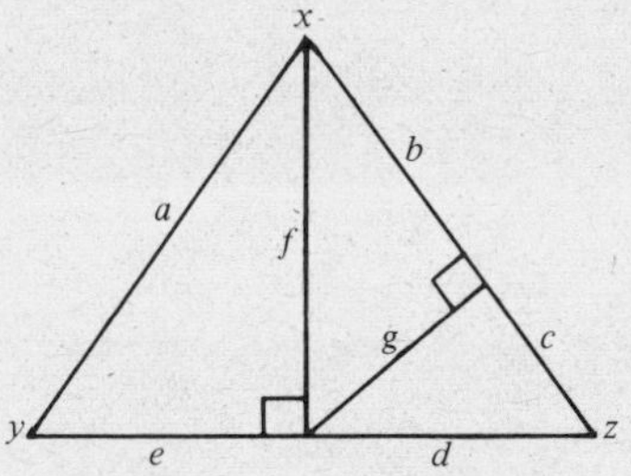

Triangle xyz
Right angles as indicated
a, b, c, d, e, f, g are the lengths of line segments

16.	g^2	bc
17.	$a + b + c$	$e + d$
18.	g	e

x is a positive integer

19.	40	$\frac{40}{x}$

$x^4 = 16$

20.	x	2

	Column A	*Column B*

$\frac{r}{8} = \frac{s}{9}, r > 0, s > 0$

21. $8r$ | $9s$

x is positive

22. $x^2 - 12x + 24$ | 0

23. number of different four-player teams that can be formed from seven players | number of different three-player teams that can be formed from seven players

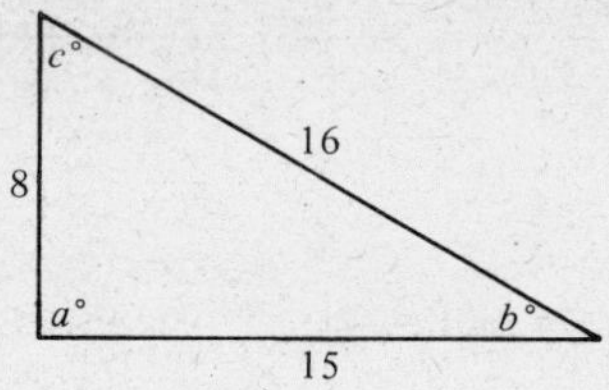

24. a^0 | $b^0 + c^0$

25. $\frac{a + 3}{a}$ | $1 + \frac{3}{a}$

Part B: Data Interpretation

Time: 15 minutes

14 questions

Directions: This section consists of various displays of data. Each display is followed by questions based on its content. After studying the display, select the best answer to each question on the basis of the information presented or implied in the display.

SEASON JAI ALAI AVERAGES
FROM DECEMBER 26TH, 1975, TO JULY 24TH, 1976

Name	Times Singles	Player in Doubles	Played Total	Times placed 1st	2d	3d	Averages
Ereño	160	146	306	70	44	31	.359
Valdez	365	303	668	122	77	84	.302
Espitia	116	397	513	76	75	84	.301
Marcelino	218	586	804	129	117	91	.295
Hernandez	268	687	955	146	134	116	.287
Juan	238	662	900	130	141	99	.286
Eduardo	281	728	1,009	132	133	119	.267
Fernando	253	730	983	121	130	133	.267
Milo	340	746	1,086	150	139	133	.265
Carasa	381	667	1,048	128	131	150	.261
Tito	340	785	1,125	136	133	148	.260
Stephen	353	320	673	95	73	88	.257
Victor	498	469	957	219	125	127	.255
Beltran	530	467	997	126	139	127	.255
Onaindia	246	718	964	129	120	109	.255
Elias	316	784	1,100	53	123	129	.255
Sergio	162	535	697	81	94	108	.254
Zaran	139	130	269	37	30	32	.251
Antonio	173	160	333	36	52	38	.250
Steve	237	647	884	122	122	133	.248
Jara	154	419	573	63	79	83	.248
Salinas	402	735	1,137	128	155	139	.244
Irusta	133	148	281	39	29	27	.240
Garcia	225	552	777	96	79	112	.236
Lalo	45	50	95	21	20	33	.232
Armando	184	722	906	85	103	99	.230
Davila	359	829	1,188	134	141	122	.225
Ramos	52	123	175	20	16	25	.233
Zamalloa	283	324	607	50	89	71	.215
Humberto	24	63	87	5	10	15	.191

Note: Averages are computed in the following manner: Three times the number of first place finishes plus two times the number of second place finishes plus the number of third place finishes are all divided by three times the number of total games played.

1. What percentage of his total games did Sergio win?

(A) 12% (B) 15% (C) 25% (D) 50% (E) It cannot be determined from the information given.

2. How many more second place finishes did the player with the most wins have than did the player with the best average?

   (A) 8 (B) 44 (C) 81 (D) 125 (E) 149

3. What percentage of his singles matches did Onaindia win?

   (A) 13% (B) 18% (C) 52% (D) 63% (E) It cannot be determined from the information given.

4. How many consecutive games would Zamalloa have to win in order to have the same percentage of first place finishes as Ramos?

   (A) 4 (B) 12 (C) 17 (D) 19 (E) It cannot be determined from the information given.

5. For the player who has played the most total games, what percentage of the number of times he has played singles is the number of times he has played doubles?

   (A) 30% (B) 43% (C) 131% (D) 143% (E) 231%

6. If Antonio had won 16 more games than he did, and his other totals were the same as on the chart, what would his average have been?

   (A) .160 (B) .300 (C) .250 (D) .305 (E) It cannot be determined from the information given.

7. How many other players have the same average as the player who has played 91 more games than Eduardo?

   (A) 0 (B) 1 (C) 2 (D) 3 (E) 4

BALANCE OF PAYMENTS IN FOUR COUNTRIES
(Billions of dollars)

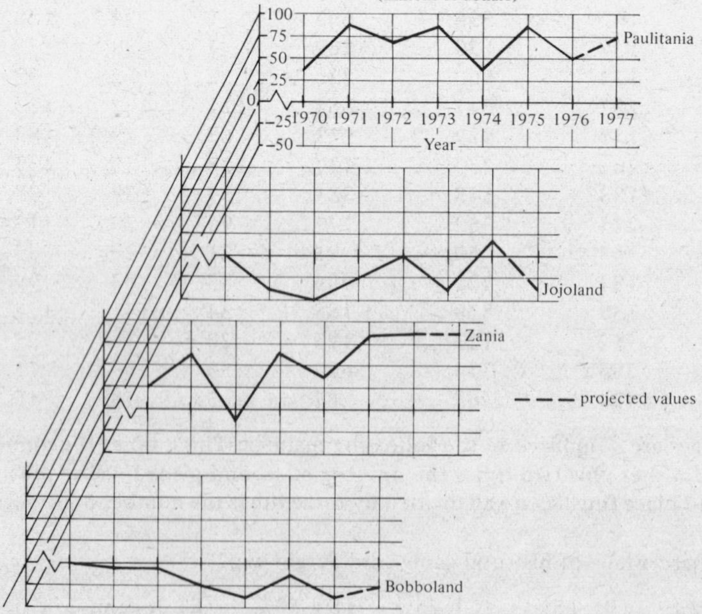

8. Which countries had identical balances of payments in 1970?

I. Paulitania II. Jojoland III. Zania IV. Bobboland

(A) I and III (B) II and IV (C) I and II (D) II, III, and IV
(E) None of these

9. In the year in which Bobboland had its highest balance of payments, what was Paulitania's balance of payments?

(A) \$38 billion (B) \$42 billion (C) \$60 billion (D) \$90 billion
(E) It cannot be determined from the information given.

10. In the year in which Zania had a negative balance of payments, what was the difference between Zania's balance of payments and Jojoland's?

(A) \$0 (B) \$10 billion (C) \$15 billion (D) \$35 billion
(E) It cannot be determined from the information given.

11. The country(ies) which never had an even balance of payments (equal to zero) during the period shown on the graph is/(are):

I. Paulitania II. Jojoland III. Zania IV. Bobboland

(A) I only (B) I and III (C) I and IV (D) I, III, and IV
(E) None of these

12. What is the total balance of payments for the four countries for 1973?

(A) \$40 billion (B) \$80 billion (C) \$100 billion (D) \$125 billion
(E) It cannot be determined from the information given.

13. If the 1977 projection for Paulitania is correct, and the balance of payments continues to increase at the same rate in 1978, what will be the percent increase from 1977 to 1978?

(A) 25% (B) $33\frac{1}{3}\%$ (C) 50% (D) 75% (E) 100%

14. In what year was the ratio of Zania's balance of payments to Paulitania's the highest?

(A) 1970 (B) 1971 (C) 1973 (D) 1974 (E) 1976

STOP

IF YOU FINISH BEFORE THE TIME IS UP,
CHECK YOUR WORK ON THIS SECTION ONLY.
DO NOT LOOK AT ANY OTHER SECTION IN THE TEST.
WHEN THE TIME IS UP, GO ON TO THE NEXT SECTION.

Section III: Practical Judgment

Time: 40 minutes
50 questions

Directions: In this section you will be presented with long passages followed by two sets of questions: data evaluation and data application. Both sets of questions focus on the relative importance of various facts and issues in the passage. Specific instructions will follow each passage.

Passage I

In April, 1972, Dr. William Burgess, a general practitioner in Chicago, received an inheritance of $20,000. Dr. Burgess decided to use the money in fulfilling his ambition of moving his family and his medical practice from their present location in the city to a house in one of the metropolitan suburbs. At the time, the Burgesses lived in a condominium in a residential Chicago neighborhood; the physician rented professional offices in the downtown area. Dr. Burgess felt that the condominium was too small for his family, while the downtown area did not offer much hope for growth in his medical practice due to an ongoing shift of population from the central city to the suburbs. Dr. Burgess hoped to locate a suburban home large enough to accommodate both his family and his professional offices. He believed that maintaining offices in his home would be more convenient for patients and would also eliminate such overhead costs as rent and travel to and from his offices.

Because he could not guarantee that his practice would flourish in a new area, Dr. Burgess did not wish to commit himself to any long-term financial obligations, such as a mortgage, in purchasing the house. In addition to the $20,000 inheritance, the physician estimated that he would receive $30,000 from the sale of the condominium. Thus he would have a financial base of $50,000 for purchasing a house outright. In case he could not find a house for $50,000 or less, he was also willing to use up to $20,000 from his savings of $35,000. Dr. Burgess wished to retain $15,000 in his savings account in order to provide a financial cushion for his family in case of emergencies. Besides this $70,000 sum made up of his inheritance, condominium, and savings, Dr. Burgess was also willing to liquidate all or part of his $20,000 securities holdings if additional funds were required. However, since these securities were high-grade bonds which paid 9% annual interest, he decided to include the loss of interest on any liquidated securities as part of his estimate of the total cost of houses priced over $70,000. He would not include the loss of interest on his savings in these cost calculations because the interest rate was lower and because he had accumulated those funds for the express purpose of buying a house.

In consulting with real estate brokers, Dr. Burgess stipulated that he required a house with at least 10 rooms, seven for his family and three for his professional offices. He had no rigid specifications regarding the layout of the house and was willing to make alterations in order to install offices. His chief criterion for the suburb itself was that it offer him a reasonable opportunity to establish a successful medical practice. As a general practitioner, Dr. Burgess ordinarily treated patients for less serious ailments and injuries, referring more serious cases to specialists. It was therefore important that his new location have a large and growing number of well-established families that would come to rely on him as their family doctor. Whether an area was particularly affluent did not matter to him, since he was not a specialist whose fees might be prohibitive for some families.

Finally, he felt it would be wise to locate in an area which was not already saturated with general practitioners.

The first suburb Dr. Burgess considered was Alton, an older suburb located quite close to the central city. Alton had grown steadily over the years, but its growth had slowed appreciably since 1965 as it became increasingly affected by the problems of the city. A number of general practitioners had offices in the suburb, but Dr. Burgess thought that the community would support his practice for the time being. However, he was concerned that the town's proximity to Chicago might cause it to lose population at some point in the future as the trend toward the outlying suburbs continued. He was far from certain that his practice would maintain steady growth in Alton. On the other hand, though, an attractive house was available in Alton for the reasonable price of $45,000. It had eleven rooms and would be suitable for residential and professional use if certain minor renovations were made. Dr. Burgess estimated that these renovations would cost $3,000, bringing the total cost of the house to $48,000.

A second suburb, Ventura, had experienced considerable recent growth. A newly developed area, it had few doctors and seemed to offer excellent prospects for establishing a medical practice. The population was young and relatively affluent; a series of articles in a local newspaper had documented the need for more physicians in the area. Unfortunately, no house was available in Ventura at the time. According to one broker, the demand for large houses had been relatively small because most new residents were young couples who intended to limit the size of their families. The broker speculated that a house might become available in the next few months, but he cautioned Dr. Burgess that prices in the area were rising rapidly due to the generally high demand for housing.

In Chester, another community which had undergone rapid growth in recent years, Dr. Burgess located a medium-sized nine-room house for $60,000. An addition to his house would be necessary in order to install offices. This addition could be built for $13,000. Chester was a commuter suburb, comprised chiefly of young professional and managerial families whose heads had not yet reached the peak of their careers. As a result, a large, constant turnover of population occurred as new families moved in and older, more successful families moved out. Dr. Burgess realized that this instability in the population, combined with a large number of community-based general practitioners, would probably make it more difficult for him to establish a successful practice in Chester than elsewhere.

Broadwood Heights, the fourth suburb, was an affluent, growing community. Its population, slightly older, on the average, than that of the other suburbs, was relatively settled. Dr. Burgess noted that a number of successful physicians, many of them specialists, had homes in the community. Nevertheless, advertisements in a number of medical journals indicated that Broadwood Heights, like Ventura, was suffering a shortage of general practitioners. A 12-room house was available for $70,000. Included in the house was a suite of professional offices which its present owner, an attorney, had installed. Minor alterations costing $2,000 would be necessary to convert these rooms for medical use, but otherwise the house was in move-in condition.

Weldon, the last suburb considered, was an older, more conservative area which had grown steadily over the years. Dr. Burgess found it difficult to evaluate his professional prospects in this community. He felt he would suffer a distinct disadvantage as a newcomer to the suburb, since most of its residents had long-standing relationships with various other physicians. However, he discovered that an elderly practitioner in the area had offered both his house and his professional practice for sale. The house, consisting of eight rooms and a four-room professional suite, was priced at $65,000. The professional practice, which included the doctor's office facilities and a complete listing of his patients, was offered at $35,000. Though the combined cost of $100,000 was beyond

Dr. Burgess's means, he estimated that he could sell the other physician's medical equipment, which he did not need, for $15,000, reducing the total cost of the combination to $85,000 plus the loss of interest on the securities he would have to sell. Dr. Burgess considered the other doctor's practice to be an excellent one, and he realized that it offered him the only real hope of establishing a successful practice in Weldon.

In deciding which house to buy, Dr. Burgess felt it was most important to choose a location which would provide an optimum combination of comfort for his family with good prospects for professional growth.

Data Evaluation

Directions: Each of the items below relates to the passage you just read. Select answer

(A) if the item is a *Major Objective* in the decision—the result desired by the decision-maker.

(B) if the item is a *Major Factor* in the decision—something specifically mentioned and important in reaching the decision relating to a Major Objective.

(C) if the item is a *Minor Factor* in the decision—something specifically mentioned that affects a Major Factor but relates only indirectly to a Major Objective.

(D) if the item is a *Major Assumption* underlying the decision—an expectation or projection taken for granted by the decision-maker before the alternatives are examined.

(E) if the item is an *Unimportant Issue* in the decision—something neither relevant nor significant.

1. Assurance that medical practice will grow

2. Amount of money received as an inheritance

3. Loss of interest on savings

4. Plausibility of selling condominium for $30,000

5. Total cost of acquiring each house considered

6. Number of rooms in each house considered

7. Number of specialists practicing in each suburb considered

8. Prospects for establishing a successful medical practice in each suburb

9. Loss of interest from the sale of securities

10. Selection of a suitable relocation area

11. Sufficiency of cushion provisions for emergencies

12. Number of general practitioners practicing in each suburb considered

13. Continuation of population shift to the suburbs

14. Diversification of his professional practice

15. Interest rates on mortgage and loans

16. Relocation of family and practice to suburbs

17. Distance of each suburb from present downtown offices

18. Availability of a suitable house in each suburb

19. Availability of a professional practice in each suburb

Data Application

Directions: Each of the questions below relates to the passage you have just read. Select the best of the five choices.

20. For which of the following reasons did Dr. Burgess wish to relocate his family and professional practice in the suburbs?

    I. Likelihood that practice would not grow in present location
    II. Deteriorating conditions in the home neighborhood
    III. Insufficiency of present living accommodations

    (A) I only (B) II only (C) I and II (D) I and III (E) I, II, and III

21. Of the five locations considered, which had houses which Dr. Burgess could have purchased without selling any securities?

    I. Alton II. Ventura III. Chester IV. Broadwood Heights
    V. Weldon

    (A) I only (B) I and V (C) III and IV (D) II and V (E) I, II, and III

22. In which of the five areas could Dr. Burgess be *least* certain of the total cost of relocation?

    (A) Alton (B) Ventura (C) Chester (D) Broadwood Heights
    (E) Weldon

23. Of the following factors, which is the greatest disadvantage of relocation in Chester?

    (A) The cost of building an addition to the house
    (B) The number of general practitioners already established in the area
    (C) The occupational status of its population
    (D) The difficulty of establishing a regular practice
    (E) The age of the house available there

24. Keeping in mind the loss of interest from securities, the total cost of Dr. Burgess's fifth alternative would be approximately:

(A) \$100,000 (B) \$85,000 (C) \$89,000 (D) \$86,350 (E) \$83,650

25. Of the five locations, which would be Dr. Burgess's best choice?

(A) Alton (B) Ventura (C) Chester (D) Broadwood Heights (E) Weldon

Passage II

In December, 1969, Mr. George Selby, president of the Selby Home Products Company, held a meeting with the firm's sales director, comptroller, and product manager. The purpose of the meeting was to discuss an apparent lag in the growth of the company's sales. Sales revenues in 1968 had totaled \$14 million, up 15% from 1967, but figures for 1969 had shown an increase of less than \$100,000, well below the 10% increase targeted for the year. The firm's executives had concluded that this slowdown in growth was not caused by deficiencies in advertising, distribution, or in the products themselves. Rather, the company's sales force had become apathetic, showing little motivation toward opening new accounts and expanding existing ones. A study of the sales force had shown that the present practice of paying salesmen a commission of 6% on gross sales volume did not provide a sufficient stimulus for more aggressive selling. Most salesmen earned a modest but comfortable income from their present sales volume and, since no additional incentives were offered for selling above this level, they tended to avoid the extra effort involved in increasing sales. One veteran salesman, Mr. Harold Champlain, who was an old friend of the sales director, Mr. Erwin Harris, had suggested that the company increase its commission rate to 8% on all sales. Personally, Mr. Harris thought that his friend's suggestion would not remedy the situation, since it would provide no additional stimulus for higher selling, but he agreed to bring the proposal up at the December meeting.

Reaction to the proposal was unfavorable. The officers were agreed that the present commission structure was inadequate, but none of them felt that a simple increase in commissions would provide an incentive which would be likely to increase sales. Mr. Selby pointed out that it amounted to a raise in pay for the sales force, which he felt was unwarranted, given their 1969 performance. Mr. Richard Shelton, the controller, added that the lag in 1969 sales had weakened the company's financial position to a point where it could not afford to grant such an increase. Furthermore, Mr. Karl Green, the production manager, observed that production employees would probably demand a raise if sales employees received one, and the company's inability to meet their demands might well lead to strikes or other delays in production which the firm could not afford.

Mr. Green then suggested that the company release those employees whose 1969 sales records had been below average. Mr. Harris quickly vetoed the suggestion, saying that the less productive salespersons were mainly junior salesmen who showed signs of becoming successful company representatives and in whose training the company had invested heavily. Also, Mr. Harris felt that the present sales staff of 50 persons was an ideal size for the company. Markets for its products were spread out over a wide area, and, in his view, the company must retain a relatively large sales force in order to give customers adequate service. What was needed, said Mr. Harris, was an incentive plan which would provide salesmen with above-average remuneration for an above-average sales record.

Mr. Harris then proposed a plan which would provide such incentives. His plan involved paying bonuses, in the form of stock in the company, to employees with large sales volumes. The average yearly sales total of Selby sales representatives had been $250,000 in 1969. Under Mr. Harris's plan, a salesman selling this amount or less would receive no stock bonus at all, only his regular 6% commission. A salesman with a total volume above $250,000 would receive, in addition to his 6% commission, a bonus of Selby stock equal in value to a fixed percentage of his sales over $250,000. This percentage would increase in successive steps, as shown below.

Proposed Schedule of Stock Bonuses for Selby Sales Personnel

Bonus Rate	*Sales Volume*
1%	First $100,000 over $250,000
2%	First $100,000 over $350,000
3%	All sales over $450,000

Thus, in addition to the regular commission, a salesman with total sales of $550,000 would receive stock bonuses worth $6,000: $1,000 for sales between $250,000 and $350,000; $2,000 for sales between $350,000 and $450,000; and $3,000 for sales above $450,000. Mr. Harris recommended that the par value of the stock, $25.00 per share, be used as the basis for figuring the actual number of shares due a salesman, since this value would not vary with fluctuations in market prices of the stock. Thus, a salesman entitled to a $2,500 bonus would receive 100 shares of Selby stock.

Mr. Shelton then proposed a plan for increasing the cash commission on sales in accordance with increases in sales volume, as shown below.

Proposed Schedule of Cash Incentive Commissions for Selby Sales Personnel

Sales Volume	*Cash Commission*
$300,000 or less	6%
First $100,000 over $300,000	8%
First $100,000 over $400,000	9%
All sales over $500,000	10%

Under this plan, a salesman with annual sales of $550,000 would receive total cash commissions of $40,000: $18,000 for the first $300,000 at 6%; $8,000 for the next $100,000 at 8%; $9,000 for the next $100,000 at 9%; and $5,000 for the $50,000 at 10%.

Mr. Shelton felt that his plan was preferable, since the incentives it provided would come from the firm's current revenues, not from its financial reserves. At the time, Selby Company held a large number of shares of its own stock. These shares could be liquidated at a profit, since the market value of the shares was currently greater than their par value. Thus, in case of emergencies, cash could be raised simply by selling some of these shares. By distributing portions of this holding through the stock bonus plan, argued Mr. Shelton, the company depleted its reserves and would, in effect, lose money on them. By contrast, the cash commission plan would not really undermine the firm's financial position, since funds distributed through it would come only from cash actually on hand. As the company's sales increased, he reasoned, so would its ability to pay extra cash commissions, while distributing its reserves of securities would entail risks at all times. Finally, he said, the cash plan would offer a more effective incentive to employees, since the value of their reward for exceptional performance would not depend on variations in the market value of the company's stock.

Mr. Harris replied that the stock-bonus plan would actually provide a greater incentive than the cash-commission plan. He pointed out that the disparity between par value and current market value of the company's stock would provide an added incentive for employees to earn more shares by increasing sales, since the shares so earned could be sold at an immediate profit. Furthermore, he said that increasing employee ownership of Selby stock would improve company morale and lead to a greater sense of involvement in the company's future, both of which would be necessary for future corporate growth. Finally, he argued that the effect of the plan on future company finances would probably not be extensive, since few salesmen would earn more than 100 shares per year under it.

Mr. Selby then observed that the issues were complex and should be studied further before action was taken. After assigning an executive to review each plan, he named a date for a second meeting and closed the present one.

Data Evaluation

Directions: Each of the items below relates to the passage you just read. Select answer

(A) if the item is a *Major Objective* in the decision—the result desired by the decision-maker.

(B) if the item is a *Major Factor* in the decision—something specifically mentioned and important in reaching the decision relating to a Major Objective.

(C) if the item is a *Minor Factor* in the decision—something specifically mentioned that affects a Major Factor but relates only indirectly to a Major Objective.

(D) if the item is a *Major Assumption* underlying the decision—an expectation or projection taken for granted by the decision-maker before the alternatives are examined.

(E) if the item is an *Unimportant Issue* in the decision—something neither relevant nor significant.

26. Losses from the distribution of securities as bonuses

27. Adoption of a system of sales incentives

28. Incentives provided under each plan

29. Probability that production workers would demand matching wage increases

30. Lack of advertising and distribution

31. Present market value of Selby stock

32. Establishment of company reputation

33. Lag in growth of overall sales volume

34. Necessity for retaining present size of sales force

35. Improvement in growth of sales

36. Amount of stock bonuses payable on sales under $250,000

37. Desire of sales personnel to increase annual incomes

38. Percentage scales specified under each plan

39. Financial position of the Selby Company

40. Present commission rates

41. Guaranteeing that incentives chosen will increase sales

42. Acquisition of additional capital for production increases

43. Relationship between stock ownership and morale

44. Relationship between Mr. Champlain and Mr. Harris

Data Application

Directions: Each of the questions below relates to the passage you have just read. Select the best of the five choices.

45. Which of the following actions was apparently most acceptable to the Selby Company executives?

    (A) Laying off salesmen
    (B) Paying stock bonuses
    (C) Reducing commission rates
    (D) Retaining the present commission structure
    (E) Making an across-the-board increase in commission rates

46. Which of the following persons participated *least* in the discussion described in the passage?

    (A) Mr. Selby (B) Mr. Green (C) Mr. Harris (D) Mr. Shelton
    (E) Participation was roughly equal.

47. You can infer that approximately what percent of the 1969 sales of the Selby Company were made directly, with no assistance from any member of the firm's sales force?

    (A) 0% (B) 17% (C) 0.07% (D) 11% (E) 25%

48. In order for a salesman to receive stock bonuses worth $2,500 under Mr. Harris's plan, his annual sales volume would have to total:

    (A) $550,000 (B) $175,000 (C) $475,000 (D) $41,667 (E) $425,000

49. According to the passage, Mr. Champlain's suggestion was rejected mainly because:

    (A) it would encourage production workers to demand a stock-option plan.
    (B) it would cause salesmen to lose faith in management.
    (C) it would provide no real incentive and would be too costly.
    (D) it would have no effect on junior salesmen.
    (E) the executives felt he was uninformed about corporate affairs.

50. You can infer that an employee with gross sales of $400,000 would receive approximately what percent more in total compensation under the stock-bonus plan than under the cash-incentive plan?

(A) 8%　(B) 0%　(C) 15%　(D) 2%　(E) 22%

STOP

IF YOU FINISH BEFORE THE TIME IS UP,
CHECK YOUR WORK ON THIS SECTION ONLY.
DO NOT LOOK AT ANY OTHER SECTION IN THE TEST.
WHEN THE TIME IS UP, GO ON TO THE NEXT SECTION.

Section IV: Principles and Cases

Time: 40 minutes

30 questions

Part A

Directions: In this section you will be presented with some legal principles that may or may not be real. You are to accept them as valid. Following each principle will be several short cases. For each case, you will be presented with four possible applications of the principle to that case. Answer each question by selecting the most reasonable application.

These questions assume no prior legal knowledge on your part; answer them using only ordinary logical reasoning.

Principle 1

A person is guilty of murder when, with the intent to cause the death of any person, he causes the death of that person or another. A person is guilty of murder when acting either alone or with one or more other persons, he commits or attempts to commit robbery, burglary, kidnapping, arson, rape, and in the course of, or furtherance of, such crime or of immediate flight, the death of a person is caused.

A person is justified in using deadly physical force in self-defense only when his or another's life is in danger and there is no other reasonable alternative. Force less than deadly physical force can be used to the extent that it is reasonable.

1. Black and Green quarrel at a party, and Black goes home to get his gun, which he believes to be empty. He then goes back to the party with the intent of scaring Green. Green sees Black coming and pulls a knife. Black, in a panic, pulls the trigger. The gun has a cartridge in the chamber and it kills Green. When Black is tried for murder, he will be found:

   (A) guilty, because he had intent to use the gun.
   (B) guilty, because he pulled the trigger.
   (C) innocent, because he thought the gun was empty.
   (D) innocent, because he wanted to scare Green.

2. Doe and Jones quarrel at a party. Doe pulls a gun and tells Jones to leave. Jones leaves and hooks up explosives to the ignition of Doe's car. Doe lends his car to Smith, who is killed in the explosion. When Jones is tried for murder, he will be found:

   (A) guilty, because he had intent to kill Doe.
   (B) guilty, because Smith died in the explosion.
   (C) innocent, because he had no intent to kill Smith.
   (D) innocent, because the explosives were planted in self-defense.

3. Davis, Sullivan, and O'Malley decide to rob a bank. On the day of the crime, O'Malley waits in the car while Davis and Sullivan enter the bank. A policeman draws his gun, and Davis shoots at him, but Sullivan gets in the line of fire and is killed by Davis' shot. When O'Malley is tried for murder, he will be found:

(A) guilty, because the killing occurred as part of the robbery.
(B) guilty, because he knew Davis would shoot at the policeman.
(C) innocent, because he wasn't in the bank.
(D) innocent, because it was a robber who got killed.

4. Burns, an arsonist, sets fire to Dirty Ernie's Greasy Spoon. As he is driving away from the fire, Burns is spotted by a man. Three hours later, while still trying to decide what to do, he accidentally runs over and kills Notlob, a plainclothes policeman, who was crossing the street. In prosecution of Burns for the murder of Notlob, Burns will be found:

(A) guilty, because he was escaping from the scene of the crime.
(B) guilty, because he had intent to kill Notlob.
(C) innocent, because he did not know that Notlob was a policeman.
(D) innocent, because he was not in immediate flight from the scene of the crime.

Principle 2

An agent may bind his principal to a written or oral contract. The existence of an agency relationship may be established in one of three ways:

1. *The principal may appoint the agent by either an oral or written communication to the agent.*
2. *The principal may authorize the agent by communication to the third party with whom the agent is to deal.*
3. *The principal may ratify the acts of another purportedly acting on his behalf (affirming a previously unauthorized act).*

A minor or an adjudicated incompetent cannot be bound by the acts of an agent even if specifically authorized. A minor or an adjudicated incompetent can, however, act as an agent for another.

5. Mr. Holmes, owner of the Zeke's Nest Night Club, is a great fan of Lulu Belle, a beautiful young starlet. He asks his friend Spangle to engage the services of Ace Anderson in signing Ms. Belle for an engagement at the Club. Anderson and Ms. Belle sign a contract, but Mr. Holmes changes his mind and refuses to accept it. When Ms. Belle sues to compel performance, she will:

(A) win, because Mr. Anderson was the agent of Mr. Holmes.
(B) win, because Spangle was the agent of Mr. Holmes.
(C) lose, because Mr. Holmes refused to ratify the contract.
(D) lose, because Mr. Holmes did not appoint Mr. Anderson personally.

6. Mr. Rich calls Mark's Garage to tell Mark that he is sending over his son, Little Rich, with his car and instructions. Little Rich, age 16, drives to the garage and tells Mark to overhaul the engine. In fact, all the car needs is an oil change, which is what

Mr. Rich told Little Rich to ask for. Mr. Rich refuses to pay for the job. When Mark sues him, he will:

(A) lose, because Little Rich was a minor.
(B) win, because Mr. Rich communicated with Little Rich.
(C) lose, because Little Rich exceeded his authorization.
(D) win, because Mr. Rich told Mark that Little Rich would instruct him.

7. Billy Boffo, janitor for the Acme Jewelry Company, meets Sneaky Pete at a cocktail party. Pete offers to sell Billy a diamond ring (that actually cuts glass) for $100. Billy agrees to buy it for his company. When he tells Mr. Dithers, his employer, that he has purchased a genuine diamond ring for the company for only $100, Mr. Dithers pays Pete the $100 for the ring and congratulates Billy on his quick thinking. A week later, when he finds out that the ring is a fake, Mr. Dithers sues Pete to get his money back. He will:

(A) win, because Billy was not a proper agent.
(B) lose, because he ratified Billy's act.
(C) lose, because Billy was an employee of the company and therefore had authority.
(D) win, because the ring was not worth $100.

8. Sixteen-year-old Burt tells his friend Steve, age 17, to purchase a bicycle for him. On Burt's behalf, Steve enters into an agreement with Willy Wheels, and returns to report to Burt. Burt is delighted to hear the good news, and calls Willy to tell him so. By the next day, however, he changes his mind. When Willy sues to force Burt to go through with the purchase, he will:

(A) win, because Burt ratified the agreement.
(B) win, because Burt appointed Steve to be his agent.
(C) lose, because Burt was a minor.
(D) lose, because Steve was a minor.

9. Peter Principal calls Sam Seller and says, "My agent, Algernon, is on his way to your office to make a deal." On his way to Seller's office, Algernon is attacked and replaced by Benny, Peter's competitor. Benny introduces himself as Algernon and negotiates a horrible deal for Peter. When Seller sues Peter to force him to honor the deal, he will:

(A) win, because Peter authorized Algernon to him by direct communication.
(B) lose, because Benny had no authority.
(C) win, because he thought that Benny was authorized.
(D) lose, because Peter did not ratify the deal negotiated by Benny.

Part B

Directions: Each case in this part is followed by several principles, which may or may not be real principles of law. You are to accept them as valid. Each principle is followed by a question with four possible answers, each a potential factor in the application of the principle to the case. In each question, you are to select the choice which is the major factor. Answer based on what is stated or implied in the principle and the case. Each of these questions is independent of all of the others.

These questions assume no prior legal knowledge on your part; answer them using only ordinary logical reasoning.

Case 1

On a snowy afternoon, Nerdle is driving his car along Main Street at 45 mph without lights. The speed limit is 45 mph. Lopes, whose license and insurance have expired, is driving along Side Street towards Main Street and skids right through the stop sign, despite the fact that he is going only 10 mph, and tries as hard as he can to stop his car. Nerdle, when he is still one block from the intersection, sees Lopes skidding towards the corner, but makes no effort to stop himself because he assumes that Lopes will obey the stop sign. Nerdle and Lopes collide, and both cars are wrecked.

10. In a suit for damages, brought by Lopes against Nerdle, the court holds for Nerdle on the following principle:

    In case of an accident, if either driver is in violation of a safety statute, he is automatically presumed to be at fault.

    Which of the following conditions was the major factor in the disposition of the case?

    (A) Lopes' license has expired.
    (B) Nerdle was driving too fast for the weather conditions, and should have had lights on..
    (C) Lopes went through a stop sign.
    (D) Lopes was not insured.

11. A suit for damages, brought by Lopes against Nerdle, is held for Lopes on the following principle:

    When one person sues another for damages for negligence he must, in order to collect, show himself to be free of negligence.

    Which of the following was the major factor in the disposition of the case?

    (A) Nerdle was negligent, since he was driving too fast and without lights.
    (B) Nerdle could have stopped if he had tried.
    (C) Lopes did everything in his power to try to stop.
    (D) Lopes was going only 10 mph.

12. A suit for damages, brought by Lopes against Nerdle, is held for Lopes on the following principle:

    The party who has the last clear chance to avoid an accident is considered to be at fault if he fails to do so.

    Which of the following was the major factor in the disposition of the case?

    (A) Nerdle was driving too fast.
    (B) Lopes was unable to avoid the accident.
    (C) Lopes tried as hard as he could to avoid the accident.
    (D) Nerdle could have avoided the accident if he had tried to stop when he first saw Lopes.

13. A suit for damages, brought by Lopes against Nerdle, is held for Lopes on the following principle:

In case of an accident, the party who is more negligent than the other is liable for all damages. Violation of a safety statute is considered to be some evidence of negligence.

Which of the following was the major factor in the disposition of the case?

(A) Nerdle's actions were more negligent than Lopes'.
(B) The licensing statute is not a safety statute.
(C) Speeding is a more serious offense than running a stop sign.
(D) Lopes tried to stop at the stop sign.

Case 2

Nelson will be 21 years old on October 12. On that day he will inherit the Rockhead family fortune. On October 6, he stops at the neighborhood Rolls Royce dealer and orders a fleet of 17 Rolls Royces, to be delivered on November 3, by which time he is to have paid for them. The dealer, who is well aware of Nelson's impending wealth, gladly agrees. On October 10, Nelson makes an initial payment of $3,000. On October 13, he tells his banker that he is looking forward to owning the fleet, and he pays the balance of his bill on October 21. On October 31, he is run over and killed.

14. A suit for a refund, brought by Nelson's estate against the Rolls Royce dealer, is held for the estate on the following principle:

A minor is not bound by contracts entered into before his 21st birthday.

Which of the following was the major factor in the disposition of the case?

(A) Nelson would have been over 21 at the time of delivery.
(B) Nelson was not yet 21 when he made the first payment.
(C) Nelson was not yet 21 when he placed the order.
(D) The dealer knew that Nelson was not yet 21.

15. A suit for a refund, brought by Nelson's estate against the Rolls Royce dealer, is held for Rolls Royce on the following principle:

A contract made by a minor is enforcible against him if he clearly reratifies it after reaching majority.

Which of the following was the major factor in the disposition of the case?

(A) Nelson said, after reaching majority, that he was looking forward to owning the fleet of Rolls Royces.
(B) The contract was made only a week before Nelson's birthday, and the dealer knew that Nelson would be able to pay for the cars and that he really wanted them.
(C) The cars were to be delivered after Nelson's 21st birthday.
(D) Nelson made a payment on the cars after his 21st birthday.

16. A suit for a refund, brought by Nelson's estate against the Rolls Royce dealer, is held for Rolls Royce on the following principle:

Once performance of a contract is begun by one of the parties, that party can no longer utilize what would otherwise have been a valid defense, if the defense existed before performance was begun.

Which of the following was the major factor in the disposition of the case?

(A) Nelson partially performed the contract after reaching majority.
(B) Nelson made partial payment on October 10.
(C) Nelson had fully performed his part of the contract before he died.
(D) Rolls Royce had not yet begun performance of the contract when Nelson died.

17. A suit for refund, brought by Nelson's estate against the Rolls Royce dealer, is held for Rolls Royce on the following principle:

Any disability which occurs after a valid contract is made will not render the contract invalid.

Which of the following was the major factor in the disposition of the case?

(A) Nelson would no longer have been a minor at the date of delivery.
(B) Nelson died after entering into a valid contract.
(C) The estate has enough money to pay all of Nelson's debts.
(D) Nelson had already reached his 21st birthday when he died.

Case 3

Bad Bart enters Prudence Goodheart's house at 4:00 P.M. on July 14 by breaking a window. He intends to steal her famous butterfly collection, which is located in a safe which stands in the dining room against the wall of Ms. Goodheart's bedroom. Unknown to Bart, this is the first day that Ms. Goodheart has stayed home from work in the entire course of her 23-year career. Bart sets off a stick of dynamite in order to open the safe. Unfortunately, it accidentally misfires and kills Ms. Goodheart, who is asleep on the other side of the wall. Bart becomes frightened and flees without ever opening the safe.

18. When Bart is tried for first-degree burglary, he is found innocent on the following principle:

First-degree burglary takes place when one enters a private dwelling at night with the intention of committing larceny therein.

Which of the following was a major factor in the disposition of the case?

(A) Bart did not actually steal anything.
(B) Bart entered the house at 4:00 P.M.
(C) Murder is a more serious crime and takes precedence over burglary.
(D) Larceny only includes items of known value, not things like a butterfly collection.

19. When Bart is tried for second-degree burglary, he is found guilty on the following principle:

Second-degree burglary takes place when one person enters the dwelling of another during the day with the intention of committing larceny therein.

Which of the following was a major factor in the disposition of the case?

(A) Bart actually committed the crime of murder after he broke into the house.
(B) Ms. Goodheart lived in an apartment house.
(C) Bart intended to steal the butterflies.
(D) Bart succeeded in setting off the dynamite.

20. When Bart is tried for murder, he is found guilty on the following principle: *When a person is involved in the commission of a serious crime, he is guilty of murder if any other person dies as a result of the crime.*

Which of the following was a major factor in the disposition of the case?

(A) Bart knew that the dynamite was powerful enough to kill if anybody was on the other side of the wall.
(B) Bart should have known that Ms. Goodheart was home.
(C) Bart should have checked to see if Ms. Goodheart was home.
(D) Bart was committing burglary at the time that he accidentally killed Ms. Goodheart.

21. When Bart is tried for murder, he is found innocent on the following principle: *A person is guilty of murder when he intentionally injures another person and that person dies as a result.*

Which of the following was a major factor in the disposition of the case?

(A) Bart did not intend to injure Ms. Goodheart.
(B) Bart thought Ms. Goodheart was at work.
(C) Bart should have checked to see if anybody was at home.
(D) Bart did not intend to kill Ms. Goodheart.

Part C

Directions: This section consists of several groups of cases. Each case ends with a judicial holding and a set of four legal principles. You must select the *narrowest* principle that reasonably explains the judicial decision but is *not inconsistent* with any previous holdings in that group of cases.

For the first case in each group, eliminate any principles that do not conform to the facts of the case and do not provide a reasonable explanation of the holding. Then select the narrowest of the reasonable principles.

In the remaining cases in that group, the basic procedure is the same, but you must also eliminate any principles that contradict earlier answers in the group before you select the narrowest principle.

These questions assume no prior legal knowledge on your part; answer them using only ordinary logical reasoning.

Group 1

22. Just after sunset on May 13, Barney Google crashes his car into the back of Mr. Bluster's tractor. Mr. Bluster sues Barney, who claims that the rear lights of the tractor were not on at the time of the accident. As proof, Barney offers a statement

that Billy Bluster, Mr. Bluster's nephew from a neighboring state who was visiting him at the time of the accident, made to Mr. Wilson, who lives about $\frac{1}{2}$ mile from the Blusters. Mr. Wilson is prepared to testify that on May 14 Billy told him that the rear lights on the tractor had been broken for about a month. Billy is no longer visiting and is not available at the trial. Mr. Wilson's testimony is not admitted.

The *narrowest principle* that *reasonably explains* this action is:

(A) The report of a statement by a declarant who is a minor and is not available at trial is hearsay evidence and is not admissible.
(B) The report of a statement by a declarant who is not available at trial is not admissible unless the declarant's domicile is outside the state in which trial is being held.
(C) The report of a statement by a declarant who is not available at trial is hearsay evidence and inadmissible if not corroborated by at least two witnesses to the statement.
(D) No statements may be offered at a criminal trial unless the party against whom the statements are offered has an opportunity to cross-examine the declarant.

23. Mr. Twiggy has been arrested for stealing candy he had promised his wife from Baby's Candy Store. The prosecution wishes to call Mrs. Twiggy as a witness in order to ask her if Mr. Twiggy offered anyone candy on the night of the theft. Mrs. Twiggy's answer would be "yes," but her evidence is not admitted.

The *narrowest principle* that *reasonably explains* this action, and is *not inconsistent with the ruling given in the first case,* is:

(A) Hearsay evidence may not be admitted in any case involving the theft of foodstuffs.
(B) One spouse cannot testify to a statement by the other in a criminal prosecution against the second spouse if they are legally married at the time of the trial.
(C) The report of a statement by a declarant who is not available at trial is not admissible unless the declarant's domicile is outside the state in which the trial is being held.
(D) No statements may be offered at a criminal trial unless the party against whom the statements are offered has an opportunity to cross-examine the declarant.

24. On August 4, Mr. Hogwash, an eccentric old man, made the following statement to his daughter Bubbles and wife LaVerne: "I am Napoleon, Emperor of all Gaul! Kneel before me, peasants!" After the death of Mr. Hogwash, his sanity is at issue: A suit has been brought to void his will which had left his entire (vast) fortune to a racehorse named Brotherhood of Elba. Bubbles and LaVerne offer to testify as to his earlier statement, and their testimony is admitted.

The *narrowest principle* that *reasonably explains* this action, and is *not inconsistent with the rulings given in the cases already cited,* is:

(A) All reports of statements made by a person which reflect as to his sanity are admissible in a probate case.

(B) The members of a man's immediate family may always enter any testimony relating to the sanity of the head of the family.
(C) Reports of a statement by a declarant when the statement was against the declarant's own interest at the time it was made are admissible when the declarant is deceased.
(D) If a report of a statement is offered by only two witnesses to the statement, the reports are only admissible if the purpose of the testimony is to show something other than the truth of the subject matter of the statement.

25. On May 16, Notlob robs a Widget factory. He tells Margie, his fiancee, he would like her to have a widget. Thrilled, Margie accepts. On May 20, Notlob and Margie are married. Reading a paper one day in June, Margie learns of the robbery, infers Notlob's participation in it, and files for divorce. Divorce is granted on June 30. Notlob stands trial for theft in August. The prosecutor calls Margie as a witness to identify which widget Notlob wished her to have. Her testimony is admitted.

The *narrowest principle* that *reasonably explains* this action, and is *not inconsistent with the rulings given in the cases already cited,* is:

(A) The testimony of a receiver of stolen goods as to the nature of the goods received and the identity of the person from whom they were received is admissible in a trial for theft of such goods.
(B) One spouse can be compelled to testify against the other if they were not legally married at the time the act to be testified to occurred.
(C) The testimony of a receiver of stolen goods need not be corroborated.
(D) A husband and wife who are divorced are legally considered never to have been married.

26. Mr. and Mrs. Primp are arrested for theft. While questioning Mr. Primp, the police beat him. He admits his participation in the robbery and also implicates his wife. Mrs. Primp, furious, files for divorce. After the divorce comes through, Mr. and Mrs. Primp are tried separately for the theft. At Mrs. Primp's trial, Mr. Primp's statements to the police are not admitted.

The *narrowest principle* that *reasonably explains* this action, and is *not inconsistent with the rulings given in the cases already cited,* is:

(A) A report of a statement by a declarant who is not available at trial is not admissible and is hearsay evidence if not corroborated by at least two witnesses to the statement.
(B) One spouse cannot legally testify to a statement made by the other if they are legally married.
(C) Statements made as a result of duress or coercion are not admissible as evidence at trial.
(D) Statements which are relevant to a divorce action cannot be admitted in a criminal trial.

Group 2

27. On April 1, Mr. Sellers sends Mr. Von Beyer a letter offering to sell him 10 tons of coal at $3 per ton. The letter arrives on April 15, and Mr. Von Beyer immediately sends back a letter accepting the terms proposed by Mr. Sellers. On April 20, the

price of coal goes up to $25 per ton. Mr. Sellers telephones Mr. Von Beyer to tell him to forget the whole thing. Mr. Von Beyer does not want to forget the whole thing. His letter reaches Mr. Sellers on April 30. When Mr. Sellers refuses to send the coal, Mr. Von Beyer sues him. *Held,* for Von Beyer.

The *narrowest principle* that *reasonably explains* this action, is:

(A) Once a seller makes an offer, he cannot revoke it for a period of 30 days.
(B) If a buyer, upon receipt of an offer, accepts the offer within a reasonable period of time, using an equivalent method of communication, a valid sales contract is formed, providing the offer has not been revoked at the time he accepts it.
(C) In order to be effectively revoked, an offer of sale must be rescinded by the seller before the intended purchaser's acceptance is received.
(D) In order to be valid, revocation of an offer must be made within 10 days of the offer itself.

28. Mr. Shill mails Mr. Board a letter offering to sell him 3,000 darts at 20¢ per dart. The letter arrives on May 12. Mr. Board writes back immediately ordering 2,000 darts at 20¢ per dart. On May 14, the price of a dart rises to 50¢. Mr. Shill refuses to fill Mr. Board's order, which arrives on May 30, and Mr. Board sues Mr. Shill. *Held,* for Mr. Shill.

The *narrowest principle* that *reasonably explains* this result, and is *not inconsistent with the ruling given in the first case,* is:

(A) If a buyer, upon receipt of an offer, accepts the offer within a reasonable period of time, using an equivalent method of communication, a valid sales contract is formed, providing the offer has not been revoked at the time he accepts it.
(B) If an offer is not accepted in its entirety, it is deemed not to have been accepted at all.
(C) If acceptance of an offer does not reach the seller within two weeks, the seller is no longer obligated to honor his offer.
(D) A seller may not revoke an offer simply because the price rises.

29. On October 31, Mr. Soloman sends a letter to Mr. Benson offering to sell him some merchandise. When the letter arrives on November 3, Mr. Benson telephones Mr. Soloman and accepts his offer. Mr. Benson also writes a letter of acceptance which is still sitting on his desk when Mr. Soloman calls him on November 5 to tell him that he no longer wishes to sell the merchandise. Mr. Benson mails the letter, but Mr. Soloman still does not want to sell, so Mr. Benson sues him. *Held,* for Benson.

The *narrowest principle* that *reasonably explains* this action, and is *not inconsistent with the rulings given in the cases already cited,* is:

(A) If a buyer, upon receipt of an offer, accepts the offer within a reasonable period of time using an equivalent method of communication, a valid sales contract is formed, providing the offer has not been revoked at the time he accepts it.
(B) In order for a revocation of an offer to be valid it must be made before the acceptance has been dispatched by an equivalent means of communication.
(C) An offer made by letter may not be revoked by telephone.

(D) If a buyer, upon receipt of an offer, accepts the offer within a reasonable period of time, using an equivalent or faster method of communication, a valid sales contract is formed, providing the offer has not been revoked at the time he accepts it.

30. On June 14, Sifter writes to Bretchy offering to sell merchandise. The letter arrives on June 25. On June 26, Sifter writes to Bretchy cancelling his offer. The second letter arrives on July 3. Before it does, however, on June 28, Bretchy writes to Sifter accepting his offer. Sifter refuses to sell, and Bretchy sues. *Held,* for Sifter.

The *narrowest principle* that *reasonably explains* this action, and is *not inconsistent with the rulings given in the cases already cited,* is:

(A) Prior to acceptance, an offer to sell is freely revocable by the seller.
(B) If a buyer, upon receipt of an offer, accepts the offer within a reasonable period of time, using an equivalent method of communication, a valid sales contract is formed, providing the offer has not been revoked at the time he accepts it.
(C) An offer to sell may be revoked at any time prior to receipt by the seller of the buyer's acceptance.
(D) An offer to sell may be revoked freely up until the time it is received by the potential buyer.

STOP

IF YOU FINISH BEFORE THE TIME IS UP,
CHECK YOUR WORK ON THIS SECTION ONLY.
DO NOT LOOK AT ANY OTHER SECTION IN THE TEST.
WHEN THE TIME IS UP, GO ON TO THE NEXT SECTION.

Section V: Error Recognition

Time: 20 minutes
35 questions

Directions: This section consists of individual sentences. Some of the sentences are correct, but some are incorrect in standard written English for one of the following reasons.

Poor Diction: Usage that is incorrect either because a word's meaning is inappropriate in the sentence or because the word is not acceptable in standard written English.
Examples: I am waiting for the medicine to take *affect.*
The new symphony is *out of sight.*

Verbosity: Repetitious elements which do not add meaning to the sentence, and which are not justified for special emphasis.
Examples: All of the judges were in *agreement* and there was no *dissent.*
With *great speed,* he *quickly* ran home.

Faulty Grammar: Grammatical or structural word forms and expressions that are improper in standard written English, such as errors in case, number or parallelism.
Examples: Each of the boys must bring *their* own baseball equipment.
My sister is studying reading, writing and *how to do arithmetic.*

Be sure to use these definitions of the errors, rather than your own ideas. No sentence contains more than one type of error. Select choice

(A) if the sentence contains a *diction* error.
(B) if the sentence contains a *verbosity* error.
(C) if the sentence contains a *grammar* error.
(D) if the sentence contains *no* error.

1. Although our current process may seem difficult at first, we have found that, ultimately, it causes less complications than the one we used previously.

2. Neither his acting style nor his delivery are adequate to the role.

3. Elizabeth, who is beautiful, intelligent, and charming, is now at lunch.

4. Ten people decided to join us on our expedition to the recently discovered cave, despite our warnings that the journey would be strenuous, the work exhausting, and the area dangerous.

5. The reason that Gertrude, in spite of her intelligence, wit and education, is now a beggar, is that she married unfortunately, lived succulently and squandered her resources.

6. To find the needed information, the whole book had to be read.

7. The principle figure in the drama, a young girl about to assume a position as governess to the children of a nobleman, was very appealing.

8. The text of the poem and the commentary following were assigned last week.

9. I disagree with your contention that when the true facts of the case emerge, he will be vindicated and totally cleared.

10. "I have said that honey and vinegar makes a healthy tonic," remarked Mr. Doan.

11. Because she was so charming and vivacious, Mary was the perfect compliment to our little dinner party.

12. "Play it cautious" was his considered advice.

13. Our major support in this endeavor are our representatives in your organization.

14. I earnestly wish that I was in a position to be of assistance to your committee, but prior commitments make it impossible for me to attend the meeting.

15. He is one of those men who never care how they look.

16. Poet Percy Bysshe Shelley, the master of verse, who married Godwin's daughter Mary, was born in the year of 1799.

17. Since he has arrived in our town and assumed complete responsibility for the organization.

18. I implore you to reconsider my offer, because I have little faith that anyone beside you can satisfactorily complete the assignment.

19. Neither you nor your brother seems to understand the quotation.

20. He realized that the report he had received on the behavior of his subordinate, while superficially quite complimentary, seemed to infer, on closer examination, that the latter's conduct during the trial had been less than ethical.

21. We would appreciate your reply to the invitation immediately, either by telephone call or by letter.

22. The triumphant winner was victorious.

23. The rise upward of the rate of street crime in New York City has been popularly attributed by the public to a wide range of sociological and environmental factors.

24. I was extremely disappointed that, although he and George both promised to attend, the last decided that he had too much work to do, and failed to appear.

25. I know that, based on your evaluation of his past performance, you are convinced that Frank can conduct a more thorough investigation than me.

26. Although her manner was very convincing, and the temptation to suspend my disbelief was great, the gypsy's prophecy was too general for me to take seriously.

27. The policeman was lauded for his brave act of courage.

28. You may raise my salary, increase my vacation periods, and remodel my office; I still remain completely disinterested in your suggestion that I retract my resignation and remain in your employ.

29. He was successful in maintaining the allusion that he was reliable and competent for quite a long time before we discovered his chronic carelessness.

30. Getting on the plane, a loud backfire could be heard, which, since I find flying unpleasant under the best circumstances, was quite disconcerting.

31. We definitely cannot attempt to make a decision on something as crucial as this before we can be altogether to discuss it.

32. Although we assured him that it was merely a practice test, John studied for the examination like he believed his entire future as a physician depended on the results.

33. It is true that, except for you and I, everyone in the group voted against the proposed change in the admission procedure.

34. Just let me alone for a few minutes and I will be fine.

35. That might be a common mistake, but me, being a linguist and having studied the subject for years, knows better.

STOP

IF YOU FINISH BEFORE THE TIME IS UP,
CHECK YOUR WORK ON THIS SECTION ONLY.
DO NOT LOOK AT ANY OTHER SECTION IN THE TEST.
WHEN THE TIME IS UP, GO ON TO THE NEXT SECTION.

Section VI: Sentence Correction

Time: 20 minutes
25 questions

Directions: Each sentence in this section is either partially or totally underlined. For each sentence, you are given five possible phrasings of the underlined part. Choice (A) is always the same as the original, but choices (B) through (E) all offer alternative versions of the underlined part. You are to choose the best phrasing.

Sometimes the original sentence is most effective; sometimes another phrasing will be preferable in standard written English. In selecting your answer, consider grammar, diction, sentence construction, and punctuation. The best choice should be clear and exact, not awkward or ambiguous. Do not change the meaning of the original sentence.

1. Marcia leaves Salt Lake City tonight; she will arrive in Denver on Tuesday, and she remains there 2 days.

   (A) tonight; she will arrive in Denver on Tuesday, and she remains there 2 days.
   (B) tonight, she will arrive in Denver on Tuesday, and she remains there 2 days.
   (C) tonight; she will arrive in Denver on Tuesday, and she will remain there 2 days.
   (D) tonight, she will arrive in Denver on Tuesday, and she will remain there 2 days.
   (E) tonight; she will arrive in Denver on Tuesday, and remains there 2 days.

2. My father enjoys fresh air, sunshine, and to take long walks.

   (A) fresh air, sunshine, and to take long walks.
   (B) fresh air, sunshine, and long walks.
   (C) fresh air, sunshine: and to take long walks.
   (D) fresh air; sunshine; and taking long walks.
   (E) fresh air, sunshine, and taking long walks.

3. The students in the dormitories were forbidden, unless they had special passes, from staying out after 11:30 P.M.

   (A) forbidden, unless they had special passes, from staying out
   (B) forbidden unless they had special passes, to stay out
   (C) forbidden unless they had special passes, from staying out
   (D) forbidden unless they had special passes to stay out
   (E) forbidden, unless they had special passes, to stay out

4. Everybody was agreed that two representatives should be sent, you and me.

   (A) Everybody was agreed that two representatives should be sent, you and me.
   (B) Everybody were agreed that two representatives should be sent, you and me.
   (C) Everybody were agreed that two representatives should be sent, you and I.
   (D) Everybody was agreed that two representatives should be sent, you and I.
   (E) Everybody was agreed that two representatives should be sent. You and me.

5. None of the rocks which form the solid crust of our planet are more than two billion years old.

(A) rocks which form the solid crust of our planet are
(B) rocks, which form the solid crust of our planet, are
(C) rocks which form the solid crust of our planet, is
(D) rocks which form the solid crust of our planet is
(E) rocks which form the solid crust of our planet, are

6. Parents are the ones whom we believe ought to insist upon their childrens' obeying orders.

(A) whom we believe ought to insist upon their childrens'
(B) whom we believe ought to insist upon their children's
(C) who we believe ought to insist upon their childrens'
(D) who we believe ought to insist upon their children
(E) who we believe ought to insist upon their children's

7. The reason for the strike, you may recall, was because the union demanded a closed shop.

(A) The reason for the strike, you may recall, was because
(B) The reason for the strike, you may recall, was that
(C) The reason for the strike, you may recall was that
(D) The reason for the strike, you may recall was because
(E) The reason for the strike you may recall was because

8. The Smokies are the home of the descendants of this brave tribe: a series of records are being published about them.

(A) The Smokies are the home of the descendants of this brave tribe: a series of records are
(B) The Smokies is the home of the descendants of this brave tribe; a series of records is
(C) The Smokies is the home of the descendants of this brave tribe; a series of records are
(D) The Smokies are the home of the descendants of this brave tribe; a series of records are
(E) The Smokies are the home of the descendants of this brave tribe; a series of records is

9. Visiting the scenes of the past, our interest in American history is renewed and enlivened.

(A) Visiting the scenes of the past, our interest
(B) While visiting the scenes of the past, our interest
(C) While we are visiting the scenes of the past, our interest
(D) Visiting the scenes of the past. Our interest
(E) Visiting the scenes of the past; our interest

10. My experience in South Africa taught me that the climate there is quite different from ours.

(A) South Africa taught me that the climate there is quite different from ours.
(B) South Africa. Taught me that the climate there is quite different from ours.
(C) South Africa, taught me that the climate there is quite different from ours.
(D) South Africa, taught me that the climate there is quite different from our's.
(E) South Africa taught me that the climate there is quite different from our's.

11. I, who am your best friend, should have at least a fair chance of winning the prize.

(A) I, who am your best friend, should
(B) I who are your best friend, should
(C) I, who are your best friend, should
(D) I who am your best friend, should
(E) I who am your best friend should

12. I do not understand why mother should object to me playing the piano at the party.

(A) mother should object to me playing
(B) Mother should object to my playing
(C) mother should object to my playing
(D) Mother should object to me playing
(E) Mother would object to my playing

13. It seems to me that everyone of the waiters is able to do their share of the work.

(A) everyone of the waiters is able to do their share
(B) everyone of the waiters is able to do his share
(C) every one of the waiters is able to do their share
(D) every one of the waiters is able to do his share
(E) everyone of the waiters is able to do there share

14. The company have moved into their new building.

(A) have moved into their
(B) has moved into its
(C) have moved into its
(D) has moved into their
(E) has moved into it's

15. Sandburg's autobiography, as well as his poems, are familiar to many readers.

(A) autobiography, as well as his poems, are
(B) autobiography as well as his poems, are
(C) autobiography, as well as his poems are
(D) autobiography, as well as his poems, is
(E) autobiography as well as his poems are

16. Spotting the principal, the chewing gum was placed under the seat by the students.

(A) Spotting the principal, the chewing gum was placed under the seat by the students.
(B) Spotting the principal, the students placed the chewing gum under the seat.

(C) Spotting the principal, the students placed their chewing gum under their seats.
(D) The chewing gum was placed under the seat by the students after spotting the principal.
(E) The chewing gum was placed under the seat by the students after their spotting of the principal.

17. Deep in the forest, warmed by the dying embers of our campfire, sat the scoutmaster and I.

(A) campfire, sat the scoutmaster and I.
(B) campfire, sat the scoutmaster and me.
(C) campfire. Sat the scoutmaster and me.
(D) campfire; sat the scoutmaster and me.
(E) campfire; sat the scoutmaster and I.

18. She asked "Who do you think is going to win the tennis match?"

(A) She asked "Who
(B) She asked, "Whom
(C) She asked, "Who
(D) She asked "Whom
(E) She asked, "who

19. Students who plan to become doctors are advised to study Biology, Chemistry, and German.

(A) Biology, Chemistry, and German.
(B) biology, Chemistry, and German.
(C) biology, Chemistry, and german..
(D) biology, chemistry, and German.
(E) Biology, chemistry, and German.

20. My diagnoses is worth more than a surgeons.

(A) diagnoses is worth more than a surgeons.
(B) diagnoses is worth more than a surgeons'.
(C) diagnosis is worth more than a surgeon's.
(D) diagnosis is worth more than a surgeons.
(E) diagnosis is worth more than a surgeons'.

21. On the corner was a house that was unlocked and with no occupants.

(A) unlocked and with no occupants.
(B) unlocked, and with no occupants.
(C) unlocked, and unoccupied.
(D) unlocked and unoccupied.
(E) unlocked; and with no occupants.

22. My uncle who was taken ill suddenly, is now feeling well.

(A) My uncle who was taken ill suddenly, is now feeling well.
(B) My uncle, who was taken ill suddenly, is now feeling good.
(C) My uncle, who was taken ill suddenly, is now feeling well.

(D) My uncle who was taken ill suddenly, is now feeling good.
(E) My Uncle, who was taken ill suddenly, is now feeling well.

23. He would not accept of my hospitality.

(A) accept of (B) except of (C) accept (D) except (E) accept from

24. The birds here are very much like North America.

(A) are very much like
(B) are very much like those of
(C) are very much like the birds of
(D) are more like those of
(E) are very much similar to

25. To be a teacher is not as difficult as being a secretary.

(A) as being a secretary.
(B) as doing secretarial work.
(C) as to do secretarial work.
(D) as to be a secretary.
(E) as to work as a secretary.

STOP

IF YOU FINISH BEFORE THE TIME IS UP,
CHECK YOUR WORK ON THIS SECTION ONLY.
DO NOT LOOK AT ANY OTHER SECTION IN THE TEST.
WHEN THE TIME IS UP, CHECK YOUR ANSWERS AGAINST THE ANSWER KEY
AND EXPLANATIONS BEGINNING ON THE FOLLOWING PAGE.

Answers to Final Self-Test B

Section I Answers

1. (C) The basic idea of both is that you get back what you put in.

2. (B) If Mark wears a green tie, he must not be fat, which means he must be skinny. But if he is skinny, he must wear a blue shirt. As for the other statements, they can be true if Keith is skinny and Richard is fat.

3. (D) The pattern is this:
    rush hour . . . crowd
    not rush hour . . . no crowd
    happy . . . quickly
    not happy . . . not quickly (slowly)
   The two are logically identical. In (C), for example, losing weight is not exactly the opposite of being fat.

4. (C) This man fits neither of the two molds. He voluntarily takes a risk and avoids recognition for it.

5. (A) We have a contrast being set up—the "in reality" tips us off. The fact that the governors are steered by *popular* applause indicates that they probably serve the populace, or multitude.

6. (E) The blank will be filled here by something the author approves of (we can tell from the tone); and the best fit is (E).

7. (D) If you were the goose, wouldn't this bother you? There is nothing philanthropic about man's caring for the goose; Choice (D) reveals the true motive.

8. (B) In fact, his whole point seems to be that people, like the goose, really *can't* get something for nothing; there is always a catch.

9. (A) For *I* to be true, the box would have to contain blue nerdles and at least one trifle. The other choices are possible.

10. (C) He clearly favors the English, and the tone is more appropriate to a journalist than to a diplomat.

11. (D) *II* and *IV* are actually stated; *I* is not even implied. Note that the question asks only for claims which the advertiser does not actually make.

12. (E) A "number . . . are ignorant in spite of experiences."

13. (B) The answer will involve some sort of financial setback, and the more global one seems to fit better than the personal one.

14. (C) The word desired will be something extremely substantial—"the home" seems to fit best.

15. (B) The implication is that if you don't buy one, you don't really love America.

16. (A) All he does is attack his opponent; he never gets to the issue. While (D) and (E) may be true, the real problem is the politician's failure to confront the issue.

17. (A) This answer is parallel in structure to the statement about hope and maintains the tone of the sentence.

18. (C) Two assumptions are made: one, that the fact that Goldstein was a good player means he can manage (statement *I*) and two, that even if he can, it will help the Bimbos (statement *III*). Statement *II* is offered as a fact.

19. (E) If (E) is true, the Silly Party probably caused more unemployment in Millertown than would have occurred otherwise.

20. (A) The first four lines basically say that the eagle supplied the implement of his own destruction. Choice (A) finishes the thought by identifying the implement.

21. (D) The fact that the eagle was killed by a dart fashioned from one of his own feathers is ironic.

22. (C) Of the five, only this one is in no substantial way a victim of circumstances.

23. (C) The artist is supposed to work hard, but the harder he works the less visible his work should be. A paradox is a seeming self-contradiction. This statement certainly sounds like one.

24. (E) Choices (B) and (D) are way off. As for (A), no suggestion is made that artists should not work hard: "Industry in art is a necessity." Neither is any suggestion made [as in (C)] that hard work is not appreciated, only that it should not be obvious.

25. (A) *Inductive reasoning* is the drawing of a general rule from a series of specific observations. *Deductive reasoning* is just the opposite: a conclusion about a specific from some general facts.

Section II, Part A Answers

1. (C) Both angles are inscribed in arc AD. Therefore, both angles have the same measure (they are equal to half of the arc).

2. (C)

The man and his shadow become the legs of an isosceles right triangle. (Any right triangle that contains a 45° angle must be isosceles.)

3. (A) Both are just larger than a half. Column A exceeds a half by $\frac{1}{42}$, Column B by only $\frac{1}{106}$. Thus, Column A is larger.

4. (C) Only two possibilities exist: heads or tails. The chance of four heads is the same as the chance of four tails (no heads) if the coin is honest.

5. (D) It depends entirely on what x is. For example, compare the results if $x = 3$ and if $x = -2$.

6. (A) In each case, we will be dealing with $\frac{\text{difference}}{\text{original}}$, and in each case, the difference will be the same. But the original is smaller in the case of Mike's age, since Mike is younger.

7. (C) Anything to the zero power = 1; 1 to any power = 1.

8. (C) The area of the rectangle = bh, of each triangle = $\frac{1}{2}bh$. The heights are all the same, and the bases of the triangles add up to the same length as the base of the rectangle. Therefore the shaded part is exactly half of the rectangle, and equal to the unshaded part.

9. (C) This problem is a hard one, unless you already know that the area of the inscribed square is half the area of the circumscribed square. Otherwise, draw some radii of the circle as follows:

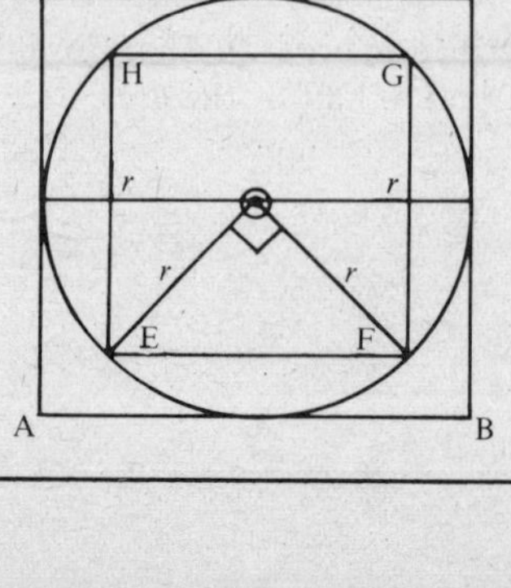

The side of the large square = $2r$. The side of the small square = $r\sqrt{2}$ (use the Pythagorean theorem). The areas, then, are $4r^2$ and $2r^2$, respectively.

10. (D) Remember, these diagrams are not drawn to scale; $\angle ABC$ might be an acute angle.

11. (D) It depends on the value of x (try $x = 0$ and $x = 10$).

12. (A) Translated to fractions, the two sides read $\frac{3}{8} \cdot \frac{1}{3} \cdot 8{,}000$ and $\frac{1}{7} \cdot \frac{7}{8} \cdot 7{,}000$. Column A $\left(\frac{1}{8} \cdot 8{,}000\right)$ is larger than Column B $\left(\frac{1}{8} \cdot 7{,}000\right)$.

13. (C) $\angle d + \angle e + \angle f = 180°$ (sum of the angles of a triangle). $\angle a + \angle b + \angle c = 360°$ (the exterior angles of any polygon always add up to 360°).

14. (B) Column B ends up positive, Column A ends up negative, so Column B must be larger.

15. (A) 16π (50.27) is larger than 49.

16. (C) This problem is a very hard one. The fact that $g^2 = bc$ is a somewhat obscure theorem of plane geometry. If you remembered it, fine. If not, you can get it with similar triangles (which we did not discuss) or with several applications of the Pythagorean theorem, as follows (remember, each letter represents the length of a line segment in the diagram):

$$g^2 + c^2 = d^2$$
$$g^2 + b^2 = f^2$$
$$f^2 + d^2 = (b + c)^2 = b^2 + 2bc + c^2$$

Add them up.

$$2g^2 + c^2 + b^2 + f^2 + d^2 = 2bc + c^2 + b^2 + f^2 + d^2$$

Drop the terms that appear on both sides.

$$2g^2 = 2bc$$
$$g^2 = bc$$

17. (A) Easy one. The sum of any two sides (a and $b + c$) of a triangle must be larger than the third side ($e + d$).

18. (D) We have no way of determining any relationship between these two lines.

19. (D) If $x = 1$, the columns are equal.

20. (D) What if $x = -2$?

21. (B) Cross-multiply. $9r = 8s$, which means s is bigger than r. Then $9s$ is bigger than $9r$, so it is certainly bigger than $8r$.

22. (D) The expression is usually positive, but not always. Try $x = 3$, for example.

23. (C) The process is the same. For every distinct team of three formed, an equally distinct nonteam of four is also formed. In one case we select four to be on the team; in the other case we select four to be off the team.

24. (B) If the sides were 8, 15, and 17, a° would be 90° (8, 15, and 17 is a Pythagorean triplet). Since the side opposite the a° angle is less than 17, a° must be less than 90°. Therefore, $b^\circ + c^\circ$ must be more than 90°.

25. (C) Divide each term of the numerator in Column A by the denominator, and you end up with the expression in Column B.

Part B Answers

1. (A) Sergio played 697 games and won 81 of them. He won about 12%.

2. (C) The player with the most wins is Victor. The player with the best average is Ereño. Victor was second 125 times; Ereño, 44 times. The difference is 81.

3. (E) The number of wins is not broken down separately for singles and doubles. Without further information, this question cannot be answered.

4. (E) Ramos has won 11% of his games, and Zamalloa has won only 8% of his. The trick is that the number of games we are looking for must be added both to the number of wins and the number of games played. The equation we need is:

$$\frac{50 + x}{607 + x} = .11 \qquad (= 11\%)$$

Solving, x turns out to be 18.84. Since Zamalloa can't play a fractional number of games, he must win 19 games in a row. He will then have won 69 out of 626, which is about 11%.

5. (E) The player who has played the most is Davila. He has played 829 doubles matches and 359 singles matches.

$$\frac{829}{359} = 2.31, \text{ or } 231\%$$

6. (B) Antonio's line would then look like this:

Played	*Won*	*Second*	*Third*
333	52	52	38

Calculate the average according to the note.

$$\frac{3(52) + 2(52) + 38}{3(333)} = \frac{298}{999} = .300$$

7. (D) Eduardo has played 1,009 games. We are, then, interested in a player who has played 1,100 games. That is Elias. Elias has a .255 average. So do Victor, Beltran, and Onaindia.

8. (B) Both were exactly 0. Zania had a balance of \$25 billion and Paulitania about \$35 billion.

9. (A) The year was 1970, when Bobboland reached the lofty peak of 0. After that, simply read the Paulitania graph.

10. (D) Zania had a negative balance only in 1972. (The balance then was –\$12 billion.) Jojoland had a balance of about –\$50 billion in that year.

11. (B) Jojoland and Bobboland both had balances of 0 in 1970. Paulitania's balance was always positive, and Zania, while its graph crossed the axis, never had a balance of exactly 0 in any year.

12. (C)

Paulitania	+\$85 billion
Jojoland	–\$25 billion
Zania	+\$65 billion
Bobboland	–\$25 billion
Total	+\$100 billion

13. (B) If the increase continues, Paulitania will reach a balance of \$100 billion in 1978. To find the percent increase, take the difference and divide by the original.

$$\frac{\text{difference}}{\text{original}} = \frac{25 \text{ billion}}{75 \text{ billion}} = \frac{1}{3} = 33\frac{1}{3}\%$$

14. (E) Only in this year was Zania's balance significantly higher than Paulitania's.

Section III Answers

1. (A) His current practice is not growing. When he moves, he feels it is necessary to find a location where it can grow.

2. (C) This factor is a partial determinant of his ability to pay; it relates to factor 5—the total cost of each house.

3. (E) This factor is not taken into account at all in reaching a decision.

4. (D) He *believes* it is plausible, but is it? He'll find out. A typical assumption.

5. (B) This factor is important in comparing all five locations, since his funds are limited.

6. (C) This factor is one component of the overall suitability of each house.

7. (E) The good doctor is a general practitioner and does not compete with specialists.

8. (B) Another important way to compare all five—without the prospect of establishing a practice, the doctor cannot afford to move.

9. (C) This factor is mentioned; it figures in the total cost (factor 5) of each house.

10. (A) This event is what will be accomplished once the decision is made.

11. (D) Is his cushion sufficient? He *thinks* it is. Note the abstract noun which is the first word; it's a tipoff that this is an assumption.

12. (C) This component–the competition–relates to the doctor's prospects of establishing a practice.

13. (D) Will the trend continue? Dr. Burgess *thinks* so, but time will tell.

14. (E) The passage gives no indication that Dr. Burgess has even considered this.

15. (E) Irrelevant, since he does not intend to use financing.

16. (A) Dr. Burgess wants to do precisely this.

17. (E) Who cares? He's moving his practice to the suburbs.

18. (B) The third way to compare all five alternatives: without a suitable house, Dr. Burgess will not move.

19. (C) This is a subpoint of factor 8–the prospects of establishing a practice.

20. (D) *I* and *III* are mentioned in the first paragraph, but *II* is not mentioned at all.

21. (B) The house in Alton costs $48,000, and the house in Weldon costs $65,000. Dr. Burgess has $70,000 to invest before he touches any of his securities. All of the other three houses cost more. (Note that the cost of the practice in Weldon is not included in the cost of the house.)

22. (B) No house is available in Ventura right now, so the cost of one is hard to determine.

23. (D) (D) represents the real problem. Choices (B) and (C) are partial answers, (E) is unimportant, and (A) could be arranged.

24. (D) The cost would be $85,000 plus 9% of the $15,000 worth of securities that would have to be sold.

25. (D) A house is available in Broadwood Heights, it is not overly expensive, and Dr. Burgess is fairly sure of the need for doctors there.

26. (C) This factor contributes to the company's financial position (factor 39).

27. (A) The entire decision is geared toward this event.

28. (B) This criterion is important in comparing plans. How much incentive will each provide?

29. (D) Will they? It seems likely, but at the moment it is not proven; it is an assumption.

30. (E) These were not the problem areas.

31. (C) This relates to factor 39, the financial position of the company.

32. (E) This was not mentioned at all.

33. (B) This problem precipitated the need for the decision in the first place.

34. (D) Harris *believes* this is optimal. He might be right and he might be wrong.

35. (A) This is what the group wants to accomplish.

36. (E) None were payable. This is not important.

37. (D) This assumption–that they will actually respond to these incentives–is a key one.

38. (C) This is a subcategory of factor 28 of the incentives.

39. (B) This is another major problem. Can the company afford the plans?

40. (C) This is a contributing factor to factor 33, the lag on the growth of sales volume.

41. (A) This is a necessity if the company is to go ahead with a plan.

42. (E) Nobody said anything at all about this.

43. (D) This is unproven; it is strictly an assumption.

44. (E) They seem to disagree on the issue, but this item does not really have any importance.

45. (B) This was discussed at great length. Choice (C) was not mentioned, (D) was untenable, and (A) and (E) were ruled out.

46. (A) All he really did was to close the meeting.

47. (D) Fifty salesmen averaged \$250,000 each in sales–for a total of \$12.5 million. The company's total sales were \$14 million dollars. Therefore, \$1.5 million dollars worth of sales were direct (14 – 12.5).

$$\frac{1.5}{14} = 11\%$$

48. (E) Under Mr. Harris' plan, a salesman would get \$1,000 (1%) for his sales between \$250,000 and \$350,000. After that, he would get 2% of the next \$100,000 worth of sales. With another \$75,000 worth of sales, he would earn a \$1,500 bonus: \$350,000 + \$75,000 = \$425,000.

49. (C) This was clearly stated in the first two paragraphs.

50. (B) *Stock Plan:*

Commission = 6% of $400,000	= $24,000
Bonus = 1% of $100,000 and 2% of $50,000 =	2,000
	$26,000

Cash Plan:

6% of $300,000 =	$18,000
8% of $100,000 =	8,000
	$26,000

A salesman making $400,000 worth of sales would get exactly the same under either plan.

Section IV Answers

1. (C) The key point is that Black had no *intent* to kill Green. Choice (D) is close, but does not rule out the possibility that Black intended to kill Green after he scared him. As long as he believed the gun empty, however, he cannot be said to have intended to kill with it.

2. (A) The first sentence of the principle allows us to transfer the intent. As long as intent to kill someone is shown, that is enough.

3. (A) Somebody merely needs to die during the robbery, which is one of the crimes mentioned in the principle. Somebody did.

4. (D) No intent to kill existed—the death was an accident. Departure 3 hours after the robbery is not immediate flight.

5. (D) Spangle may have been Holmes' agent, and Anderson may have been Spangle's agent, but no agency relationship existed between Holmes and Anderson.

6. (D) A definite communication had gone from Mr. Rich to Mark. Little Rich, therefore, was the authorized agent of Mr. Rich, and Mark was correct to follow his instructions.

7. (B) Billy had no authority when he made the deal, but when Mr. Dithers paid for the ring, he ratified Billy's acts in his behalf.

8. (C) Appointment and ratification mean nothing. The provision about minority overrides everything; Burt is a minor and cannot appoint an agent.

9. (B) Peter appointed Algernon, not Benny. That's all there is to it.

10. (C) The law about stopping at a stop sign is obviously a safety regulation; the other factors are more administrative in nature.

18. (A) "Beside" means "next to." We need "besides."

19. (D) This is fine. In "neither one seems to," there is perfect agreement.

20. (A) The report *implies;* the reader *infers.*

21. (C) As the sentence stands, "immediately" could refer to the reply or the appreciation. It should read "your immediate reply."

22. (B) This sentence holds too much triumph for ordinary emphasis: "triumphant . . . winner . . . victorious."

23. (B) This sentence is verbose in two ways. "To rise" is "to move upward"; "popularly" means "by the public."

24. (C) The *latter,* not the *last.*

25. (C) More thorough than *I* (could).

26. (D) Nothing wrong.

27. (B) "Brave" and "courage" are repetitious.

28. (A) "Disinterested" means "impartial." This speaker is *uninterested* (not interested).

29. (A) He maintained an *illusion.* An *allusion* is a reference.

30. (C) Something is dangling. The sentence reads as though the backfire was getting on the plane.

31. (A) "Altogether" means "entirely," which is not at all appropriate in this sentence. We want to be *together* or, if you must, *all together.*

32. (A) He studied *as if* he believed that.

33. (C) Except for *us* (you and me)—we need the objective case.

34. (A) Wrong verb—*leave* me alone. "To let" is "to allow"; our speaker wants to be *left* alone.

35. (C) It comes down to "me knows," a very definite grammar error.

Section VI Answers

1. (C) The semicolon is fine, but what comes after it should be parallel. If she "arrives," she then "remains"; if she "will arrive," she then "will remain."

2. (B) Parallelism! We have a string of nouns; the third element must also be a noun.

3. (E) The commas were correct, but forbidden takes *to.*

4. (D) "Everybody" takes a singular verb. The agreement was that you and *I* should be sent.

5. (D) No commas are necessary, but "none" (which means "not one") takes a singular verb.

6. (E) We need the nominative case—we believe *they* ought to. . . . "Children" is already a plural word without an extra *s*.

7. (B) Reasons are never "because." The existence of a reason implies some causality. The commas are necessary to set off the parenthetical phrase, "you may recall."

8. (E) *A* series—singular. The Smokies are a collection of mountains; they need a plural verb.

9. (C) This choice is the only one that corrects the problem—something is dangling. The sentence reads as though "our interest" is visiting.

10. (A) Nothing wrong here. The original is best.

11. (A) "I" takes "am." A mental reorganization of the sentence shows this. The commas are necessary to set off the parenthetical phrase.

12. (B) "Mother" is a proper name (capitalized); we then need the possessive pronoun. Choice (E) changes the meaning.

13. (D) "Every one" is two words; every *one* does *his* share.

14. (B) "Company" is singular. The possessive of "it" is "its." "It's" means "it is."

15. (D) His autobiography *is*—the parenthetical phrase between does not change that, although it must be set off with commas.

16. (B) As this sentence is written, it sounds as if the chewing gum spotted the principal. (D) has much the same problem. (C) changes the meaning of the sentence slightly, and (E) is extremely awkward.

17. (A) This sentence is perfectly correct. (We sat.)

18. (C) We need the nominative case, but we also need a comma before the quote.

19. (D) The name of a language is capitalized, but the other subjects are not.

20. (C) A simple matter of the possessive case, and a singular use of "diagnosis."

21. (D) This choice is the most effective. The others are all quite awkward.

22. (C) Commas around the parenthetical phrase. To describe health, we need the adverb "well."

23. (C) The word "of" is unnecessary, but "accept" is correct.

24. (B) As the sentence is written, we are comparing birds to a continent. Choice (C) is not as effective as (B); it is too repetitious. Choice (D) changes the meaning, and (E) suffers from the same defect as the original.

25. (D) Make it parallel, but do not change the meaning of the sentence, as (B), (C), and (E) do.

APPENDIX A

Experimental Sections

The Educational Testing Service constantly tests new types of sections for possible use on the LSAT. Most of these sections are scrapped after a year or so of testing, but some—most recently the Logical Reasoning, Practical Judgment, and Quantitative Comparison sections—become regular sections of the exam. We include here the types that have been tested recently. The chances are that they will not appear on your test, but if they do, they should not be totally unfamiliar to you. Remember, the last section is *usually* experimental, in which case it will not count toward your score, but you should take it seriously in any case.

First, let us try a new variation of logical reasoning. You are asked five questions on a fairly complex set of data. For example:

A is the brother-in-law of B.
C is the sister-in-law of E.
F and G have a daughter named H. (F is the father, G the mother.)
E is the sister of B. They have no other siblings.
Neither A nor C has any siblings.
H is married to D and they have a son named I.
D is the child of C.
No one has been married more than once.

1. **A is married to**

   (A) E (B) C (C) G (D) H (E) None of these

2. **I's grandfather is**

   (A) A (B) B (C) C (D) D (E) None of these

3. **The mother-in-law of H is**

   (A) E (B) C (C) G (D) A (E) B

4. **Which of the following has no blood relative mentioned?**

   (A) A (B) B (C) C (D) D (E) I

5. **Who is not a grandparent of I?**

   (A) B (B) C (C) E (D) F (E) G

The important thing to do in this type of question is to set up a diagram. The key provisions here are that E and B are siblings and that A and C are only children. The only way for A to be the brother-in-law of B and C to be the sister-in-law of E is for A to be married to E and B to C. So we get:

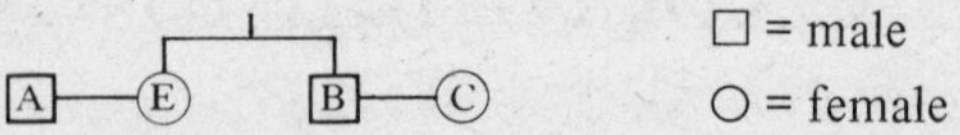

Add in the rest of the facts:

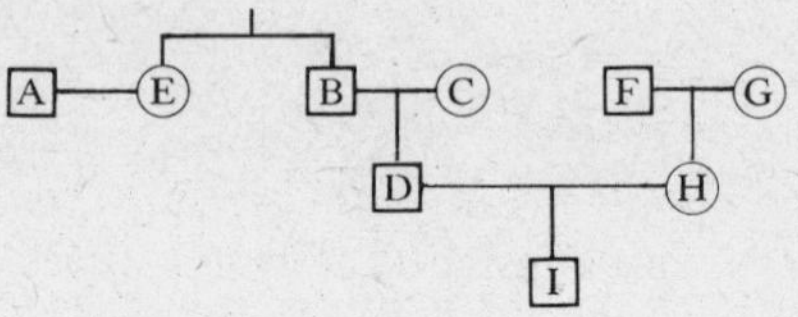

Now, the questions are easy.

1. (A) A is married to E.

2. (B) I has two grandfathers, but only one is listed (F is the other).

3. (B) D's mother—C.

4. (A) A is the only one with no siblings, parents, or children.

5. (C) B, C, F, and G are the grandparents.

Our next experimental sample involves a new variety of Principles and Cases. You are given a case and two principles which apply to it. You are then faced with several questions. You do not answer these questions, given the facts of the case. For each question, you are to choose the most appropriate alternative.

(A) The question presents a *major issue* requiring a choice between the two principles.
(B) The question presents a *major issue* requiring additional facts or principles, but no choice between the two given principles.
(C) The question presents a *major issue* which can be resolved by application of the given principles.
(D) The question presents a *minor issue* which is either unimportant or unlikely in light of the facts and the principles.

Case

The Reverend Loon is standing on the corner preaching his new religion when Bingo walks up and calls him a "rotund dotard." Loon picks up a books and says, "Hold it, this Bible is loaded." Bingo, who is hard of hearing, thinks that he said, "Why, you're loaded." He is very afraid that Loon is about to throw the book at

him, and has a heart attack. Mrs. Peabody, who is blind, is standing right next to Loon and hears exactly what he says. She starts to run away.

Principle I

No person may be punished for speaking any words whatsoever.

Principle II

A person is liable for assault when, by words or actions, he places another in apprehension of an injurious, unrequested and unprivileged touching.

1. Can Bingo win a suit against Loon? Ⓐ Ⓑ Ⓒ Ⓓ

2. Can Mrs. Peabody win a suit against Loon? Ⓐ Ⓑ Ⓒ Ⓓ

3. Would an ordinary person in Bingo's position have been afraid that Loon would throw the book? Ⓐ Ⓑ Ⓒ Ⓓ

4. Can Loon win a suit against Bingo for defamation of character? Ⓐ Ⓑ Ⓒ Ⓓ

5. Will Loon be guilty of murder if Bingo dies? Ⓐ Ⓑ Ⓒ Ⓓ

— —

Once you understand the directions, these are not as bad as they seem at first.

1. (C) The speech is not at issue, since Bingo did not hear what was said—he was frightened solely by Loon's actions, and Principle II governs.

2. (A) Mrs. Peabody did not see the actions—she was frightened solely by the words, and the two principles are in direct conflict.

3. (D) This is totally unimportant—Bingo *was* afraid, and that is all that the principle requires.

4. (C) No problem here—the first principle clearly governs.

5. (B) We would have to know something about the relevant law of murder to answer this one.

The next question type is a sort of combination of Principles and Cases and Practical Judgment. You are given a fact pattern and a conclusion which might be drawn from it. You will then be given a series of additional facts and asked if each of them

(A) proves, or nearly proves the conclusion
(B) supports, but does not prove the conclusion
(C) disproves, or nearly disproves the conclusion

(D) weakens, but does not disprove the conclusion
(E) is irrelevant or nearly irrelevant to the conclusion

Case

Bruno and Igor have never gotten along. When Bruno is found brutally murdered, Igor is brought in for questioning. He claims that he was taking a long walk alone on the other side of town at the time of the murder. Gorgo, Bruno's best friend, claims that he saw Igor leaving the scene of the murder moments after it happened. *Conclusion:* **Igor murdered Bruno.**

1. **Ten nuns saw Igor on the other side of town at the exact time of Bruno's death.** Ⓐ Ⓑ Ⓒ Ⓓ Ⓔ

2. **Gorgo and Igor never liked each other.** Ⓐ Ⓑ Ⓒ Ⓓ Ⓔ

3. **Two days ago, Igor swore in front of five witnesses that he would kill Bruno.** Ⓐ Ⓑ Ⓒ Ⓓ Ⓔ

4. **Igor's fingerprints are on a knife found in Bruno's stomach.** Ⓐ Ⓑ Ⓒ Ⓓ Ⓔ

5. **Igor claims he was walking past a bar at the exact time of Bruno's death and heard a song which was in fact playing in the bar at that time.** Ⓐ Ⓑ Ⓒ Ⓓ Ⓔ

How did you do?

1. **(C) This seems to be an air-tight alibi.**

2. **(E) This does not really add to the evidence and does not make his story less credible.**

3. **(B) This is one more piece of evidence but hardly conclusive proof.**

4. **(A) This seems to be proof.**

5. **(D) While the story could be faked, it certainly strengthens Igor's case.**

The next experimental question type is a new variety of writing ability questions, more specifically, error recognition. You are given a sentence with four parts underlined and labeled A–D and asked to select the part that contains an error. If there is no error you are to answer E.

Try these:

1. **Richard was <u>fat,</u> (A) foolish and <u>becoming bald</u> (B), but <u>he was a</u> (C) very <u>nice person.</u> (D) <u>No error.</u> (E)** Ⓐ Ⓑ Ⓒ Ⓓ Ⓔ

2. Tom, who (A) was (B) a great musician, was (C) never on time for an (D) appointment. No error. (E) Ⓐ Ⓑ Ⓒ Ⓓ Ⓔ

3. Mike would like to know what affect (A) the weather (B) will have on (C) tomorrow's game. (D) No error. (E) Ⓐ Ⓑ Ⓒ Ⓓ Ⓔ

4. Bart, who (A) we consult (B) on legal questions, is (C) really a dangerous radical. (D) No error. (E) Ⓐ Ⓑ Ⓒ Ⓓ Ⓔ

— — — — — — — — — — — — — — — — — — — —

1. **(B)** The problem here is a lack of parallelsim.

2. **(E)** There is nothing wrong here.

3. **(A)** The word we need here is "effect."

4. **(A)** We consult *him*—we need the objective case, which is "whom."

Remember, you may not find any of these sections on your actual test, but it is always best to be prepared.

APPENDIX B

Law Schools on the Approved List of the American Bar Association, 1976

American Bar Association Approval. Since the adoption of the first law school accreditation standards by the American Bar Association in 1922, state supreme courts and other bar admitting authorities have encouraged the ABA's accreditation efforts, and the vast majority of states rely upon ABA accreditation to determine whether an applicant meets the educational requirements for admission to the bar. Graduation from an ABA approved law school satisfies the legal education requirements for admission to the bar in all jurisdictions in the United States. Graduation from a state approved law school may qualify a person to take the bar exam in the state in which the school is located but, generally, does not qualify the person for the examination in other states.

The United States Commissioner of Education, Department of Health, Education and Welfare, has recognized the Association officially as a "nationally recognized accrediting agency." The Council on Postsecondary Accreditation similarly has recognized the American Bar Association's program of accreditation.

Law Schools are approved by the American Bar Association upon application of a school and after a finding that the school offers a sound program of legal education which complies with the Standards for the Approval of Law Schools by the American Bar Association. A law school is approved by action of the House of Delegates of the Association. Responsibility for administering the Association's program of accreditation has been placed with the Council of the Section of Legal Education and Admissions to the Bar.

Applications for provisional approval are not considered until a law school has completed the first academic year of its program. Therefore, the charter class of a new law school enrolls in an "ABA unapproved" school.

A law school will be granted provisional approval when it establishes that it substantially complies with the Standards and gives assurances that it will be in full compliance with the Standards within three years after receiving provisional approval. Only when the applicant school establishes its substantial compliance, when it gives assurances that it will be in full compliance with the Standards within three years, and when the institution appears to have the necessary resources to accomplish these assurances, may the school be granted provisional approval.

A law school which has been provisionally approved for two years will be considered for full approval by the House of Delegates of the American Bar Association when the Council finds, after inspection, that the school fully meets the Standards established by the American Bar Association as interpreted by the Council on a basis that assures continued compliance with the letter and the spirit of the Standards, with particular emphasis on a steady improvement in the quality of its educational program.

The students at provisionally approved law schools and persons who graduate while a school is provisionally approved are entitled to the same recognition accorded to students and graduates of fully approved law schools.

Membership in the Association of American Law Schools is separate and apart from American Bar Association approval. A law school is not eligible for AALS membership until the school has been in operation five years and has graduated three classes. A total of 132 of the 163 American Bar Association approved law schools granting the J.D. degree are members of the Association of American Law Schools. While ABA and AALS are separate organizations, both are interested in quality legal education and maintain a close working relationship toward that end.

No rating of law schools beyond the simple statement of their accreditation status is attempted or advocated by the official organizations in legal education. Qualities that make one kind of school good for one student may not be as important to another. The American Bar Association and its Section of Legal Education and Admissions to the Bar have issued disclaimers of any law school rating system. Prospective law students should consider a variety of factors in making their choice among approved schools.

For many years the first degree in almost all law schools was the Bachelor of Laws (LL.B.). A few gave the Juris Doctor (J.D.) to all students, while others reserved the J.D. for students graduating with honors. In recent years all schools have changed to granting the J.D. There is no difference in the nature of the course of study for the two degrees. The Master's degree (LL.M.) usually involves a one-year program combining course work and research beyond the J.D.; the Doctorate of Juridical Sciences (S.J.D.) is a graduate academic research degree that involves major academic advanced publishable work; and the Master's in Comparative Law (M.C.L.) involves advanced work for foreign-educated lawyers.

Reading the Approved Law School Table. The table lists the 164 law schools approved by the American Bar Association, arranged alphabetically by states. The figures in parentheses following the name of the school indicate the year the school received provisional approval by the American Bar Association. The name, mailing address, and telephone number are given for each school in the table.

The enrollment figures are in terms of head count. The figures beneath the name of the school show the enrollment by each class or year and by division. "F" indicates the full-time program and "P" indicates the part-time program. Students are classified for purposes of the enrollment statistics on the basis of the program in which they are enrolled and not upon the basis of whether they are carrying a full load in the division in which they are enrolled. The figures not in parentheses indicate the number of men and women enrolled; the numbers in parentheses indicate the number of these students who are women. Minority group enrollment is the total enrollment reported of students who would classify themselves as Black, not of Hispanic Origin; American Indian or Alaskan Native; Asian or Pacific Islander; Mexican American; Puerto Rican; and Other Hispano-American. Puerto Rican law students enrolled in the three approved law schools in Puerto Rico are not classified as minority students.

"Joint Degrees" indicates whether the law school, in conjunction with some other college or school, offers a program leading to a joint degree. "MPA," for example, indicates that the law school offers with another college a joint Juris Doctor-Master of Public Administration degree, and "MBA" indicates that a joint Juris Doctor-Master of Business Administration degree is offered. The figure following the letters indicates the number of each of these degrees awarded during the 1975–76 academic year. Where the school reported that it had no joint degree program, this is indicated by "N."

The "Degrees Awarded" column gives the total number of each of the specified degrees awarded by each school since the start of the 1975–76 academic year, including the 1976 summer session. The number of degrees awarded to graduates of each division is stated separately. The figure in parentheses indicates the number of degrees, within the total number awarded, which were awarded to women. The figure in brackets indicates the number of degrees, within the total, which were awarded to minorities.

Under the heading "Annual Tuition and Fees," "r" stands for resident and "n" stands for nonresident. If the amount is not followed by a symbol, it is the same for both resident and nonresident. The figure given shows what each student is required to pay for the 1975–76 academic year, excluding summer session, and includes both tuition and fees.

The number of academic years of college study required for admission to each approved law school is indicated by a number where a degree is not required and by "degree" where a baccalaureate degree is required for admission. The letter "s" after the number of weeks indicates the school is on a semester basis. The letter "q" indicates the school is on a quarterly basis. The adjacent column states the minimum number of weeks required to complete the full-time program of law study. Weeks of class and of examination are included, but weeks of vacation and registration are excluded in this statement.

In the next column, "Y" (Yes) is indicated in parentheses where a school will accept transfer credit for courses successfully completed by students in summer sessions at other institutions. Where a school permits students to accelerate their graduation by attending summer sessions at other institutions, this is indicated by "Y" in brackets. An "N" indicates the school does not do so.

The next two columns list the total number of full- and part-time teachers engaged in the school's teaching program. The number of women teachers within the total is given in parentheses. The dean, librarian with academic rank, and those associate and assistant deans who teach are not included in the count of full-time teachers. They are shown separately in the next column.

"Total Volumes" refers to the total number of volumes of law and law-related books held by the law school at the end of its 1975–76 fiscal year. "Volume" means a physical unit of any printed, typewritten, handwritten, mimeographed or processed work contained in one binding or portfolio, hardbound or paperbound, which has been catalogued, classified, or made ready for use.

"Microform Equivalents" are also reported as the total number held at the end of the 1975–76 fiscal year. The U.S. Office of Education, National Center for Educational Statistics, has not yet achieved general agreement among librarians on a definition. In the interim, law librarians were instructed to use the following method for determining volume equivalents of microform materials:

(1) If the original material (hard copy) was in countable volumes, use that number as volume equivalents. The number of volumes of the original material is usually available from the bibliographic description.

(2) If the original material was not in countable volumes, figure 800 pages of original material as the equivalent of one volume.

For additional information, please contact:

James P. White, Consultant on Legal Education
to the American Bar Association
Indiana University
355 North Lansing Street
Indianapolis, IN 46202

or

Frederick R. Franklin, Staff Director
Section of Legal Education and Admissions
to the Bar
American Bar Association
1155 East 60th Street
Chicago, IL 60637
(312) 947-3856

LAW SCHOOLS ON THE APPROVED LIST OF THE AMERICAN BAR ASSOCIATION, 1976

	School		*First Year*	*Second Year*	*Third Year*	*Fourth Year*	*Graduate*	*Other*	*Minority Groups*	*Total Enrollment 1976*	*Joint Degrees*	*Degrees Awarded 1975–76*	*Tuition and Fees*	*Years College Required*	*Credits Required*	*Weeks Required*	*Summer Program*	*Full-time Teachers*	*Full-time Deans*	*Part-time Teachers*	*Total Volumes*	*Microform Equivalents*
AL	University of Alabama (1926) School of Law P.O. Box 1435 University, Alabama 35486 205/348-5930	F	163(28)	151(35)	148(25)	....	1	....	18	463(88)	MPA MBA 4	JD 151(14)[4]	$ 434 r 806 nr	degree	90s	90	(Y)[Y]	23(1)	3(1)	6	142,083	14,156
		P																				
	Samford University (1949) Cumberland School of Law 800 Lakeshore Drive Birmingham, Alabama 35209 205/870-2701	F	273(42)	230(33)	210(25)	....	....	....	9	713(100)	MBA	JD 205(26)[3]	$2,078	degree	88s	90	(Y)[Y]	20(2)	4(1)	15	74,026	740
		P	1	....	....	....	....	....	....	1			1,290			120						
										714(100)												
AZ	Arizona State University (1969) College of Law Tempe, Arizona 85281 602/965-6181	F	142(55)	110(27)	127(41)	....	....	....	33	379(123)	N	JD 116(17)[12]	$ 514 r 1,704 nr	degree	87s	99	(Y)[Y]	18(1)	3	2	133,102	3,998
		P	....	....	....	....	....	6(5)	....	6(5)												
										385(128)												
	University of Arizona (1930) College of Law Tucson, Arizona 85721 602/884-1373	F	149(48)	144(46)	127(37)	....	....	18(5)	33	438(136)	N	JD 124(40)[9]	$ 520 r 1,710 nr	degree	85s	96	(Y)[Y]	21(1)	1	7(1)	118,716	12,631
		P																				
AR	University of Arkansas (1926) School of Law Fayetteville, Arkansas 72701 501/575-5600	F	209(45)	177(27)	162(19)	....	....	....	19	548(91)	N	JD 130(16)[10]	$ 400 r 930 nr	degree	84s	98	(Y)[Y]	18	4(1)	7(1)	86,726	0
		P																				
	University of Arkansas (1969) School of Law 400 West Markham Little Rock, Arkansas 72201 501/371-1071	F																				
		P	138(54)	113(38)	46(9)	39(8)	1	6(4)	....	343(113)	N	JD 53(5)	$ 400 r 950 nr	degree	84s	120	(Y)[Y]	11	2(1)	2	57,799	18,742

I (AR)

LAW SCHOOLS ON THE APPROVED LIST OF THE AMERICAN BAR ASSOCIATION, 1976

	School		First Year	Second Year	Third Year	Fourth Year	Graduate	Other	Minority Groups	Total Enrollment 1976	Joint Degrees	Degrees Awarded 1975–76	Tuition and Fees	Years College Required	Credits Required	Weeks Required	Summer Program	Full-time Teachers	Full-time Deans	Part-time Teachers	Total Volumes	Microform Equivalents
CA	University of California (1923) School of Law Boalt Hall Berkeley, California 94720 415/642-1741	F P	293(98)	301(100)	298(105)	....	24(5)	2(1)	216	918(309)	MSW MA/PhD 3 MPP 1 MLS MCP 1 MBA 1	SJD/JSD 1 LLM 26(1) JD 292(99)[86]	$ 707 r 2,612 nr	degree	81s	90	(Y)[N]	41(3)	1	9(1)	349,075	42,765
	University of California (1968) School of Law Davis, California 95616 916/752-0243	F P	189(84)	139(62)	166(81)	....	....	....	124	494(227)	Philo. Engin. Econ. Ecol. Anthro. Reg. Pl. PhD MPA MBA Rhet. Int.Aff.	JD 165(71)[59]	$ 680 r 2,585 nr	degree	84s	98	(Y)[Y]	19(4)	4	6(1)	142,021	27,379
	University of California (1950) School of Law 405 Hilgard Avenue Los Angeles, California 90024 213/825-4841	F P	306(104)	336(111)	344(96)	....	....	....	216	986(311)	Econ. Reg.Pl. MBA 1	JD 300(94)[59]	$ 706 r 2,611 nr	degree	127q	90	(Y)[Y]	43(6)	....	4(1)	251,666	2,999
	University of California (1939) Hastings College of Law 198 McAllister Street San Francisco, California 94102 415/557-1320	F P	505(167)	518(163)	503(161)	....	....	....	292	1,536(491)	N	JD 518(157)	$ 370 r 1,322 nr	degree	87s	96	(Y)[Y]	50(4)	11(5)	24(2)	131,745	11,300
	California Western School of Law (1962) 350 Cedar Street San Diego, California 92101 714/239-0391	F P	244(55)	228(53)	161(15)	....	....	....	34	633(123)	N	JD 142(19)[8]	$2,972	degree	90s	99	(Y)[Y]	13(1)	3	13	53,608	3,162

CA1	Golden Gate University (1956) School of Law 536 Mission Street San Francisco, California 94105 415/391-7800									MS Tax 1											
	F	204(91)	142(62)	162(81)	....	....	....	53	508(234)	MBA2	JD 159(65)[8]	$ 92 r unit	degree	84s	96	(Y)[Y]	20(2)	....	7(3)	76,061	161
	P	98(42)	71(29)	58(24)	56(17)	....	16(2)	49	299(112)		JD 28(6)	$ 99 nr unit			128						
									807(348)												
CA2	Loyola University (1935) School of Law 1440 West Ninth Street Los Angeles, California 90015 213/642-2900																				
	F	289(108)	274(84)	239(80)	....	....	11(5)	....	813(277)	N	JD 228(49)	$2,919	degree	87s	102	(Y)[Y]	31(4)	3(1)	36(2)	137,447	38,650
	P	109(49)	107(30)	145(51)	130(33)	....	8(3)	....	499(166)		JD 127(30)	$1,761			161						
									1,312(443)												
CA3	University of the Pacific (1969) McGeorge School of Law 3200 Fifth Avenue Sacramento, California 95817 916/452-6051									Manag. Acc. PAA											
	F	298(61)	221(41)	186(23)	....	....	....	21	705(125)	MBA	JD 203(39)[6]	$2,991	degree	129q	111	(Y)[N]	26(3)	3	6(1)	87,489	27,735
	P	231(49)	176(44)	125(23)	122(23)	....	6(2)	....	660(141)		JD 121(16)[7]	1,767			160						
									1,365(266)												
CA4	Pepperdine University (1972) School of Law 1520 South Anaheim Boulevard Anaheim, California 92805 714/776-4490																				
	F	215(34)	174(17)	149(23)	....	....	....	....	538(73)	N	JD 174(14)	$3,090	degree	84s	90	(Y)[Y]	18(1)	3(1)	14	47,496	16,758
	P	....	29(8)	26(4)	29(5)	....	....	....	84(17)		JD 31(5)	$2,320			120						
									622(86)												
CA5	University of San Diego (1961) School of Law Alcala Park San Diego, California 92110 714/291-6480									Int.Aff.											
	F	243(67)	237(60)	211(41)	....	....	2(1)	52	693(169)	MBA	JD 196(34)[13]	$2,615	degree	85s	102	(Y)[Y]	34(1)	4(1)	18(1)	92,000	5,795
	P	102(30)	56(20)	47(18)	41(9)	....	41(10)	7	287(87)		JD 46(5)[1]	1,845			136						
									980(256)												
CA6	University of San Francisco (1935) School of Law Kendrick Hall San Francisco, California 94117 415/666-6307																				
	F	207(80)	189(76)	154(54)	....	....	5(2)	124	555(212)	N	JD 158(51)[24]	$2,985	degree	82s	90		23(4)	2	1	72,732	28,366
	P	48(22)	47(22)	58(21)	42(15)	....	....	32	195(80)		JD 68(18)[7]	1,087			120	(Y)[Y]					
									750(292)												

LAW SCHOOLS ON THE APPROVED LIST OF THE AMERICAN BAR ASSOCIATION, 1976

School		First Year	Second Year	Third Year	Fourth Year	Graduate	Other	Minority Groups	Total Enrollment 1976	Joint Degrees	Degrees Awarded 1975–76	Tuition and Fees	Years College Required	Credits Required	Weeks Required	Summer Program	Full-time Teachers	Full-time Deans	Part-time Teachers	Total Volumes	Microform Equivalents
University of Santa Clara (1937) School of Law Santa Clara, California 95053 408/984-4361	F	282(102)	177(56)	243(48)	....	....	7(3)	140	709(209)	MBA	JD 233(41)[34]	$2,715	degree	86s	90	(Y)[Y]	25(4)	3(1)	4	86,749	7,081
	P	43(18)	40(19)	52(20)	31(10)	....	2(1)	23	168(68) 877(277)		JD 47(7)[1]	1,914			120						
Stanford Law School (1923) Stanford, California 94305 415/497-2465	F	171(39)	158(41)	149(34)	....	3	7(3)	67	488(117)	MA Econ. 1 MA Hist. 2 MBA 9	JM 1 JSD 1 JSM 3(1) JD 148(27)[28]	$4,465	degree	89s	108	(Y)[Y]	26(2)	3	8	236,592	0
University of Southern California (1924) Law Center University Park Los Angeles, California 90007 213/746-6473	F	180(51)	176(50)	184(61)	....	....	3	89	543(163)	MA PhD PAA 6 MBA 4	JD 159(48)[6]	$1,896	degree	88s	96	(Y)[Y]	20(1)	1	13	143,678	20,948
	P																				
Southwestern University (1970) School of Law 675 South Westmoreland Avenue Los Angeles, California 90005 213/380-4800	F	285(100)	268(62)	258(62)	....	....	114(35)	....	925(259)	N	JD 225(26)	$2,430	3 yrs.	84s	96	(Y)[N]	37(5)	9(5)	31(3)	84,482	2,397
	P	258(61)	202(66)	184(42)	139(22)	....	....	....	783(191) 1,708(450)		JD 174(19)	1,380			128						
CO University of Denver (1928) College of Law 200 West 14th Avenue Denver, Colorado 80204 303/753-2645	F	192(69)	183(50)	180(50)	....	44(13)	14(5)	39	613(188)	Int.Aff.1 Reg.Pl. PhD PAA MSBA 1 MBA 1	MSJA 16(5) LLM 4 JD 181(53)[16]	$3,396	degree	130q	90	(Y)[Y]	28(3)	4	9(9)	106,291	19,491
	P	101(39)	77(27)	51(20)	64(13)	58(10)	8(2)	26	360(111) 73(299)		JD 87(15)[3] MSJA 1(1)	75/qtr.hr.									
University of Colorado (1923) School of Law Boulder, Colorado 80309 303/492-8047	F	151(47)	148(47)	145(37)	....	....	1(1)	60	445(132)	N	JD 145(35)[20]	$ 788 r 2,520 nr	degree	86s	90	(Y)[Y]	17(2)	3	14(4)	140,000	6,000
	P																				

CT	IV CT1	University of Connecticut (1933) School of Law Greater Hartford Campus West Hartford, Connecticut 06117 203/523-4841, ext. 341										MSLS											
		F	138(41)	150(54)	163(57)	....	....	7	37	458(152)	MSW	JD 155(39)[12]	$1,365 r 1,965 nr	degree	86s	99	(Y)[Y]	25(1)	2(1)	19(1)	99,463	25,476
		P	74(35)	63(27)	43(14)	52(10)	....	3(1)		235(87) 693(239)		JD 34(7)[1]	1,000			147						
		Yale Law School (1923) 127 Wall Street New Haven, Connecticut 06520 203/436-2211									MD 2 MA 2 PhD	Jnt. 3(1) SJD/JSD 3 LLM 29(1)[1]										
		F	165(43)	174(47)	171(38)	....	46(13)	24(3)	58	580(144)	MBA	JD 177(35)[23]	$4,150	degree	81s	102	(N)[N]	34(2)	1(1)	5(1)	559,709	8,167
		P																				
DE	V DE1	Delaware Law School (1975) Widener College 2001 Washington Street Wilmington, Delaware 19802 302/658-8531																				
		F	150(28)	151(24)	107(10)	....	....	....	18	408(62)	N	JD 99(6)	$2,120	degree	84s	96	(Y)[Y]	15(2)	4	12	56,875	9,386
		P	84(20)	75(21)	57(2)	44(5)	....	....		260(48) 668(110)		JD 98(5)[1]	1,620			128						
DC	DC1	American University (1940) Washington College of Law Massachusetts & Nebraska Avenues, N.W. Washington, D.C. 20016 202/686-2600																				
		F	167(74)	129(46)	134(44)	....	....	....	60	430(164)	N	JD 127(35)[13]	$3,090	degree	84s	102	(Y)[Y]	21(3)	2(1)	34(7)	78,185	13,972
		P	62(27)	47(19)	51(13)	85(22)	....	31(5)	23	276(86) 706(250)		JD 47(15)[2]	1,880			154						
		Antioch School of Law (1973) 1624 Crescent Place, N.W. Washington, D.C. 20009 202/265-9500																				
		F	127(57)	101(49)	101(42)	....	14(6)	50(34)	142	393(188)	N	JD 95(37)[26]	$3,630	degree	92s	124	(Y)[Y]	19(5)	2	10(1)	50,907	0
		P																				
	DC2	Catholic University of America (1925) School of Law Washington, D.C. 20064 202/635-5144									City Pl. Phil. Hist. Pol. Econ.											
		F	161(63)	144(61)	174(70)	....	....	3(2)	47	482(196)	MSLS	JD 150(57)[16]	$3,147	degree	84s	96	(Y)[Y]	16(3)	1	22(2)	85,350	541
		P	69(23)	63(30)	58(31)	58(18)	....	9(2)	28	257(104) 739(300)		JD 49(22)[7]	1,800			128						

LAW SCHOOLS ON THE APPROVED LIST OF THE AMERICAN BAR ASSOCIATION, 1976

	School		*First Year*	*Second Year*	*Third Year*	*Fourth Year*	*Graduate*	*Other*	*Minority Groups*	*Total Enrollment 1976*	*Joint Degrees*	*Degrees Awarded 1975–76*	*Tuition and Fees*	*Years College Required*	*Credits Required*	*Weeks Required*	*Summer Program*	*Full-time Teachers*	*Full-time Deans*	*Part-time Teachers*	*Total Volumes*	*Microform Equivalents*
	Georgetown University (1924) Law Center 600 New Jersey Avenue, N.W. Washington, D.C. 20001 202/624-8000											MCL 3(1) LLM Tax 12(3) LLM 11(4) JD 452(86)[38] JD 114(23)[10] LLM 23 LLM Tax 89 MCL 4(1)										
		F	519(184)	490(165)	504(133)	....	90(20)	7(4)	242	1,610(506)	MSFS		$3,375	degree	81s	96		44(3)	4	80(20)	188,932	10,620
		P	130(62)	113(44)	117(24)	129(37)	371(32)	94(27)	83	954(226)			116/hr.			128	(Y)[Y]					
										2,564(732)												
	George Washington University (1923) National Law Center 720 20th Street, N.W. Washington, D.C. 20052 202/676-6260										Int.Aff. Reg.Pl. PAA	MCL(AP) 3(2) MCL 3 LLM 35(3) JD 349(104)[34] JD 72(20)[5] LLM 56(6) MCL 6 SJD 3 MCL(AP) 5										
		F	342(125)	335(117)	262(84)	....	40(4)	22(1)	80	1,001(331)	MBA		$2,701	degree	84s	102	(Y)[Y]	40(3)	3	37(3)	149,745	0
		P	116(55)	133(50)	101(38)	93(30)	194(12)	66(12)	20	703(197)			102/hr.			136						
										1,704(528)												
	Howard University (1931) School of Law 2935 Upton Street, N.W. Washington, D.C. 20008 202/686-6573																					
		F	185(65)	142(55)	121(30)	....	14(1)	....	359	462(151)	MBA	JD 103(35)[83]	$1,663	degree	88s	96	(Y)[N]	28(3)	4	9	138,645	19,660
		P																				
FL	University of Florida (1925) College of Law Gainesville, Florida 32611 904/392-0421											LLM 44(1)										
		F	457(122)	333(87)	168(33)	....	41(3)	....	102	999(245)	N	JD 418(84)[25]	$1,020 r	degree	126q	96	(Y)[Y]	37(2)	1	2	157,803	174,059
		P	....	....	....	....	18(3)	....		18(3)			2,820 nr									
										1,017(248)												
	Florida State University (1968) College of Law Tallahassee, Florida 32306 904/644-3400										Int.Aff. 1 Reg.Pl. PhD PAA											
		F	182(45)	160(48)	171(51)	....	....	3(2)	46	516(146)	MBA 2	JD 131(28)[13]	$ 990 r	degree	135q	90	(Y)[Y]	20(2)	3	....	70,607	52,425
		P											2,790 nr									

	University of Miami (1941) School of Law P.O. Box 248087 Coral Gables, Florida 33124 305/284-2392	F P	360(85) 67(21)	359(80) 25(3)	345(55) 17(2)	.... 20(4)	51(4) 86(7)	6(3) 2	52 20	1,121(227) 217(37) 1,338(264)	N	MCL 7 LLM 48(2) JD 291(43)[14] JD 26(4)[5] LLM 12 MCL 1	$3,510 $2,640	degree	88s	96 128	(N)[Y]	41(1)	1	20(3)	202,655	7,813
	Nova University (1975) Center for the Study of Law 3301 College Avenue Fort Lauderdale, Florida 33314 305/587-6660, ext. 323	F P	177(58)	157(32)	147(19)	....	....	....	22	481(109)	N	....	$2,950	degree	87s	96	(Y)[Y]	18(3)	5(2)	2	60,973	32,677
	Stetson University (1930) College of Law 1401 61st Street, South St. Petersburg, Florida 33707 813/347-4560	F P	208(56)	90(31)	170(24)	....	....	1	18	469(111)	N	JD 158(21)	$2,645	degree	86s	102	(Y)[Y]	17(1)	3	11	86,563	8,383
GA	Emory University (1923) School of Law Atlanta, Georgia 30322 404/329-6815	F P	259(76)	220(60)	213(78)	...	50(5)	....	41	742(219)	MBA 1	MCL 1 LLM 8(1) JD 231(58)[7]	$3,100	degree	88s	93	(Y)[Y]	26(4)	3(1)	14(2)	111,151	9,329
	University of Georgia (1930) School of Law Athens, Georgia 30602 404/542-7140	F P	210(46)	198(54)	208(37)	....	1	....	24	617(137)	MBA 3	LLM 1 JD 216(34)[4]	$ 711 r 1,662 nr	degree	135q	99	(Y)[Y]	19(2)	1	4	225,897	26,373
	Mercer University (1925) Walter F. George School of Law Macon, Georgia 31207 912/745-6811, ext. 346	F P	99(16)	78(11)	75(8)	....	....	....	3	252(35)	N	JD 73(7)[1]	$2,150	degree	135q	99	(Y)[Y]	8	2(1)	6(1)	73,709	14,000
HI	University of Hawaii (1974) School of Law 1400 Lower Campus Road Honolulu, Hawaii 96822 808/948-7966	F P	76(27)	62(21)	64(21)	....	....	1	143	203(69)	N	JD 51(18)[36]	$ 665 r 1,600 nr	degree	84s	90	(Y)[N]	10(1)	3	9(1)	110,105	37,045

LAW SCHOOLS ON THE APPROVED LIST OF THE AMERICAN BAR ASSOCIATION, 1976

State	School		First Year	Second Year	Third Year	Fourth Year	Graduate	Other	Minority Groups	Total Enrollment 1976	Joint Degrees	Degrees Awarded 1975–76	Tuition and Fees	Years College Required	Credits Required	Weeks Required	Summer Program	Full-time Teachers	Full-time Deans	Part-time Teachers	Total Volumes	Microform Equivalents
ID	University of Idaho (1925) College of Law Moscow, Idaho 83843 208/885-6422	F	98(15)	87(17)	75(17)	....	....	....	5	260(49)	N	JD 95(10)[3]	$ 640 r 1,840 nr	degree	84s	96	(Y)[Y]	11(1)	3	1	65,538	2,465
		P																				
IL	University of Chicago (1923) Law School 1111 East 60th Street Chicago, Illinois 60637 312/753-2401	F	170(44)	171(43)	164(35)	....	4(1)	3(2)	26	512(125)	MBA 3	SJD 1 LLM 4 JD 161(29)[8]	$4,144	3 yrs.	135q	99	(N)[N]	26	1	....	333,370	7,222
		P																				
	DePaul University (1925) College of Law 25 East Jackson Boulevard Chicago, Illinois 60604 312/321-7700	F	287(112)	185(63)	196(70)	....	....	1(1)	95	669(246)	N	JD 195(73)[16]	$2,717	degree	86s	102	(Y)[Y]	27(1)	5(4)	20(1)	93,492	27,149
		P	113(42)	98(36)	76(30)	73(14)	....	9(2)	76	369(124) 1,038(370)		JD 76(16)[16]	1,867			136						
	University of Illinois (1923) College of Law Champaign, Illinois 61820 217/333-0930	F	223(60)	219(40)	200(32)	....	26(6)	....	44	668(138)	Lab.Ind. Acct. Int.Aff. Reg.Pl. PhD PAA MBA 1	SJD 1 MCL 13(2) LLM 5 JD 187(17)[9]	$ 712 r 1,702 nr	degree	90s	99	(Y)[Y]	27(2)	3	9(3)	285,101	0
		P																				
	Illinois Institute of Technology (1936) Chicago-Kent College of Law 77 South Wacker Drive Chicago, Illinois 60606 312/567-5000	F	227(94)	204(59)	157(36)	....	....	....	....	588(189)	N	JD 177(21)	$2,580	3 yrs.	90s	96	(Y)[Y]	18(2)	1	27(5)	58,671	19,978
		P	102(43)	74(23)	64(18)	80(16)	....	....	....	320(100) 908(289)		JD 79(15)	1,730			128						
	John Marshall Law School (1951) 315 South Plymouth Court Chicago, Illinois 60604 312/427-2737	F	388(61)	301(37)	231(18)	....	1	....	35	921(116)	N	JD 373(29)[2]	$2,420	degree	86s	102	(Y)[Y]	42(4)	6(4)	28(1)	56,104	16,041
		P	176(35)	97(16)	101(14)	99(12)	100(9)	1		574(86) 1,495(202)		JD 85(10)[3] LLM 7(2)	1,740			136						

	Loyola University (1925) School of Law 41 East Pearson Street Chicago, Illinois 60611 312/670-2920																					
		F	167(71)	137(51)	151(58)	....	....	....	7	455(180)	N	JD 120(39)[5]	$2,400	degree	86s	96	(Y)[Y]	19(2)	2(1)	20(3)	72,713	6,541
		P	85(35)	57(22)	52(20)	40(10)	....	....	17	258(29) 713(272)		D 46(11)[1]	1,805			96						
	Northwestern University (1923) School of Law 357 East Chicago Avenue Chicago, Illinois 60611 312/649-8462																					
		F	174(47)	176(56)	183(63)	....	7(2)	3(1)	99	543(169)	MM 5 PhD 1	SJD 1 LLM 7 JD 185(51)[24]	$4,290	degree	90s	99	(Y)[Y]	37(3)	3(1)	16	335,115	7,881
		P																				
	Southern Illinois University (1974) School of Law Carbondale, Illinois 62901 618/536-7711																					
		F	99(20)	84(15)	75(17)	....	....	....	10	258(52)	MBA	JD 72(12)	$ 596 r 1,650 nr	degree	90s	90	(Y)[Y]	14(2)	3	2	66,690	34,121
		P																				
IN	Indiana University (1923) School of Law Bloomington, Indiana 47401 812/337-5588																					
		F	207(61)	178(47)	175(44)	....	7	22(9)	59	589(161)	PhD PAA MBA 8	JD 152(33)[11]	$ 868 r 1,932 nr	degree	82s	96	(Y)[Y]	22(2)	5	8(4)	152,143	0
		P																				
	Indiana University (1936) School of Law-Indianapolis 735 West New York Street Indianapolis, Indiana 46202 317/264-8523																					
		F	166(47)	146(32)	90(17)	....	....	....	....	402(96)	MBA	JD 108(19)	$ 843 r 1,953 nr	degree	85s	90	(Y)[Y]	25(3)	3	6(1)	190,721	32,881
		P	161(48)	96(26)	131(24)	....	....	15(4)	....	403(102) 805(198)		JD 107(14)	563 r 1,303 nr			120						
	Notre Dame Law School (1925) Notre Dame, Indiana 46556 219/283-6626																					
		F	146(43)	154(41)	152(40)	12(2)	....	14(2)	44	478(128)	MTH 1 MS MBA 4	JD 144(27)[9]	$3,067	degree	84s	96	(Y)[Y]	16(1)	3	10(1)	95,104	1,873
		P																				
	Valparaiso University (1929) School of Law Valparaiso, Indiana 46383 219/464-5434																					
		F	114(29)	105(28)	96(19)	....	....	....	44	315(76)	N	JD 107(24)[10]	$2,656	degree	90s	96	(Y)[Y]	11(1)	2	3	86,671	120
		P	1(1)	....	....	....	....	....		1(1) 316(77)			70/hr.									

LAW SCHOOLS ON THE APPROVED LIST OF THE AMERICAN BAR ASSOCIATION, 1976

			First Year	*Second Year*	*Third Year*	*Fourth Year*	*Graduate*	*Other*	*Minority Groups*	*Total Enrollment 1976*	*Joint Degrees*	*Degrees Awarded 1975–76*	*Tuition and Fees*	*Years College Required*	*Credits Required*	*Weeks Required*	*Summer Program*	*Full-time Teachers*	*Full-time Deans*	*Part-time Teachers*	*Total Volumes*	*Microform Equivalents*
IA	Drake University (1923) Law School Des Moines, Iowa 50311 515/271-2824	F	225(33)	112(18)	145(26)	....	....	18(8)	29	500(85)	MBA 4	JD 143(19)[5]	$3,230	degree	90s	102	(Y)[Y]	17(2)	3	9(1)	87,439	2,400
		P																				
	University of Iowa (1923) College of Law Iowa City, Iowa 52242 319/353-5742	F	221(67)	206(48)	172(28)	....	....	....	....	599(143)	Any Univ. Dept.	JD 208(41)	$ 780 r 1,720 nr	degree	90s	96	(Y)[Y]	28(4)	1	3	267,835	20,345
		P																				
KS	University of Kansas (1923) School of Law Lawrence, Kansas 66045 913/867-4550	F	158(40)	144(42)	155(38)	....	....	....	37	457(120)	Econ. 1 PAA 4 MBA 2	JD 142(24)[14]	$ 677 r 1,517 nr	degree	90s	90	(Y)[Y]	19(2)	3(1)	3	158,584	17,077
		P																				
	Washburn University of Topeka (1923) School of Law 1700 College Topeka, Kansas 66621 913/295-6660	F	200(33)	201(37)	194(22)	....	....	2	13	597(92)	N	JD 195(21)[2]	$1,430 r 1,790 nr	degree	90s	92	(Y)[Y]	19(2)	2	20(1)	65,499	19,722
		P																				
KY	University of Kentucky (1925) College of Law Lexington, Kentucky 40506 606/257-1678	F	179(56)	158(45)	148(31)	....	....	....	20	485(132)	N	JD 157(42)[8]	$ 480 r 1,210 nr	degree	87s	90	(Y)[Y]	18(2)	2(1)	6	148,518	16,654
		P																				
	University of Louisville (1931) School of Law Belknap Campus 2301 South 3rd Street Louisville, Kentucky 40208 502/588-6358	F	158(53)	143(30)	162(34)	....	....	4(2)	14	467(119)	MA	JD 159(27)[3]	$ 680 r 1,980 nr	degree	84s	99	(Y)[Y]	21(4)	3	20(2)	81,033	4,076
		P	73(18)	35(5)	53(11)	26(4)	....	5(2)	14	192(40) 659(159)		JD 38(2)[3]				132						

	Northern Kentucky University (1954) Salmon P. Chase College of Law 1401 Dixie Highway Covington, Kentucky 41011 606/292-5340																						
		F	79(7)	64(10)	....	....	....	1(1)	2	144(18)	N		$ 766 r 1,406 nr	degree	84s	96	(Y)[N]	19(2)	2	5	73,399	36,140
		P	104(22)	71(12)	133(23)	129(18)	....	....	18	438(75) 582(93)		JD 106(9)[2]	582 r 1,068 nr			150						
LA	Louisiana State University (1926) Law School Baton Rouge, Louisiana 70803 504/388-8491																					
		F	386(89)	317(58)	317(44)	....	3	1	43	1,024(191)	N	JD 278(28)[3]	$ 630 r 830 nr	degree	97s	99	(Y)[Y]	32(3)	....	14	219,912	14,723
		P																				
	Loyola University (1931) School of Law 6363 St. Charles Avenue New Orleans, Louisiana 70118 504/865-2011																					
		F	206(48)	179(49)	170(35)	....	....	....	30	555(132)	N	JD 174(31)[7]	$2,240	96 hrs.	90s	90	(Y)[N]	19(2)	2	9	63,188	4,343
		P	96(34)	70(25)	36(12)	39(13)	....	....	14	241(87) 796(216)		JD 38(5)[5]	1,607			130						
	Southern University (1953) School of Law Southern Branch Post Office Baton Rouge, Louisiana 70813 504/771-3776																					
		F	77(10)	63(11)	45(9)	....	....	....	133	185(30)	N	JD 37(5)[30]	$ 362 r 1,082 nr	degree	90s	90	(Y)[N]	10(1)	3	4(1)	59,802	0
		P																				
	Tulane University (1925) School of Law New Orleans, Louisiana 70118 504/866-2751																					
		F	222(59)	178(57)	194(42)	....	21(4)	....	12	615(162)	MA MS MBA	MCL 1(1) LLM 3(1) JD 188(36)[4]	$3,330	3 yrs.	90s	96	(Y)[N]	18(2)	4	6	138,365	8,000
		P																				
ME	University of Maine (1962) School of Law 246 Deering Avenue Portland, Maine 04102 207/773-2981																					
		F	70(15)	91(22)	77(26)	....	....	....	1	238(63)	N	JD 79(19)[1]	$ 915 r 2,365 nr	degree	88s	96	(Y)[Y]	12(1)	4(1)	3	123,000	154
		P																				

LAW SCHOOLS ON THE APPROVED LIST OF THE AMERICAN BAR ASSOCIATION, 1976

State	School		*First Year*	*Second Year*	*Third Year*	*Fourth Year*	*Graduate*	*Other*	*Minority Groups*	*Total Enrollment 1976*	*Joint Degrees*	*Degrees Awarded 1975–76*	*Tuition and Fees*	*Years College Required*	*Credits Required*	*Weeks Required*	*Summer Program*	*Full-time Teachers*	*Full-time Deans*	*Part-time Teachers*	*Total Volumes*	*Microform Equivalents*
MD	University of Baltimore (1972) School of Law Charles at Mount Royal Baltimore, Maryland 21201 301/727-6350	F	152(32)	188(44)	140(20)	....	....	....	58	480(96)	MBA	JD 133(11)[2]	$1,060 r 1,760 nr	3 yrs.	84s	96	(Y)[Y]	21(2)	5(3)	13	59,769	8,000
		P	156(28)	172(32)	104(12)	116(12)	....	....	12	548(84) 1,028(180)		JD 120(11)[1]	940 r 940 nr			128						
	University of Maryland (1930) School of Law •500 West Baltimore Street Baltimore, Maryland 21201 301/528-7214	F	172(63)	167(59)	182(62)	....	....	....	108	521(184)	Reg.Pl. PhD 1 PAA MBA	JD 177(48)[21]	$ 459 r 1,296 nr	3 yrs.	84s	90	(Y)[Y]	30(2)	5	17(2)	111,342	11,957
		P	80(35)	70(24)	46(5)	70(13)	....	8(2)		274(79) 795(263)		JD 52(13)[5]	324 r 952 nr			120						
MA	Boston College (1932) Law School 885 Centre Street Newton Centre, Massachusetts 02159 617/969-0100, ext. 4340	F	266(88)	249(66)	253(80)	....	....	4(2)	86	772(236)	N	JD 227(64)[22]	$3,200	degree	85s	94	(Y)[N]	21(3)	1	14	114,165	4,680
		P																				
	Boston University (1925) School of Law 765 Commonwealth Avenue Boston, Massachusetts 02215 617/353-3100	F	381(126)	349(108)	335(101)	....	....	41(3)	53	1,106(338)	N	LLM 87(6) JD 427(110)[11]	$3,628	degree	84s	90	(N)[N]	34(2)	2	6	133,849	170
		P	....	....	....	....	195(20)	....	....	195(20) 1,301(358)												
	Harvard Law School (1923) Cambridge, Massachusetts 02138 617/495-3100	F	546(138)	529(106)	538(111)	....	93(15)	55(11)	192	1,761(381)	AM 1 MPP 11 PhD 3 MPA 1 MBA 13	SJD 5 LLM 93(11) JD 525(94)[57]	$3,415	degree	83s	93	(N)[N]	53(3)	2(1)	19(2)	1,274,862	16,591
		P	....	....	....	....	15(4)	10(3)		25(7) 1,786(388)												

	New England School of Law (1969)																				
	126 Newbury Street																				
	Boston, Massachusetts 02116																				
	617/267-9655																				
	F	185(42)	182(43)	181(40)	....	....	....	6	548(125)	N	JD 191(49)[2]	$2,355	degree	84s	105	(Y)[Y]	17(1)	4	14	71,357	7,007
	P	116(21)	90(23)	77(17)	65(20)	....	....	2	348(81)		JD 70(5)	1,780			140						
									896(206)												
	Northeastern University (1969)																				
	School of Law																				
	400 Huntington Avenue																				
	Boston, Massachusetts 02115																				
	617/437-3335																				
	F	131(70)	128(66)	130(66)	....	....	5(2)	29	394(204)	N	JD 121(61)[6]	$3,330	degree	99q	80	(Y)[N]	10(2)	4(1)	7(2)	85,758	1,901
	P																				
	Suffolk University (1953)																				
	Law School																				
	41 Temple Street																				
	Boston, Massachusetts 02114																				
	617/723-4700										LLM 1										
	F	342(101)	309(85)	307(74)	....	....	....	93	958(260)	BS 2	JD 274(52)[4]	$2,310	degree	88s	90	(Y)[Y]	33(5)	6(1)	49(2)	83,588	2,812
	P	233(63)	209(62)	205(63)	202(43)	1	6		856(231)		JD 296(39)[5]	$1,735			120						
									1,814(491)												
	Western New England College (1974)																				
	School of Law																				
	1215 Wilbraham Road																				
	Springfield, Massachusetts 01119																				
	413/783-6131																				
	F	177(57)	143(36)	130(13)	....	....	....	18	450(106)	N	JD 142(7)[2]	$2,875	degree	86s	96	(Y)[N]	19(2)	3	32(2)	48,869	10,050
	P	102(27)	78(15)	63(16)	50(8)	....	48(3)		341(69)		JD 114(8)[1]	$1,747			128						
									791(175)												
MI	Thomas M. Cooley Law School (1975)																				
	217 South Capitol Avenue																				
	Lansing, Michigan 48933																				
	517/371-5140																				
	F	398(79)	262(46)	164(24)	....	....	....	47	824(149)	N	JD 168(16)[1]	$1,809	degree	90s	90	(N)[N]	9(1)	5	25	39,232	26,965
	P																				
	Detroit College of Law (1941)																				
	136 East Elizabeth Street																				
	Detroit, Michigan 48201																				
	313/965-0150																				
	F	213(47)	146(29)	174(10)	....	....	1	23	534(86)	N	JD 133(20)[1]	$2,020	degree	85s	96	(Y)[Y]	16	2	30	42,248	27,221
	P	196(37)	90(20)	89(14)	92(9)	....	1		468(80)		JD 104(4)	1,520									
									1,002(166)												
	University of Detroit (1933)																				
	School of Law																				
	651 East Jefferson Avenue																				
	Detroit, Michigan 48226																				
	313/927-1541																				
	F	142(36)	112(23)	122(26)	....	....	....	....	376(85)	MBA	JD 110(15)	$2,550	degree	86s	96	(Y)[Y]	18(1)	5(5)	13(1)	68,507	28,000
	P	98(21)	109(13)	91(17)	83(11)	....	3(1)	....	384(63)		JD 64(9)	83/hr.			128						
									760(148)												

LAW SCHOOLS ON THE APPROVED LIST OF THE AMERICAN BAR ASSOCIATION, 1976

	School	Row	First Year	Second Year	Third Year	Fourth Year	Graduate	Other	Minority Groups	Total Enrollment 1976	Joint Degrees	Degrees Awarded 1975–76	Tuition and Fees	Years College Required	Credits Required	Weeks Required	Summer Program	Full-time Teachers	Full-time Deans	Part-time Teachers	Total Volumes	Microform Equivalents
	University of Michigan (1923) Law School 304 Hutchins Hall 621 South State Street Ann Arbor, Michigan 48109 313/764-5278	F	369(89)	335(78)	397(79)	....	46(5)	24(7)	150	1,171(258)	PhD	SJD 5(2) MCL 6(1) LLM 17 JD 353(84)[24]	$1,540 r 3,536 nr	degree	82s	96	(Y)[Y]	47(3)	6(1)	3	461,465	9,642
		P																				
	Wayne State University (1936) Law School Detroit, Michigan 48202 313/577-3930	F	251(93)	240(79)	253(66)	....	....	4(3)	138	748(241)	MA	JD 204(48)[18]	$1,372 r 2,878 nr	degree	120q	90	(Y)[Y]	31(5)	2	18(1)	156,026	38,558
		P	107(35)	56(22)	62(14)	71(19)	127(7)	2		425(97) 1,173(338)		JD 51(9)[10] LLM 11(1)	1,153 r 2,404 nr			120						
MN	Hamline University (1975) School of Law 1536 Hewitt Avenue St. Paul, Minnesota 55104 612/641-2345	F	182(43)	141(31)	271(41)	....	....	....	7	594(115)	N	JD 105(8)[4]	$2,528	degree	86s	96	(Y)[Y]	18(1)	5(1)	13	54,809	11,887
		P										JD 7										
	University of Minnesota (1923) Law School 125 Fraser Hall Minneapolis, Minnesota 55455 612/373-2717	F	251(80)	228(73)	231(75)	....	....	1	44	711(228)	Int.Aff. Reg.Pl. PhD PAA MBA 1	JD 233(48)[15]	$1,135 r 2,902 nr	degree	133q	99	(Y)[Y]	24(3)	2	4	370,621	0
		P																				
	William Mitchell College of Law (1938) 875 Summit Avenue St. Paul, Minnesota 55105 612/227-9171	F																				
		P	299(94)	329(91)	239(78)	252(58)	....	1	....	1,120(321)	N	JD 195(27)	$1,758	degree	88s	144	(Y)[Y]	15(1)	5(1)	51(7)	56,540	14,070
MS	University of Mississippi (1930) School of Law University, Mississippi 38677 601/232-7361	F	311(60)	163(18)	116(16)	....	22(1)	4	34	616(95)	N	LLM 1(1) JD 164(13)	$ 451 r 826 nr	degree	90s	96	(Y)[Y]	19(1)	2	5	87,347	22,500
		P																				

MO	University of Missouri (1923) School of Law 114 Tate Hall Columbia, Missouri 65201 314/882-6539																					
		F	157(43)	128(35)	117(19)	....	....	....	7	402(87)	N	JD 137(13)[1]	$ 644 r 1,844 nr	3 yrs.	86s	96	(Y)[Y]	16(1)	4(1)	3	145,619	38,000
		P																				
	University of Missouri (1936) School of Law 5100 Rockhill Road Kansas City, Missouri 64110 816/276-1644																					
		F	166(58)	157(44)	157(25)	....	14	....	26	494(127)	MA	LLM 17(8)[1] JD 163(32)[10]	$ 670 r 1,870 nr	3 yrs.	86s	96	(Y)[Y]	19(2)	4(1)	7	82,598	113
		P	....	....	....	....	42(1)	58(11)		100(12) 594(139)		LLM 9	37/hr									
	St. Louis University (1924) School of Law 3642 Lindell Boulevard St. Louis, Missouri 63108 314/535-3300, ext. 335																					
		F	183(50)	161(42)	180(40)	....	....	....	46	524(132)	MHA MA 2 MBA 1	JD 166(25)[8]	$2,750	degree	84s	96	(Y)[Y]	21(1)	1	7	137,750	12,661
		P										JD 8(1)	105/hr.									
	Washington University (1923) School of Law Lindell & Skinker Boulevards St. Louis, Missouri 63130 314/863-0100, ext. 4883																					
		F	212(57)	186(80)	242(53)	....	16(1)	....	46	656(191)	MSW 6 Econ MBA 3	LLM 6 JD 165(40)[11]	$3,300	degree	86s	90	(Y)[Y]	28(3)	1	....	142,797	20,760
		P	2	....	....	....	29(6)	....		31(6) 687(197)		LLM 11	140/hr.									
MT	University of Montana (1923) School of Law Missoula, Montana 59801 406/243-4311																					
		F	75(25)	70(14)	74(8)	....	....	....	4	219(47)	N	JD 66(7)	$ 724 r 1,696 nr	degree	90s	96	(Y)[N]	11	2	4	80,016	801
		P																				
NB	Creighton University (1924) School of Law 2133 California Street Omaha, Nebraska 68178 402/449-2872																					
		F	191(38)	163(32)	167(26)	....	....	1	18	522(86)	N	JD 200(25)[3]	$2,780	3 yrs.	84s	94	(Y)[N]	20(1)	3	12	82,046	7,620
		P																				

LAW SCHOOLS ON THE APPROVED LIST OF THE AMERICAN BAR ASSOCIATION, 1976

		First Year	Second Year	Third Year	Fourth Year	Graduate	Other	Minority Groups	Total Enrollment 1976	Joint Degrees	Degrees Awarded 1975–76	Tuition and Fees	Years College Required	Credits Required	Weeks Required	Summer Program	Full-time Teachers	Full-time Deans	Part-time Teachers	Total Volumes	Microform Equivalents
	University of Nebraska (1923) College of Law Lincoln, Nebraska 68583 402/472-2161																				
	F	163(52)	156(36)	153(30)	....	....	....	4	472(118)	PhD MBA	JD 150(33)	$ 371 r 910 nr	3 yrs.	96s	90	(Y)[Y]	18(1)	4(2)	9	113,029	5,890
	P	....	....	....	....	....	2(1)		2(1) 474(118)												
NH	Franklin Pierce Law Center (1975) Concord, New Hampshire 03301 603/225-6671																				
	F	118(30)	114(21)	108(19)	....	....	....	6	340(70)	N	JD 87(7)[1]	$2,700	degree	84s	96	(Y)[Y]	14(2)	2	8	43,665	0
	P	5(2)	1	2	....	....	....		8(2) 348(72)			90/cr.			160						
NJ	Rutgers University (1951) School of Law Fifth and Penn Streets Camden, New Jersey 08102 609/757-6185																				
	F	206(55)	188(58)	162(40)	....	....	....	35	556(153)	Reg.Pl.	JD 151(31)[23]	$1,143 r 1,163 nr	degree	84s	96	(Y)[Y]	26(5)	2(1)	6(1)	144,093	22,369
	P	50(11)	27(4)	....	....	....	....	5	77(15) 633(168)			45/hr.r 65/hr.nr			136						
	Rutgers University (1941) School of Law 180 University Avenue Newark, New Jersey 07102 201/648-5561																				
	F	185(90)	240(95)	255(78)	....	....	6(1)	173	686(264)	Int.Aff. PhD PAA Reg.Pl. MBA	MCRP 1 LLM 1 JD 222(89)[41]	$1,207 r 1,687 nr	degree	84s	99	(Y)[N]	32(7)	3	14	217,715	25,115
	P	61(13)	53(25)	....	....	....	....	31	114(38) 800(302)		LLM 1	757 r 1,077 nr			132						
	Seton Hall University (1951) School of Law 1111 Raymond Boulevard Newark, New Jersey 07102 201/642-8500																				
	F	199(59)	185(59)	206(42)	....	....	....	48	590(160)	N	JD 167(46)[9]	$2,536	degree	84s	96	(Y)[Y]	24(2)	4	19(1)	85,401	9,905
	P	155(39)	132(23)	110(19)	125(26)	....	7(3)	58	529(110) 1,119(270)		JD 106(11)[8]	1,906			128						

NM	University of New Mexico (1948) School of Law 1117 Stanford Albuquerque, New Mexico 87131 505/277-2146																						
		F	106(33)	104(40)	127(42)	....	....	....	119	337(115)	PAA 1 MBA 1	JD 101(29)[16]	$ 524 r 1,520 nr	degree	86s	102	(Y)[N]	23(3)	2	4	135,527	30,129
		P																				
NY	Brooklyn Law School (1937) 250 Joralemon Street Brooklyn, New York 11201 212/625-2200																						
		F	277(111)	239(85)	230(76)	....	....	....	24	746(272)	MUP MA	JD 241(46)[11]	$2,780	degree	84s	96	(Y)[N]	28(5)	2	15(3)	116,947	2,887
		P	78(29)	65(22)	63(21)	53(10)	....	4(1)	25	263(83) 1,009(355)		JD 103(16)[8] LLM 1	2,092			128						
	Columbia University (1923) School of Law 435 West 116th Street New York, New York 10027 212/280-2671																						
		F	303(99)	280(90)	303(83)	....	54(6)	5	....	945(278)	Journ. IA 1 RP PA MBA 2	LLM 32(6) JD 297(71)	$4,162	degree	83s	96	(N)[N]	40(2)	....	23(3)	577,953	54,997
		P																				
	Cornell Law School (1923) Myron Taylor Hall Ithaca, New York 14853 607/256-3626																						
		F	167(42)	168(41)	171(45)	....	6	3(1)	48	515(129)	PhD MBA 8	SJD 1 LLM 1 JD 157(23)[12]	$4,050	3 yrs.	84s	96	(Y)[N]	22	3(2)	2	314,832	98
		P																				
	Fordham University (1936) School of Law 140 West 62nd Street New York, New York 10023 212/956-3783																						
		F	237(68)	225(69)	211(48)	....	....	....	62	735(185)	N	JD 193(40)[1]	$3,000	degree	81s	96	(Y)[N]	26(1)	2	37(6)	168,571	1,141
		P	116(33)	96(32)	101(21)	108(17)	....	....		421(103) 1,094(288)		JD 102(16)[1]	2,250			128						
	Hofstra University (1971) School of Law Hempstead, New York 11550 516/560-3636																						
		F	232(115)	222(105)	244(111)	....	....	....	60	698(331)	MBA 2	JD 206(53)[10]	$3,480	degree	87s	....	(Y)[Y]	22(4)	4	10(1)	127,487	14,924
		P																				
	New York Law School (1954) 57 Worth Street New York, New York 10013 212/966-3500																						
		F	322(89)	213(58)	226(50)	....	....	3(1)	42	764(198)	MBA	JD 132(22)[1]	$2,630	degree or 3 yrs.	85s	96	(Y)[N]	26(5)	2	31	90,392	14,932
		P	145(31)	114(22)	88(21)	57(13)	....	11(3)	36	415(90) 1,179(288)		JD 75(12)	1,768			128						

LAW SCHOOLS ON THE APPROVED LIST OF THE AMERICAN BAR ASSOCIATION, 1976

	First Year	Second Year	Third Year	Fourth Year	Graduate	Other	Minority Groups	Total Enrollment 1976	Joint Degrees	Degrees Awarded 1975–76	Tuition and Fees	Years College Required	Credits Required	Weeks Required	Summer Program	Full-time Teachers	Full-time Deans	Part-time Teachers	Total Volumes	Microform Equivalents
New York University (1930) School of Law 40 Washington Square South New York, New York 10012 212/598-2511																				
F	377(139)	361(118)	344(100)	....	268(30)	34(10)	....	1,384(397)	Reg.Pl. PAA 2 MBA 5	MCL 38(3) LLM 444(26) JD 361(112)	$1,775	degree or 3 yrs.	81s	96	(Y)[Y]	55(7)	6	42(2)	438,631	41,764
P	....	....	4(2)	....	1186(130)	25(7)	....	1,215(139)			1,331									
								2,599(536)												
St. John's University (1937) School of Law Fromkes Hall Jamaica, New York 11439 212/969-8000																				
F	219(69)	236(72)	238(58)	....	....	....	37	693(199)	N	JD 237(62)[8]	$2,650	degree	83s	96	(Y)[N]	22(3)	3	9	133,372	13,874
P	117(32)	94(22)	81(22)	95(13)	....	....		387(89)		JD 87(11)[3]	1,950			128						
								1,080(288)												
State University of New York at Buffalo (1936) School of Law John Lord O'Brian Hall Amherst Campus Buffalo, New York 14260 716/636-2060																				
F	226(78)	256(55)	243(62)	....	....	....	41	725(195)	Hum. 21 Soc.Sci. 9 Reg.Pl. 1 PhD 4 MBA 17	JD 266(57)[15]	$2,055 r 3,055 nr	degree	81s	96	(Y)[Y]	32(6)	2	18	209,126	109,451
P	17(7)	10(4)	8(3)	19(6)	....	....		54(20)		JD 6(2)	83/hr.r 125/hr.nr			128						
								779(215)												
Syracuse University (1923) College of Law Ernest I. White Hall Syracuse, New York 13210 315/423-2524																				
F	246(72)	190(46)	227(47)	....	....	....	49	663(165)	ML 1 MSA 3 PAA 3 MBA 3	JD 175(44)[7]	$3,751	3 yrs.	88s	96	(Y)[Y]	22(1)	1	13(3)	107,012	2,699
P	2(1)	9(2)	....	....	....	2(1)		13(4)			160/hr.			128						
								676(169)												
Union University (1930) Albany Law School 80 New Scotland Avenue Albany, New York 12208 518/434-0136																				
F	266(76)	247(72)	221(46)	....	....	5(2)	....	739(196)	BBA BA MBA	JD 227(51)	$2,500	3 yrs.	90s	90	(Y)[N]	17(2)	1	5	100,782	482
P																				

NC	Duke Univesrity (1931) School of Law Durham, North Carolina 27706 919/684-5824	F	217(52)	148(31)	148(28)	....	....	....	....	523(118)	MD MHA MBA 3	LLM 2(1) JD 145(21)	$3,310	3 yrs.	84s	90	(Y)[Y]	20(2)	3(1)	6	201,080	14,201
		P																				
	North Carolina Central University (1950) School of Law 1801 Fayetteville Street Durham, North Carolina 27707 919/683-6333	F	95(21)	55(15)	47(10)	....	....	....	119	197(46)	N	LLB 1 JD 109(17)[62]	$ 487 r 2,153 nr	3 yrs.	80s	90	(Y)[N]	15(4)	....	....	25,333	306
		P														120						
	University of North Carolina (1923) School of Law Chapel Hill, North Carolina 27514 919/933-5106	F	234(71)	208(48)	213(47)	....	....	....	53	655(166)	MA 1 Reg.Pl. 4 MBA 7	JD 216(47)[13]	$ 498 r 2,142 nr	degree	85s	96	(Y)[Y]	29(2)	2	....	174,448	30,156
		P																				
	Wake Forest University (1935) School of Law Box 7206 Reynolds Station Winston-Salem, North Carolina 27109 919/761-5434	F	151(30)	161(29)	165(29)	....	....	....	10	477(88)	N	JD 144(18)[1]	$2,300	degree	84s	102	(Y)[N]	16(1)	3	2	66,043	0
		P																				
ND	University of North Dakota (1923) School of Law University Station Grand Forks, North Dakota 58202 701/777-2104	F	101(21)	67(14)	79(17)	....	....	....	....	247(52)	N	JD 94(13)	$ 677 r 1,405 nr	degree	90s	96	(Y)[Y]	9(1)	2	4	103,210	53,000
		P																				
OH	University of Akron (1961) C. Blake McDowell Law Center Akron, Ohio 44325 216/375-7331	F	96(31)	88(19)	94(20)	....	....	3	11	281(70)	N	JD 97(7)[4]	$1,053 r 1,305 nr	degree	126q	96	(Y)[Y]	14(1)	8(3)	4	110,892	9,9€0
		P	99(30)	86(24)	81(20)	68(8)	....	4	24	338(82) 619(152)		JD 45(4)[2]	693 r 855 nr			144						

OH1

LAW SCHOOLS ON THE APPROVED LIST OF THE AMERICAN BAR ASSOCIATION, 1976

School		First Year	Second Year	Third Year	Fourth Year	Graduate	Other	Minority Groups	Total Enrollment 1976	Joint Degrees	Degrees Awarded 1975–76	Tuition and Fees	Years College Required	Credits Required	Weeks Required	Summer Program	Full-time Teachers	Full-time Deans	Part-time Teachers	Total Volumes	Microform Equivalents
Capital University (1950) Law School 2199 East Main Street Columbus, Ohio 43209 614/236-6395	F	132(40)	107(24)	105(24)	....	....	....	32	344(88)	N	JD 110(19)[1]	$2,802	degree	84s	96	(Y)[Y]	18(3)	2	....	68,964	3,049
	P	76(16)	58(16)	52(6)	50(6)	....	2		238(44)		JD 43(7)[1]	1,802			146						
									582(132)												
Case Western Reserve University (1923) School of Law 11075 East Boulevard Cleveland, Ohio 44106 216/368-3280	F	241(74)	219(59)	204(56)	....	....	....	48	664(189)	Hist.	LLM 2 JD 229(44)[11]	$3,326	degree	88s	104	(Y)[Y]	23(1)	1	8(1)	157,622	19,680
	P																				
University of Cincinnati (1923) College of Law 301 Taft Hall Cincinnati, Ohio 45221 513/475-6805	F	128(46)	116(38)	112(38)	....	....	3(1)	26	359(123)	N	JD 113(27)[7]	$1,200 r 2,325 nr	degree	88s	102	(Y)[Y]	16(1)	4	7	87,212	16,594
	P																				
Cleveland State University (1957) Cleveland-Marshall College of Law Cleveland, Ohio 44115 216/687-2344	F	221(63)	182(69)	216(53)	....	....	....	44	619(185)	N	JD 191(42)[5]	$1,125 r 2,250 nr	degree	126q	90	(Y)[Y]	31(3)	5(2)	15	86,444	31,047
	P	188(60)	144(42)	72(17)	94(13)	8(1)	12(1)	75	518(134) 1,137(319)		JD 75(12)[6] LLM 1	783 r 1,566 nr			120						
University of Dayton (1975) School of Law 300 College Park Drive Dayton, Ohio 45469 513/229-3211	F	154(49)	141(20)	107(25)	....	....	....	20	402(94)	MA MS MBA	....	$2,700	degree	84s	90	(Y)[Y]	14(1)	1	7(1)	70,753	39,853
	P																				

	Ohio Northern University (1948) Claude W. Pettit College of Law Ada, Ohio 45810 419/634-9921, ext. 225																					
		F	198(16)	166(24)	154(26)	....	....	....	10	518(66)	N	JD 148(5)[6]	$2,811	degree	129q	90	(Y)[Y]	15(2)	3	....	80,946	4,610
		P	3(2)	1	2	....	....	1		7(2)			78/hr.									
										525(68)												
	Ohio State University (1923) College of Law 1659 North High Street Columbus, Ohio 43210 614/422-2631																					
		F	241(59)	214(52)	222(42)	....	....	....	55	677(153)	Pol.Sci. 1 Hist. 1 Int.Aff. Reg.Pl. 1 PhD 1 PAA MBA	JD 209(30[15]	$1,050 r 2,400 nr	degree	128q	97	(Y)[Y]	26(4)	2	5	338,888	21,770
		P																				
	University of Toledo (1939) College of Law 2801 West Bancroft Street Toledo, Ohio 43606 419/537-2282																					
		F	192(41)	190(31)	209(23)	....	....	1	24	592(95)	N	JD 183(23)[10]	$1,110 r 2,370 nr	degree	126q	99	(Y)[Y]	30(3)	5(2)	3	92,465	12,408
		P	105(20)	96(19)	35(7)	44(10)	....	....	16	280(56)		JD 40(5)	740 r 1,580 nr			132						
										872(151)												
OK	Oklahoma City University (1960) School of Law 2501 North Blackwelder Oklahoma City, Oklahoma 73106 405/525-5411																					
		F	123(24)	84(17)	94(12)	....	....	....	22	301(53)	N	JD 79(13)[1]	$2,064	degree	90s	90	(Y)[Y]	13(1)	3	10(2)	42,104	5,150
		P	196(36)	66(10)	36(7)	....	....	1		299(53)		JD 74(11)[3]	1,383			120						
										600(106)												
	University of Oklahoma (1923) Law Center 300 Timberdell Road Norman, Oklahoma 73069 405/325-3711																					
		F	206(51)	250(60)	183(30)	....	....	....	38	639(141)	MBA 1	JD 165(22)[7]	$ 682 r 1,882 nr	degree	90s	102	(Y)[Y]	25(1)	3(2)	6	109,409	10,913
		P																				
	University of Tulsa (1950) College of Law 3120 East 4th Place Tulsa, Oklahoma 74104 918/939-6351, ext. 401																					
		F	160(36)	166(37)	114(24)	....	....	....	39	440(97)	N	JD 142(26)[3]	$ 70/hr.	degree	88s	96	(Y)[Y]	18(2)	4	9(2)	70,406	6,677
		P	72(17)	56(7)	29(9)	14(1)	....	....		171(34)		JD 9(2)				144						
										611(131)												

LAW SCHOOLS ON THE APPROVED LIST OF THE AMERICAN BAR ASSOCIATION, 1976

State	School		First Year	Second Year	Third Year	Fourth Year	Graduate	Other	Minority Groups	Total Enrollment 1976	Joint Degrees	Degrees Awarded 1975–76	Tuition and Fees	Years College Required	Credits Required	Weeks Required	Summer Program	Full-time Teachers	Full-time Deans	Part-time Teachers	Total Volumes	Microform Equivalents
OR	Lewis and Clark College (1970) Northwestern School of Law 10015 S.W. Terwilliger Boulevard Portland, Oregon 97219 503/244-1181	F	150(33)	121(37)	102(32)	....	....	....	....	373(102)	N	JD 118(28)	$2,725	degree	86s	102	(Y)[Y]	18(2)	2	19(1)	77,605	20,842
		P	97(32)	101(23)	63(14)	69(10)	....	....		330(79)		JD 97(18)	1,725			136						
										703(181)												
	University of Oregon (1923) School of Law 1275 Kincaid Street Eugene, Oregon 97403 503/686-3852	F	169(54)	156(39)	165(40)	....	....	8(4)	26	498(137)	N	JD 144(34)[12]	$1,411	degree	85s	90	(Y)[Y]	21(2)	2	2	94,955	9,076
		P																				
	Willamette University (1938) College of Law Salem, Oregon 97301 503/370-6380	F	141(32)	120(27)	115(27)	....	10(2)	10(2)	15	396(90)	MA	JD 120(13)[6]	$2,754	degree	88s	96	(Y)[Y]	14(1)	1	3	70,093	1,552
		P																				
PA	Dickinson School of Law (1931) 150 South College Street Carlisle, Pennsylvania 17013 717/243-4611	F	158(41)	145(39)	153(25)	....	1(1)	11(3)	9	468(109)	N	MCL 4 JD 137(17)[1]	$1,887 r 2,187 nr	degree	88s	97	(Y)[N]	12(1)	1	11(1)	70,500	7,500
		P																				
	Duquesne University (1960) School of Law 600 Forbes Avenue Pittsburgh, Pennsylvania 15219 412/434-6300	F	118(30)	93(28)	90(12)	....	....	....	19	301(70)	N	JD 88(13)[3]	$2,410	degree	88s	99	(Y)[Y]	16(2)	1	13	61,843	0
		P	120(35)	82(28)	73(22)	66(10)	....	....	9	341(95)		JD 62(6)[3]	88/hr			132						
										641(165)												

	University of Pennsylvania (1923) Law School 3400 Chestnut Street Philadelphia, Pennsylvania 19174 215/243-7483										MA Reg.Pl. 1 PhD 2	LLM 5									
	F	207(89)	208(61)	191(55)	....	9(1)	....	113	615(206)	MBA 8	JD 200(48)[29]	$4,190	degree	90s	99	(N)[N]	25(1)	1	8(1)	272,653	0
	P																				
	University of Pittsburgh (1923) School of Law 3900 Forbes Avenue Pittsburgh, Pennsylvania 15260 412/624-6200																				
	F	238(60)	205(42)	185(32)	....	....	....	42	628(134)	N	JD 105(19)[4]	$1,404 r 2,804 nr	degree	86s	96	(Y)[N]	21(1)	2	10(1)	91,518	9,257
	P																				
	Temple University (1933) School of Law 1719 North Broad Street Philadelphia, Pennsylvania 19122 215/787-7863											LLM 5(2)									
	F	281(119)	258(94)	277(93)	....	14(2)	....	118	830(308)	N	JD 274(84)[24]	$1,600 r 3,100 nr	degree	83s	102	(Y)[N]	37(4)	2	16(2)	220,302	16,640
	P	99(40)	80(23)	69(20)	51(13)	142(9)	....	35	441(105) 1,271(413)		JD 75(18)[4] LLM 18(2)	1,400 r 2,790 nr			136						
	Villanova University (1954) School of Law Villanova, Pennsylvania 19085 215/527-2100																				
	F	225(81)	212(80)	196(61)	....	....	1	24	634(222)	N	JD 212(47)[8]	$2,855	degree	86s	102	(N)[N]	20(1)	3(1)	3	178,862	13,576
	P																				
PR	Catholic University of Puerto Rico (1967) School of Law Ponce, Puerto Rico 00731 809/844-4150, ext. 267																				
	F	61(20)	49(7)	57(12)	....	....	....		167(39)	N	JD 55(8)	$2,380	degree	....	96	(N)[N]	10(1)	1	15(2)	63,562	531
	P	49(7)	37(5)	33(5)	42(7)	....	....		161(24) 328(63)		JD 34(2)	1,808			128						
	Inter-American University of Puerto Rico (1969) School of Law P.O. Box 8897 Fernandez Juncos Station Santurce, Puerto Rico 00910 809/724-1930																				
	F	184(62)	175(55)	91(33)	....	....	....		450(150)	N	JD 76(25)	$1,842	degree	90s	102	(Y)[N]	23(7)	2	15(2)	53,375	6,476
	P	127(37)	131(39)	74(25)	87(13)	....	5		424(114) 874(264)		JD 139(39) LLM 3	1,362			136						

LAW SCHOOLS ON THE APPROVED LIST OF THE AMERICAN BAR ASSOCIATION, 1976

State	School	First Year	Second Year	Third Year	Fourth Year	Graduate	Other	Minority Groups	Total Enrollment 1976	Joint Degrees	Degrees Awarded 1975–76	Tuition and Fees	Years College Required	Credits Required	Weeks Required	Summer Program	Full-time Teachers	Full-time Deans	Part-time Teachers	Total Volumes	Microform Equivalents
	University of Puerto Rico (1945) School of Law Box AZ, University Station San Juan, Puerto Rico 00931 809/767-6208																				
	F	97(47)	116(44)	140(54)	....	....	....	....	353(145)	N	JD 121(45)	$ 514 r 954 nr	degree	92s	102	(Y)[N]	21(3)	11(7)	14(1)	95,487	69
	P	59(18)	47(10)	53(9)	43(11)	....	....		202(48) 555(193)			364 r 664 nr			140						
SC	University of South Carolina (1925) Law Center Columbia, South Carolina 29208 803/777-6617																				
	F	250(55)	267(56)	323(52)	....	....	....	45	840(163)	Acct. 2 Econ. 1 MBA 6	JD 277(34)[9]	$ 662 r 1,662 hr	degree	80s	96	(Y)[Y]	30(1)	1	6(1)	129,024	53,327
	P																				
SD	University of South Dakota (1923) School of Law Vermillion, South Dakota 57069 605/677-5361																				
	F	66(15)	67(14)	67(18)	....	....	....	....	200(47)	Hist. Ed.Ad. Pol. Sci. Econ. PAA 1 MBA 5	JD 70(7)[2]	$1,029 r 1,817 nr	degree	90s	102	(Y)[Y]	10(2)	5	2	76,428	0
	P																				
TN	Memphis State University (1965) School of Law Memphis, Tennessee 38152 901/454-2421																				
	F	159(34)	131(33)	103(13)	....	....	....	7	393(80)	N	JD 156(22)[1]	$ 448 r 1,384 nr	degree	84s	93	(Y)[Y]	21(1)	3(2)	5	95,749	25,111
	P	48(10)	45(16)	23	13(3)	....	10	7	139(29) 532(109)		JD 10	23/hr.r 62/hr.nr			142						
	University of Tennessee (1925) College of Law 1505 West Cumberland Avenue Knoxville, Tennessee 37916 615/974-2521																				
	F	232(67)	203(53)	176(36)	....	....	....	20	611(156)	MBA	JD 203(38)[4]	$ 525 r 1,425 nr	degree	126q	90	(Y)[Y]	26(1)	3	3	101,095	15,100
	P																				

	Vanderbilt University (1925)									Eng.											
	School of Law									M											
	Nashville, Tennessee 37240									MD											
	615/322-2615									PhD											
										MM											
	F	174(31)	162(43)	165(31)	....	....	6(1)	36	507(106)	MBA 1	JD 167(27)[12]	$3,410	degree	88s	96	(Y)[Y]	23(1)	3	9	107,102	8,338
	P																				
TX	Baylor University (1931)																				
	Law School																				
	Waco, Texas 76703																				
	817/755-1911																				
	F	162(30)	112(15)	121(16)	....	....	....	....	395(61)	N	JD 140(9)	$1,363	3 yrs.	120q	106	(Y)[Y]	9	4(3)	5(1)	75,334	173
	P	1	....	12(1)	....	....	....		13(2)		JD 140(9)	45/hr.									
									108(63)												
	University of Houston (1950)																				
	Bates College of Law																				
	4800 Calhoun Road																				
	Houston, Texas 77004																				
	713/749-1422																				
	F	281(89)	368(121)	210(54)	....	....	....	....	859(264)	N	JD 238(54)	$ 372 r 1,452 nr	degree	88s	90	(Y)[Y]	29(2)	11(4)	13(1)	128,774	32,247
	P	77(20)	122(36)	36(12)	....	....	....		235(68)			342 r			120						
									1,094(332)			1,042 nr									
	St. Mary's University (1948)																				
	School of Law																				
	One Camino Santa Maria																				
	San Antonio, Texas 78284																				
	512/436-3424																				
	F	270(59)	244(56)	176(25)	....	....	....	57	690(140)	N	JD 191(19)[16]	$2,400	degree	90s	96	(Y)[Y]	18(1)	5(2)	10	75,591	2,932
	P																				
	Southern Methodist University (1927)																				
	School of Law										SJD 1										
	Dallas, Texas 75275										MCL 14										
	214/692-2618									PAA 2	LLM 23(1)										
	F	223(62)	201(66)	258(63)	....	43(4)	22	19	747(195)	MBA 2	JD 236(40)[9]	$1,742	degree	88s	90	(Y)[Y]	20(2)	4	21(5)	210,230	13,498
	P	....	9(2)	17(5)	....	57(9)	6(1)		89(17)		LLM 2	118									
									836(212)												
	South Texas College of Law (1959)																				
	1303 San Jacinto Street																				
	Houston, Texas 77002																				
	713/659-8040																				
	F											$1,452	degree	90s	108						
	P	441(87)	273(33)	190(18)	92(9)	....	7	47	1,003(147)	N	JD 202(20)[4]	1,052			148	(Y)[Y]	11	4	23(1)	67,235	11,544
	Texas Southern University (1949)									MA											
	Thurgood Marshall School of Law									Int.Aff.											
	3201 Wheeler Avenue									Reg.Pl.											
	Houston, Texas 77004									PhD											
	713/527-7112									PAA											
	F	147(49)	77(20)	109(26)	....	....	....	....	333(95)	MBA	JD 77(13)	$ 188 r 764 nr	degree	90s	96	(Y)[Y]	16(1)	4	4(1)	64,720	20,237
	P																				

LAW SCHOOLS ON THE APPROVED LIST OF THE AMERICAN BAR ASSOCIATION, 1976

		First Year	Second Year	Third Year	Fourth Year	Graduate	Other	Minority Groups	Total Enrollment 1976	Joint Degrees	Degrees Awarded 1975–76	Tuition and Fees	Years College Required	Credits Required	Weeks Required	Summer Program	Full-time Teachers	Full-time Deans	Part-time Teachers	Total Volumes	Microform Equivalents
	Texas Tech University (1969) School of Law P.O. Box 4030 Lubbock, Texas 79409 806/742-3791																				
	F	162(37)	147(25)	158(21)	....	....	....	54	467(83)	MBA 6	JD 135(19)[7]	$ 371 r 1,451 nr	degree	90s	102	(Y)[Y]	19	4(1)	3(1)	108,895	3,297
	P																				
	University of Texas (1923) School of Law 2500 Red River Street Austin, Texas 78705 512/471-1621																				
	F	536(173)	568(147)	495(102)	....	20	4(2)	175	1,623(424)	N	MCL 6 LLM 3(1) JD 570(83)[23]	$ 336 r 1,180 nr	degree	84s	96	(Y)[Y]	50(4)	6(1)	9(1)	366,199	9,351
	P																				
UT	Brigham Young University (1974) J. Reuben Clark Law School Provo, Utah 84602 801/374-1211, ext. 4274																				
	F	150(12)	150(6)	154(7)	....	....	....	....	454(25)	PAA MBA	JD 143(8)	$1,320 r 1,970 nr	degree	87s	90	(Y)[Y]	19(1)	4	3	194,782	38,768
	P	1	....	....	....	....	....	....	1 455(25)												
	University of Utah (1927) College of Law Salt Lake City, Utah 84112 801/581-6833																				
	F	144(35)	132(29)	139(29)	....	....	....	25	415(93)	MBA 1	JD 136(27)[9]	$ 282 r 695 nr	3 yrs.	110s	90	(Y)[Y]	21(1)	1	4	150,700	22,652
	P																				
VT	Vermont Law School (1975) South Royalton, Vermont 05068 802/763-8303																				
	F	98(26)	108(18)	128(7)	....	....	....	4	334(51)	N	JD 80(3)	$3,015	degree	135q	110	(Y)[Y]	13	2	2	41,225	3,368
	P																				

VA	Judge Advocate General's School (1965; offers post J.D. degree programs only) U.S. Army Charlottesville, Virginia 22901 804/924-7343	F	....	....	....	....	....	....	....	....	....	....	....	....	....	....	....	27	6(2)	....	15,410	481
		P																				
	University of Richmond (1928) T. C. Williams School of Law Richmond, Virginia 23173 804/285-6336	F	138(27)	134(24)	135(15)	....	....	....	12	408(66)	N	JD 152(4)[1]	$2,700	3 yrs.	90s	96	(Y)[Y]	13	....	12(1)	64,327	0
		P	....	....	....	....	....	1		1 409(66)			131/hr.									
	University of Virginia School of Law Charlottesville, Virginia 22901 804/924-7343	F	359(96)	365(71)	357(66)	....	20(3)	....	....	1,101(236)	Hist. 1 Int.Aff. Reg.Pl. PhD PAA MBA	SJD 2 MCL 3(1) LLM 13 JD 332(58)	$1,036 r 2,496 nr	degree	86s	99	(Y)[N]	43(1)	5	25	243,285	75,405
		P	....	....	2(1)	....	5	....		7(1) 1,108(237)												
	Washington and Lee University (1923) School of Law Lexington, Virginia 24450 703/463-9111	F	114(14)	75(10)	71(10)	....	....	5(1)	11	265(35)	N	JD 76(6)[3]	$2,500	degree	85s	96	(Y)[Y]	14(1)	1	3	117,484	36,216
		P																				
	College of William and Mary (1932) Marshall-Wythe School of Law Williamsburg, Virginia 23185 804/229-3000, ext. 304	F	151(43)	142(32)	148(35)	....	7	....	19	448(110)	N	JD 144(27)[5]	$ 968 r 2,264 nr	degree	90s	90	(Y)[Y]	19	2	4	91,000	10,000
		P																				
WA	Gonzaga University (1951) School of Law East 600 Sharp Spokane, Washington 99202 509/326-5310	F	199(31)	151(14)	160(20)	....	....	....	30	510(65)	MBA	JD 155(9)[2]	$1,209	degree	90s	90	(Y)[Y]	26(1)	1	9	88,000	3,000
		P	129(20)	91(6)	101(13)	30(1)	....	3		354(40) 864(105)		JD 135(16)[5]	1,023			120						
	University of Puget Sound (1973) School of Law 8811 South Tacoma Way Tacoma, Washington 98499 206/756-3322	F	277(45)	232(54)	173(37)	....	....	....	28	682(136)	N	JD 186(30)[11]	$1,350	degree	90s	90	(Y)[Y]	18(2)	3(1)	15(3)	65,232	27,729
		P	84(28)	48(18)	43(9)	39(8)	....	....		214(63) 896(199)		JD 41(3)[1]	900			135						

LAW SCHOOLS ON THE APPROVED LIST OF THE AMERICAN BAR ASSOCIATION, 1976

State	School		First Year	Second Year	Third Year	Fourth Year	Graduate	Other	Minority Groups	Total Enrollment 1976	Joint Degrees	Degrees Awarded 1975–76	Tuition and Fees	Years College Required	Credits Required	Weeks Required	Summer Program	Full-time Teachers	Full-time Deans	Part-time Teachers	Total Volumes	Microform Equivalents
	University of Washington (1924) School of Law Condon Hall 1100 N.E. Campus Parkway Seattle, Washington 98195 206/543-4550	F	156(50)	166(56)	161(51)	....	30(4)	3(2)	71	516(163)	Int.Aff. Reg.Pl. PhD PAA MBA 4	LLM 10 JD 160(42)[18]	$ 624 r 1,641 nr	degree	135q	99	(Y)[Y]	30(2)	4(1)	4(2)	245,602	20,196
		P																				
WV	West Virginia University (1924) College of Law Morgantown, West Virginia 26506 304/293-5301	F	131(30)	138(30)	127(24)	....	....	....	8	396(84)	N	JD 103(16)[1]	$ 216 r 715 nr	degree	85s	102	(Y)[N]	18(2)	4(1)	5	103,226	4,744
		P																				
WI	Marquette University (1925) Law School 1103 West Wisconsin Avenue Milwaukee, Wisconsin 53233 414/224-7090	F	158(25)	134(30)	139(22)	....	....	3(2)	15	434(79)	MBA 3	JD 129(10)[4]	$2,930	degree	90s	94	(Y)[N]	12(2)	3	8	87,152	2,622
		P																				
	University of Wisconsin (1923) Law School Madison, Wisconsin 53706 608/262-2240	F	293(109)	304(82)	276(91)	....	5(1)	4(1)	58	882(284)	MBA	SJD 1 LLM 2(1) JD 291(71)[24]	$ 959 r 2,987 nr	degree	90s	96	(Y)[Y]	40(2)	2	25(1)	187,921	15,915
		P																				
WY	University of Wyoming (1923) College of Law P.O. Box 3035 University Station Laramie, Wyoming 82071 307/766-6416	F	79(18)	62(16)	70(17)	....	....	....	1	211(51)	N	JD 62(9)	$ 434 r 1,400 nr	degree	86s	96	(Y)[Y]	10	4(2)	1	62,556	14,848
		P																				

Answer Sheet for Chapter Self-Tests

Data Interpretation
Self-Test A

1. Ⓐ Ⓑ Ⓒ Ⓓ Ⓔ
2. Ⓐ Ⓑ Ⓒ Ⓓ Ⓔ
3. Ⓐ Ⓑ Ⓒ Ⓓ Ⓔ
4. Ⓐ Ⓑ Ⓒ Ⓓ Ⓔ
5. Ⓐ Ⓑ Ⓒ Ⓓ Ⓔ
6. Ⓐ Ⓑ Ⓒ Ⓓ Ⓔ
7. Ⓐ Ⓑ Ⓒ Ⓓ Ⓔ
8. Ⓐ Ⓑ Ⓒ Ⓓ Ⓔ
9. Ⓐ Ⓑ Ⓒ Ⓓ Ⓔ
10. Ⓐ Ⓑ Ⓒ Ⓓ Ⓔ
11. Ⓐ Ⓑ Ⓒ Ⓓ Ⓔ
12. Ⓐ Ⓑ Ⓒ Ⓓ Ⓔ
13. Ⓐ Ⓑ Ⓒ Ⓓ Ⓔ
14. Ⓐ Ⓑ Ⓒ Ⓓ Ⓔ
15. Ⓐ Ⓑ Ⓒ Ⓓ Ⓔ
16. Ⓐ Ⓑ Ⓒ Ⓓ Ⓔ
17. Ⓐ Ⓑ Ⓒ Ⓓ Ⓔ
18. Ⓐ Ⓑ Ⓒ Ⓓ Ⓔ
19. Ⓐ Ⓑ Ⓒ Ⓓ Ⓔ
20. Ⓐ Ⓑ Ⓒ Ⓓ Ⓔ
21. Ⓐ Ⓑ Ⓒ Ⓓ Ⓔ
22. Ⓐ Ⓑ Ⓒ Ⓓ Ⓔ
23. Ⓐ Ⓑ Ⓒ Ⓓ Ⓔ
24. Ⓐ Ⓑ Ⓒ Ⓓ Ⓔ
25. Ⓐ Ⓑ Ⓒ Ⓓ Ⓔ
26. Ⓐ Ⓑ Ⓒ Ⓓ Ⓔ
27. Ⓐ Ⓑ Ⓒ Ⓓ Ⓔ
28. Ⓐ Ⓑ Ⓒ Ⓓ Ⓔ

Data Interpretation
Self-Test B

1. Ⓐ Ⓑ Ⓒ Ⓓ Ⓔ
2. Ⓐ Ⓑ Ⓒ Ⓓ Ⓔ
3. Ⓐ Ⓑ Ⓒ Ⓓ Ⓔ
4. Ⓐ Ⓑ Ⓒ Ⓓ Ⓔ
5. Ⓐ Ⓑ Ⓒ Ⓓ Ⓔ
6. Ⓐ Ⓑ Ⓒ Ⓓ Ⓔ
7. Ⓐ Ⓑ Ⓒ Ⓓ Ⓔ
8. Ⓐ Ⓑ Ⓒ Ⓓ Ⓔ
9. Ⓐ Ⓑ Ⓒ Ⓓ Ⓔ
10. Ⓐ Ⓑ Ⓒ Ⓓ Ⓔ
11. Ⓐ Ⓑ Ⓒ Ⓓ Ⓔ
12. Ⓐ Ⓑ Ⓒ Ⓓ Ⓔ
13. Ⓐ Ⓑ Ⓒ Ⓓ Ⓔ
14. Ⓐ Ⓑ Ⓒ Ⓓ Ⓔ
15. Ⓐ Ⓑ Ⓒ Ⓓ Ⓔ
16. Ⓐ Ⓑ Ⓒ Ⓓ Ⓔ
17. Ⓐ Ⓑ Ⓒ Ⓓ Ⓔ
18. Ⓐ Ⓑ Ⓒ Ⓓ Ⓔ
19. Ⓐ Ⓑ Ⓒ Ⓓ Ⓔ
20. Ⓐ Ⓑ Ⓒ Ⓓ Ⓔ
21. Ⓐ Ⓑ Ⓒ Ⓓ Ⓔ
22. Ⓐ Ⓑ Ⓒ Ⓓ Ⓔ
23. Ⓐ Ⓑ Ⓒ Ⓓ Ⓔ
24. Ⓐ Ⓑ Ⓒ Ⓓ Ⓔ
25. Ⓐ Ⓑ Ⓒ Ⓓ Ⓔ
26. Ⓐ Ⓑ Ⓒ Ⓓ Ⓔ
27. Ⓐ Ⓑ Ⓒ Ⓓ Ⓔ
28. Ⓐ Ⓑ Ⓒ Ⓓ Ⓔ

Quantitative Comparison
Self-Test

1. Ⓐ Ⓑ Ⓒ Ⓓ
2. Ⓐ Ⓑ Ⓒ Ⓓ
3. Ⓐ Ⓑ Ⓒ Ⓓ
4. Ⓐ Ⓑ Ⓒ Ⓓ
5. Ⓐ Ⓑ Ⓒ Ⓓ
6. Ⓐ Ⓑ Ⓒ Ⓓ
7. Ⓐ Ⓑ Ⓒ Ⓓ
8. Ⓐ Ⓑ Ⓒ Ⓓ
9. Ⓐ Ⓑ Ⓒ Ⓓ
10. Ⓐ Ⓑ Ⓒ Ⓓ
11. Ⓐ Ⓑ Ⓒ Ⓓ
12. Ⓐ Ⓑ Ⓒ Ⓓ
13. Ⓐ Ⓑ Ⓒ Ⓓ
14. Ⓐ Ⓑ Ⓒ Ⓓ
15. Ⓐ Ⓑ Ⓒ Ⓓ

Reading Comprehension Self-Test

1. Ⓐ Ⓑ Ⓒ Ⓓ Ⓔ
2. Ⓐ Ⓑ Ⓒ Ⓓ Ⓔ
3. Ⓐ Ⓑ Ⓒ Ⓓ Ⓔ
4. Ⓐ Ⓑ Ⓒ Ⓓ Ⓔ
5. Ⓐ Ⓑ Ⓒ Ⓓ Ⓔ
6. Ⓐ Ⓑ Ⓒ Ⓓ Ⓔ
7. Ⓐ Ⓑ Ⓒ Ⓓ Ⓔ
8. Ⓐ Ⓑ Ⓒ Ⓓ Ⓔ
9. Ⓐ Ⓑ Ⓒ Ⓓ Ⓔ
10. Ⓐ Ⓑ Ⓒ Ⓓ Ⓔ
11. Ⓐ Ⓑ Ⓒ Ⓓ Ⓔ
12. Ⓐ Ⓑ Ⓒ Ⓓ Ⓔ
13. Ⓐ Ⓑ Ⓒ Ⓓ Ⓔ
14. Ⓐ Ⓑ Ⓒ Ⓓ Ⓔ
15. Ⓐ Ⓑ Ⓒ Ⓓ Ⓔ
16. Ⓐ Ⓑ Ⓒ Ⓓ Ⓔ
17. Ⓐ Ⓑ Ⓒ Ⓓ Ⓔ
18. Ⓐ Ⓑ Ⓒ Ⓓ Ⓔ
19. Ⓐ Ⓑ Ⓒ Ⓓ Ⓔ
20. Ⓐ Ⓑ Ⓒ Ⓓ Ⓔ
21. Ⓐ Ⓑ Ⓒ Ⓓ Ⓔ
22. Ⓐ Ⓑ Ⓒ Ⓓ Ⓔ
23. Ⓐ Ⓑ Ⓒ Ⓓ Ⓔ
24. Ⓐ Ⓑ Ⓒ Ⓓ Ⓔ
25. Ⓐ Ⓑ Ⓒ Ⓓ Ⓔ

Reading Recall Self-Test

1. Ⓐ Ⓑ Ⓒ Ⓓ Ⓔ
2. Ⓐ Ⓑ Ⓒ Ⓓ Ⓔ
3. Ⓐ Ⓑ Ⓒ Ⓓ Ⓔ
4. Ⓐ Ⓑ Ⓒ Ⓓ Ⓔ
5. Ⓐ Ⓑ Ⓒ Ⓓ Ⓔ
6. Ⓐ Ⓑ Ⓒ Ⓓ Ⓔ
7. Ⓐ Ⓑ Ⓒ Ⓓ Ⓔ
8. Ⓐ Ⓑ Ⓒ Ⓓ Ⓔ
9. Ⓐ Ⓑ Ⓒ Ⓓ Ⓔ
10. Ⓐ Ⓑ Ⓒ Ⓓ Ⓔ
11. Ⓐ Ⓑ Ⓒ Ⓓ Ⓔ
12. Ⓐ Ⓑ Ⓒ Ⓓ Ⓔ
13. Ⓐ Ⓑ Ⓒ Ⓓ Ⓔ
14. Ⓐ Ⓑ Ⓒ Ⓓ Ⓔ
15. Ⓐ Ⓑ Ⓒ Ⓓ Ⓔ
16. Ⓐ Ⓑ Ⓒ Ⓓ Ⓔ
17. Ⓐ Ⓑ Ⓒ Ⓓ Ⓔ
18. Ⓐ Ⓑ Ⓒ Ⓓ Ⓔ
19. Ⓐ Ⓑ Ⓒ Ⓓ Ⓔ
20. Ⓐ Ⓑ Ⓒ Ⓓ Ⓔ
21. Ⓐ Ⓑ Ⓒ Ⓓ Ⓔ
22. Ⓐ Ⓑ Ⓒ Ⓓ Ⓔ
23. Ⓐ Ⓑ Ⓒ Ⓓ Ⓔ
24. Ⓐ Ⓑ Ⓒ Ⓓ Ⓔ
25. Ⓐ Ⓑ Ⓒ Ⓓ Ⓔ
26. Ⓐ Ⓑ Ⓒ Ⓓ Ⓔ
27. Ⓐ Ⓑ Ⓒ Ⓓ Ⓔ
28. Ⓐ Ⓑ Ⓒ Ⓓ Ⓔ
29. Ⓐ Ⓑ Ⓒ Ⓓ Ⓔ
30. Ⓐ Ⓑ Ⓒ Ⓓ Ⓔ

Principles and Cases Self-Test

1. Ⓐ Ⓑ Ⓒ Ⓓ
2. Ⓐ Ⓑ Ⓒ Ⓓ
3. Ⓐ Ⓑ Ⓒ Ⓓ
4. Ⓐ Ⓑ Ⓒ Ⓓ
5. Ⓐ Ⓑ Ⓒ Ⓓ
6. Ⓐ Ⓑ Ⓒ Ⓓ
7. Ⓐ Ⓑ Ⓒ Ⓓ
8. Ⓐ Ⓑ Ⓒ Ⓓ
9. Ⓐ Ⓑ Ⓒ Ⓓ
10. Ⓐ Ⓑ Ⓒ Ⓓ
11. Ⓐ Ⓑ Ⓒ Ⓓ
12. Ⓐ Ⓑ Ⓒ Ⓓ
13. Ⓐ Ⓑ Ⓒ Ⓓ
14. Ⓐ Ⓑ Ⓒ Ⓓ
15. Ⓐ Ⓑ Ⓒ Ⓓ
16. Ⓐ Ⓑ Ⓒ Ⓓ
17. Ⓐ Ⓑ Ⓒ Ⓓ
18. Ⓐ Ⓑ Ⓒ Ⓓ
19. Ⓐ Ⓑ Ⓒ Ⓓ
20. Ⓐ Ⓑ Ⓒ Ⓓ
21. Ⓐ Ⓑ Ⓒ Ⓓ
22. Ⓐ Ⓑ Ⓒ Ⓓ
23. Ⓐ Ⓑ Ⓒ Ⓓ
24. Ⓐ Ⓑ Ⓒ Ⓓ
25. Ⓐ Ⓑ Ⓒ Ⓓ
26. Ⓐ Ⓑ Ⓒ Ⓓ
27. Ⓐ Ⓑ Ⓒ Ⓓ
28. Ⓐ Ⓑ Ⓒ Ⓓ
29. Ⓐ Ⓑ Ⓒ Ⓓ
30. Ⓐ Ⓑ Ⓒ Ⓓ

Practical Judgment Self-Test

1. Ⓐ Ⓑ Ⓒ Ⓓ Ⓔ
2. Ⓐ Ⓑ Ⓒ Ⓓ Ⓔ
3. Ⓐ Ⓑ Ⓒ Ⓓ Ⓔ
4. Ⓐ Ⓑ Ⓒ Ⓓ Ⓔ
5. Ⓐ Ⓑ Ⓒ Ⓓ Ⓔ
6. Ⓐ Ⓑ Ⓒ Ⓓ Ⓔ
7. Ⓐ Ⓑ Ⓒ Ⓓ Ⓔ
8. Ⓐ Ⓑ Ⓒ Ⓓ Ⓔ
9. Ⓐ Ⓑ Ⓒ Ⓓ Ⓔ
10. Ⓐ Ⓑ Ⓒ Ⓓ Ⓔ
11. Ⓐ Ⓑ Ⓒ Ⓓ Ⓔ
12. Ⓐ Ⓑ Ⓒ Ⓓ Ⓔ
13. Ⓐ Ⓑ Ⓒ Ⓓ Ⓔ
14. Ⓐ Ⓑ Ⓒ Ⓓ Ⓔ
15. Ⓐ Ⓑ Ⓒ Ⓓ Ⓔ
16. Ⓐ Ⓑ Ⓒ Ⓓ Ⓔ
17. Ⓐ Ⓑ Ⓒ Ⓓ Ⓔ
18. Ⓐ Ⓑ Ⓒ Ⓓ Ⓔ
19. Ⓐ Ⓑ Ⓒ Ⓓ Ⓔ
20. Ⓐ Ⓑ Ⓒ Ⓓ Ⓔ
21. Ⓐ Ⓑ Ⓒ Ⓓ Ⓔ
22. Ⓐ Ⓑ Ⓒ Ⓓ Ⓔ
23. Ⓐ Ⓑ Ⓒ Ⓓ Ⓔ
24. Ⓐ Ⓑ Ⓒ Ⓓ Ⓔ
25. Ⓐ Ⓑ Ⓒ Ⓓ Ⓔ

Logical Reasoning Self-Test

1. Ⓐ Ⓑ Ⓒ Ⓓ Ⓔ
2. Ⓐ Ⓑ Ⓒ Ⓓ Ⓔ
3. Ⓐ Ⓑ Ⓒ Ⓓ Ⓔ
4. Ⓐ Ⓑ Ⓒ Ⓓ Ⓔ
5. Ⓐ Ⓑ Ⓒ Ⓓ Ⓔ
6. Ⓐ Ⓑ Ⓒ Ⓓ Ⓔ
7. Ⓐ Ⓑ Ⓒ Ⓓ Ⓔ
8. Ⓐ Ⓑ Ⓒ Ⓓ Ⓔ
9. Ⓐ Ⓑ Ⓒ Ⓓ Ⓔ
10. Ⓐ Ⓑ Ⓒ Ⓓ Ⓔ
11. Ⓐ Ⓑ Ⓒ Ⓓ Ⓔ
12. Ⓐ Ⓑ Ⓒ Ⓓ Ⓔ
13. Ⓐ Ⓑ Ⓒ Ⓓ Ⓔ
14. Ⓐ Ⓑ Ⓒ Ⓓ Ⓔ
15. Ⓐ Ⓑ Ⓒ Ⓓ Ⓔ
16. Ⓐ Ⓑ Ⓒ Ⓓ Ⓔ
17. Ⓐ Ⓑ Ⓒ Ⓓ Ⓔ
18. Ⓐ Ⓑ Ⓒ Ⓓ Ⓔ
19. Ⓐ Ⓑ Ⓒ Ⓓ Ⓔ
20. Ⓐ Ⓑ Ⓒ Ⓓ Ⓔ
21. Ⓐ Ⓑ Ⓒ Ⓓ Ⓔ
22. Ⓐ Ⓑ Ⓒ Ⓓ Ⓔ
23. Ⓐ Ⓑ Ⓒ Ⓓ Ⓔ
24. Ⓐ Ⓑ Ⓒ Ⓓ Ⓔ
25. Ⓐ Ⓑ Ⓒ Ⓓ Ⓔ

Error Recognition Self-Test

1. Ⓐ Ⓑ Ⓒ Ⓓ
2. Ⓐ Ⓑ Ⓒ Ⓓ
3. Ⓐ Ⓑ Ⓒ Ⓓ
4. Ⓐ Ⓑ Ⓒ Ⓓ
5. Ⓐ Ⓑ Ⓒ Ⓓ
6. Ⓐ Ⓑ Ⓒ Ⓓ
7. Ⓐ Ⓑ Ⓒ Ⓓ
8. Ⓐ Ⓑ Ⓒ Ⓓ
9. Ⓐ Ⓑ Ⓒ Ⓓ
10. Ⓐ Ⓑ Ⓒ Ⓓ
11. Ⓐ Ⓑ Ⓒ Ⓓ
12. Ⓐ Ⓑ Ⓒ Ⓓ
13. Ⓐ Ⓑ Ⓒ Ⓓ
14. Ⓐ Ⓑ Ⓒ Ⓓ
15. Ⓐ Ⓑ Ⓒ Ⓓ
16. Ⓐ Ⓑ Ⓒ Ⓓ
17. Ⓐ Ⓑ Ⓒ Ⓓ
18. Ⓐ Ⓑ Ⓒ Ⓓ
19. Ⓐ Ⓑ Ⓒ Ⓓ
20. Ⓐ Ⓑ Ⓒ Ⓓ
21. Ⓐ Ⓑ Ⓒ Ⓓ
22. Ⓐ Ⓑ Ⓒ Ⓓ
23. Ⓐ Ⓑ Ⓒ Ⓓ
24. Ⓐ Ⓑ Ⓒ Ⓓ
25. Ⓐ Ⓑ Ⓒ Ⓓ
26. Ⓐ Ⓑ Ⓒ Ⓓ
27. Ⓐ Ⓑ Ⓒ Ⓓ
28. Ⓐ Ⓑ Ⓒ Ⓓ
29. Ⓐ Ⓑ Ⓒ Ⓓ
30. Ⓐ Ⓑ Ⓒ Ⓓ
31. Ⓐ Ⓑ Ⓒ Ⓓ
32. Ⓐ Ⓑ Ⓒ Ⓓ
33. Ⓐ Ⓑ Ⓒ Ⓓ
34. Ⓐ Ⓑ Ⓒ Ⓓ
35. Ⓐ Ⓑ Ⓒ Ⓓ

Sentence Correction Self-Test

1. Ⓐ Ⓑ Ⓒ Ⓓ Ⓔ
2. Ⓐ Ⓑ Ⓒ Ⓓ Ⓔ
3. Ⓐ Ⓑ Ⓒ Ⓓ Ⓔ
4. Ⓐ Ⓑ Ⓒ Ⓓ Ⓔ
5. Ⓐ Ⓑ Ⓒ Ⓓ Ⓔ
6. Ⓐ Ⓑ Ⓒ Ⓓ Ⓔ
7. Ⓐ Ⓑ Ⓒ Ⓓ Ⓔ
8. Ⓐ Ⓑ Ⓒ Ⓓ Ⓔ
9. Ⓐ Ⓑ Ⓒ Ⓓ Ⓔ
10. Ⓐ Ⓑ Ⓒ Ⓓ Ⓔ
11. Ⓐ Ⓑ Ⓒ Ⓓ Ⓔ
12. Ⓐ Ⓑ Ⓒ Ⓓ Ⓔ
13. Ⓐ Ⓑ Ⓒ Ⓓ Ⓔ
14. Ⓐ Ⓑ Ⓒ Ⓓ Ⓔ
15. Ⓐ Ⓑ Ⓒ Ⓓ Ⓔ
16. Ⓐ Ⓑ Ⓒ Ⓓ Ⓔ
17. Ⓐ Ⓑ Ⓒ Ⓓ Ⓔ
18. Ⓐ Ⓑ Ⓒ Ⓓ Ⓔ
19. Ⓐ Ⓑ Ⓒ Ⓓ Ⓔ
20. Ⓐ Ⓑ Ⓒ Ⓓ Ⓔ
21. Ⓐ Ⓑ Ⓒ Ⓓ Ⓔ
22. Ⓐ Ⓑ Ⓒ Ⓓ Ⓔ
23. Ⓐ Ⓑ Ⓒ Ⓓ Ⓔ
24. Ⓐ Ⓑ Ⓒ Ⓓ Ⓔ
25. Ⓐ Ⓑ Ⓒ Ⓓ Ⓔ

Answer Sheet for Final Self-Test A

Section I
Reading Comprehension

1. Ⓐ Ⓑ Ⓒ Ⓓ Ⓔ
2. Ⓐ Ⓑ Ⓒ Ⓓ Ⓔ
3. Ⓐ Ⓑ Ⓒ Ⓓ Ⓔ
4. Ⓐ Ⓑ Ⓒ Ⓓ Ⓔ
5. Ⓐ Ⓑ Ⓒ Ⓓ Ⓔ
6. Ⓐ Ⓑ Ⓒ Ⓓ Ⓔ
7. Ⓐ Ⓑ Ⓒ Ⓓ Ⓔ
8. Ⓐ Ⓑ Ⓒ Ⓓ Ⓔ
9. Ⓐ Ⓑ Ⓒ Ⓓ Ⓔ
10. Ⓐ Ⓑ Ⓒ Ⓓ Ⓔ
11. Ⓐ Ⓑ Ⓒ Ⓓ Ⓔ
12. Ⓐ Ⓑ Ⓒ Ⓓ Ⓔ
13. Ⓐ Ⓑ Ⓒ Ⓓ Ⓔ
14. Ⓐ Ⓑ Ⓒ Ⓓ Ⓔ
15. Ⓐ Ⓑ Ⓒ Ⓓ Ⓔ
16. Ⓐ Ⓑ Ⓒ Ⓓ Ⓔ
17. Ⓐ Ⓑ Ⓒ Ⓓ Ⓔ
18. Ⓐ Ⓑ Ⓒ Ⓓ Ⓔ
19. Ⓐ Ⓑ Ⓒ Ⓓ Ⓔ
20. Ⓐ Ⓑ Ⓒ Ⓓ Ⓔ
21. Ⓐ Ⓑ Ⓒ Ⓓ Ⓔ
22. Ⓐ Ⓑ Ⓒ Ⓓ Ⓔ
23. Ⓐ Ⓑ Ⓒ Ⓓ Ⓔ
24. Ⓐ Ⓑ Ⓒ Ⓓ Ⓔ
25. Ⓐ Ⓑ Ⓒ Ⓓ Ⓔ

Section II
Data Interpretation

1. Ⓐ Ⓑ Ⓒ Ⓓ Ⓔ
2. Ⓐ Ⓑ Ⓒ Ⓓ Ⓔ
3. Ⓐ Ⓑ Ⓒ Ⓓ Ⓔ
4. Ⓐ Ⓑ Ⓒ Ⓓ Ⓔ
5. Ⓐ Ⓑ Ⓒ Ⓓ Ⓔ
6. Ⓐ Ⓑ Ⓒ Ⓓ Ⓔ
7. Ⓐ Ⓑ Ⓒ Ⓓ Ⓔ
8. Ⓐ Ⓑ Ⓒ Ⓓ Ⓔ
9. Ⓐ Ⓑ Ⓒ Ⓓ Ⓔ
10. Ⓐ Ⓑ Ⓒ Ⓓ Ⓔ
11. Ⓐ Ⓑ Ⓒ Ⓓ Ⓔ
12. Ⓐ Ⓑ Ⓒ Ⓓ Ⓔ
13. Ⓐ Ⓑ Ⓒ Ⓓ Ⓔ
14. Ⓐ Ⓑ Ⓒ Ⓓ Ⓔ
15. Ⓐ Ⓑ Ⓒ Ⓓ Ⓔ
16. Ⓐ Ⓑ Ⓒ Ⓓ Ⓔ
17. Ⓐ Ⓑ Ⓒ Ⓓ Ⓔ
18. Ⓐ Ⓑ Ⓒ Ⓓ Ⓔ
19. Ⓐ Ⓑ Ⓒ Ⓓ Ⓔ
20. Ⓐ Ⓑ Ⓒ Ⓓ Ⓔ
21. Ⓐ Ⓑ Ⓒ Ⓓ Ⓔ
22. Ⓐ Ⓑ Ⓒ Ⓓ Ⓔ
23. Ⓐ Ⓑ Ⓒ Ⓓ Ⓔ
24. Ⓐ Ⓑ Ⓒ Ⓓ Ⓔ
25. Ⓐ Ⓑ Ⓒ Ⓓ Ⓔ
26. Ⓐ Ⓑ Ⓒ Ⓓ Ⓔ
27. Ⓐ Ⓑ Ⓒ Ⓓ Ⓔ
28. Ⓐ Ⓑ Ⓒ Ⓓ Ⓔ

Section III
Reading Recall

1. Ⓐ Ⓑ Ⓒ Ⓓ Ⓔ
2. Ⓐ Ⓑ Ⓒ Ⓓ Ⓔ
3. Ⓐ Ⓑ Ⓒ Ⓓ Ⓔ
4. Ⓐ Ⓑ Ⓒ Ⓓ Ⓔ
5. Ⓐ Ⓑ Ⓒ Ⓓ Ⓔ
6. Ⓐ Ⓑ Ⓒ Ⓓ Ⓔ
7. Ⓐ Ⓑ Ⓒ Ⓓ Ⓔ
8. Ⓐ Ⓑ Ⓒ Ⓓ Ⓔ
9. Ⓐ Ⓑ Ⓒ Ⓓ Ⓔ
10. Ⓐ Ⓑ Ⓒ Ⓓ Ⓔ
11. Ⓐ Ⓑ Ⓒ Ⓓ Ⓔ
12. Ⓐ Ⓑ Ⓒ Ⓓ Ⓔ
13. Ⓐ Ⓑ Ⓒ Ⓓ Ⓔ
14. Ⓐ Ⓑ Ⓒ Ⓓ Ⓔ
15. Ⓐ Ⓑ Ⓒ Ⓓ Ⓔ
16. Ⓐ Ⓑ Ⓒ Ⓓ Ⓔ
17. Ⓐ Ⓑ Ⓒ Ⓓ Ⓔ
18. Ⓐ Ⓑ Ⓒ Ⓓ Ⓔ
19. Ⓐ Ⓑ Ⓒ Ⓓ Ⓔ
20. Ⓐ Ⓑ Ⓒ Ⓓ Ⓔ
21. Ⓐ Ⓑ Ⓒ Ⓓ Ⓔ
22. Ⓐ Ⓑ Ⓒ Ⓓ Ⓔ

Section III
Reading Recall (cont.)

23.	Ⓐ	Ⓑ	Ⓒ	Ⓓ	Ⓔ
24.	Ⓐ	Ⓑ	Ⓒ	Ⓓ	Ⓔ
25.	Ⓐ	Ⓑ	Ⓒ	Ⓓ	Ⓔ
26.	Ⓐ	Ⓑ	Ⓒ	Ⓓ	Ⓔ
27.	Ⓐ	Ⓑ	Ⓒ	Ⓓ	Ⓔ
28.	Ⓐ	Ⓑ	Ⓒ	Ⓓ	Ⓔ
29.	Ⓐ	Ⓑ	Ⓒ	Ⓓ	Ⓔ
30.	Ⓐ	Ⓑ	Ⓒ	Ⓓ	Ⓔ

Section IV
Principles and Cases

1.	Ⓐ	Ⓑ	Ⓒ	Ⓓ	Ⓔ
2.	Ⓐ	Ⓑ	Ⓒ	Ⓓ	Ⓔ
3.	Ⓐ	Ⓑ	Ⓒ	Ⓓ	Ⓔ
4.	Ⓐ	Ⓑ	Ⓒ	Ⓓ	Ⓔ
5.	Ⓐ	Ⓑ	Ⓒ	Ⓓ	Ⓔ
6.	Ⓐ	Ⓑ	Ⓒ	Ⓓ	Ⓔ
7.	Ⓐ	Ⓑ	Ⓒ	Ⓓ	Ⓔ
8.	Ⓐ	Ⓑ	Ⓒ	Ⓓ	Ⓔ
9.	Ⓐ	Ⓑ	Ⓒ	Ⓓ	Ⓔ
10.	Ⓐ	Ⓑ	Ⓒ	Ⓓ	Ⓔ
11.	Ⓐ	Ⓑ	Ⓒ	Ⓓ	Ⓔ
12.	Ⓐ	Ⓑ	Ⓒ	Ⓓ	Ⓔ
13.	Ⓐ	Ⓑ	Ⓒ	Ⓓ	Ⓔ
14.	Ⓐ	Ⓑ	Ⓒ	Ⓓ	Ⓔ
15.	Ⓐ	Ⓑ	Ⓒ	Ⓓ	Ⓔ
16.	Ⓐ	Ⓑ	Ⓒ	Ⓓ	Ⓔ
17.	Ⓐ	Ⓑ	Ⓒ	Ⓓ	Ⓔ
18.	Ⓐ	Ⓑ	Ⓒ	Ⓓ	Ⓔ
19.	Ⓐ	Ⓑ	Ⓒ	Ⓓ	Ⓔ
20.	Ⓐ	Ⓑ	Ⓒ	Ⓓ	Ⓔ
21.	Ⓐ	Ⓑ	Ⓒ	Ⓓ	Ⓔ
22.	Ⓐ	Ⓑ	Ⓒ	Ⓓ	Ⓔ
23.	Ⓐ	Ⓑ	Ⓒ	Ⓓ	Ⓔ
24.	Ⓐ	Ⓑ	Ⓒ	Ⓓ	Ⓔ
25.	Ⓐ	Ⓑ	Ⓒ	Ⓓ	Ⓔ
26.	Ⓐ	Ⓑ	Ⓒ	Ⓓ	Ⓔ
27.	Ⓐ	Ⓑ	Ⓒ	Ⓓ	Ⓔ
28.	Ⓐ	Ⓑ	Ⓒ	Ⓓ	Ⓔ
29.	Ⓐ	Ⓑ	Ⓒ	Ⓓ	Ⓔ
30.	Ⓐ	Ⓑ	Ⓒ	Ⓓ	Ⓔ

Section V
Error Recognition

1.	Ⓐ	Ⓑ	Ⓒ	Ⓓ	Ⓔ
2.	Ⓐ	Ⓑ	Ⓒ	Ⓓ	Ⓔ
3.	Ⓐ	Ⓑ	Ⓒ	Ⓓ	Ⓔ
4.	Ⓐ	Ⓑ	Ⓒ	Ⓓ	Ⓔ
5.	Ⓐ	Ⓑ	Ⓒ	Ⓓ	Ⓔ
6.	Ⓐ	Ⓑ	Ⓒ	Ⓓ	Ⓔ
7.	Ⓐ	Ⓑ	Ⓒ	Ⓓ	Ⓔ
8.	Ⓐ	Ⓑ	Ⓒ	Ⓓ	Ⓔ
9.	Ⓐ	Ⓑ	Ⓒ	Ⓓ	Ⓔ
10.	Ⓐ	Ⓑ	Ⓒ	Ⓓ	Ⓔ
11.	Ⓐ	Ⓑ	Ⓒ	Ⓓ	Ⓔ
12.	Ⓐ	Ⓑ	Ⓒ	Ⓓ	Ⓔ
13.	Ⓐ	Ⓑ	Ⓒ	Ⓓ	Ⓔ
14.	Ⓐ	Ⓑ	Ⓒ	Ⓓ	Ⓔ
15.	Ⓐ	Ⓑ	Ⓒ	Ⓓ	Ⓔ
16.	Ⓐ	Ⓑ	Ⓒ	Ⓓ	Ⓔ
17.	Ⓐ	Ⓑ	Ⓒ	Ⓓ	Ⓔ
18.	Ⓐ	Ⓑ	Ⓒ	Ⓓ	Ⓔ
19.	Ⓐ	Ⓑ	Ⓒ	Ⓓ	Ⓔ
20.	Ⓐ	Ⓑ	Ⓒ	Ⓓ	Ⓔ
21.	Ⓐ	Ⓑ	Ⓒ	Ⓓ	Ⓔ
22.	Ⓐ	Ⓑ	Ⓒ	Ⓓ	Ⓔ
23.	Ⓐ	Ⓑ	Ⓒ	Ⓓ	Ⓔ
24.	Ⓐ	Ⓑ	Ⓒ	Ⓓ	Ⓔ
25.	Ⓐ	Ⓑ	Ⓒ	Ⓓ	Ⓔ
26.	Ⓐ	Ⓑ	Ⓒ	Ⓓ	Ⓔ
27.	Ⓐ	Ⓑ	Ⓒ	Ⓓ	Ⓔ
28.	Ⓐ	Ⓑ	Ⓒ	Ⓓ	Ⓔ
29.	Ⓐ	Ⓑ	Ⓒ	Ⓓ	Ⓔ
30.	Ⓐ	Ⓑ	Ⓒ	Ⓓ	Ⓔ
31.	Ⓐ	Ⓑ	Ⓒ	Ⓓ	Ⓔ
32.	Ⓐ	Ⓑ	Ⓒ	Ⓓ	Ⓔ
33.	Ⓐ	Ⓑ	Ⓒ	Ⓓ	Ⓔ
34.	Ⓐ	Ⓑ	Ⓒ	Ⓓ	Ⓔ
35.	Ⓐ	Ⓑ	Ⓒ	Ⓓ	Ⓔ

Section VI
Sentence Correction

1. Ⓐ Ⓑ Ⓒ Ⓓ Ⓔ
2. Ⓐ Ⓑ Ⓒ Ⓓ Ⓔ
3. Ⓐ Ⓑ Ⓒ Ⓓ Ⓔ
4. Ⓐ Ⓑ Ⓒ Ⓓ Ⓔ
5. Ⓐ Ⓑ Ⓒ Ⓓ Ⓔ
6. Ⓐ Ⓑ Ⓒ Ⓓ Ⓔ
7. Ⓐ Ⓑ Ⓒ Ⓓ Ⓔ
8. Ⓐ Ⓑ Ⓒ Ⓓ Ⓔ
9. Ⓐ Ⓑ Ⓒ Ⓓ Ⓔ
10. Ⓐ Ⓑ Ⓒ Ⓓ Ⓔ
11. Ⓐ Ⓑ Ⓒ Ⓓ Ⓔ
12. Ⓐ Ⓑ Ⓒ Ⓓ Ⓔ
13. Ⓐ Ⓑ Ⓒ Ⓓ Ⓔ
14. Ⓐ Ⓑ Ⓒ Ⓓ Ⓔ
15. Ⓐ Ⓑ Ⓒ Ⓓ Ⓔ
16. Ⓐ Ⓑ Ⓒ Ⓓ Ⓔ
17. Ⓐ Ⓑ Ⓒ Ⓓ Ⓔ
18. Ⓐ Ⓑ Ⓒ Ⓓ Ⓔ
19. Ⓐ Ⓑ Ⓒ Ⓓ Ⓔ
20. Ⓐ Ⓑ Ⓒ Ⓓ Ⓔ
21. Ⓐ Ⓑ Ⓒ Ⓓ Ⓔ
22. Ⓐ Ⓑ Ⓒ Ⓓ Ⓔ
23. Ⓐ Ⓑ Ⓒ Ⓓ Ⓔ
24. Ⓐ Ⓑ Ⓒ Ⓓ Ⓔ
25. Ⓐ Ⓑ Ⓒ Ⓓ Ⓔ

Answer Sheet for Final Self-Test B

Section I
Logical Reasoning

1. Ⓐ Ⓑ Ⓒ Ⓓ Ⓔ
2. Ⓐ Ⓑ Ⓒ Ⓓ Ⓔ
3. Ⓐ Ⓑ Ⓒ Ⓓ Ⓔ
4. Ⓐ Ⓑ Ⓒ Ⓓ Ⓔ
5. Ⓐ Ⓑ Ⓒ Ⓓ Ⓔ
6. Ⓐ Ⓑ Ⓒ Ⓓ Ⓔ
7. Ⓐ Ⓑ Ⓒ Ⓓ Ⓔ
8. Ⓐ Ⓑ Ⓒ Ⓓ Ⓔ
9. Ⓐ Ⓑ Ⓒ Ⓓ Ⓔ
10. Ⓐ Ⓑ Ⓒ Ⓓ Ⓔ
11. Ⓐ Ⓑ Ⓒ Ⓓ Ⓔ
12. Ⓐ Ⓑ Ⓒ Ⓓ Ⓔ
13. Ⓐ Ⓑ Ⓒ Ⓓ Ⓔ
14. Ⓐ Ⓑ Ⓒ Ⓓ Ⓔ
15. Ⓐ Ⓑ Ⓒ Ⓓ Ⓔ
16. Ⓐ Ⓑ Ⓒ Ⓓ Ⓔ
17. Ⓐ Ⓑ Ⓒ Ⓓ Ⓔ
18. Ⓐ Ⓑ Ⓒ Ⓓ Ⓔ
19. Ⓐ Ⓑ Ⓒ Ⓓ Ⓔ
20. Ⓐ Ⓑ Ⓒ Ⓓ Ⓔ
21. Ⓐ Ⓑ Ⓒ Ⓓ Ⓔ
22. Ⓐ Ⓑ Ⓒ Ⓓ Ⓔ
23. Ⓐ Ⓑ Ⓒ Ⓓ Ⓔ
24. Ⓐ Ⓑ Ⓒ Ⓓ Ⓔ
25. Ⓐ Ⓑ Ⓒ Ⓓ Ⓔ

Section II
Part A
Quantitative Comparison

1. Ⓐ Ⓑ Ⓒ Ⓓ
2. Ⓐ Ⓑ Ⓒ Ⓓ
3. Ⓐ Ⓑ Ⓒ Ⓓ
4. Ⓐ Ⓑ Ⓒ Ⓓ
5. Ⓐ Ⓑ Ⓒ Ⓓ
6. Ⓐ Ⓑ Ⓒ Ⓓ
7. Ⓐ Ⓑ Ⓒ Ⓓ
8. Ⓐ Ⓑ Ⓒ Ⓓ
9. Ⓐ Ⓑ Ⓒ Ⓓ
10. Ⓐ Ⓑ Ⓒ Ⓓ
11. Ⓐ Ⓑ Ⓒ Ⓓ
12. Ⓐ Ⓑ Ⓒ Ⓓ
13. Ⓐ Ⓑ Ⓒ Ⓓ
14. Ⓐ Ⓑ Ⓒ Ⓓ
15. Ⓐ Ⓑ Ⓒ Ⓓ
16. Ⓐ Ⓑ Ⓒ Ⓓ
17. Ⓐ Ⓑ Ⓒ Ⓓ
18. Ⓐ Ⓑ Ⓒ Ⓓ
19. Ⓐ Ⓑ Ⓒ Ⓓ
20. Ⓐ Ⓑ Ⓒ Ⓓ
21. Ⓐ Ⓑ Ⓒ Ⓓ
22. Ⓐ Ⓑ Ⓒ Ⓓ
23. Ⓐ Ⓑ Ⓒ Ⓓ
24. Ⓐ Ⓑ Ⓒ Ⓓ
25. Ⓐ Ⓑ Ⓒ Ⓓ

Part B
Data Interpretation

1. Ⓐ Ⓑ Ⓒ Ⓓ Ⓔ
2. Ⓐ Ⓑ Ⓒ Ⓓ Ⓔ
3. Ⓐ Ⓑ Ⓒ Ⓓ Ⓔ
4. Ⓐ Ⓑ Ⓒ Ⓓ Ⓔ
5. Ⓐ Ⓑ Ⓒ Ⓓ Ⓔ
6. Ⓐ Ⓑ Ⓒ Ⓓ Ⓔ
7. Ⓐ Ⓑ Ⓒ Ⓓ Ⓔ
8. Ⓐ Ⓑ Ⓒ Ⓓ Ⓔ
9. Ⓐ Ⓑ Ⓒ Ⓓ Ⓔ
10. Ⓐ Ⓑ Ⓒ Ⓓ Ⓔ
11. Ⓐ Ⓑ Ⓒ Ⓓ Ⓔ
12. Ⓐ Ⓑ Ⓒ Ⓓ Ⓔ
13. Ⓐ Ⓑ Ⓒ Ⓓ Ⓔ
14. Ⓐ Ⓑ Ⓒ Ⓓ Ⓔ

Section III
Practical Judgment

1. Ⓐ Ⓑ Ⓒ Ⓓ Ⓔ
2. Ⓐ Ⓑ Ⓒ Ⓓ Ⓔ
3. Ⓐ Ⓑ Ⓒ Ⓓ Ⓔ
4. Ⓐ Ⓑ Ⓒ Ⓓ Ⓔ
5. Ⓐ Ⓑ Ⓒ Ⓓ Ⓔ
6. Ⓐ Ⓑ Ⓒ Ⓓ Ⓔ
7. Ⓐ Ⓑ Ⓒ Ⓓ Ⓔ
8. Ⓐ Ⓑ Ⓒ Ⓓ Ⓔ
9. Ⓐ Ⓑ Ⓒ Ⓓ Ⓔ
10. Ⓐ Ⓑ Ⓒ Ⓓ Ⓔ
11. Ⓐ Ⓑ Ⓒ Ⓓ Ⓔ
12. Ⓐ Ⓑ Ⓒ Ⓓ Ⓔ
13. Ⓐ Ⓑ Ⓒ Ⓓ Ⓔ
14. Ⓐ Ⓑ Ⓒ Ⓓ Ⓔ
15. Ⓐ Ⓑ Ⓒ Ⓓ Ⓔ
16. Ⓐ Ⓑ Ⓒ Ⓓ Ⓔ
17. Ⓐ Ⓑ Ⓒ Ⓓ Ⓔ
18. Ⓐ Ⓑ Ⓒ Ⓓ Ⓔ
19. Ⓐ Ⓑ Ⓒ Ⓓ Ⓔ
20. Ⓐ Ⓑ Ⓒ Ⓓ Ⓔ
21. Ⓐ Ⓑ Ⓒ Ⓓ Ⓔ
22. Ⓐ Ⓑ Ⓒ Ⓓ Ⓔ
23. Ⓐ Ⓑ Ⓒ Ⓓ Ⓔ
24. Ⓐ Ⓑ Ⓒ Ⓓ Ⓔ
25. Ⓐ Ⓑ Ⓒ Ⓓ Ⓔ
26. Ⓐ Ⓑ Ⓒ Ⓓ Ⓔ
27. Ⓐ Ⓑ Ⓒ Ⓓ Ⓔ
28. Ⓐ Ⓑ Ⓒ Ⓓ Ⓔ
29. Ⓐ Ⓑ Ⓒ Ⓓ Ⓔ
30. Ⓐ Ⓑ Ⓒ Ⓓ Ⓔ
31. Ⓐ Ⓑ Ⓒ Ⓓ Ⓔ
32. Ⓐ Ⓑ Ⓒ Ⓓ Ⓔ
33. Ⓐ Ⓑ Ⓒ Ⓓ Ⓔ
34. Ⓐ Ⓑ Ⓒ Ⓓ Ⓔ
35. Ⓐ Ⓑ Ⓒ Ⓓ Ⓔ
36. Ⓐ Ⓑ Ⓒ Ⓓ Ⓔ
37. Ⓐ Ⓑ Ⓒ Ⓓ Ⓔ
38. Ⓐ Ⓑ Ⓒ Ⓓ Ⓔ
39. Ⓐ Ⓑ Ⓒ Ⓓ Ⓔ
40. Ⓐ Ⓑ Ⓒ Ⓓ Ⓔ
41. Ⓐ Ⓑ Ⓒ Ⓓ Ⓔ
42. Ⓐ Ⓑ Ⓒ Ⓓ Ⓔ
43. Ⓐ Ⓑ Ⓒ Ⓓ Ⓔ
44. Ⓐ Ⓑ Ⓒ Ⓓ Ⓔ
45. Ⓐ Ⓑ Ⓒ Ⓓ Ⓔ
46. Ⓐ Ⓑ Ⓒ Ⓓ Ⓔ
47. Ⓐ Ⓑ Ⓒ Ⓓ Ⓔ
48. Ⓐ Ⓑ Ⓒ Ⓓ Ⓔ
49. Ⓐ Ⓑ Ⓒ Ⓓ Ⓔ
50. Ⓐ Ⓑ Ⓒ Ⓓ Ⓔ

Section IV
Principles and Cases

1. Ⓐ Ⓑ Ⓒ Ⓓ
2. Ⓐ Ⓑ Ⓒ Ⓓ
3. Ⓐ Ⓑ Ⓒ Ⓓ
4. Ⓐ Ⓑ Ⓒ Ⓓ
5. Ⓐ Ⓑ Ⓒ Ⓓ
6. Ⓐ Ⓑ Ⓒ Ⓓ
7. Ⓐ Ⓑ Ⓒ Ⓓ
8. Ⓐ Ⓑ Ⓒ Ⓓ
9. Ⓐ Ⓑ Ⓒ Ⓓ
10. Ⓐ Ⓑ Ⓒ Ⓓ
11. Ⓐ Ⓑ Ⓒ Ⓓ
12. Ⓐ Ⓑ Ⓒ Ⓓ
13. Ⓐ Ⓑ Ⓒ Ⓓ
14. Ⓐ Ⓑ Ⓒ Ⓓ
15. Ⓐ Ⓑ Ⓒ Ⓓ
16. Ⓐ Ⓑ Ⓒ Ⓓ
17. Ⓐ Ⓑ Ⓒ Ⓓ
18. Ⓐ Ⓑ Ⓒ Ⓓ
19. Ⓐ Ⓑ Ⓒ Ⓓ
20. Ⓐ Ⓑ Ⓒ Ⓓ
21. Ⓐ Ⓑ Ⓒ Ⓓ
22. Ⓐ Ⓑ Ⓒ Ⓓ
23. Ⓐ Ⓑ Ⓒ Ⓓ
24. Ⓐ Ⓑ Ⓒ Ⓓ
25. Ⓐ Ⓑ Ⓒ Ⓓ
26. Ⓐ Ⓑ Ⓒ Ⓓ
27. Ⓐ Ⓑ Ⓒ Ⓓ
28. Ⓐ Ⓑ Ⓒ Ⓓ
29. Ⓐ Ⓑ Ⓒ Ⓓ
30. Ⓐ Ⓑ Ⓒ Ⓓ

Section V
Error Recognition

1. Ⓐ Ⓑ Ⓒ Ⓓ
2. Ⓐ Ⓑ Ⓒ Ⓓ
3. Ⓐ Ⓑ Ⓒ Ⓓ
4. Ⓐ Ⓑ Ⓒ Ⓓ
5. Ⓐ Ⓑ Ⓒ Ⓓ
6. Ⓐ Ⓑ Ⓒ Ⓓ
7. Ⓐ Ⓑ Ⓒ Ⓓ
8. Ⓐ Ⓑ Ⓒ Ⓓ
9. Ⓐ Ⓑ Ⓒ Ⓓ
10. Ⓐ Ⓑ Ⓒ Ⓓ
11. Ⓐ Ⓑ Ⓒ Ⓓ
12. Ⓐ Ⓑ Ⓒ Ⓓ
13. Ⓐ Ⓑ Ⓒ Ⓓ
14. Ⓐ Ⓑ Ⓒ Ⓓ
15. Ⓐ Ⓑ Ⓒ Ⓓ
16. Ⓐ Ⓑ Ⓒ Ⓓ
17. Ⓐ Ⓑ Ⓒ Ⓓ
18. Ⓐ Ⓑ Ⓒ Ⓓ
19. Ⓐ Ⓑ Ⓒ Ⓓ
20. Ⓐ Ⓑ Ⓒ Ⓓ
21. Ⓐ Ⓑ Ⓒ Ⓓ
22. Ⓐ Ⓑ Ⓒ Ⓓ
23. Ⓐ Ⓑ Ⓒ Ⓓ
24. Ⓐ Ⓑ Ⓒ Ⓓ
25. Ⓐ Ⓑ Ⓒ Ⓓ
26. Ⓐ Ⓑ Ⓒ Ⓓ
27. Ⓐ Ⓑ Ⓒ Ⓓ
28. Ⓐ Ⓑ Ⓒ Ⓓ
29. Ⓐ Ⓑ Ⓒ Ⓓ
30. Ⓐ Ⓑ Ⓒ Ⓓ
31. Ⓐ Ⓑ Ⓒ Ⓓ
32. Ⓐ Ⓑ Ⓒ Ⓓ
33. Ⓐ Ⓑ Ⓒ Ⓓ
34. Ⓐ Ⓑ Ⓒ Ⓓ
35. Ⓐ Ⓑ Ⓒ Ⓓ

Section VI
Sentence Correction

1. Ⓐ Ⓑ Ⓒ Ⓓ Ⓔ
2. Ⓐ Ⓑ Ⓒ Ⓓ Ⓔ
3. Ⓐ Ⓑ Ⓒ Ⓓ Ⓔ
4. Ⓐ Ⓑ Ⓒ Ⓓ Ⓔ
5. Ⓐ Ⓑ Ⓒ Ⓓ Ⓔ
6. Ⓐ Ⓑ Ⓒ Ⓓ Ⓔ
7. Ⓐ Ⓑ Ⓒ Ⓓ Ⓔ
8. Ⓐ Ⓑ Ⓒ Ⓓ Ⓔ
9. Ⓐ Ⓑ Ⓒ Ⓓ Ⓔ
10. Ⓐ Ⓑ Ⓒ Ⓓ Ⓔ
11. Ⓐ Ⓑ Ⓒ Ⓓ Ⓔ
12. Ⓐ Ⓑ Ⓒ Ⓓ Ⓔ
13. Ⓐ Ⓑ Ⓒ Ⓓ Ⓔ
14. Ⓐ Ⓑ Ⓒ Ⓓ Ⓔ
15. Ⓐ Ⓑ Ⓒ Ⓓ Ⓔ
16. Ⓐ Ⓑ Ⓒ Ⓓ Ⓔ
17. Ⓐ Ⓑ Ⓒ Ⓓ Ⓔ
18. Ⓐ Ⓑ Ⓒ Ⓓ Ⓔ
19. Ⓐ Ⓑ Ⓒ Ⓓ Ⓔ
20. Ⓐ Ⓑ Ⓒ Ⓓ Ⓔ
21. Ⓐ Ⓑ Ⓒ Ⓓ Ⓔ
22. Ⓐ Ⓑ Ⓒ Ⓓ Ⓔ
23. Ⓐ Ⓑ Ⓒ Ⓓ Ⓔ
24. Ⓐ Ⓑ Ⓒ Ⓓ Ⓔ
25. Ⓐ Ⓑ Ⓒ Ⓓ Ⓔ